Systemic Phonology
Recent Studies in English

Systemic Phonology
Recent Studies in English

Edited by
Wendy L. Bowcher and Bradley A. Smith

SHEFFIELD UK   BRISTOL CT

Published by Equinox Publishing Ltd.

UK: Office 415, The Workstation, 15 Paternoster Row, Sheffield, South Yorkshire
      S1 2BX
USA: ISD, 70 Enterprise Drive, Bristol, CT 06010

www.equinoxpub.com

First published 2014

ISBN   978 1 84553 939 9   (hardback)
ISBN   978 1 84553 946 7   (paperback)

British Library Cataloguing-in-Publication Data

A catalogue record for this book is available from the British Library.

Library of Congress Cataloging-in-Publication Data

Systemic phonology : recent studies in English / Edited by Wendy L. Bowcher and Bradley A. Smith.
      pages cm. – (Functional Linguistics)
   Includes bibliographical references and index.
   ISBN 978-1-84553-939-9 (hb) – ISBN 978-1-84553-946-7 (pb)
   1. English language–Phonology. 2. Phonetics. I. Bowcher, Wendy L. II. Smith, Bradley A.
   PE1133.S97 2013
   421.5–dc23
   2013000308

Typeset by S.J.I. Services, New Delhi
Printed and bound by Lightning Source Inc. (La Vergne, TN), Lightning Source UK Ltd. (Milton Keynes), Lightning Source AU Pty. (Scoresby, Victoria).

Contents

Acknowledgements

The editors would like to express their appreciation to Ms Xia Jinping, Ms Zhang Zhenzhen and Mr Yu Xinle for assistance during the preparation of this book manuscript.

Every effort has been made to acknowledge ownership of copyright material in this book. Should any copyright holder not be properly acknowledged, the editors offer their sincere apologies and request that the copyright holders make contact with the publishers in order to rectify the situation.

Introduction

Wendy L. Bowcher[a] and Bradley A. Smith[b]

1   Introduction

This long-awaited volume presents a selection of current research on English phonology within the theoretical framework of systemic functional linguistics (SFL). Not since Tench's volume, *Studies in Systemic Phonology*, published in 1992, has there been a volume devoted to phonology within the body of literature in SFL. Phonology can perhaps be considered the 'poor cousin' of other fields in SFL in that it is one of the areas in which the least amount of research takes place, and is an aspect of language

a   **Wendy L. Bowcher** is a professor in the School of Foreign Languages at Sun Yat-sen University, China. She has worked as a consultant forensic linguist in Australia, and for several years as Associate Professor of Linguistics at Tokyo Gakugei University, Japan. She has taught in secondary schools, worked as a multicultural education consultant, and taught linguistics and applied linguistics at both undergraduate and graduate level. She has also taught on teacher training courses, most notably as adjunct lecturer for Columbia University Teachers College, MA TESOL program (Tokyo campus). She received her PhD in linguistics from the University of Liverpool, England. Her research interests include multimodal discourse analysis of Japanese and English texts, context in Systemic Functional Linguistic theory, language education, and English intonation. She was instrumental in the formation of the Japan Association of Systemic Functional Linguistics (JASFL). She is editor of *Multimodal Texts from Around the World: Cultural and Linguistic Insights* (2012) and co-editor with Terry D. Royce of *New Directions in the Analysis of Multimodal Discourse* (2007).

b   **Bradley A. Smith** is a Research Fellow in the School of Education at Curtin University, Australia. He has previously worked in a learning and teaching centre at the University of Melbourne, and in the Multimodal Analysis Lab at the National University of Singapore. His PhD thesis (2008, Macquarie University) is entitled 'Intonation and Register: A Multidimensional Exploration'. His major research interests are intonation, register, communication in higher education, and multimodality, with a focus on the roles of sound-based semiotic resources within cultures. His publications include (with William S. Greaves) the chapter on intonation for the forthcoming *Bloomsbury Companion to Halliday*, co-editor (with Kay L. O'Halloran) of *Multimodal Studies: Exploring Issues and Domains* (2011), as well as several journal articles, book chapters, two invited encyclopaedia entries in the *Wiley-Blackwell Encyclopedia of Applied Linguistics* (2013) and an invited review for *Linguistics and the Human Sciences* 4(1) of Halliday and Greaves (2008) *Intonation in the Grammar of English*.

that is seldom addressed in more general or applied linguistics tasks. As a result, our knowledge and understanding of phonological and related phenomena have failed to grow and develop to the same extent as other areas of SFL theory and description.

One of the most common reasons for the paucity of research seems to be a professed insecurity by many scholars and students that they 'cannot trust their ears' when it comes to phonological analyses, particularly analyses of intonation. And yet, for those who have tackled intonational or other phonological analysis, the difficulties one encounters are in essence the same as for other analyses: there is a learning curve to be undertaken, and there are always those specific instances of analysis that are not as clear cut as others. However, one common problem seems to be viewing phonology as only 'sound', or analysing intonation as only 'shapes' of sound, which is akin to viewing language as only made of 'structures'. A focus on language structure at the expense of meaning, or function, misses the point of language as social semiotic (Halliday, 1978), a key characteristic of the SFL approach to language and an essential part of this approach to phonological description and analysis.

When we engage in spoken interaction we are not thinking, 'oh, which tone choice shall I make next?', or 'which syllable shall I assign tonic prominence to?'. And in the process of interacting with another speaker, we are not in general consciously analysing the phonological choices made by a speaker with whom we are interacting. Rather, as speakers and hearers of a language, we make or interpret those selections in an unconscious, 'taken-for-granted' manner, because our priority is to 'make meaning', and the choices we make and comprehend are a natural consequence of this. And yet, in a sense we are making that analysis, in that in interaction we differentiate certain choices from others that are possible, because such choices do realize meaning and are a part of our language potential.

Halliday (1975) shows how, for an infant learner of language, the learning of phonology – the systematization of sounds into meaning-bearing patterns – is integral to the very earliest language experiences. A basic distinction that is made is between rising and falling pitch – a crucial component of the early childhood semiotic repertoire and the basis of later adult language intonation systems. Social semiosis, as representing and interacting with our social world, is encountered, learnt and used through physical expression, form and function as one. Thus, for analysts too, it goes without saying that phonology is very much about both sound and its social semiotic functions, its role in making meaning.

And this perspective informs both the description of intonation within SFL theory and its analysis in text.

The last century in language study has seen the development of a wide variety of sophisticated theoretical models for analysing spoken language and rich descriptions of the phonological systems and structures of English and of other languages, and other semiotic resources (cf. van Leeuwen, 1999). Meanwhile, with increasingly sophisticated and accessible technologies we are able to scrutinize the sounds of language more thoroughly and in a way that supports our aural analytical skills and our search for the ways in which phonological systems serve to realize meaning. This current volume, presenting phonological research within the systemic tradition, evidences an important aspect of the SFL approach to phonology: as for the infant learning language, so with the researcher studying language, both the expression and content planes are equally involved – the meanings together with the means by which they are made.

2   The orientations, purposes and value of researching phonology

In the opening lines of the first chapter of *An Introduction to Descriptive Linguistics*, Gleason observes:

> As you listen to an unfamiliar language you get the impression of a torrent of disorganised noises carrying no sense whatever. To the native speaker it is quite otherwise. (Gleason, [1955] 1961: 1)

For the student of phonology, Gleason's comments recall Trubetzkoy's ([1935] 1968: 1) observation that '[u]ntil recently, most students of language regarded the phonic side of human speech as a meaningless jumble of acoustic and motor phenomena', and also, much later, Brazil *et al.*'s (1980: xiv) reference to the second language learner's perception of intonation as an 'ocean of near-chaos'.

Research into the 'sounds' of English, however, has had a long and illustrious history, dating back at least as far as Hart's ([1551] 1955) treatise on the reform of English spelling in relation to English pronunciation (see also Dobson, 1968; see Crystal, 1969 for a historical review of the literature on English prosody). The study of phonology in general can be traced back more than two millennia to the ancient Sanscrit scholar Pāṇini (see Fischer-Jorgensen, 1975 for a historical overview of phonological theory).

In modern times, many scholars such as Henry Sweet, a major influence on Firth, have considered phonetics to be 'the indispensable foundation of all study of language – whether that study be purely theoretical, or practical as well' (Sweet, 1877: v). Fischer-Jorgensen (1975: 6) points out that in many early works on phonetics, the 'descriptions, on the whole, are restricted to sound differences which have a distinctive function', the basic principle of phonological description.

The early interest by Sweet and others in the sounds of language often related to a pedagogic purpose, the teaching and learning of English both in terms of elocution for native speakers and as a second language, as well as having the theoretical purpose Sweet mentions in the quote above. The pedagogical interests in phonology spawned a school of American elocutionists (cf. Crystal, 1969: 32–4). In England the early pedagogic purposes of the study of phonology are summed up in Jones's *The Pronunciation of English*: 'primarily designed for the use of ... students in training-colleges and teachers whose aim is to correct cockneyisms or other undesirable pronunciation in their scholars' (Jones, [1909] 1937: vii). The teaching of pronunciation gave rise to an interest in both the segmental and prosodic aspects of language. However, in works on teaching English as a second language such as those by Armstrong and Ward (1926), Kingdon (1958), Schubiger (1958) and Halliday (1970), one tends to find a dedicated focus on intonation, especially in terms of its communicative functions, alongside an inclusion of supporting phonetic and phonological description.

The invention and increasing availability of recording and other technologies in the late nineteenth and early twentieth centuries coincided with an increasing interest in the study of language in general, arising out of the earlier comparative historical studies of the nineteenth century. This gave impetus to a dramatic increase in the study of the sounds of language as an area of theoretical and descriptive interest. The first generation of scholars with access to early recording technologies, such as Daniel Jones, continued the interest in pedagogic concerns such as pronunciation (e.g. Jones, [1909] 1937), but the use of technology enabled detailed empirical study of actual speech, leading to an 'instrumental' tradition in the study of spoken language. This has become the basis for most modern studies of phonetics, and a significant influence on the study of phonology in the second half of the twentieth century. It is perhaps the link between the instrumental, technical science of phonetics and the development of mainstream phonological studies, more than any other factor, which has made the study of intonation and other phonological systems so daunting to those coming from a humanities background, and particularly the grammar and discourse analysis traditions.

The distinction between the sciences of phonetics and phonology has been an important one in the development of phonology. Trubetzkoy discusses this distinction in the preface to his influential 1935 work, *Introduction to the Principles of Phonological Descriptions*. He points to a 'methodological gulf between phonetics and the other branches of linguistic studies' deriving from a perception that speech could only be studied 'using physical or physiological methods' (Trubetzkoy, [1935] 1968: 1). He notes that this situation changed once it was

> logically inferred, from the long-accepted fact that speech sounds have a distinctive function and significatory value, that it was precisely these significatory values which represented the most significant element in linguistics … since the world of these values lying behind the empirical sounds of human speech was seen to constitute an orderly system comparable … with the system of grammatical values. (*Ibid.*: 1)

Trubetzkoy goes on to write that phonetics could thus be 'given its proper place … in the field of natural sciences quite separate from language studies' (*ibid.*: fn1; see also a discussion in Halliday and Greaves, 2008: 10–11). Kohler discusses the wider consequences of such a distinction:

> Theoretical and methodological paradigms in speech research determine the design of data collection, their analysis and their interpretation. The scientific approaches to spoken language have been shaped by the dominating influence of the dichotomy of *phonology*, dealing with discrete mental objects, and *phonetics*, dealing with infinitely fine gradation of physical manifestation. They have been associated with the humanities and the sciences, respectively, since the first half of the twentieth century. (Kohler, 2006: 123)

However, phoneticians such as Lehiste (1970), a pioneer in the phonetics-based approach to the study of suprasegmentals, and Ladefoged (1975) challenged this dichotomy. These scholars laid the groundwork for an integrated but phonetics-driven approach to phonological theory and description. Johnson notes that Ladefoged, for instance, 'engaged with the theory of phonological distinctive features, establishing the idea that the building blocks of phonological structure emerge from phonetic structure' (Johnson, 2011: 4).

Much subsequent research within mainstream phonological studies follows in this instrumental, phonetics-oriented tradition, which attempts to bridge the disciplinary and theoretical gulf between sciences which in systemic functional theory are located at the two strata of the expression plane of language (cf. Kingston and Beckman, 1990). And because 'phonetic studies of prosody were instrumental in establishing phonetics as one of the major subdisciplines in linguistics in American universities' (Johnson, 2011: 5), the dominant approach to intonation study has also been a 'bottom-up' view of phonology (e.g. Ladd, 2008; Gussenhoven, 2004; Beckman *et al.*, 2005; cf. Chapter 10 of this volume for a discussion). Kohler however, makes an interesting point with regard to modern research trends. He observes that in recent experimental prosodic analysis, 'an increasing number of phonologists take their phonological solutions to the laboratory to fill them post hoc with phonetic measurement', so that 'linguistic form takes precedence over phonetic substance' (Kohler, 2006: 123).

Another dominant influence on the development of phonological science has been the choice of methods, with traditions of experimental, laboratory methods (such as Kohler, 2006) in contradistinction to observation of naturally occurring discourse (Halliday's work on intonation being an example).

Within the study of intonation, two major theoretical issues have been how to interpret pitch movements phonologically, and whether or to what extent to include intonation as a part of the grammar of language. In terms of the former, according to Crystal (1969: 45) 'Bloomfield (1933) was the first to apply the prior determined techniques of segmental phonemic analysis to intonation, notating distinctive segments only'. Three decades later, Bolinger notes:

> There is wide agreement among linguists on the units of sound that make distinctions in word meanings. There is no such agreement on the units of intonation ... Some have argued that an intonation contour consists of a succession of levels, others that it is a succession of changes in direction. (Bolinger, [1964] 1972: 14)

Bolinger was a significant influence on the debate as to whether to include intonation as part of language, claiming that the 'encounters between intonation and grammar are casual, not causal', and that 'intonation is not grammatical' (Bolinger, 1958: 37). For Bolinger, intonation is a 'half-tamed servant of language' (Bolinger, [1964] 1972: 29), not as '"central" to communication as some of the other traits of language. If it were, we could not understand someone who speaks in a monotone' (*ibid.*: 20). However, in these, as in other accounts of intonation and other phonological phenomena, the theory of 'grammar' and 'language' is crucial to one's interpretation of such phenomena: one can surely understand certain meanings in language spoken on a monotone, but there are crucial meanings which would be lost – in systemic functional terms, interpersonal and textual meanings. These are captured only if one's theory of language is adapted to handle such meanings.

In regard to this, Pike's reflection on the relationship between theory and description can be applied to the study of phonology. He argues that

> The list and kind of things men will find will vary radically if they adopt different *theories as tools* with which to search for these units. The theory is part of the observer; a different theory makes a different observer; a different observer sees different things, or sees the same things as structured differently. (Pike, 1982: 3; emphasis in the original)

As the discussion above shows, there have been various theoretical and applied traditions in the study of phonology, each with its own orientations, purposes and areas of concern (see Halliday and Greaves, 2008, for example, for a discussion). Pike's comments are certainly applicable to, for example, the treatments of pitch movement as contour or segmental structure, as well as to the appeal to 'scientific' experimental, laboratory, instrumental or other methods, or to the differences between studies for pedagogic or other more 'purely' theoretical purposes (cf. Smith, 2011 for discussion of this point).

In terms of purposes, there is a rich vein of work focusing on the structural features of spoken language with a view to comparing these features with those of other languages (e.g. Hirst and Di Cristo, 1998; Gussenhoven, 2004; Jun, 2005). Other work focuses more on the tunes and pitch changes with reference to the possible connections between these and semantic features of the language (e.g. Fletcher *et al.*, 2005; Pierrehumbert and Hirschberg, 1990). And there is a plethora of work within specific socio-discoursal traditions (e.g. Johns-Lewis, 1986; Couper-Kuhlen and Selting, 1996). There is also a rich history of the study of so-called 'paralinguistic' features such as tempo, timbre and other vocal qualities (e.g. Crystal, 1969; Jenks, 2011; Tench, 1990), including van Leeuwen's (1999) systemic functional approach to looking at the semiotics of sound: sound-as-sound, sound-as-language and sound-as-music. All of these works bring new perspectives, by their own purposes, orientations and focuses, to speech phenomena.

3   The systemic approach

As discussed in the previous section, although it is near impossible to discuss phonology without reference to meaning in some shape or form, the theoretical view one holds of the concept of meaning in relation to language bears a critical role in how one goes about investigating and presenting phonological phenomena. In this volume we present studies within the SFL framework. The SFL approach to the study of phonology has connections, at least in terms of a general philosophy of phonology as being 'meaningful' and 'communicative', with work by Brazil (1995), Couper-Kuhlen (1986), Crystal (1969) and Schubiger (1958), to name just a few. However, of significance in the SFL view of phonology is the influence of Firth (e.g. 1957, 1968), who is perhaps best known within phonological studies for his prosodic approach to the study of the expression plane, and his situating 'meaning' at the centre of all linguistic pursuits. Tench (1992) provides a comprehensive summary of Firth's view on phonology, and a detailed discussion of the concepts of hierarchy (rank) and system networks in the SFL view of phonology as developed by Halliday. Rank and system networks are two means by which linguistic phenomena are modelled in SFL. Rank is used to model structure in lexicogrammar and phonology, and presents 'a hierarchy in which a unit of any rank consists of one or more units of rank next below' (Halliday and Webster, 2009: 237). System 'is the organizing concept for modelling paradigmatic relations in language' (*ibid.*: 232), and rank and system are related in that 'each system in grammar and phonology has its point of origin at a particular structural rank ... and a set of related systems is modelled as a system network' (*ibid.*: 232). Rather than reiterate Tench's summary here, we encourage readers to consult Tench (1992) as background to the contributions in this volume. In the next few paragraphs we briefly discuss some other influences on research into phonology within SFL theory.

As already noted, Firth's work plays a central role in the development of SFL phonology, and characteristic of his work is his focus on meaning. Meaning, for Firth, does not reside 'in words and sentences as if they somehow could have meanings in and by themselves' (Firth, 1968: 12). Rather, each level of language organization, including the phonology of a language, is a 'mode of meaning' (*ibid.*: 33), and must be seen in relation to, and as interdependent on, other levels of linguistic abstraction such as grammar. Meaning is the result of the action and interaction of all the levels of language. Linguistic abstraction 'must always presuppose communicativeness or tendency to diffusion of experience as a human predisposition' (*ibid.*: 14). Hence, a systemic phonology, including any 'phonetic descriptions of features of the phonic material selected' (*ibid.*: 184) must have 'renewal of connection with the processes and patterns of life' (*ibid.*: 19), and 'renewal of connection in experience with the language under description' (*ibid.*: 185). Thus a systemic phonological analysis of English is conducted with a view to understanding more about how meaning in English is organized and expressed phonologically: how, and why, it is not a 'torrent of disorganised' nonsensical noises for its speakers. 'Phonology', within the systemic tradition, is often seen as synonymous with 'intonation', and indeed, much research has been devoted to this. Halliday's ([1963] 2005) pioneering discussion of the tones of English set out how, abstracting from observations of the 'mass of noise' of English, the system of phonology could be described through utilizing 'a simple set of contrastive exponents' (*ibid.*: 240). He proposed the four ranks of 'tone group', 'foot', 'syllable' and 'phoneme', and identified the systems of TONALITY (the distribution of sound into tone groups with tone group boundaries), TONICITY (the assignment of prominence in a tone group) and the choice of primary or secondary TONE. All these systems represent potentials for 'distinct meaningful choices, or sets of choices', which he 'subsumed under the single heading of "intonation"' (*ibid.*: 247).

The phonological stratum is located within the 'expression' plane of language. The expression plane itself is stratified; the higher stratum is phonology and the lower stratum is phonetics, the materiality of sound and the 'interface to the human articulatory and auditory systems' (Matthiessen *et al.*, 2010: 159). The role of phonology is to realize worded meaning within context of situation.

Within SFL theory, when analysing features at any strata of language, we have a means of 'validating' our analytical hypotheses. That is, features at each stratum are viewed 'from three related perspectives: from above ... from their own stratum ... and from below' (Hasan, 1995: 220).

Thus, the reach of phonology within the SFL theoretical model is simultaneously upwards as it plays a role in the realization of lexicogrammatical features, semantic features, and features of the context of situation; and downwards, as its expression is in the materiality of sound waves. At the level of lexicogrammar, intonational systems (systems of grammar realized through intonation) interact 'around' with other systems such as MOOD and THEME, and must be interpreted within the context of such interactions (for example, systems of KEY, realized through choice of tone, are more delicate options within the MOOD network). As with the other strata of language within the architecture of SFL, the relationship between features in the system of phonology with those in other strata are theoretically motivated, and correlate in a non-random way with the metafunctions of language. Table 1 outlines the features of phonology within the strata of language (Note that in Chapter 11 of this volume, Fawcett presents an alternative view of intonation within a bi-stratal model in the systemic theoretical tradition).

Table 1 Phonology and its place in the language strata (adapted from Bowcher, 1998a: 52; see also Halliday, 1985a: 60).

Language strata				
Meaning (meta-functions)	Ideational		Interpersonal	Textual
	Experiential	Logical		
Lexico-grammar	Transitivity	Hypotaxis, Parataxis	Mood, Key	Information unit
Phonology	Rhythm can foreground lexical items (content words) and background others. Word accent allows us to distinguish between words such as desert/dessert.	Rhythm plays a role in distinguishing relations between such clauses as non-defining relatives and defining relative clauses. Tone sequences e.g. a rising tone followed by a falling tone may realize a co-ordinate relation.	Tone group choice (system of TONE) e.g. a choice of rising or falling pitch may realize a specific speech function.	Assignment of Tonic prominence (TONICITY), realizes 'New'. The organization of spoken language into tone groups (TONALITY).
Phonetics	'The interface between the language system and human articulatory and auditory systems' (Matthiessen *et al.* 2010: 159).			

(Left margin: Realization/construal — vertical arrow. Right margin braces: CONTENT, EXPRESSION.)

Table 1 shows how certain systems and features of phonology relate to the metafunctions of language. Rhythm, for example, plays an important role in distinguishing between certain words and clausal elements (see Chapter 9 this volume). Choice of tone plays a role in realizing logical, textual, and interpersonal meanings (see Chapters 1–3 and 5–6 in this volume). And the assignment of tonic prominence plays a role in distinguishing the location of 'New' information in an utterance (see Chapters 1–3 in this volume).

At the level of sounding, an analysis of phonological patterns can provide insights into the meaning potential of a language, and as we move from the potential to an instance of language in use, we see how phonological choices pattern within certain registers. For example, radio sports commentaries, auctions, newsreading and even television soap operas exhibit certain register-specific intonational choices (see e.g. Crystal and Davy 1969; Tench, 1988; van Leeuwen, 1985, 1992; Bowcher, 1998b; Kuiper, 1996; Smith, 2008; Chapters 2 and 4, this volume). We know this because when hearing only the distant soundings of these registers and yet not being able to make out the specific wordings, we can still identify, to a fairly successful degree, the kind of language that is taking place. Thus, the study of choices within the phonological system of a language can enhance a description of the features of specific registers, and the roles these features play in construing contextual meanings.

The chapters within this volume illustrate how a study of phonology within the multidimensional SFL approach may involve a wide range of phenomena at all strata, and across all dimensions of the theory including rank, metafunction, instantiation and axis. Moreover, the contributions focus not only on spoken but also written modes of discourse, as well as phenomena outside of language such as paralinguistic, vocal and musical phenomena (see Chapters 7 and 8, this volume). This points to a concern within this theoretical tradition to engage with 'language in its entirety, so that whatever is said about one aspect is always understood with reference to the total picture ... [and] *contributes to* the total picture' (Halliday and Matthiessen, 2014: 20, emphasis in the original).

That is, systemic analyses can best be understood in relation to other analyses and to the overall picture on a text as a 'semantic unit' in context (Halliday, 1985b: 10). Phonological analyses must be seen as interdependent with other analyses within this overall holistic view. This affects both the way we approach the description and analysis of intonational and other phonological systems, as well as how we investigate language in situations where phonology is not the dedicated focus but where its analysis may be consequential to the research.

If we lose sight of the rich meaning potential of sound, and if we forget that the phonology of a language is doing 'meaningful' work for those acculturated into its specific conventions, we are left with only sound, just as if we focus only on the structures of a language and lose sight of their role in construing meaning. The chapters in this collection have this perspective in view, and illustrate some of the fascinating research avenues that one can take in discovering relations between sound and meaning.

4   The organization of this volume

The research presented in this volume explores the relationship between sound and meaning in interesting and diverse ways. The volume is divided into five sections. Part A presents four chapters focusing on the use of intonation (and other vocal features such as pitch height) to organize text-within-context. Part B presents two chapters in which the authors explore aspects of the relationship between the spoken and written modes of discourse. The two chapters in Part C focus on the voice within music, both as part of language, and in terms of paralinguistic features of the 'sung' and 'rap' voices. Part D presents three theoretical papers which explore the representation or generation of English intonation, punctuation and other semiotic systems, with a particular concern in each for the methods and models by which we theorize, analyse and describe semiotic phenomena. The final section, Part E, presents an interactive chapter which invites readers to engage in an analysis of two different texts through not only reading the chapter, but also listening to accompanying sound files and acting out the texts for themselves. The following sections provide brief summaries of each of the chapters in this volume.

4.1　Part A: Intonation: construing the textual metafunction

The four chapters in Part A focus on the role of intonation in the realization of textual meaning, that aspect of language involved in the creation of coherent text in its social context. The section begins with O'Grady's chapter, which challenges theoretical preconceptions of 'Given' and 'New' and how they are used in the analysis of text. He discusses the domains of 'Givenness' and 'Newness' in relation to other cues in the discourse, such as cohesive recoverability, and shows that the traditional structural model of a wave of information leading to a single peak of New information does not match all the data. Through providing examples from three monologues – two speeches by the former prime minister of Great Britain, Tony Blair, and a text from Halliday's *A Course in Spoken English: Intonation* – O'Grady investigates the relationship between lexical items and tonic and pre-tonic prominence. O'Grady suggests that 'New' may be categorized as New1 or New2. New1 refers to items presented in a discourse as non-recoverable from the previous discourse, or as 'freshly' introduced. New2, on the other hand, refers to items which are given salience because they bear some kind of 'interest' in the discourse. He finds that prominence assigned to lexical items is tied to a speaker's communicative goals 'irrespective of whether or not the particular lexical items are very much in the air'. O'Grady's chapter includes a useful literature review of the concepts of Given and New across various linguistic approaches.

In Chapter 2, Lukin investigates the textual metafunction at work in a television news report on the Iraq war. Her aim is to highlight interstratal relations between textual choices in the intonational systems of INFORMATION DISTRIBUTION and INFORMATION FOCUS (realized through TONALITY and TONICITY, respectively) and the contextual parameter of Mode. Lukin's chapter demonstrates the importance of including the analysis of intonational systems within media discourse research and of contextualizing the contribution of these systems within the wider multidimensional model, which adds to our understanding both of this specific register and of the general model used for its analysis. Beginning with the mode parameter of context and working towards language, Lukin's chapter addresses an important issue in SFL: 'the consideration of how meanings made by intonation interact with other metafunctionally specific systemic choices'. Lukin shows how this is crucial to an analysis of 'the expression of the values in mode, for a given instance of register'. The analysis and discussion reveal how the multidimensional systemic approach can throw light on the often opaque and propagandist discourses of war reporting.

Shan Zhu in Chapter 3 focuses on the interplay of THEME and INFORMATION systems in news commentary, within the context of global hyperThematic and hyperNew organization (Martin's 'method of development'; Martin, 1992). A significant aspect of this chapter is the investigation of 'onset pitch' and its relation to topic change (see also Chapter 4 this volume). An important implication arising from the analysis is that intonational systems work together with choices of Theme to help realize global textual design, by creating additional layers of textual prominence through the use of onset pitch and markedness. This further adds to our understanding of the 'wave' model of the textual metafunction (Halliday, [1979] 2002), a model which has always appeared problematic in terms of the actual analysis of textual systems where compositional models have tended to be imposed. Zhu's chapter, like Lukin's, shows how analysis of textual choices must include consideration of the elements given textual status in the discourse: the language choices given special attention through intonation choices or Thematic prominence through placement. This chapter is also important in that most work on macro-textual organization looks at written text, whereas this chapter focuses on spoken text (see also Bowcher, 2004).

Chapter 4 presents an investigation by Iwamoto of a novel area for the systemic research tradition: the notion of a spoken paragraph, or paraphone. Iwamoto provides a valuable review of literature within the field, his discussion demonstrating the importance of understanding and incorporating work outside of the SFL tradition. The comprehensive and integrated theory of SFL allows him to locate work from disparate theoretical and disciplinary backgrounds in relation to one another within this framework. As elsewhere in this volume, an important aspect of Iwamoto's approach is to interpret spoken paragraphing multidimensionally. This avoids the common trap of working exclusively from the 'bottom up' when dealing with phonetic phenomena, in terms of their identification and interpretation. He argues that 'paraphoning is a textual process to organize the ideational and interpersonal choices made in phonology, lexicogrammar and semantics, according to the context of situation in which the text is created'. Iwamoto's analysis indicates that pitch levels play a key role in realizing paraphone boundaries, and he argues for the importance of these in linguistic descriptions of spoken discourse. The study of paraphone is an important area for future research, with Iwamoto a pioneer within the SFL treatment of this area.

4.2 Part B: The interface between written and spoken language

The two chapters in Part B explore relations between the spoken and written modes of discourse, addressing issues of importance within literate cultures which prize so highly written texts: texts such as religious works, poems and other literary texts. Such texts may provide a valuable record of cultures from the ages before sound recording, but do not contain a record of any intended or appropriate intonational reading (see Smith, 2011 for a discussion). Davies in Chapter 5 continues and concludes his long-running series of studies (dating back to the late 1960s) of 'what people do when they read aloud'. He discusses why certain spoken interpretations, but not others, of written text are considered acceptable. The chapter builds upon Davies' fundamental insight that the interpretation of information systems in a written text derives crucially from consideration of the cohesive properties of that text, with the result that people generally are able to work out the correct choices of TONALITY and TONICITY in reading aloud, an interesting conclusion for teachers of English. Davies draws attention to the important relation between information structure and ellipsis, and shows also how cohesion helps determine the extent of New and Given. To illustrate this point, he provides nine different possible interpretations of a short sentence, each disambiguated by a simple preceding co-text, a question. The chapter includes humorous instances of misreadings of intonation and includes an interesting experiment: recording readings of a transcription (without markup for intonation) of one of Halliday's 1970 texts, analysed in terms of differences between the original and the read aloud text.

In Chapter 6 Cummings offers an exciting new addition to our understanding of the interpretation of written text in terms of choices in information systems. His sample texts are designed to be read as writing, and not written to be read aloud. As with the other chapters in this section, the issue addressed is how a reciter of such a written English prose text decides, just on the basis of the text, how to distribute and realize the focus or foci of information in each clause, and also how the reciter determines the extent of New-Given information. The chapter draws on the author's earlier computational work, where the intonational interpretation of clauses is based on their grammatical and lexical cohesion identified from a computerized analysis of the whole text. The algorithms used in this analysis measure relative distances between some lexical item or equivalent proforms in the text and their preceding lexis in order to derive a value for the relative degree of lexical cohesion. However, in this chapter Cummings uses 'a more intuitive method, based on the identification of anaphoric reference', and in doing so he draws on Martin's 1992 work in this area. Certain principles governing interpretation are derived, and seven 'rules' are applied 'after the interpretation of anaphoric reference and lexical identity as Given' to two quite dissimilar written texts. A key conclusion is 'that the location of the tonic in the recitation of a text written originally to be read as written may proceed mainly from principles of lexicogrammar'.

4.3   Part C: The interface between music and language

This section takes the systemic approach to phonology into the domain of music, showing how there are rich fields of study available to social semiotic theorists who venture beyond language as the conventional and usually sole focus of phonological studies. Banks presents a focused study in Chapter 7 of the sung interpretation of what Halliday and Matthiessen (2014: 3) refer to as a valued text, an 'artefact', Handel's *Messiah*. In particular, Banks focuses on the vocal interpretation of the '-ed' endings of the simple past form and the past participle as a separate syllable in certain parts of the sung performance. Banks points out that this pronunciation was obsolete by Handel's time, and analyses its use in the *Messiah* using the appraisal framework and interprets its use against the socio-cultural context. Banks shows that such an unusual choice by

Handel, and in certain parts only of the oratorio, added value to the text: a sense of gravitas befitting the privileged status of the oratorio, derived from the Bible, as 'ancient, sacred, revered'. The application of the appraisal framework to an entire text as text and to a rank below the word, the rank of morpheme, is suggested as a novel aspect of the chapter. The chapter draws on a diverse range of historical, literary and other cultural knowledge sources in an informed account showing again, as elsewhere throughout the volume, how an account of phonological phenomena informed by higher-strata perspectives – context and other linguistic phenomena – is enriched.

Caldwell takes the study of systemic phonology into the domain of paralanguage in Chapter 8, in a study of the differences between the sung and rap vocal styles. Applying van Leeuwen's (1999) pioneering social semiotics approach to the study of sound, Caldwell draws on work within a range of traditions and disciplines, including phonetics, SFL and other traditions of phonology, music studies and SFL and social semiotic work in general, and presents novel and interesting visual representa-tions of the analyses of various features of vocal performances. A crucial point is that paralanguage features operate alongside but not within the phonology of language (hence the term 'paralanguage'!), as 'a distinct and interacting modality'. The chapter draws on van Leeuwen's modelling of binary, non-discrete (gradient) parametric systems (2009), but adds the feature of probabilistic weighting to these systems (cf. Halliday, 1991; see Fawcett, this volume). For example, he finds that there is a higher probability for the sung voice to slide its consonant aspiration. Caldwell presents a valuable description of several new features of the human semiotic potential within contemporary culture, and draws the attention to the rich field of the social semiotics of sound, both outside and within language as conventionally understood.

4.4   Part D: Modelling intonation

The chapters in Part D remind us that the ongoing development of a theory is itself an important area of study. Chapter 9 presents Tench's attempt to describe word phonology in English using the SFL tool of system networks. The chapter begins with a discussion of the relationship between lexicogrammar and phonology. Then, through the use of system networks, Tench lays the groundwork for modelling word phonology in English by concentrating on words in citation form and specifically monomorphemic words. He explains that system networks to represent the 'options' available for phonological features of words for speakers of English are different from system networks at other levels of language such as the level of intonation or lexicogrammar in that rather than being systems of 'options from which a speaker chooses to create meaning', system networks at the level of the word are 'specifications of what the speakers of a language recognize as having been established in, or "chosen" by, the language' itself. This chapter complements work by Young (1992) who develops a systemic description of consonant clusters in accented syllables. Some of the system networks included in Tench's chapter are those for syllable structure, syllable peaks and syllable margins, and he briefly covers other dimensions of word phonology, such as allophonic variation, phonotactics and sound symbolism. His discussion of the cultural associations between certain sounds and qualities is particularly enlightening, and he makes suggestions for how this particular area of systemic phonology could be further investigated. Although Tench concentrates his discussion of word phonology to Southern England Standard Pronunciation, the principles for modelling word phonology are applicable to any accent.

Chapter 10, by Smith, Fasciani and O'Halloran, discusses the role and value of technology in the study of phonology. It primarily focuses on two software applications supporting phonological research: Praat, and software currently under development. The latter, designed for multimodal research in general, is being developed with reference to the principles and framework of SFL. The chapter also mentions other digital resources useful for the study of sound and video.

Smith *et al.*'s starting point is the observation that 'progress throughout the last century of language studies in general and studies of speech in particular has been intimately linked to the development and increasingly widespread availability of technological resources enabling and supporting such study'. They identify a compartmentalization in the study of phono-logical phenomena, in terms of purposes and objects of study, with technology-based approaches tending to focus on the lower strata, while higher-strata phenomena remain the preserve of teachers of English and other humanities-based scholars and interests. As a result, there is much knowledge within each tradition that remains under-exploited because of a lack of a holistic approach to the study of speech and other sounds.

Software such as Praat offer exciting new opportunities, as studies within this volume show, for the integration of polysystemic analyses across multiple dimensions – metafunctions, ranks, strata – and so help to move us towards a synthesis of analysis and findings, which has eluded scholars of language, in particular those conducting software-based analyses. The new software adapted for large-scale SFL analyses moves us further along the path of integrated holistic views on text that are nevertheless grounded in empirical detail. The grounding in computational databases of systemic analyses offers a range of potentialities for exploitation in terms of further computational, mathematical and other processing, including, importantly, visualization techniques of large analytical data sets and their various post-processing forms, thus extending the human capacities for perception. Computer-based studies of the semiotics of sound in general, including music, are also discussed.

Chapter 11 presents for the first time how intonation and punctuation are generated within the Cardiff model of SFL. A feature of Fawcett's work within SFL in general has been his willingness to challenge key assumptions, perhaps as a result of his long-standing engagement with computational linguistics. This characteristic is particularly important in phonological and especially intonation studies, where the phenomena are often difficult to account for and where there has been disagreement over the interpretation of some basic features. The chief value of Fawcett's approach in this chapter is in the overall Cardiff framework, the model of systemic linguistics within which his description of intonation systems sits. His chapter provides a discussion of the relevant aspects of the general linguistic model within which a description of intonation and punctuation is to be located and understood. That is, Fawcett models language as a bi-stratal semiotic phenomenon, and this perspective informs his account of intonation and punctuation. A central claim is that 'the meanings that are built into a language are realized as either (i) syntax, (ii) items (words and morphemes) or (iii) one of intonation (in speech) or punctuation'. Another important feature of Fawcett's model is the probabilities assigned to systemic options.

Fawcett presents thirteen steps, as well as eight 'final adjustment rules', for the realization of intonation in form. He argues that these rules are as central to a complete model of the 'grammar' of intonation as they are to any complete model of syntax and items. The chapter illustrates (i) the sort of system networks that are needed, (ii) the sort of realization rules that are needed and (iii) the type of representation of the outputs that one should aim for in developing a theoretically motivated description of intonation and punctuation in language.

This chapter represents the outcome of many years of work by Fawcett in modelling language and language generation within the general framework of SFL theory, and builds on work by Halliday and Tench in particular. We are fortunate to have this important work included within this collection.

4.5   Part E: Interacting with systemic phonology

In the last chapter of the collection, Greaves offers an opportunity for the reader to become listener and analyst through interacting with the text, the sound files and Praat software. The data focused on in this chapter are two well-known genres of English: a sonnet and a limerick. The chapter begins with the concept of context in SFL followed by a discussion of the importance of rhythm. Reader–listeners are asked to actively participate in the exercise of 'feeling the rhythm' of a limerick and through this they become acquainted with the notational conventions used in analysing intonation in SFL. Through interacting with the sounds, the notational conventions, Praat graphs of the lines of the limerick, and his discussion of the context construed by the limerick, the reader–listener is provided with a rich experience of various aspects of the genre of a limerick.

The next part of Greaves' chapter presents a study of a very different type of text, a sonnet. The sonnet chosen for analysis is Milton's 'On his blindness'. Greaves' analysis of the sonnet, from its context, features of its lexicogrammar, to its manipulation of sound are combined with an analysis of Robert Speaight's reading of the poem. The reader–listener is led through a discussion of tones chosen by Speaight and what these choices mean in relation to the sonnet itself.

Greaves' chapter steps across the customary boundary of what constitutes the academic author–reader relationship, both in tenor and mode, and creates a new way of 'doing' academic discourse that befits our interactive digital age in the early twenty-first century. As with other chapters, rather than being a study of phonological phenomena as such, alone and in isolation from other semiotic phenomena, Greaves presents a discussion of the two texts in terms of various systems. But of course, he crucially involves a discussion of intonational systems, thus showing the important role these systems play in the meaning-making process of the text. This is the ultimate goal of systemic phonology studies: to bring analysis of intonation and other phonological phenomena to any study where they are relevant, rather than being the dedicated and sole focus within the work of a few 'experts' in the area. Moreover, Greaves demonstrates how an interpretation of an artistic text across a number of its features can be grounded in theory and analysis rather than via ad hoc commentary.

5 Concluding remarks

This collection adds rich analytical detail to the corpus of research in SFL phonology and offers original and cutting edge insights into the meaning-making potential of phonological systems in English. As discussed above, and as the contributions demonstrate, choices in phonology are not just about sound, but very much about meaning, and it is the understanding of the relationship between sound and meaning that is a major strength of the SFL approach to phonology. Meaning, as Firth put it, is 'the whole complex of functions which a linguistic form may have' and each function is 'the use of some language form or elements in relation to some context' (Firth, 1935: 72, 54). This conceptualization of meaning and function applies to all levels of language.

This volume presents work which focuses on English, but the approach employed may be adapted to investigating phonological phenomena in other languages. However, it should be remembered that systemic phonology is a 'non-universalist approach to the description of the phonology of a language' (Tench, 1992: 15). Investigations from an SFL perspective aim to describe and account for the variety of potentialities afforded by languages and choices made in actual texts, and the reasons why these choices and not others have been made. It is through such investigations that the researcher can begin to 'reveal how speakers increase their cultural repertoire, register by register', and how linguistic description can become 'a kind of cartography, a mapping of the "meaning potential" in the dynamic, open-ended spiral of community and personal experience' (Butt, 2001: 1819).

We hope that the research reported in this volume will inspire more SFL scholars to investigate phonological phenomena and to add to our understanding of the meaning potential of language.

References

Armstrong, L. E. and Ward, I. C. (1926) *Handbook of English Intonation*. Leipzig: Teubner.

Beckman, M. E., Hirschberg, J. and Shattuck-Hufnagel, S. (2005) The original ToBI system and the evolution of the ToBI framework. In S.-A. Jun (ed.) *Prosodic Typology: The Phonology of Intonation and Phrasing* 9–54. Oxford: Oxford University Press.

Bloomfield, L. (1933) *Language*. London: George Allen and Unwin.

Bolinger, D. L. M. (1958) Intonation and grammar. *Language Learning* 8: 31–7.

Bolinger, D. L. M. ([1964] 1972) Around the edge of language: intonation. *Harvard Educational Review* 34 (2): 282–93. Reprinted in D. L. M. Bolinger (ed.) *Intonation: Selected Readings* 19–29. Harmondsworth: Penguin.

Bowcher, W. L. (1998a) Intonation in English: workshop. *JASFL Occasional Papers* 1(1): 51–68.

Bowcher, W. L. (1998b) Intonation in radio sports commentating: towards an analysis and interpretation. In Y. Nagahara (ed.) *Descriptions and Theoretical Studies of Sentence Subordination*. Japanese Ministry of Education Research grant no. 07451097.

Bowcher, W. L. (2004) Theme and new in radio sports commentary. In D. Banks (ed.) *Text and Texture: Systemic Functional Viewpoints on the Nature and Structure of Text* 455–93. Paris: L'Harmattan.

Brazil, D. (1995) *A Grammar of Speech*. Oxford: Oxford University Press.

Brazil, D., Coulthard, M. and Johns, C. (1980) *Discourse Intonation and Language Teaching*. London: Longman.

Butt, D. (2001) Firth, Halliday, and the development of Systemic Functional theory. In S. Auroux, E. F. K. Koerner, H-J. Niederehe, and K. Versteegh (eds.) *History of the Languages Sciences: An International Handbook on the Evolution of the Study of Language from the Beginnings to the Present* 1806–38. Berlin: Walter de Gruyter.

Couper-Kuhlen, E. (1986) *An Introduction to English Prosody*. London: Arnold.

Couper-Kuhlen, E. and Selting, M. (eds) (1996) *Prosody in Conversation: Interactional Studies*. Cambridge: Cambridge University Press.

Crystal, D. (1969) *Prosodic Systems and Intonation in English*. Cambridge: Cambridge University Press.

Crystal, D. and Davy, D. (1969) *Investigating English Style*. London: Longman.

Dobson, E. J. (1968) *English Pronunciation 1500–1700 (Volume II: Phonology)*. Oxford: Clarendon Press.

Firth, J. R. (1935) The technique of semantics. *Transactions of the Philological Society* 34(1): 36–72.

Firth, J. R. (1957) *Papers in Linguistics: 1934–1951*. Oxford: Oxford University Press.

Firth, J. R. (1968) The language of linguistics. In F. R. Palmer (ed.) *Selected Papers of J. R. Firth: 1952–59* 27–34. London: Longman.

Fischer-Jorgensen, E. (1975) *Trends in Phonological Theory: A Historical Introduction*. Copenhagen: Akademisk Forlag.

Fletcher, J., Grabe, E. and Warren, P. (2005) Intonational variation in four dialects of English: the high rising tone. In S.-A. Jun (ed.) *Prosodic Typology: The Phonology of Intonation and Phrasing* 390–409. Oxford: Oxford University Press.

Gleason, H. A. ([1955] 1961) *An Introduction to Descriptive Linguistics* (revised edition). New York: Holt, Rinehart & Winston.

Gussenhoven, C. (2004) *The Phonology of Tone and Intonation*. Cambridge: Cambridge University Press.

Halliday, M. A. K. ([1963] 2005) The tones of English. *Archivum Linguisticum* 15(1): 1–28. Reprinted in J. J. Webster (ed.) (2005) *Studies in English Language, Volume 7 in the Collected Works of M. A. K. Halliday.* London: Continuum.

Halliday, M. A. K. (1970) *A Course in Spoken English: Intonation.* Oxford: Oxford University Press.

Halliday, M. A. K. (1975) *Learning How to Mean.* London: Arnold.

Halliday, M. A. K. (1978) *Language as Social Semiotic.* London: Arnold.

Halliday, M. A. K. ([1979] 2002) Modes of meaning and modes of expression: types of grammatical structure and their determination by different semanticfunctions. In D. J. Allerton, E. Carney and D. Holdcroft (eds) *Function and Context in Linguistic Analysis: A Festschrift for William Haas* 196–218. Cambridge: Cambridge University Press. Reprinted in M. A. K. Halliday and J. Webster (eds) *On Grammar* 57–79. London: Continuum.

Halliday, M. A. K. (1985a) *Spoken and Written Language.* Geelong, Vic: Deakin University Press.

Halliday, M. A. K. (1985b) Part A. In M. A. K. Halliday and R. Hasan *Language, Context and Text: Aspects of Language in a Social-Semiotic Perspective.* Geelong, Vic: Deakin University Press.

Halliday, M. A. K. (1991) Towards probabilistic interpretations. In E. Ventola (ed.) *Trends in Linguistics Studies and Monographs 55: Functional and Systemic Linguistics Approaches and Uses* 39–61. Berlin: Mouton de Gruyter.

Halliday, M. A. K. and Greaves, W. S. (2008) *Intonation in the Grammar of English.* London: Equinox.

Halliday, M. A. K. and Matthiessen, C. M. I. M. (2014) *Halliday's Introduction to Functional Grammar* (4th Edition). Abingdon: Routledge.

Halliday, M. A. K. and Webster, J. J. (2009) Keywords. In M. A. K. Halliday and J. J. Webster (eds) *Continuum Companion to Systemic Functional Linguistics* 229–53. London: Continuum.

Hart, J. ([1551] 1955) The opening of the unreasonable writing of our inglish toung. In B. Danielsson (ed.) *John Hart's Works on English Orthography and Pronunciation (1551, 1569, 1570) Part I.* Stockholm: Alqvist and Wiksell.

Hasan, R. (1995) The conception of context in text. In P. H. Fries and M. Gregory (eds) *Discourse in Society: Systemic Functional Perspectives. Meaning and Choice in Language: Studies for Michael Halliday* 183–283. Norwood, NJ: Ablex.

Hirst, D. and Di Cristo, A. (eds) (1998) *Intonation Systems: A Survey of Twenty Languages.* Cambridge: Cambridge University Press.

Jenks, C. J. (2011) *Transcribing Talk and Interaction: Issues in the Representation of Communication Data.* Amsterdam: John Benjamins.

Johns-Lewis, C. (ed.) (1986) *Intonation in Discourse.* London: Croom Helm.

Johnson, K. (2011) Ilse Lehiste. *UC Berkeley Phonology Lab Annual Report.* Available at http://linguistics.berkeley.edu/phonlab/annual_report/documents/2011/Ilse. pdf (accessed 19 June 2012).

Jones, D. ([1909] 1937) *The Pronunciation of English* (2nd edition). Cambridge: Cambridge University Press.

Jun, S.-A. (ed.) (2005) *Prosodic Typology: The Phonology of Intonation and Phrasing.* Oxford: Oxford University Press.

Kingdon, R. (1958) *The Groundwork of English Intonation.* London: Longman.

Kingston, J. and Beckman, M. E. (eds) (1990) *Papers in Laboratory Phonology I: Between the Grammar and Physics of Speech.* Cambridge: Cambridge University Press.

Kohler, K. J. (2006) Paradigms in experimental prosodic analysis: from measurement to function. In S. Sudhoff, M. Lenertova, R. Meyer, S. Pappert, P. Augurzky, I. Mleinek, N. Richter and J. Schieber (eds) *Methods in Empirical Prosody Research* 123–52. Berlin: Walter de Gruyter.

Kuiper, K. (1996) *Smooth Talkers: The Linguistic Performance of Auctioneers and Sportscasters.* Mahwah, NJ: Lawrence Erlbaum & Associates.

Ladd, D. R. (2008) *Intonational Phonology* (2nd edition). Cambridge: Cambridge University Press.

Ladefoged, P. (1975) *A Course in Phonetics.* Orlando, FL: Harcourt Brace.

Lehiste, I. (1970) *Suprasegmentals.* Cambridge, MA: MIT Press.

Martin, J. R. (1992) *English Text: System and Structure.* Amsterdam: John Benjamins.

Matthiessen, C. M. I. M., Teruya, K. and Lam, M. (2010) *Key Terms in Systemic Functional Linguistics.* London: Continuum.

Pierrehumbert, J. and Hirschberg, J. (1990) The meaning of intonational contours in the interpretation of discourse. In P. R. Cohen, J. Morgan and M. E. Pollack (eds) *Intentions in Communication* 271–311. Cambridge, MA: MIT Press.

Pike, K. L. (1982) *Linguistic Concepts: An Introduction to Tagmemics.* Lincoln, NE: University of Nebraska Press.

Schubiger, M. (1958) *English Intonation: Its Form and Function.* Tubingen: Max Niemeyer Verlag.

Smith, B. A. (2008). *Intonational systems and register: A multidimensional exploration.* PhD thesis, Macquarie University, Sydney. Available at www.isfla. org/Systemics/Print/Theses.html.

Smith, B. A. (2011). Speech and writing: intonation within multimodal studies. In K. L. O'Halloran and B. A. Smith (eds) *Multimodal Studies: Exploring Issues and Domains* 39–54. London: Routledge.

Sweet, H. (1877) *A Handbook of Phonetics: Including a Popular Exposition of the Principles of Spelling Reform.* Oxford: Clarendon Press.

Tench, P. (1988) The stylistic potential of intonation. In N. Coupland (ed.) *Styles of Discourse* 50–84. London: Croom Helm.

Tench, P. (1990) *The Role of Intonation in English Discourse.* Frankfurt: Peter Lang.

Tench, P. (1992) From prosodic analysis to systemic phonology. In P. Tench (ed.) *Studies in Systemic Phonology* 1–17. London: Pinter.

Trubetzkoy, N. S. ([1935] 1968) *Introduction to the Principles of Phonological Descriptions* (trans. L. A. Murray, ed. H. Bluhme). The Hague: Martinus Nijhoff.

van Leeuwen, T. (1985) Persuasive speech: the intonation of the live radio commercial. *Australian Journal of Communication* 7: 25–34.

van Leeuwen, T. (1992) Rhythm and social context: accent and juncture in the speech of professional radio announcers. In P. Tench (ed.) *Studies in Systemic Phonology* 231–62. London: Pinter.

van Leeuwen, T. (1999) *Speech, Music, Sound.* Basingstoke: Palgrave Macmillan.

van Leeuwen, T. (2009) Parametric systems: the case of voice quality. In C. Jewitt (ed.) *The Routledge Handbook of Multimodal Analysis* 68–77. New York: Routledge

Young, D. (1992) English consonant clusters: a systemic approach. In P. Tench (ed.) *Studies in Systemic Phonology* 44–69. London: Pinter.

Part A

Intonation: Construing the Textual Metafunction

1   An investigation of how intonation helps signal information structure

Gerard O'Grady[a]

1.1   Tonicity and the projection of Given and New

There is widespread acceptance in the literature that speakers, operating in real time in pursuit of their individual communicative goals, use intonation to package their message into Given and New lexical elements. However, it is still not entirely clear what the terms Given and New refer to, nor how information structure relates to tonic and pre-tonic prominence. This chapter briefly examines the second issue in §1.2 before returning to the first one in §1.3. According to Halliday (1994: 296), 'information ... is the tension between what is already known or predictable and what is new or unpredictable'. Speakers make tonicity selections in order to project the status of lexical items within the tone unit as New or Given. In the unmarked case the tonic syllable occurs within the final lexical item in the tone unit. The placement of the tonic syllable signals unambiguously the culmination of the New but the boundary between the Given and

---

a   **Gerard O'Grady** is a Senior Lecturer in Language and Communication (phonology) at the Centre for Language and Communication Research, Cardiff University. His main research interests are intonation, spoken information structure, critical discourse analysis and linear grammars. He is active in the SFL community and co-organized the European Systemic Functional Linguistics Conference and Workshop in 2009. He is also a co-founder of the LinC research network at Cardiff University with Tom Bartlett and Lise Fontaine. His recent publications include two books, *A Grammar of Spoken English Discourse: The Intonation of Increments* (2010) and *Key Concepts in Phonetics and Phonology* (2012), as well as the article 'The unfolded imagining of Segolene Royal' in the *Journal of Pragmatics* (2011). He co-edited the volumes, *Systemic Functional Linguistics: Exploring Choice* (Cambridge 2013) and *Choice in Language: Applications in Text Analysis* (Equinox 2013).

New is not signalled solely by the phonology. Interlocutors utilize the previous linguistic and situational context to project Given and New material (Halliday and Greaves, 2008). Thus, in examples such as (1) which are uttered out of the blue, the tonic placement on *bank* signals that it is projected unambiguously as New:

(1) || mary /went to the /BANK ||

New

The domain of Newness spreads back through the tone unit. The entire tone unit is projected as New. However, consider this (albeit unlikely) example:

(2)   What happened to Mary?
        || mary /went to the /BANK ||

Given   New

Here, *bank* is projected as New while *Mary*, despite being prosodically prominent, cannot be New because she has been referred to previously. Example (3) is a more likely answer to the question: what happened to Mary?

(3) || ∧ she /went to the /BANK ||

Given   New

In example (3) the tonic placement on *bank* signals that it is unambiguously New and as in example (2) the boundary between the Given and New is the start of the second foot. However, unlike example (2) the Givenness of *she* is signalled by a lack of prosodic prominence. Halliday (1967a: 206–207) argues that in any non-initial information unit recoverable information tends to be represented anaphorically, by reference, substitution or ellipsis. In addition non-anaphoric closed-system items such as verbal auxiliaries and prepositions are, he states, inherently Given. To illustrate, consider example (1) reprinted as example (4):

(4) || mary /went to the /BANK ||

New

Within the all-New tone unit, we find *to* which as a non-anaphoric closed class item is inherently Given as a recoverable closed-system item found among lexical items which have been projected as New. Speakers are of course entirely free to make closed class items tonic in pursuit of their individual communicative goals. Consider example (5) and the slightly more difficult to explain example (6), both adapted from Lambrecht (1994: 254):

(5)   *A mother to her daughter: Did you do that?*
      The daughter pointing at her brother: || ∧ no /HE did ||

(6)   A: *Let's go the kitchen and get something to eat*
      B: || ∧ there's nothing /TO eat ||

In example (5) the daughter makes the closed class item *he* tonic not only to project her innocence but also to draw attention to her claim that her brother and not she was responsible. In example (6) Lambrecht (1994: 254) argues that the placement of the tonic on 'the semantically empty function word *to*' arose by default. Any other tonic placement could have resulted in an unwarranted contrast. But as Lambrecht notes the speaker's tonicity selection is motivated by not signalling other possible information structures. If the speaker had chosen to make *no(thing)* tonic his/her utterance would have signalled an explicit contrast between *no* and *some*, the utterance would represent an explicit face threatening denial of the previous utterance. A tonic placement on *eat* would leave open the theoretical possibility that there might be something to drink in the kitchen. The tonic choice in (6) alone signals a non-face threatening correction.

From the discussion so far, as a first approximation, three conclusions can be drawn:

1.   Lexical items are projected as New if they are tonic.
2.   Lexical items are projected as New if they (a) contain prominent syllables, (b) are found in pre-tonic position and (c) are neither recoverable from the physical context nor the co-text.
3.   Closed-system items are Given unless the speaker chooses to make them tonic.

1.2   How long does a lexical item remain recoverable?

There is dispute in the literature as to the length of time in which a lexical item remains recoverable from the context. Givón (1983: 352–4) argues that it is possible to quantify a limit beyond which a previously mentioned element is no longer recoverable from the context. He is cited, in a personal communication, by Geluykens (1989: 135), as proposing a limit of twenty preceding clauses. However, as his limit is based on unspecified psycholinguistic constraints, his reasons are neither transparent nor entirely convincing. Geluykens points out that as speech is full of pauses, false starts and hesitations, and is composed of variations in speech rate, clauses are not the ideal measure of distance. He identifies three further complicating factors in measuring the recoverability of lexical items in speech, namely turn taking, the number of speakers and the nature of the intervening material (*ibid.*: 135–6). Intuitively, it appears that a correlation should exist between the number of conversation turns, topic shifts, speakers and the recoverability of a lexical item. Similarly, if the intervening material is related to the previously mentioned lexical element, it should remain potentially recoverable.

Chafe (1987) defines recoverability in terms of whether or not an 'item' is present in the listener's short-term memory. Once an item has passed out of short-term memory it can no longer be considered Given. In line with the psychological literature, he argues that short-term memory can only hold seven items plus or minus two. It is unclear whether item refers to a word, a phrase or a tone unit. In an analysis of a monologue, he rules out a priori the possibility that a second mention of *old world* could be Given information even though the two mentions were separated by only 29 tone units (Chafe, 1994: 29). On the other hand, he states that references to 'participants' in events or states remain potentially recoverable even after they have left the listener's short-term memory (*ibid.*: 67). Unfortunately he does not suggest how long the reference remains potentially recoverable.

In contrast, Halliday (1967a: 209) reports an example where the lexical item 'student' remained recoverable even though its previous mention had been 83 information units earlier. Prince (1992: 309) seemingly goes further and suggests that once a speaker has introduced an entity into a discourse, hearers are assumed to be able to remember it until the completion of the entire discourse (also Allerton, 1978: 142 for a similar view). To conclude, it can be said that the concept of recoverability is at least, in theory, ambiguous, in that unless a lexical item is tonic, it is not unambiguously New. An example demonstrates:

(7) || ∧ he brought /Mary to the /PARty ||

In example (7) *Mary* is a pre-tonic prominence and thus, likely to be projected by the speaker as part of the New. However, in order to establish whether Mary is in fact projected as part of the New, an analyst must investigate the context to see whether or not there has been a previous mention of *Mary*. If there has been a recent mention of *Mary* the lexical item is recoverable and not projected as part of the New. However, if there has been a previous but distant mention of *Mary*, the analyst is forced to make a subjective judgement as to whether or not the speaker's placement of a pre-tonic prominence on *Mary* was intended to project her status as New or whether or not the prominence in the context was informationally redundant. We can conclude that pre-tonic prosodic prominences are ambiguous in signalling information structure (Halliday, 1967b; Halliday and Greaves, 2008).

Taglicht (1984: 34) raises what he considers to be a problem with Halliday's theory of intonation. In example (8), adapted from Taglicht (*ibid.*: 34, ex. 9), he points out that in response to a question such as 'what happened?', the respondent might produce the following response:

(8) || John /phoned /MAry || ∧ and /Peter phoned /JANE ||

　　　　New　　　　　　　　Given　　　　　　　　New

In the first tone unit the tonic item *Mary* is projected by the speaker as being unambiguously New. As the other lexical items in the first tone unit are not recoverable from the context, they too are projected as New. In the second tone unit the tonic syllable *Jane is* projected as New, but the non-prosodically prominent lexical item *phoned* is recoverable from the context and, thus, must represent the boundary between the New and the Given elements in the second tone unit. However, this seems problematic. In the context *Peter* seems as New as *John*. There is no reason to suppose that a hearer could have recovered *Peter* from the context more easily than any of the other participants. In the context, none of the participants have been referred to previously. Additionally, *Pe(ter)* is as prosodically prominent as the New lexical item *John*. In short the Givenness of *Peter* seems awkward and motivated only by theoretical preconceptions.

The claim that a tonic accent on the final lexical item of a tone unit represents the unmarked or neutral case[1] does not appear to apply to all types of utterances. Examples (9a) and (9b), based on Newman (1946), illustrate this point:

(9a) || ∧ I have in /STRUCtions to /leave ||

　　　　　　　　New

(9b) || ∧ I have in /structions to /LEAVE ||

　　　　　　　　New

Both (9a) and (9b) would appear to be possible, but different, answers to a question such as *what are you doing?* Crucially there does not appear to be any means available for the speakers to signal the difference in meaning other than through their tonicity selections. It is clearly not sufficient to claim that in (9a) the verbal item is Given, as this would imply that (9a) is synonymous with (9c), which appears open to two contextually different readings:

(9c) || ∧ I have in /STRUCtions ||

The first reading is that the speaker has some instructions he/she has been asked to leave as in (9a), and the second that the speaker has been instructed to do something as in (9b). The combination of the lexicogrammar and the prosodic prominence pattern in (9a) of a tonic followed by a prominent syllable realizes a different meaning than it does in combination with the prosodic prominence pattern in (9b) of a pre-tonic prominence followed by a tonic. This suggests that in English, not only does prosodic prominence play a role in signalling the lexical items speakers intend their hearers to attend to, but also a post-tonic prominence may signal that it is part of the New. Indeed, as numerous authors, such as Cruttenden (1997: 78), Gussenhoven (1983: 25ff.) and Ladd (2008: 244ff.) have documented, there exists a class of constructions known as eventive constructions. In eventive constructions a tonic placement on the nominal rather than the final verbal element appears to project that the entire utterance is New. Consider the following pairs:

(10a) || ∧ the /BAby /cried ||
         ←―――
        New

(10b) || ∧ the /baby /TALKED ||
        ←―――――――
        New

(11a) || ∧ the /KETtle /boiled ||
        ←―――
        New

(11b) || ∧ the /kettle ex/PLODED ||
        ←―――――――
        New

It is easy to imagine a context where neither the verbal nor the nominal element in each of the above examples was recoverable. While the lexical items *cried* and *boiled* are not tonic, they do not appear to be projected as

Given. Instead, they appear to make up the non-focal component of the New. In contrast the tonic verbs *talked* and *exploded* are both focal and New.

Bolinger (1986: 11–126) posits four reasons, of which the first three are of relevance to the present discussion,[2] for the potential deaccenting of content words in English as in examples (9) to (11):

1. Meanings already implied in the context.
2. Meanings which are so ubiquitous in a culture that they can be taken for granted.
3. Meanings sacrificed to a nearby focal meaning.

The deaccenting of *cried* and *boiled* can be explained by any of the three reasons. Kettles, after all, are devices for boiling water, and it is likely that an utterance such as (11a) is either an invitation to have tea or a reminder to make some! The tonic placement on *ba(by)* projects that it is the baby who needs attending to and not the crying. In (10b) and (11b) the verbs *talked* and *exploded* are the focus of the utterance; it is not every day that babies start talking and kettles explode! The difference in the tonicity selections between the (a) and the (b) examples moves the primary focus but does not in these examples change the extent of the new elements. In other words, it is argued that the information structure of (10a) and (11a) reprinted as (12) and (13) is:

(12) || ∧ the /BAby /cried ||

⟵⟶
New

(13) || ∧ the /KETtle /boiled ||[3]

⟵⟶
New

To summarize the preceding discussion, it is suggested that tonic placement signals that the tonic lexical item is projected as the focus of the information contained within the tone unit. Other prosodically prominent syllables may signal contextually non-recoverable or recoverable elements. Thus far, this chapter has not yet addressed the question set out earlier: what do the terms Given and New refer to?

1.3 The meaning of Given and New

Prince (1981: 226ff.), in a rigorous review of the literature on Given and New, which did not however examine the role of intonation in projecting lexical items as Given or New, identified three differing and not always compatible uses of the terms:

- Given/New1 – recoverability/predictability
- Given/New2 – saliency (interest)
- Given/New3 – shared knowledge

The first use, which is identical to Halliday's, was examined in §1.1. The third, for two reasons, is outside the scope of this chapter. First, any discussion of how to identify shared knowledge and what it means to share knowledge requires at least a chapter of its own (see O'Grady, 2010: 52ff.). Second, speakers, as previously noted, are free to manipulate the information structure that best achieves their ends. We can easily imagine a speaker attempting to project information as shared in order to downplay its significance, or as not shared to heighten its freshness. The equation of Given with shared knowledge and New with non-shared knowledge presupposes that speakers do not attempt to manipulate hearers in the pursuit of their communicative goals. Prince's second use of the term is similar to the theory of information structure developed by Bolinger (1972), known as 'Focus to Accent', which claims that speakers highlight the words which are of importance to their conversational ends. According to this view, the information status of *Mary* presented earlier in examples (1) and (2), reprinted as (14) and (15), is (somewhat counterintuitively) the same. The accented words *Mary, went* and *bank* are highlighted as being of particular interest to the hearer:

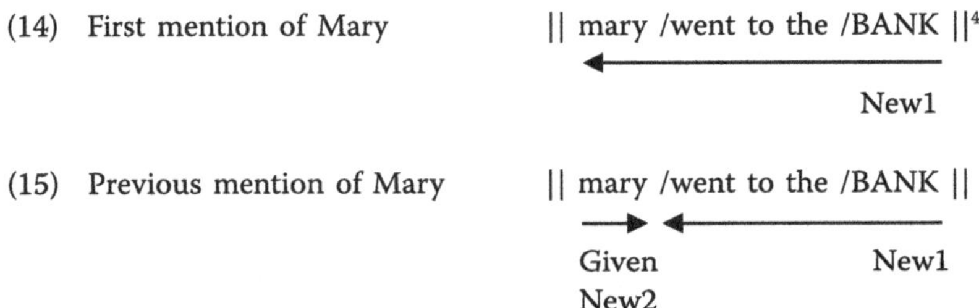

Yet, despite the prosodic prominence on *Ma(ry)* in example (15) the referent is recoverable from the context. *Mary*, while recoverable, is projected as representing a selection from what Brazil (1997: 23) labelled an existential paradigm: the set of available possibilities in the context. Out of the available possibilities the speaker chose one that meant that the person who did the act was not *John, Jane, Mike, Tom* (etc.), the act they did was not to *stay, come, leave* (etc.), and the place connected with the act was not the *shop, park, university, coffee shop* (etc.). There is no reason why the prosodically prominent item chosen from the set of available possibilities must be non-recoverable. To summarize, in example (14) the speaker projects *Mary* as being new in the sense of New1 (not recoverable) and New2 (interest), whereas in example (15) *Mary* is projected as New only in the sense of New2 (interest) but Given in the sense of New1.

Tonic syllables are, as example (16) from Halliday (1970) illustrates, not always contained in non-recoverable lexical items:

(16) || ʌ by the /time the /Great /CENtral was /built the || trains could manage the /gradients/ much more /EASily and the || great /CENtral || LINE || .... 23 tone groups ... || ʌ like the /Great /CENtral ||

The second and third instances of *Central* are recoverable though the speaker's tonicity selections project a context in which they are New2 information. The speaker for his own purposes makes tonic recoverable items and the hearer is instructed to focus on them as points of interest. What appears clear from the previous discussion is that the information status of an item in English depends on a combination of numerous factors: notably its syntactic realization, lack of previous or recent mention, unavailability in the situational context, and prosodic prominence. It is also clear as demonstrated by example (16) that speakers are free to manipulate their projection of an item's information status. As a result, it appears that, were we to follow Prince (1981, 1992) and attempt to examine the information status of spoken lexical items by examining only written scripts, our analysis could be incomplete at best.

This chapter attempts to illustrate the contribution of intonation in projecting information structure by examining:

1. The relationship between tonic syllables and lexical items. It is expected that the overwhelming majority of tonic syllables will be contained within lexical items, and furthermore that those lexical items will have been freshly introduced to the discourse. Thus, tonic syllables are likely to project items as New1 (but see example (16)).

2. The relationship between pre-tonic prosodic prominence and lexical items. It is expected that the overwhelming majority of non-tonic prominences will be contained within lexical items. The investigation aims to explicate whether pre-tonic prosodic prominences tend to project items as New1 or New2.

As noted earlier the issue of how long an item remains recoverable from the co-text remains in some dispute. Accordingly, this chapter examines the contribution intonation makes to projecting information structure under two conditions, A and B. Condition A stipulates that a lexical item is considered recoverable if it has been previously mentioned earlier in the discourse, while Condition B stipulates that a lexical item is considered recoverable if it has been previously mentioned within the previous 20 tone units.[5]

1.4   The texts

The three texts chosen for examination are monologues. Monologues were chosen for investigation as they allow for pre-planned, extended speaker turns which allow speakers the time and space to achieve their communicative purposes. Geluykens, as discussed previously, noted that the recoverability of a lexical item was dependent among other things on the number of speakers, the intervening number of speaker turns and the nature of the intervening material. Because of the absence of interruptions, turns, competition for the floor, and irrelevant intervening material, in the three texts used here, we can consider that once the speaker has introduced a lexical item that it remains potentially recoverable under Condition A for the entire discourse and Condition B for twenty tone units.

Texts 1 and 2 were spoken by the former UK prime minister, Tony Blair. Text 1 is his initial public response to the London bombings in July 2005 while Text 2 is his extended reply to a journalist's question at a White House press conference later the same year. Table 1.1 indicates that, despite Text 1 and Text 2 being spoken by the same speaker, there are considerable differences between them. Text 1 is spoken at an extremely slow rate with some considerable pauses between tone units. Text 2 is spoken with a far faster delivery, which (to my ears at least) approaches Blair's normal speaking rate. Two of the other factors which Geluykens proposed as influencing the length of time in which a lexical item remains recoverable are speaking rate and pausing. This suggests that a decrease in speaking rate coupled with an increased length of pausing may have influenced Blair's projection of his information structure by resulting in an increased number of tone units and concomitantly tonic syllables. For comparative purposes, study unit 35, 'Spontaneous monologue', from Halliday (1970), referred to here as Text 3, is also examined in case Blair's choices of prosodic prominence proved to be idiosyncratic.

Texts 1 and 2 were initially transcribed by ear and then rechecked using Praat software (Boersma and Weenink, 2008). As Text 3 is a commercially available transcription, the audio recording was not listened to; instead the printed transcription was taken to be the definitive intonation transcription.

Table 1.1 Description of the three texts.

	Text 1	*Text 2*	*Text 3*
Length of text	195 s	342 s	N/A
Number of tone units	96	191	72
Average number of words per tone unit	4.17	4.61	5.54
Average number of syllables per tone unit	6.01	6.25	6.4
Number of prosodic prominences	171.0	371	166
Average number of prosodic prominences per tone unit	1.78	1.91	2.3
Percentage of syllables which are tonic	16.6	16	15.6
Percentage of syllables which are prominent	13.0	15.1	20.4

Table 1.1 shows that Text 1 contains the fewest words and syllables per tone unit. However, the difference in tone unit length is much reduced if the tone units are measured in terms of syllables. Text 3 contains 33 per cent more words on average per tone unit than Text 1, but only 6 per cent more syllables. The percentage of tonic syllables across the three texts is roughly equivalent though as is to be expected there are more prosodically prominent syllables found on average in the Texts which have longer tone units. Each text contains tone units which on average contain around two prominences: the mandatory tonic and an optional pretonic. To conclude, the differences between the lengths of the tone units in the three texts do not appear to be large enough to have influenced the length of time which an item remains recoverable, especially under Condition B. Text 2 is a far longer text than the other two texts combined. However, under Condition B where an item is considered to be freshly introduced, if it has not appeared in the immediately preceding twenty tone units there should be no reason other than the speaker's motivated selections for differences in the projection of recoverable lexical items as New.

1.4.1 Tonic prominence

As anticipated, Table 1.2 indicates that the speakers overwhelmingly made tonic lexical items. Though on occasions, especially in Texts 1 and 2, the speaker chose to make tonic closed-system items which were projected

Table 1.2 Percentage of tonics on lexical versus closed items.

	Lexical Items	*Closed Items*
Text 1	96.9%	3.1%
Text 2	91.6%	8.4%[6]
Text 3	96.8%	4.2%

as being significant for the management of the discourse. In Text 1 the formulaic expression *thank you* was presented in its own tone group with *thank* tonic. And in Text 2 the fixed expressions *you know* and *at all,* were repeatedly placed into their own tone groups with *know* and *all* tonic. Had these been excluded only 2.1 per cent and 2.6 per cent of tonic placements would have occurred on closed-system items in both Texts 1 and 2 respectively. The significance of tonic closed-system items is examined below.

Table 1.3 presents the percentage of tonic syllables which occurred on lexical items that had been previously mentioned in the texts under Conditions A and B. Text 2 contains the highest percentage of tonic syllable selection on lexical items which have been previously introduced into the discourse. However, Text 2 is a far longer text than the other two texts and if Condition B is applied it contains a lower percentage of tonic syllable selections on previously mentioned lexical items than Text 1 does. Text 3, the shortest text, contains the lowest percentage of tonic syllable selections under both conditions. It is noticeable that the percentage of tonic syllable selections on previously mentioned lexical items is much reduced under Condition B for all texts, and especially Texts 2 and 3. Yet even under Condition B between 8 and 14 per cent of tonic syllables selections were on previously mentioned lexical items. This suggests that speakers in the pursuit of their communicative goals make syllables tonic irrespective of the objective status of the item as Given or New if they require their hearer to focus on the particular lexical item.

Table 1.3 Percentage of tonic syllables on previously repeated lexical items.

	Condition A	*Condition B*
Text 1	19.8%	14.6%
Text 2	24.6%	13.1%
Text 3	16.6%	8.3%

Example (17) from Text 1 illustrates a representative example of a tonic syllable being chosen on a repeated lexical item.

(17) || /each of /THE || /countries around that /table has some ex/PErience || ∧ of the e/ffects of /TERrorism || ∧ and all the /LEADers || ∧ as they will /INdicate || ∧ a little /bit /LAter || /share our com/plete reso/LUtion || ∧ to de/feat this /**TERr**orism ||

The second mention of terrorism, presented in bold, is redundant, and no meaning would apparently have been lost had the speaker ellipted it and made *defeat* tonic. Yet he chose not to do so. He chose to present it as New2 in order to emphasize that in the pursuit of his individual communicative purpose that he projects 'terrorism' to be of interest to his hearers.

Of further interest in example (17) is the tonic placement in the initial tone unit on the closed-system item *the*. This does not appear to be an example of a default accent as had the speaker chosen to place the tonic syllable on *each* no unwarranted contrasts would have been generated. The placing of the tonic syllable on *the* results from the speaker's marked tonality selection and serves the communicative function of managing his discourse by signalling a suspensive pause. He simulates that he is unsure of his next word and invites his hearers to fill in the missing word. The tonicity selection neither signals that the lexical item is New1 nor New2. Despite the tonic placement on *the* the initial two tone units of example (17) form a single all new information unit. The tonic on *the* while of significance for the management of the unfolding discourse is redundant informationally in that *the* does not represent a selection from an existential paradigm. To conclude this section, tonic syllable selections tend to occur on lexical items which are freshly introduced and project that the lexical item is New1. Speakers though are free to project a lexical item as being New2 through their tonicity selections. The significance of New2 selections will be examined in §1.5.

1.4.2   Pre-tonic prominences

Across all three texts, as expected, pre-tonic prosodic prominences tended to occur on full lexical items, see Table 1.4. Text 1 had a higher percentage of pre-tonic prosodically prominent closed-system items but as will be discussed below this arose chiefly because of the speaker's decision to repeatedly make prominent personal pronouns – see example (18).

Table 1.4 Percentage of pre-tonic prominences on lexical and non-lexical items.

	Lexical Items	*Closed-system items*
Text 1	84%	16%
Text 2	92.7%	7.3%
Text 3	93.6%	6.4%

Table 1.5 presents the percentage of pre-tonic prominent syllables that occurred on lexical items that had been previously mentioned under Conditions A and B. As with tonic syllable selections far fewer pre-tonic prominences were found on previously mentioned lexical items under

Table 1.5 Percentage of pre-tonic prominences on previously repeated lexical items.

	Condition A	*Condition B*
Text 1	9.3%	4%
Text 2	20%	13.9%
Text 3	13.9%	10.6%

Condition B. Yet, even under Condition B, between 4 and 14 per cent of pre-tonic prominent syllables occurred on lexical items, which had been previously mentioned.

The previous mention of a pre-tonic prosodically prominent lexical item, except in one case, was itself either a tonic or pre-tonic prosodic prominence. In Text 1, 50 per cent of the previous mentions were tonic prominences, while 50 per cent were pre-tonic prominences. In Text 2, 56.5 per cent of the previous mentions were tonic prominences whereas 44.5 per cent were pre-tonic prosodic prominences. And in Text 3, only 42.8 per cent of the previous mentions were tonic prominences compared with 57.2 per cent of the previous mentions which were pre-tonic prominences. Furthermore, if there were any further occurrences of the pre-tonic prosodically prominent lexical item later in the text it was likely to be repeated as either a tonic or pre-tonic prosodic prominence. All three texts contain chains of prosodically prominent lexical items, the significance of which is examined in §1.5.

1.4.3   Closed-system items and prominence

Within the three texts, tonic and pre-tonic prosodic prominences occurred on the following items, pronouns, formulaic expressions, determiners and prepositions. Table 1.6 illustrates the distributions.

Table 1.6 The number and type of prosodically prominent closed-system items.[7]

	Pronouns	*Formulaic expressions*	*Determiners*	*Prepositions*
Text 1	13	1	1	0
Text 2	11	12	0	0
Text 3	2	0	2	1

Across all three texts the most common type of prosodically prominent closed-system item were pronouns and in the case of Text 2 formulaic expressions. In Text 3 the determiners *some* and *all* were tonic. In both cases, unlike *the* (see example 17) the tonic selection projects the determiner as representing a selection from an existential paradigm. Unlike the case of *the* (example 17), the tonic prominence is not informationally redundant and the closed-system item is projected as New1. In Text 3 the speaker made a preposition *on* tonic but informationally it seems that the speaker intended to project the lexical item *move (on)* as tonic.[8]

The following example from Text 1 illustrates the communicative significance of prosodically prominent pronouns. The relevant items are presented in bold.

(18) || ʌ it's im/portant how/EVer ||that /**those** en /gaged in /TERrorism rea|| LIZE || ʌ that /our determi/NAtion || ʌ to de/fend / our /VAlues || ʌ and /**our** /WAY of / life || is /GREATer // ʌ than /**their** deter /MINation / ʌ to /cause /death / ʌand des/TRUCtion || ʌ to /innocent /PEOple || ʌ in a de/sire / ʌ to im/pose ex/TREMism || ʌ on the /WORLD || ʌ what/ever they /DO || ʌ it is /**our** determi/NAtion || ʌ that /**they** will / ʌ never suc/CEED || ʌ in de/STROYing || ʌ what /**we** /hold /DEAR || ʌ in /**this** /COUNTry ||

The prosodically prominent pronouns in example (18) are doubly foregrounded, first, by the rarity of prosodically prominent pronouns in Text 1 in particular and in the language system in general, and, second, by the repeated prosodic re-focusing on the pronouns. Tony Blair projects the pronouns as being centres of interest to his hearers by projecting them as selections from an existential paradigm. By so doing he projects his assumed unity with his audience while simultaneously opposing himself and his audience to the terrorists. Figure 1.1 illustrates the projected existential paradigms, with the items not chosen in each paradigm notated with a strike-through.

those	our	their	they	we	this
~~all others~~	~~my~~	~~my~~	~~I~~	~~I~~	~~all other~~
	~~your~~ *sing*	~~our~~	~~we~~	~~you~~ *sing*	
	~~your~~ *plural*	~~your~~ *sing*	~~you~~ *sing*	~~you~~ *plural*	
	~~their~~	~~your~~ *plural*	~~you~~ *plural*	~~they~~	

Figure 1.1 Existential selection of pronouns in Text 1.

Through his systematic selection of prosodic prominences, Blair projects a context where he signals to his hearers that *he* and *they* share values and a common way of life. He projects a context in which he and his audience possess a mutual determination to protect what he projects as jointly shared. An analysis focused solely on the lexicogrammar would

have been unable to catch the full extent of Blair's projection of unity
with his audience and his and their joint opposition to the terrorists.

In example (19) the speaker makes a marked tonality selection:[9]

(19) || ^ you can see it in /CHECHnya || ^ you /KNOW ||

Given   New   New

The tonic selection on *(you) know* does not signal the introduction of
a non-recoverable lexical item into the discourse. Instead it signals that
the fixed expression is projected as New2 and the speaker projects his
certainty that the hearer is implied to be already aware of and in agreement
with his claim that the results of terrorism and hatred can be witnessed
in Chechnya.

(20) || ^ that is pre/pared to /use any /means at /ALL ||

New

In example (20) the speaker chooses a marked tonicity selection by making
(at) all and not *means* tonic. The closed-system item *at all* is not projected
as freshly introduced into the discourse. Instead the speaker's marked
tonicity selection projects a context where he signals to his hearers the
emphatic nature of his warning; the tonic on *(at) all* projects the speaker's
certainty and heightens the gravity of the situation.

To conclude this section we have seen, across all three texts, that tonic
and pre-tonic prosodic prominence tends to co-occur with lexical items
which are freshly introduced to the discourse or New1. We have also seen
that speakers, in the pursuit of their individual communicative goals, may
make prosodically prominent lexical items which have been previously
introduced and that this prosodic prominence signals that these items
are New2. Lexical items which are foregrounded by receiving repeated
prosodic prominences tend to be doubly foregrounded by being presented
in lexical chains which run through the texts. Speakers, in pursuit of their
individual communicative purposes, make closed-system items prosodically prominent to highlight that they are New2. Most significantly for
present purposes, the information structure projected by a speaker in
any individual text is not entirely predictable from the lexicogrammar.
In other words, an analyst who wishes to examine the actual information
structure projected in a spoken text must take into account the meaning
potential realized by the speaker's intonational choices.

1.5   Foregrounded chains

In all three texts there are chains of lexical items which are foregrounded by their repeated prominence. This section examines the significance of these chains and investigates the effect of repeated prosodic prominence on lexical items across the three texts. In Tables 1.7–1.9 small capitals indicate the first mention of a lexical item, italics indicate that the item is a pre-tonic prominence and bold indicates that it is tonic. The numbers refer to the number of intervening tone units between mentions of the lexical item.

Table 1.7 Open-class items with repeated prosodic prominence in Text 1.

Lexical item	Type of prominence
HAPPENED	... (6) **happened** ... (48) **happened**
LONDON	... (14) **London** ... (12) **London**
TRYING	... (5) *try* ... (47) **try**
INFORMATION	... (3) **information**
CLEAR	... (48) **clear**
TERRORIST	... (31) **terrorism** ... (5) **terrorism** ... (13) *terrorist* ... (11) **terrorism**
ATTACKS	... (52) **attack**
PEOPLE	... (63) **people**
DIED	... (64) **death**
GEIGHT	... (11) **Geight** ... (34) **Geight**
LEADERS	... (12) **leaders**
MEETING	... (18) **meeting**[10]
DISCUSS	... (1) **discuss**
REACH	... (1) **reach**
PROBLEMS	... (1) **problems**
DETERMINATION	... (1) **determination** ... (6) **determination**

Table 1.7 reveals that, unsurprisingly, Tony Blair's initial verbal response to the London bombings focused on the topic of terrorism, which he constantly introduced as New. His audience hardly needed to be repeatedly informed of the existence of terrorism in a public response to a terrorist bombing. Yet Blair says:

(21) || ∧ that there have been a ... ∧ a /series of /terrorist /ATTACKS in || LONdon ||

In other words he does not say:

(22) || ∧ that there have been a ... ∧ a /SEries of /terrorist /attacks in /London ||

Example (22) would appear to represent the most congruent representation of the news to his audience. After all the only (possible) newsworthy fact in the confusion of the morning which Blair could have reported was that there had been more than one bombing! However, Blair's pre-tonic prominence on *terrorist* projects the element as New2. He re-introduces the concept of *terrorism* thirty-one tone units later, which under Condition B is considered the lexical item's first mention. Nevertheless, the four subsequent mentions of *terrorism/terrorist* are certainly not freshly introduced to the discourse even under Condition B. Despite this, three of the four mentions are prominent with two of the mentions tonic.

(23)   Each of the countries around that table has some experience || ∧ of the ef/fects of /TERrorism || ∧ and all the /LEADers || ∧ as they will /INdicate || ∧ a little bit /LATer || share our com/plete reso/LUtion || ∧ to de/feat this /TERrorism || ... [8 tone groups] || ∧ just as it is rea/sonably /CLEAR || ∧ that this is a /TERrorist attack || ∧ or a /SEries of /terrorist attacks || ... [9 tone groups] || ∧ its im/portant how/EVer || ∧ that /those en/gaged in /TERrorism ||

Had Blair ellipted the second mention of *terrorism* the object of the verb *defeat* would have been recoverable to his audience. Yet by not doing so he projects a context where *terrorism* as tonic is presented both as New2 and as the focus of interest in the tone unit. It is such a vital concept required for the achievement of his communicative goal that Blair projects a context where he cannot but keep it other than in focus. The subsequent mention of terrorist (or perhaps terrorist attack) is entirely predictable and a more neutral presentation of the information structure would have been to − as Blair does in the following tone unit − choose a syllable prior to *terrorist* as tonic. Similarly the remaining tonic placement on *terrorism* is unmotivated if Blair wants to signal that the word is not recoverable, but it is motivated if he intends to project that *terrorism* is of vital interest to the achievement of his communicative intention.

The key lexical items focused on in Text 2 were *September the eleventh, America, ideology, Muslims, terrorism* and *wrong.* It is noteworthy that many of the repeated prominences tend to cluster together so that even though the lexical items are not freshly introduced, even under Condition B, they are signalled as being foci of interest or as New2. For example, towards the end of the text Blair says:

(24) || this is /WRONG || ∧ it's not /just /wrong in its /METhods || ∧ it's /wrong in its i/DEas || ∧ it's/ wrong in its ide/OLogy || ∧ it's/wrong in / every /SINgle || ...

Table 1.8 Open-class items with repeated prosodic prominence in Text 2.

Lexical item	Type of prominence
AMERICAN	... (72) **America** ... (93) *America* ... (3) **America** ... (6) **America**
CHANGED	... (1) **changed** ... (2) *changed*
POLICY	... (1) *policy* ... (2) **policy** ... (2) **policy** ... (9) *policy* ... (50) policy
SEPTEMBER	... (2) *September* ... (4) *September* ... (6) *September* ... (45) *September*
ELEVENTH	... (2) **eleventh** ... (4) *eleventh* ... (6) **eleventh** ... (45) eleventh
GLOBAL	... (1) *global* ... (106) *global* ... (1) *global*
IDEOLOGY	... (31) ideology ... (52) *ideology* ... (24) ideology ... (8) ideology ... (36) ideology ... (27) ideology ... (8) ideology
DO	... (65) **doing** ... (1) *doing* ... (88) **doing**
HAPPENING	... (44) *happened* ... (86) *happening* ... (9) happening
COUNTRIES	... (66) **countries** ... (11) **country**
PEOPLE	... (69) *people* ... (38) **people** ... (26) people
MOVEMENT	... (98) movement
TERRORISM	... (15) **terrorism** ... (2) **terrorism** ... (3) **terror** ... (1) **terror** ... (1) *terrorism* ... (5) **terrorism** ... (50) terrorism
HATRED	... (23) **hatred** ... (1) **hatred**
SEE	... (41) **see** ... (73) **saw**
PALESTINE	... (70) **Palestine** ... (32) **Palestine**
PURPOSE	... (1) **purpose** (122) *purpose*
ISLAM	... (122) **Islam** ... (3) **Islam**
REPRISAL	... (1) **reprisal**
ADDITIONAL	... (1) *additional* ... (1) *additional* ... (2) *additional*
VIEW	... (1) **view**
REASON	... (11) *reason* ... (71) **reason**
BRITAIN	... (106) **Britain**
FIGHTING	... (82) *fight* ... (46) **fight**
TOUGH	... (41) *tough* ... (24) **tough**
MIDDLE EAST	... (40) *Middle* **East**
MUSLIM	... (72) *Muslim* ... (13) **Muslims** ... (4) *Muslims*
DEMOCRACY	... (4) *democracy*
REACTIONARY	... (93) *reactionary*
CIRCUMSTANCES	... (28) **circumstances**
ISRAEL	... (9) **Israel**
STOPPED	... (62) *stop* ... (1) *stop*
LEBANON	... (24) **Lebanon**
INNOCENT	... (17) *innocent*
STAYING	... (1) **staying** ... (45) *stay*
COURSE	... (46) **course**
PROBLEM	... (47) **problem**
PROPAGANDA	... (19) *propaganda*
SUPPRESS	... (4) **suppression**
WORSHIP	... (2) **worship**
NONSENSE	... (1) **nonsense**
WRONG	... (1) *wrong* ... (1) *wrong* ... (1) *wrong* ... (1) *wrong*

The repeated pre-tonic prosodic prominence on *wrong* foregrounds not only that the word itself is of interest but also foregrounds the parallelisms in the clause structure. *Methods, ideas* and *ideology* are all, to some extent, lumped together as three similar things, which are *wrong*. Table 1.8 illustrates that Blair uses the word *ideology* eight times throughout Text 2, with seven of the repeated mentions tonic. Unlike many of the repeated prosodically prominent items there tends to be more than a twenty-tone unit distance between any two mentions of *ideology*. Hence, if we adopt Condition B we have to argue that *ideology* as a concept is of such interest to the achievement of Blair's communicative purpose that he consistently re-introduces it as New1. Otherwise, if we adopt Condition A, we can argue that even though *ideology* is not New1 Blair consistently projects it as the focus of interest or New2. However, what we are unable to say without examining the local contexts in which Blair produced the lexical item *ideology* is how it served the achievement of his communicative goal.

(25a) but actually before September the eleventh this global movement || ∧ with a / global ide/OLogy || was already in being ||

(25b) its purpose is to promote || ∧ its ide/OLogy || based upon a perversion of Islam

(25c) you got a genuine democracy of the people || how does their ide/ology / flourish in such /CIRcumstances ||

(25d) now it's a global movement || ∧ it's a /global ide/OLogy ||

(25e) because you're up against || ∧ an ide/OLogy || that is prepared to use any means at all

(25f) because the alternative || ∧ is actually /letting this ide/OLogy || grip larger and larger numbers of people

(25g) || ∧ and we're /not going to de/feat this ide/OLogy ||

(25h) || ∧ it's /wrong in its ide/OLogy ||

Blair's use of the lexical item *ideology* does not mirror the definition provided in the *Concise Oxford English Dictionary* (Allen, 1990), which states that ideology is 'the system of ideas at the basis of an economic or political theory'. Instead his use of the term seems closer to the view labeled by Eagleton (1991: 3) as the 'person-in-the-street' view. He projects that ideology is a distorted and over-simplified view of reality which arises out of an inflexible, outmoded and fanatical way of thinking. In Brazil's terms he projects that the lexical item has been selected from an existential paradigm consisting of two opposed items:

(26)

He projects the message that his enemies are irrational while implying that he himself is sensible and rational. In other words, he signals to his audience by his repeated prosodic prominences his common sense which of course contrasts with his enemies' ideology and by so doing validates his actions as perspicacious and proportionate.

Table 1.9 Open-class items with repeated prosodic prominence in Text 3.

Lexical items	Type of prominence
GREAT CENTRAL[11]	... (2) *Great* **Central** ... (29) *Great* **Central**
TRAINS	... (20) *trains* ... (3) *trains* ... (5) **trains** ... (7) *trains* (3) **trains** ... (7) *trains* ... (1) *trains* ... (14) **train**
LINE	... (13) **line** ... (9) *line* ... (5) **line**
RAILWAY[12]	... (14) **railway**
NORTH	... (54) **North**
TRACK	... (45) **track**
RUN	... (3) *run* ... (12) **run**
ELECTRICITY	... (11) *electrified*
DRIVERS	... (3) **driving**

The key concept which the speaker of Text 3 consistently chooses to make prosodically prominent is *train*, which is repeated ten times throughout the text. Only a single mention of train is projected as unambiguously Given.

(27) || trains could /manage the /gradients / much more /EASily and the ||
... [20 tone groups] || all the /trains have /been with/DRAWN || now /
if they decided to /keep the /track in /good con /DITIon and || run the
/ trains at the / speeds at / which they /COULD have been /run || ... [3
tone groups] what you /NEED for || this /PURpose is a || self / drive /
TRAIN || ...[5 tone groups] || ∧ and /THEN || ∧ in /stead of /running /
trains as they're /run at /PREsent || ∧ as /public /VEhicles || ∧ you /hire /
OUT || small /TRAINS to || indi/vidual /DRIVers [6 tone groups] || ∧ so
that /once a /train gets /into a /SECTion || no other /train can move /ON
to that /section and || ... [10 tone groups] ∧ there'd be /FAMily /trains for
|| ... [3 tone groups] || ∧ you'd have your /own /TRAIN and you'd ||

In example (27) there are three tonics on the repeated lexical item *train*. As the lexical item *train* has been previously introduced to the discourse under both Conditions A and B this is unexpected. We would have expected that the speaker would focus on the freshly introduced information, namely the type of trains, *self-drive*, *small* and *own*, and that it is these epithets which would have received the tonic. Indeed the speaker later in the text as expected focuses on the epithet *family* rather than the lexical item *train*. The significance of the repeated tonic placements on trains appears to be to signal that *train* is New2 in the sense that it is the very core of what the speaker is communicating. The focus on *train* as New2 is by the six pre-tonic prominences. The speaker could have, without compromising the comprehensibility of his message, replaced the pre-tonic prosodically prominent item *train* with closed-system items and moved the tonic to the freshly introduced epithets. The monologue could have been uttered as follows, with lexical changes indicated in small capitals and new tonic syllables indicated in bold capitals:

(28) || trains could /manage the / gradients /much more EASily and the || [20 tone groups] || all OF THEM have /been with /DRAWN || now /if they decided to /keep the /track in /good con /DITIon and || run THEM /at the /speeds at /which they /COULD /have been /run || ... [3 tone groups] what you /NEED for || this /PURpose is a || self /**DRIVE** /TRAIN || [5 tone groups] and then || ∧ in/stead of /running THEM as they're /run at / PREsent || ∧ as /public /VEhicles || ∧ you /hire /OUT || **SMALL** /TRAINS to || indi/vidual /DRIVers [6 tone groups] || ∧ so that /once ONE gets / into a /SECTion || no other ONE /can move /ON to that /section and || ... [10 tone groups] ∧ there'd be /FAMily /trains for ...[3 tone groups] || ∧ you'd have your /**OWN** /TRAIN and you'd ||

Yet the speaker chose not to produce a monologue with the prosodic prominence patterns in (28). He chose to project that the lexical item *train* was New2 and represented a selection from an existential paradigm which appears to consist of an opposition between *trains* and all other forms of *transport*. The effect of this is to signal to the hearer the aesthetic and practical value of trains as a form of transport and as a form of relaxation.

1.6   Conclusion

Examination of all three texts has revealed that the significance of speakers' tonic and pre-tonic selections can only be seen against the context in which they were uttered. A prominence normally projects an item as realizing a selection from an existential paradigm. In addition a tonic prominence signals that a particular lexical item is projected as the focus of the tone unit. However, speakers may on occasion produce prominences which, while informationally redundant, are significant for the management of the flow of their discourse by, for instance, creating expectations and, as in example (17), inviting their hearers to fill in the missing word.[13] Yet prominences on freshly introduced items project that the item is not recoverable from the context (New1), and also represent a selection from an existential paradigm (New2). The majority of tonic and pre-tonic prominences on previously mentioned lexical items in the three texts tend to co-occur with a distance of less than twenty tone units between the two mentions. This indicates that speakers in pursuit of their communicative goals may choose to make lexical items prosodically prominent in order to direct their hearers' attention to them irrespective of whether the particular lexical items are very much in the air.

Acknowledgements

I would like to thank the editors for their useful and thought-provoking comments and questions. In addition, I would like to thank Paul Tench and Martin Hewings for their informative comments on an earlier draft of this chapter. Finally, I'd like to thank Margaret Berry for useful discussions on the issues discussed in this chapter.

Notes

1. Strictly speaking, Halliday (1967b: 23) states that, 'a tone group is neutral in tonicity if the tonic falls on the last element of grammatical structure that contains a lexical item'. Though he acknowledges that 'this could be formulated even more simply by direct reference to lexis: the tonic in neutral tonicity, falls on the last lexical item in the tone group'.
2. Bolinger's fourth reason refers to meanings which the speakers choose to play down. This while unsatisfactory as an attempt to explain prosodic prominence choices is, however, well worth remembering. Speakers, as Halliday (1994: 298) states, are free to play down meanings or play up meanings in the pursuit of their individual communicative purposes. In other words, speakers' choices of which syllables to make prosodically prominent realize their assumed projection of whether a lexical item is Given or New, and not whether in fact a lexical item is objectively recoverable or not from the context. Prince (1992) notes that discourse new items may be hearer 'old' (Given) but as she

does not examine intonation is unable to make the logical corollary claim that hearer New items may be presented as Given in the discourse.

3.   An analogy may perhaps be drawn with primary and secondary lexical stress. In almost all cases secondary stress precedes the primary stress but in a few cases e.g. anecdote the primary stressed syllable precedes the secondary stressed one.

4.   Strictly speaking, as explained on page 28, the closed-system item *to* is inherently Given.

5.   The tone unit rather than the clause has been taken, albeit somewhat arbitrarily, as a more appropriate measure of speech.

6.   Three instances of *I think* and one of *I mean* with the verb tonic have been interpreted as main verbs and not as epistemic parentheticals. Dehé and Wichmann (2010) note the difficulty in deciding whether the verbs in expressions such as *I think* and *I mean* in clause initial position are main verbs or separate comment clauses. In any case they endorse Aijmer's (1997: 21) claim that the placing of expressions such as *I think* into a separate tone group, indicates less tentativeness, more deliberation and greater objectivity. The tonic placements on the verbs project that they are points of interpersonal interest or in the terms used here New2.

7.   In Text 1, two of the pronouns, the determiner and the formulaic expression were tonic. The rest of the prosodic prominences occurred on pre-tonic items. In Text 2, four of the pronouns and all of the formulaic expressions were tonic. The rest of the prosodic prominences were pre-tonic. In Text 3, two of the determiners and the preposition were tonic. The pronouns were all pre-tonic.

8.   The items *hire out, run off* and *run into* had tonic prominence on the preposition but they were classified as open-class phrasal verbs.

9.   In this analysis I assume that *you know* represents an epistemic parenthetical and not a main clause with an ellipted object. Had *you know* been interpreted as a main clause, only *know* would have been projected as New.

10.   The second mention of meeting was a non-finite verbal element.

11.   In all realizations of this lexical item both component words were prosodically prominent.

12.   The first mention of *railway* was not marked by prosodic prominence, though the second mention was!

13.   Hence, despite the tonic prominence on *the* in example (17), the tonic functions to focus the hearer's attention onto the following word by signalling that it is recoverable from the context of situation shared by the speaker and their audience.

References

Aijmer, K. (1997) I think: an English modal particle. In T. Swan and O. Jansen Westvik (eds) *Modality in Germanic languages: Historical and Comparative Perspectives* 1–47. Berlin: Mouton de Gruyter.

Allen, R. E. (ed.) (1990) *Concise Oxford English Dictionary* (8th edition). Oxford: Oxford University Press.

Allerton, D. J. (1978) The notion of 'givenness' and its relationship to presupposition and to theme. *Lingua* 44: 133–68.

Boersma, P. and Weenink, D. (2008) Praat doing phonetics by computer, version 5.0.32. Available at www.praat.org (accessed 24 November 2010).

Bolinger, D. (1972) Accent is predictable (if you're a mind reader). *Language* 48: 633–44.

Bolinger, D. (1986) *Intonation and its Parts: Melody in Grammar and Discourse.* Stanford, CA: Stanford University Press.

Brazil, D. (1997) *The Communicative Value of Intonation in English.* Cambridge: Cambridge University Press.

Chafe, W. (1987) Cognitive constraints on information flow. In R. S. Tomlin (ed.) *On Coherence and Grounding in Discourse* 21–51. Amsterdam: John Benjamins.

Chafe, W. (1994) *Discourse, Consciousness, and Time: The Flow and Displacement of Conscious Experience in Speaking and Writing.* Chicago, IL: The University of Chicago Press.

Cruttenden, A. (1997) *Intonation* (2nd edition). Cambridge: Cambridge University Press.

Déhe, N. and Wichmann, A. (2010) The multi-functionality of epistemic parentheticals in discourse. *Functions of Language* 17(1): 1–28.

Eagleton, T. (1991) *Ideology: An Introduction.* London: Verso.

Geluykens, R. (1989) Information structure in English conversation: the given–new distinction revisited. *Occasional Papers in Systemic Linguistics* 3: 129–47.

Givón, T. (1983) *Topic Continuity in Discourse: A Quantitative Cross-Language Study.* Amsterdam: John Benjamins.

Gussenhoven, C. (1983) *On the Grammar and Semantics of Sentence Accents.* Dordrect: Foris.

Halliday, M. A. K. (1967a) Notes on transitivity and theme in English. *Journal of Linguistics* 3(2): 199–244.

Halliday, M. A. K. (1967b) *Intonation and Grammar in British English.* The Hague: Mouton.

Halliday, M. A. K. (1970) *A Course in Spoken English: Intonation.* London: Oxford University Press.

Halliday, M. A. K. (1994) *An Introduction to Functional Grammar* (2nd edition). London: Arnold.

Halliday, M. A. K. and Greaves, W. S. (2008) *Intonation in the Grammar of English.* London: Equinox.

Ladd, D. R. (2008) *Intonational Phonology* (2nd edition). Cambridge: Cambridge University Press.

Lambrecht, K. (1994) *Information Structure and Sentence Form*. Cambridge: Cambridge University Press.

Newman, S. (1946) On the stress system of English. *Word* 2: 171–87.

O'Grady, G. (2010) *A Grammar of Spoken English Discourse: The Intonation of Increments*. London: Continuum.

Prince, E. F. (1981) Toward a taxonomy of given–new information. In P. Cole (ed.) *Radical Pragmatics* 223–55. New York: Academic Press.

Prince, E. F. (1992) The ZPG letter: Subjects, definiteness, and information-status. In S. Thompson and W. Mann (eds) *Discourse Description: Diverse Analyses of a Fund-Raising Text* 295–325. Amsterdam: John Benjamins.

Taglicht, J. (1984) *Message and Emphasis: On Focus and Scope in English*. London: Longman.

2

Creating a parallel universe: Mode and the textual metafunction in the study of one news story

Annabelle Lukin[a]

2.1 Introduction

In a 2003 paper titled 'On the "architecture" of human language', Halliday explicates the 'various assumptions about language' that underpin his systemic functional account of what language is like. In working through his claims about the 'all-round thickening of language' (Halliday, 2003: 29), the consistent focus in Halliday's linguistic theorizing has been on the nature of language. This may seem obvious, yet linguistic theories are remarkably varied in the way in which they delineate their object of study. An obvious contrast is with the work of Chomsky, where the focus has not been on language for its own sake, but as a window to the mind. But Halliday's focus has unequivocally been on the nature of language as a 'social semiotic'; that is, on language inextricably linked to the study of meaning in society, and language in all of its manifestations. And language 'manifest', for Halliday, is language as text instance, and as text type, or 'register'. In other words, we meet 'language' in all of our day to day dealings, and each and every instance is an instance of language

a   **Annabelle Lukin** is Senior Lecturer in Linguistics in the Centre for Language in Social Life, Macquarie University. She is interested in understanding more fully what it means to analyse text and linguistically construed social context in the terms established and developed in the work of linguists such as Halliday and Hasan. She works in particular in the areas of media and political discourse, and in literature, including literature and translation, and she has published in all these areas. She is co-editor (with Geoff Williams) of *Language Development: Functional Perspectives on Species and Individuals* (Continuum). She curates the 'SFL Linguists' site on VIMEO, and contributes to Wikipedia on topics in linguistics, especially on people and ideas from the systemic functional linguistics tradition.

related by realization to some category of a context of situation. This relationship of register to the context of situation in Halliday's theory goes back to 1964, and has remained a central premise of his model. From this recognition of the affinity of text and social context, Halliday developed his metafunctional hypothesis. An instance of text is said to conflate meanings of three kinds: ideational, interpersonal and textual, in a recapitulation of the organization of language. These meanings are configured under the pressure of the realization relation between the metafunctions, and the semiotic structure of the social context, articulated by Halliday as the parameters of 'field', 'tenor' and 'mode' (e.g. Halliday *et al.*, [1964] 2007; Halliday, [1977] 2002).

But while these terms are crucial to Halliday's account, there is no doubt they remain underdeveloped. Martin's theoretical justification for 'genre' includes the lack of agreement in the 1960s about where the contextual feature 'rhetorical mode' (as Halliday called it) or 'functional tenor' (which was Gregory's term) should be located in systemic functional theory (see Martin, 1992). While invoking an extra stratum (i.e. genre) resolved the matter for Martin, for those who follow Halliday in seeing register as a central organizing principle in the interface between language and society, the question of the metafunctional location of rhetorical mode remains unresolved.[1] But the difficulties with the application of the terms 'field', 'tenor' and 'mode' run deeper still. Hasan's 2009 paper, titled 'The place of context in a systemic functional model', sets out a fulsome critique of the lack of theoretical firepower of the notions of field, tenor and mode. Following an explication of the concepts, and including her own work in the critique, Hasan writes:

> What is interesting in the … description [of field, tenor and mode] is its vagueness, the absence of 'checkable' criteria and the reliance on 'common sense'. It is as if, other than the context's tripartite division, its description has no underlying regularities, and no reasoned framework to work with. (Hasan, 2009: 179–80)

Yet, in the face of the complexity of modelling context, Hasan urges not a turning away from the terms, or their repositioning in the theory. Instead, she argues that, given that 'relevant context' is a 'semiotic construct', it 'should be within the descriptive orbit of linguistics'. It is, therefore, 'one important function of SFL, as a social semiotic theory of language, to throw light on this construct' (*ibid.*: 181). Hasan (1999, 2004) provides argumentation for adopting the system network as the tool for modelling context of situation.

The motivation for my paper is to contribute in general terms to exploring this relationship between the parameters of context and the metafunctions of language. Given the special focus in this volume on intonation, I want to attend to this relationship by focusing on the textual function, in which intonation, via the systems of INFORMATION DISTRI- BUTION and INFORMATION FOCUS (Halliday and Greaves, 2008), plays a role. My aim is to explore the contribution of these intonation systems, within the context of the overall workings of the textual metafunction, in relation to one instance of text. The issues raised by this inquiry are both theoretical and methodological. In theoretical terms, for instance, Halliday's claim is that the systems realizing one given metafunction will display a tighter form of interaction, relative to the systems at play in the other metafunctions. To test this claim we have to see these systems 'in action', as it were; and we will see that since the textual function has as its domain the ideational and interpersonal functions, the analysis of the textual function of necessity brings in considerations of the other two. Speaking methodologically, there is the matter of how one organizes the interpretation of the findings from analysis of various systems. I am not claiming to resolve this matter here, but will simply explore how the choices from the various textual systems can be seen to be working together. From an intonation point of view, my approach allows the consideration of how meanings made by intonation interact with other metafunctionally specific systemic choices, all in the service of the expression of the values in mode, for a given instance of register.

I begin with a discussion of Halliday's textual function, before examining the contextual parameter of mode, including the developments in modelling mode systemically, drawing on Butt (2003), which sets out networks for field, tenor and mode. These networks present a hypothesis about the systemic organization of these parameters of context; they are very much a 'work in progress'. The mechanism for testing out these networks is to apply them to texts, that is, to work out whether it is viable to explain the meanings of a text in relation to some selection of features of the networks. My method then, is what Matthiessen (1993: 276) called a 'metafunctional slice through the system with multi-stratal coverage'.

The text selected for this paper is an instance of TV news reporting. It was broadcast on ABC TV (Australia's public broadcaster) on 3 April 2003, two weeks into the 'Coalition' invasion of Iraq, and about a week prior to the so-called 'fall of Baghdad'. It was the opening item of the main nightly news bulletin (7 pm), the first of six news items in the bulletin concerning the invasion of Iraq. The Appendix presents a transcript of the text, annotated with the intonation analysis. I have included the opening of the bulletin, which largely previews elements of the specific news item that follows (as well as foreshadowing one other item in the bulletin). One of the interesting features of the news report is that while something is concluded in its unfolding, the activity of reporting Iraq at that time was not encapsulated within a single news item. It was only later that 'Iraq' would come to have the status of a topic covered by a single item in a news bulletin. The correspondent presenting this news item was reporting from Qatar, where the United States Central Command had established a press briefing centre. Qatar gave journalists a place with a Middle East by-line to report from, without the dangers associated with reporting from inside Iraq.[2]

Since I am presenting the analysis of only one single text, it is important to position what the detailed study of a text like this can reveal. The text represents one instance of the practice of news reporting, where the focus of the news was events that have had significant consequences for Iraqis, for the Middle East region, and for the countries that invaded Iraq. This news item was produced in a kind of echo chamber; that is, in the context of meanings generated by some of the most powerful forces in American, British and Australian society. It was part of creating an environment in which the invasion of Iraq 'made sense'. If one takes Halliday's view that the function of language is to semioticize our eco-social environment (Halliday, 2003), then even a single text must be responsive to the complex dynamics of the social and cultural context of its production. Thus, even one instance, analysed thoroughly, can give some insights into the specific context of the ABC news reporting of the Iraq invasion, as well as the larger, geopolitical context of the Iraq invasion, in which the media had a role to play.

2.2   Halliday's textual metafunction

As Halliday has argued, it is via the textual function that 'acts of meaning become discourse, a kind of virtual reality in semiotic form' (Halliday, [1994] 2007: 321). The textual function 'breathes life into language; in another metaphor, it provides texture and without texture there is no text' (Halliday, [1976] 2003: 70). It is 'that which makes language relevant' and 'that which makes the difference between language that is suspended in vacuo and language that is operational in a context of situation' ([1975] 2007: 184). Ideational resources are freely combinable with interpersonal ones. As Halliday writes, 'you can put any interactional "spin" on any

Table 2.1 Halliday's function–rank matrix (Halliday, 2009: 85)

metafunction			ideational			interpersonal	textual	
rank	[class]		logical		experiential			(cohesive)
clause		complexes (clause-			TRANSITIVITY (process type)	MOOD MODALITY POLARITY	THEME CULMINATION VOICE	COHESIVE RELATIONS
phrase	[preposition-al]	phrase-			MINOR TRANSITIVITY (circumstance type)	MINOR MOOD (adjunct type)	CONJUNCTION	
group	[verbal]	group-	INTERDEPENDENCY (parataxis/hypotaxis) & LOGICAL-SEMANTIC RELATION (expansion/projection)	TENSE	EVENT TYPE ASPECT (non-finite)	FINITENESS	VOICE DEICTICITY	REFERENCE ELLIPSIS/ SUBSTITUTION CONJUNCTION LEXICAL COHESION *
	[nominal]			MODIFICATION	THING TYPE CLASSIFICATION EPITHESIS QUALIFICATION	PERSON ATTITUDE	DETERMINATION	
	[adverbial]			MODIFICATION	QUALITY (circumstance type)	COMMENT (adjunct type)	CONJUNCTION	
word		word)		DERIVATION	(DENOTATION)	(CONNOTA-TION)		
information unit		info. unit complex			ACCENTUATION	KEY	INFORMATION	
			complexes	simplexes				

*Lexical cohesion does not appear in the 2009 version of the matrix, but appears in the original version in Halliday (1971: 335).

representational content' (Halliday, 2003: 17). This combinatorial freedom entails a constraint: a speaker can freely combine them, but must combine them. One cannot mean, ideationally, without meaning interpersonally at the same time. And the combination of meanings relies on the textual function, and in the process 'language has to create a parallel universe of its own: a world that is made of meaning and hence instantiated in the semiotic process' (Halliday, [2001] 2003: 276).

Table 2.1 is Halliday's function–rank matrix, a visual representation of his claim concerning the metafunctional organization of language. The table sets out the three metafunctions, and under each metafunctional heading, Halliday lists, by rank (clause, phrase, group, word and information unit), the systems involved in the construal of metafunctional meanings. With regard to the textual function, the relevant systems are as follows. At clause rank: THEME, CULMINATION,[3] VOICE; at phrase rank: CONJUNCTION; at group rank: VOICE, DEICTICITY, DETERMINATION, CONJUNCTION; and as information unit: INFORMATION DISTRIBUTION and INFORMATION FOCUS. In addition, above the structural unit of clause, there are the resources involved in cohesion (reference, substitution and ellipsis, and cohesive conjunction). The methodological challenge is to visit each of these domains of choice, to build an argument out of the analysis across these systems, and to relate this description to the dimensions of mode.

2.3   Mode as 'contextualization system'

In the light of Hasan's call for a systematic description of relevant context as the 'prime mover' of discourse (Hasan, 2009), as well as her arguments for the adoption of the system network as the means to produce such descriptions (Hasan, 1995, 1999, 2004, 2009), let us consider the case study text more formally with respect to the contextualization system (Hasan, 2009) of MODE. Mode is defined by Halliday in the following terms:

> The mode of discourse refers to what part the language is playing, what it is that the participants are expecting the language to do for them in that situation; the symbolic organisation of the text, the status that it has, and its function in the context, including the channel (is it spoken or written or some combination of the two?) and also the rhetorical mode, what is being achieved by the text in terms of such categories as persuasive, expository, didactic and the like. (Halliday, 1985: 12)

Hasan (1985) articulated what can be considered 'proto-systems' for mode, which were: ROLE OF LANGUAGE, CHANNEL and MEDIUM. Role of language is described as a cline from 'constitutive' to 'ancilliary'. Channel was described as 'the modality through which the addressee comes in contact with the speaker's messages'. To this dimension she related the issue of 'process sharing'. Process sharing describes the distinction between texts in which interactants are both/all engaged in the text production process, versus those in which the text is prefabricated with a 'virtual addressee' built into the text (see Hasan, 1999). MEDIUM captures 'the pattern of the textual organization adopted when "organization" pertains to all those reactances of "spoken-ness" and "written-ness"' (Butt, 2003: 41).

Butt's (*ibid.*) mode network retains the three 'proto-systems' from Hasan, using them as a point of departure for elaborating his systemic descriptions of parameters of context (see Figure 2.1).

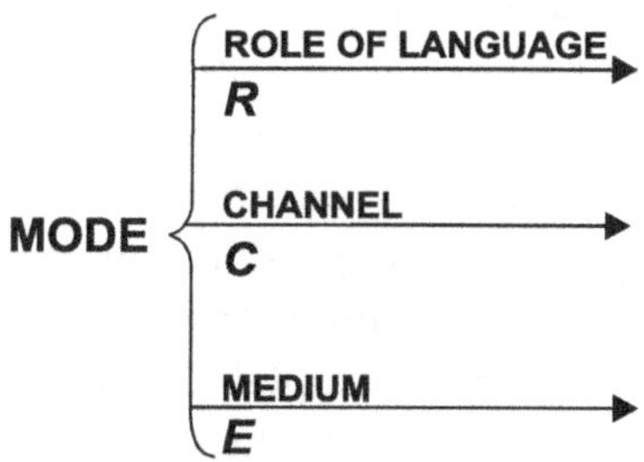

Figure 2.1 The contextualization system of MODE (Butt, 2003, based on Hasan, 1985).

The system ROLE OF LANGUAGE in Butt's network offers a primary distinction between [constitutive], [ancilliary] and [supported]. The text under consideration is multimodal, having both a verbal and a visual channel. Butt's network is designed for the description of language, as the name of the system indicates, yet the combination of the verbal and visual is a defining feature of TV news. The issues which arise at this point are complex, not least being the concept of 'multimodal text'.[4] I note a rather obvious feature of the contribution of the visual mode is its role in creating a sense of proximity to people and events in a (virtual) material situational setting (MSS) (Hasan, [1973] 2005). The possible combinations of the modes for television (the choices, for instance, of verbal modality based within the visual modality versus verbal modality overlaid on the visual modality) are clearly important to the expression of the register (see e.g. Hartley, 1982). The engendering of a sense of proximity to the MSS is enhanced by the cross-modal references in the verbal text. For instance, the correspondent's report begins with *These could well be the first shots in the final phase of the invasion*, with 'these' a reference to the visual modality. As Halliday's proposal about the relationship of text to context of situation predicts, the language here is responsive to the fact of the visual modality running in parallel, and I will return to this point later in the discussion. But it is interesting to note that the viewer is not expected to be able to retrieve the referent for 'these' him/herself. The referential meaning is disambiguated through a lexicalization (i.e. of all the possibilities in the visual image, the 'these' refers to 'shots'). I note that the visual modality has no resources for referring to itself, or to the linguistic text.

Leaving aside these complexities, and returning to the analysis of the text from the basis of the language, the text can be considered [constitutive], as the term is defined in the following way by Butt (2003): 'the activity could not exist without the language'. From the choice of [constitutive], more delicate choices are available in Butt's network (see Figure 2.2). The first is a distinction between [abstracted] and [actualized]. Since [actualized] encompasses a process of language constituting reports of actual events, this is the relevant choice for the TV news item in question. There is a further choice at this point between [displaced] and [immediate]. The text displays the feature [immediate] defined by Butt as 'dealing with an unfolding present', and is [continuing]; that is, it is 'processual, legato, incomplete'. While something is completed with the enactment of this text, the text is a product of a period when more than one news item in a bulletin was reporting a state of affairs.

The point of the analysis is to provide evidence for my claims that the context construed by this text has the features I am suggesting.[5] For

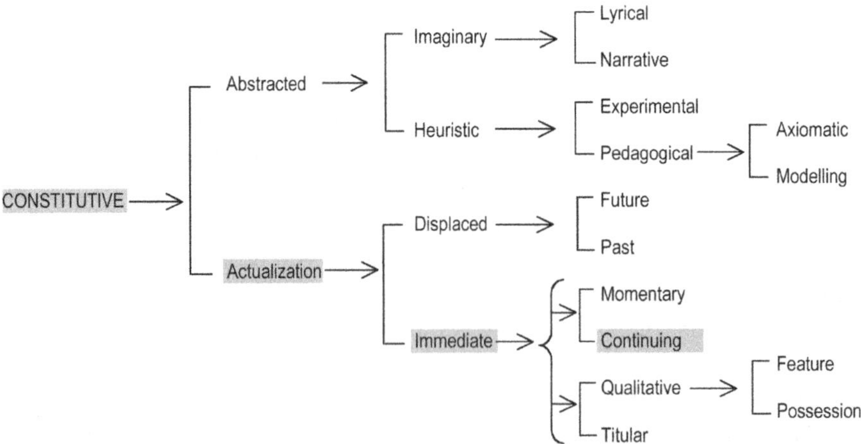

Figure 2.2 Options from the choice [constitutive] from the Mode network in Butt (2003).

instance, the systems of DEICTICITY and DETERMINATION are analysed, and will provide some evidence of my choice of [immediate: continuing] in the system of ROLE OF LANGUAGE; but note as preliminary evidence at this point that much of the primary tense selection is present, and there are instances of phoric reference which assume the viewer has been tuned in previously. I would suggest that variation in selections here realize some of the intra-registerial variation in news. For instance, it is not difficult to envisage a news text with the orientation of [constitutive: actualization: displaced: past] or as [constitutive: actualization: immediate: momentary].

In relation to CHANNEL, Butt's network offers two subsystems. The first allows the choice of [graphic] versus [phonic], the latter being the choice relevant to the verbal text. Simultaneous to this choice is a system with the primary distinction of [real time] versus [mediated] (see Figure 2.3). While the text has a drive towards a sense of immediacy, this immediacy is a linguistic artefact. It is [mediated: intervened: edited] in the terms of Butt's network. This feature is partly reflected in the thematic organization of the text, which, as we will see is not temporal. Thus, despite the orientation of the verbal group being to a here-and-now, the text does not unfold chronologically. While it is common parlance to describe news as 'stories', there is no narrative quality to the text (see Lukin, 2010; also Montgomery, 2007: ch. 5).

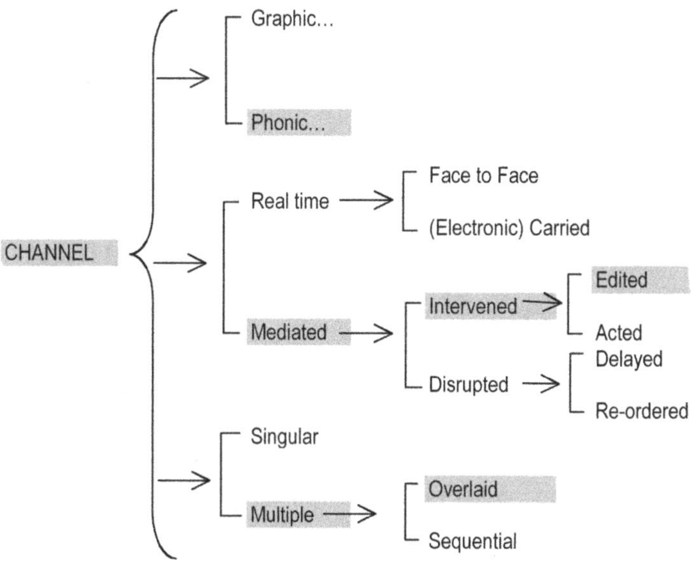

Figure 2.3 The system of CHANNEL (Butt, 2003).

We see an interesting disjuncture at this point. ROLE OF LANGUAGE includes the selection [immediate], but in CHANNEL, in the face of the option [real time] versus [mediated], the relevant choice is [mediated]. This feeling of immediacy is a function of choices in the verbal modality, including choices in DETERMINATION and DEICTICITY (meanings which cannot be generated in the visual mode). Finally, regarding MEDIUM (see Figure 2.4), the text is written to be read. It is neither spontaneous in its unfolding, nor is it densely constructed. As Butt (2003: 33) notes, the apparent binary choices represented by the first two subsystems of MEDIUM need to be considered as relative positions on a cline. In relation to the third system of MEDIUM, the selection is [constant: as fixture]. By this I am saying the settings in MEDIUM do not vary in the unfolding of the text.

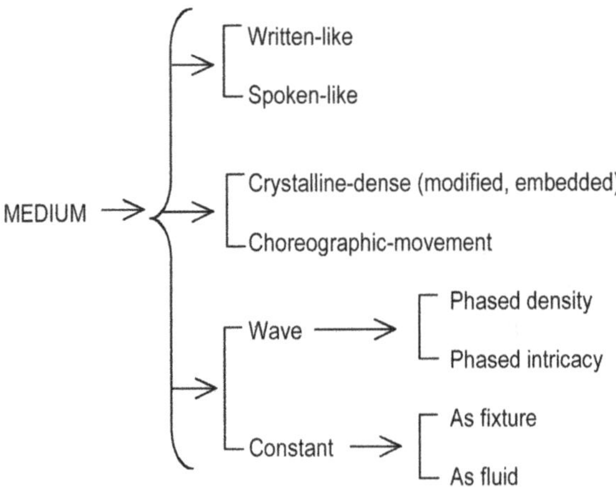

Figure 2.4 Choices in the system of MEDIUM (Butt, 2003).

2.4 The construal of textual meanings in the case study text

As I have noted, the meaning of Halliday's function–rank matrix is that the systems associated with the textual metafunction most closely conduct the work of creating the 'parallel universe', a reality made out of meanings. In any given instance, selections and co-selections from these systems combine to package up the experiential and interpersonal meanings to actualize language as text – to ground it, and to make it able to function in the life of the relevant interactants. In some sense textual meanings must be less available to 'the naked eye', being as they are responsible for the creation of coherence, and thus for the fact that we tend not to see the semiotic nature of the linguistic artefact through which we are interacting and making sense of the world.

2.4.1 Given and New; Theme and Rheme

Let us explore the relationship of mode and the textual metafunction, taking the first clause complex of the text as an example. I have analysed this opening clause complex with respect to the textual systems in Table 2.2, ignoring the systems relating to cohesion, although I will turn to them later in the chapter. What is interesting is that we see in this opening the foreshadowing of the principles for the continuity of the text. Beginning with the grammatical stratum, there are two relevant systems. One is the system of INFORMATION DISTRIBUTION, realized by the phonological system of TONALITY, and the other is the system of INFORMATION FOCUS, realized by the phonological system of TONICITY. The first system chunks the flow of discourse into information units, setting the boundaries of tone units, and relating the text to its audience by signalling to the interactant/s how much information is being carried in a given stretch of text. In the example in Table 2.2, we find three information units across two clauses. In combination with the system of INFORMATION DISTRIBUTION (ID) is the system of INFORMATION FOCUS (IF); each information unit requires a point of prominence, established by the point at which the major pitch change takes place, which is referred to as the tonic syllable. (The full transcript is set out in Table 2.A1 in the Appendix, with choice in IF denoted in bold.) The choice of IF relates the language to the context by signalling to the hearer what it is s/he ought to be attending to in the flow of the discourse; the remainder of the tone unit is considered to be information already recoverable in the context. In Halliday's terms, this is the Given–New structure, one of the meanings mapped onto the tone unit.

The mapping of the Given–New structure is 'hearer-oriented', although it is entirely at the speaker's discretion (Halliday, [1997] 2002: 34). By these choices, the speaker is 'free to use the system as he pleases, and frequently uses it to great effect as a means of constructing the environment it is designed to reflect' (*ibid.*: 34). This instance of a news report reconfirms the established tendency in news broadcasting for a higher ratio of tone units to the grammatical unit of clause (e.g. van Leeuwen, 1992; Smith, 2008). This text consists of 95 information units over 38 clauses, a ratio of 2.5 information units per clause. Figure 2.5 shows the distribution of the

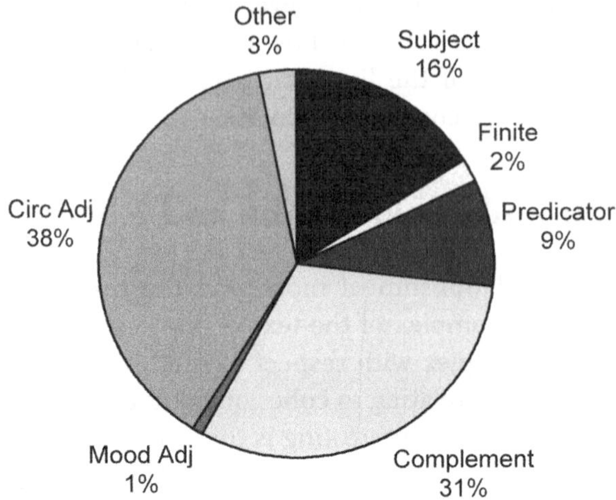

Figure 2.5 Choice of IF in terms of interpersonal clause structure.

IF in terms of its mapping onto elements of interpersonal clause structure, and one can see the possibilities when more than one information unit is available to one clause. News must be newsworthy, and what better way to present information as newsworthy than through choices in INFORMATION DISTRIBUTION? In the political economy of news, keeping viewers watching reigns supreme, even in the case of this text, produced by a public broadcaster.

Is there a metafunctionally significant pattern in what is selected for focus by the location of intonational focus? A preliminary observation on this text is the frequency (27%) with which the IF falls on the non-Head element of the group/phrase (e.g. on the numerative, classifier or qualifier of a nominal group; or on the preposition in a prepositional phrase). IUs 25–7 show a single clause element (Complement/Value: 'the first shots in the final phase of the invasion') attracting three tone units. Van Leeuwen has argued that the typical function of information focus – to differentiate the element that is treated as New, from that which is considered Given – is over-ridden in the context of broadcast news. Van Leeuwen suggests that the 'rhythmic regularization' of news 'serves to signify the impartiality of the news: to demonstrate, even if it has to be at the cost of intelligibility, that the newsreaders are not themselves involved in the message they transmit, do not themselves discriminate between what is important and what is not' (van Leeuwen, 1992: 241). In a sense this is to say that, within this register, the mere chunking into information units has a more substantial significance to the textual meanings than the units actually chosen for focus. Is this potentially a form of intonational 'de-automatization' (Halliday, [1982] 2002)?

And yet, the choices of information focus cannot fail to mean, since they signal to the hearer to 'take notice'. As Smith (2008: 326) argues, selections in IF 'are elements in the clausal flow of information considered by the speaker to be important in the situation being discussed'. For example, the selection of elements for focus can, as Smith argues, (following Matthiessen, 1992; Martin, 1992) orient the listener to either field or tenor in the context (Smith, 2008: 106). In the event that these selections are experientially oriented, as they largely are in this text, these selections form a 'mini-narrative' of the events which form the basis for the construal of the field. In the clause complex analysed in Table 2.2, three choices in IF are made: 'Commanders', 'Baghdad' and 'begun'. These can be considered instances of more general categories: person, place and process. The analysis shows attention to these categories throughout the text, with 'place' appearing more dominant than the others (see Table 2.A1 in the Appendix, showing choices in INFORMATION FOCUS against choices in THEME). In the choice of 'person' and 'place', the system of IF is reinforcing patterns established via the system of THEME. The two options account for roughly half the IF selections (48%), with these choices largely reflecting the location of IF on the elements Subject and circumstantial Adjunct (see Table 2.A1 in the Appendix). The category of 'process' is not insignificant; nearly 10 per cent of IF selections fall on the Predicator.

Table 2.2 An example, analysed for systems construing textual meanings.

RANK	SYSTEM	US commanders say the battle for Baghdad has begun	
Clause	THEME	US Commanders say	the battle for Baghdad has begun
	VOICE	middle	Middle
Phrase			
[prep]	CONJ	–	–
Group **[v]**	VOICE	middle	middle
	DEICTICITY	primary tense: present	primary tense: present
[n]	DETERMINATION	[0] US Commanders, [non-specific: partial]	[the] battle for Baghdad [specific: demonstrative & determinative: non-selective]
[adv]	CONJ	–	–
Information **Unit**	INFORMATION	//4 US Com/**manders** say//	//4 the /battle for /**Bagh**dad has be- // //1 -**gun**//

Table 2.A2 in the Appendix presents the Theme/Rheme analysis, with the thematic choices characterized as the categories 'person', 'act of war', 'place/time', the verb 'to be', and so on. The category 'person' is expressed through choices like 'US Commanders', 'tens of thousands of American troops', 'the Americans', 'British Marines' and 'American generals' – military collectives all pertaining to the Coalition invasion force. There is one instance of Iraqi soldiers being thematized, and the formulation is as 'Saddam's troops'. (I note here the impossibility of the formulations 'George's troops', or 'Tony's troops', to denote American or British forces). Textually, one vein in the text, then, is ordering by what military collectives are doing/saying. This choice combines with location, as mentioned earlier, as a mechanism for organizing the flow of information. A third important category is 'act of war', which we see in the example in Table 2.2. 'The battle for Baghdad' is thematized partly as a function of the choice in the system of VOICE. The clause is middle voice ('the battle for Baghdad has begun'), denoting a self-engendered process (Halliday and Matthiessen, 2004), i.e. the battle has begun all by itself. By being a middle voice selection, only one participant is available for thematization; that participant is the nominalization of an act of war, which the lexical choice of 'battle' construes as bi-directional (as compared with, for instance, 'attack', which is unidirectional; see Lukin (2013), for further discussion on this kind of choice). A transitive model would have provided at least two participants as possible thematic choices.

2.4.2 Cohesive relations

For thematic choices to produce coherent text, experiential continuity in thematic choice is required. This brings us to examine cohesive relations, invoking the texture-producing resources of reference, substitution/ellipsis, and cohesive conjunction. These systems are displayed in Halliday's function–rank matrix under cohesive relations, in a cell which does not specify rank, denoting the fact that cohesive ties are non-structural.

What is interesting in this text is the minimal contribution of grammatical cohesion to the creation of cohesive ties. Hasan has argued that coherence requires the working together of both grammatical and lexical cohesion (Hasan, 1985). Texture is created by continuity of two kinds: continuity by identity, and continuity by similarity (Hasan, 1984, 1985). Continuity by identity, that is, the establishment of coreferential relations by which a specific entity can recur in a text, makes very little contribution to the texture of this text (see Figure 2.A1 in the Appendix).

Note, for instance, there is no text-exhaustive identity chain. Figure 2.A2 in the Appendix sets out the cohesive chains (the continuity achieved when relations of both identity and similarity are combined), consisting of the relevant tokens for this text (Hasan, 1984, 1985). Chain (b) nets in all lexical items construing categories of military personnel ('troops', 'divisions', 'forces', 'army', etc.). This chain is built largely through relations of synonymy. Apart from a couple of grammatical choices construing coreferential relations ('Jessica Lynch' – 'her'; '30,000 men from the US 4th Division' – 'these troops'), the chain relating to belligerents unfolds in the text largely through the introduction of new instances of the same category of thing. Those who have created this state of war, the agents of the violence unfolding, get no specificity or continuity in the text, yet they get Thematic prominence.

This lack of specificity is realized by the absence of a deictic element in the nominal groups construing these referents; a choice from the system of DETERMINATION. Halliday and Matthiessen (2004: 312) note that:

> The Deictic element indicates whether or not some specific subset of the Thing is intended; and if so, which. The nature of the Deictic is determined by the system of DETERMINATION ... The primary distinction is between (i) specific or (ii) non-specific.

Figure 2.6 sets out the choices in the system of determination; and Table 2.2 shows the analysis of the nominal groups in the opening clause complex ('US Commanders' – non-specific: partial; and 'the battle for Baghdad' – specific: demonstrative & determinative: non-selective). These two instances in Table 2.2 exemplify this primary distinction between specific and non-specific. Non-specific deixis construes things as not already given. 'US Commanders' has non-specific deixis; like other references to the Coalition forces through this, and other texts: 'British forces', 'British marines', 'US forces', 'American troops', 'Republican Guard troops'. These human collectives lack specificity and therefore definiteness; they echo each other by being instances of the same more general category, not because the text tracks a specified group over some set of events.

By contrast, 'the battle for Baghdad' is specific in its deixis. The tokens of specific deixis have the feature that they can refer within the text (known as 'endophoric' reference), or outside the text to a specific material situational setting, or to a wider cultural context (known as 'exophoric' reference[6]). In doing so, they treat the thing which they point to as identifiable, along some dimension. I have mentioned previously the cross modal phoricity of the text: 'these could well be ...'; 'in this case ...'; 'these troops ...'. Such

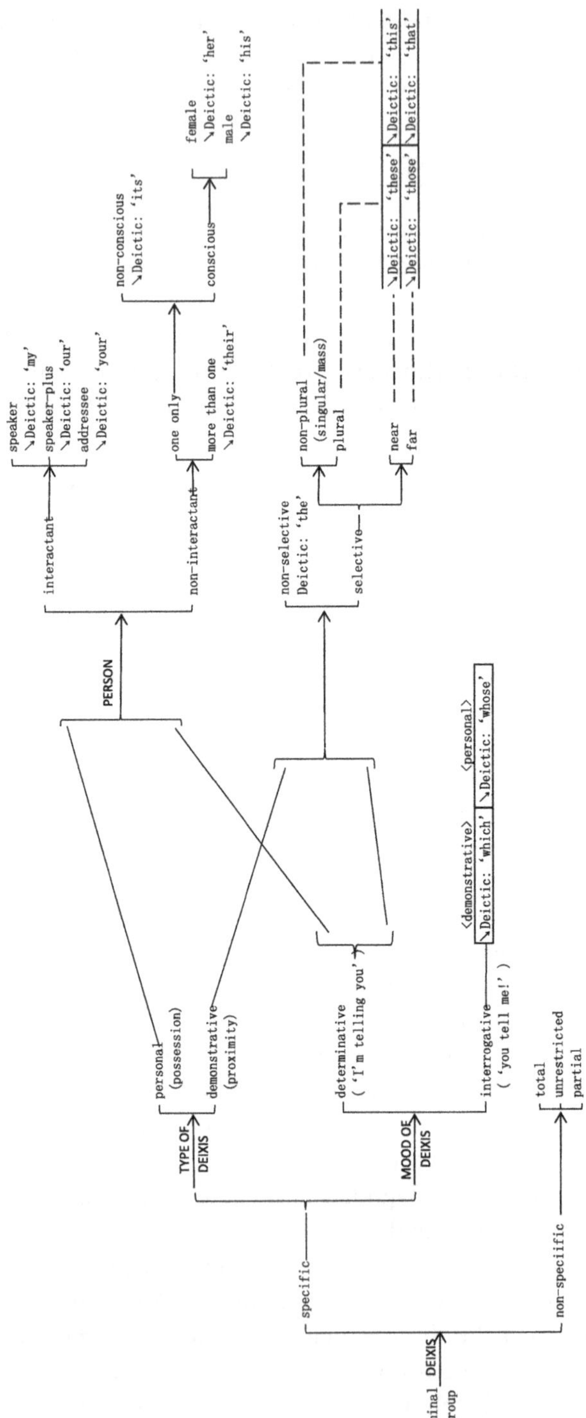

Figure 2.6 The system of DETERMINATION (Halliday and Matthiessen, 2004: 313).

references create a sense of proximity between viewer and the visual mode; it is as if the visual mode is a co-present material reality. The text also recruits an expectation of shared knowledge about preceding events. For instance, 'the aerial war isn't over yet' construes the viewer as already in the know about 'the aerial war'. At the same time, it recruits the viewer to this construal of the American bombardment of Iraq; like 'battle', war implies bi-directional action, as distinct from say, 'bombardment', which is unidirectional. The aerial bombing was, in fact, in one direction, since Iraq had no air force to speak of. Note also the specificity in 'the battle for Baghdad'. The 'the' is an instance of cataphoric reference, which presumes that the post-qualification sufficiently specifies 'which battle'. I return to this matter later, since the full impact of the 'the-ness' of 'the battle for Baghdad' needs a consideration of choices in DEICTICITY.

A full discussion of the cohesion analysis is obviously beyond the scope of this paper, but one further comment is in order. The categories of Theme foreshadowed in the opening 'person (military)' and 'act of war' are sustained strands of meaning in the text. As the cohesive chains show (see Figure 2.A2 in the Appendix), these choices in the opening clause go on to be part of text-exhaustive cohesive threads. The chain around acts of war is constituted almost in its entirety by nominalizations. The items in this chain make virtually no contact with the chain around persons capable of agentive action in relation to the invasion; while the chain around acts of war interacts with the processes of 'be' (chain (k)) and phasal meanings (chain (f)), as in 'a ground battle is under way between ...'. By way of summary, the text is populated with categories of people who lack specification and who do not, therefore, have continuity through the text other than by synonymic relations. Furthermore, in the enactment of texture, these people do not engage in the processes defining of 'war'. This point needs to be put against the orientation to field by selections in INFORMATION FOCUS, noted earlier. The intonational selections of the textual function, together with choices in Theme, create a veneer of field building, which the cohesion and cohesive harmony analysis suggests is not 'delivered on' in the texture of the text.

2.4.3 Deicticity

The full impact of the 'the-ness' of 'the battle for Baghdad' needs a consideration of choices in DEICTICITY, a system concerned with relating the process to the speaker-now (Halliday and Matthiessen, 2004: 336). Deicticity is the point of departure for the verbal group. It is realized by the finite element of the verbal group, and its primary distinction is between [temporal] and [modal]; and if [temporal], between [past], [present], [future]. In making the claim above that the text had the orientation [immediate] – to events unfolding in some kind of here-and-now – the choices in DEICTICITY are important. The text's opening, presented in Table 2.2, signals the proximity of the events to the time of speaking by the choice of [present] in regards to DEICTICITY. As in other choices we have seen, these early selections prefigure the dominant pattern in the text, which can be seen in Figure 2.7. Deicticity in the verbal group, from a mode perspective, is one resonance of the relationship of 'relevant context' to a material situational setting. Thus, despite the distance between the viewer and the events in focus, and indeed between the correspondent and these same events, the text dissolves, as far as it can, the time/space disjunction, through the choice in DEICTICITY in the verbal group. DEICTICITY combines with other systems to construe the semantics of time. Cloran, for instance, has explored the notion of EVENT ORIENTATION as semantic system, noting that it has a dispersed realization, with tense, modality, logico-semantic relations and circum-stanciation all implicated. In EVENT ORIENTATION, the question is 'the temporal direction and distance of the time of the event spoken about from the time of speaking' (Cloran, 1994: 197).

The text shows varying choices with respect to EVENT ORIENTATION. There is a brief excursus into the past. In addition, at the point where the presenter hands over to the correspondent, we find a modal deictic ['these could well be the first shots in the final phase of the invasion'], and in the closing of the news item an instance of the future tense deictic. The text is thus 'bookended' by claims about the larger significance of the details of the report: the correspondent's report begins with an instance of Cloran's Rhetorical Unit 'conjecture', defined as 'a type of activity constituted by language in which language anticipates a possible future' (Cloran, 1994: 108), and ends on a 'conjecture' followed by a 'prediction' ('with American generals predicting there could be many more casualties in the days ahead, it's likely these troops will soon be drawn northward into the battle for Baghdad'). The projecting verb 'predicting' in this instance alerts us to the status of what follows, although Cloran provides the necessary definition for this rhetorical unit should the projecting clause be absent (namely, a unit concerned with anticipated action, which may or may not be volitional, and in which the 'central entity' involved is not the speaker (*ibid.*: 112)). These are, in Cloran's terms, shifts along a cline of decontextualization, where this shift is defined as a move away from language based 'in the material here-and-now' to language use based 'in the relations created by language itself' (*ibid.*: 132). An experience of the contrast between a material 'here-and-now', versus a perspective based in the 'relations created by language itself' is, I would argue, characteristic of registers of news (see Lukin, 2010). I am suggesting that central to the experience of news is to experience a contrast along the cline of rhetorical units identified by Cloran (1994), with respect to some 'newsworthy' event. The effect of these microshifts away from the here-and-now of what unfolds in the text engenders a sense that these various events accumulate into something – that something being 'the final phase of the invasion', projected by this journalist to be 'the battle for Baghdad'. The belief that the 'war' was about to be over almost immediately following its commencement was a function of the profound conceptual failure that was the invasion of Iraq (see e.g. Ricks, 2006; Dower, 2010). Within six weeks of the invasion, the US President was trying to draw some line in the sand, with his announcement that 'major combat operations' were over. The 'the' of 'the battle for Baghdad', which both opens and closes this text, gives an identity and shape to the action distilled from the US military's own philosophy of the time: that the US could 'take' the capital, and that would signal the end of something. The General who led Coalition forces in the invasion of Iraq had, at the time, already been criticized in relation to his stewardship of the Afghanistan invasion for believing that taking an 'enemy's' capital was the same as 'winning the war' (Ricks, 2006).

2.4.4 Conjunction

Finally, what does an analysis of cohesive conjunction show? There are five instances of cohesive conjunction:

> (8) <u>And</u> in Basra, << >>, British troops are waiting for reinforcements before a final push to take the city; (15) <u>But</u> the regime is sounding as defiant as ever; (23) <u>And</u> during a battle at Nasiriyah, US special forces rescued servicewoman Jessica Lynch. (31) There's <u>also</u> been action on the northern front just two hours drive from Baghdad; (34) <u>Still</u> the preparations go on.

Four of these are conjunctions of the extending type, construing meanings associated with 'addition' (Halliday and Matthiessen, 2004: 541ff.). As Hasan has argued, conjunctions are a stamp on an already available meaning (Hasan, forthcoming). At other points in the text, despite the absence of the stamp of a conjunction, additive relations bind the elements of

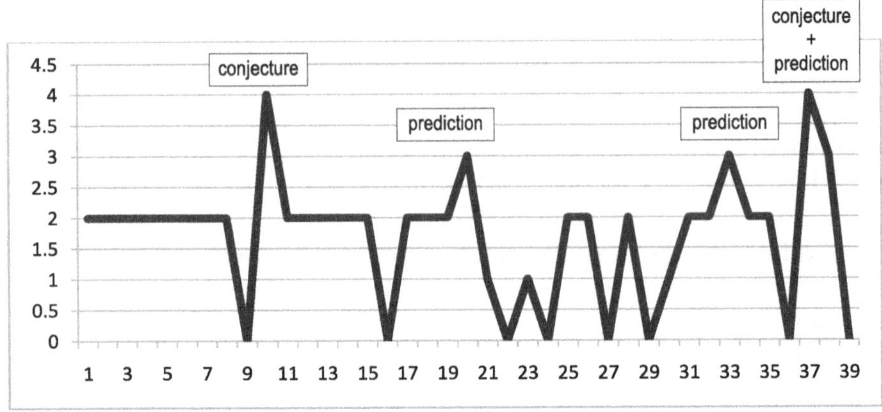

KEY	
4	modal
3	future
2	present
1	past
0	non-finite

Figure 2.7 Sample text analysed with respect to the system of DEICTICITY.

the text together, creating a looseness in the texture, a kind of bond by 'association', as Hasan has suggested (*ibid.*):

> Associative continuity is distinct from topical continuity, in that the former does not entail any continuity by identity of referents, while topical continuity almost always calls for such identity. For associative continuity, the merest peripheral contact is sufficient, hence, although such continuity can be exploited in the formation of certain very particular kinds of texts – e.g. in the writings of the 'stream of consciousness school' – it is, in general, only marginally relevant to texture. Again, it is worth noting that the only cohesive conjunctive that could be introduced between clause boundaries in [a text with texture based on associate relations] is <u>and</u> ...

2.5 Concluding remarks

I have hardly done justice to the analysis of even one metafunction of this text, but I would like to suggest that further work of this kind would complement existing contributions from linguistics to the study of media discourse. Taking up Halliday's suggestion that one angle on the organization of the semantic stratum is 'metafunctional regions defined in topological fashion', what are the meanings that the textual function engenders in this text? I suggest, tentatively, the following: a sense for the viewers of insiderness (you know some of this situation already); proximity (these distant events are not so far away from you after all); newness (events are building up into a new state in the unfolding of this war); immediacy (things are happening as we speak); and connectedness/ plausibility (this text is bringing things together for you). It may be that these meanings are in some sense prior to the experiential choices which they populate, an example of Matthiessen's claim that 'there is good reason for assuming that the textual metafunction motivates ideational decisions' (Matthiessen, 1992: 74).

The textual metafunction requires the experiential and interpersonal function over which it can work its magic, creating seamless text which ultimately obscures the role of language in semioticizing experience. Halliday has suggested that in modern, multisemiotic texts, the textual function has to integrate the different semiotic strands, with the consequence that the textual 'becomes less explicit in the text'.[7] Certainly, it is complex to distil a structure statement from this example text, providing a challenge to claims about the structure of the 'hard news genre' (e.g. Iedema *et al.*, 1994; see also Lukin, 2010), and I have suggested there is a certain 'looseness' in the texture of this text. If Halliday's point holds for the text examined here, perhaps intonation is keeping up the 'textual appearances' when other systems are becoming backgrounded. With respect to this claim, Halliday and Greaves (2008: 69) note:

> The continuous flow of melody and rhythm, as the speaker ongoingly activates the resources of the phonological system, serves both as means and as metaphor: it is the means whereby the speaker keeps the discourse flowing, and also the metaphor for the seamless flux of experience and of personal interaction.

Just as 'the war' rolls on, the reporting does too, despite the complexity of making sense of these era-changing events. The ID and IF choices help provide credibility to the idea that the events in play can be summarized in a news item lasting just under three minutes. Intonation is, perhaps, central to broadcast news because it is, potentially, impervious to questions of experiential organization. This claim would explain the character of news satire,[8] and suggests that the register defining features of news are textual and interpersonal, rather than experiential.

Notes

1. Cloran's work on the rhetorical unit, a semantic unit modelled along a cline of decontextualization, is an elaboration of the notion of rhetorical mode, and is an account from the viewpoint of mode (e.g. Cloran, 1994). More recently, Hasan has argued that the category belongs in field, since terms like 'narrating', 'informing', 'commenting' and 'describing' are more delicate descriptions of social activity (Hasan, 1999). Butt's context networks recapitulate the basic architecture of Hasan's field network, thereby supporting her position for 'rhetorical mode' to be part of field, while at the same time maintaining some semblance of Halliday's original conception within his mode network.
2. Interviewed about his experience as a reporter in Qatar, *New York Magazine*'s correspondent Michael Wolff said: 'I have never been in a situation where there were so many reporters so far from anything that was happening ... The press center could have been in Florida ... technically speaking, it would not have made a difference' (Wolff, 2003: 41).
3. Culmination is a system associated with language in the written channel (see Matthiessen, 1995), so will not be further discussed here.
4. Royce (2007) argues for the notion of 'intersemiotic complementarity', the idea that two co-occuring semiotic systems are inter-related through meanings that are metafunctionally defined. Liu and O'Halloran (2009) invoke 'intersemiotic texture', a related concept imputing a form of integration between two co-occuring modes. Both contributions essentially assume, rather than derive, a notion of a multimodal text. Further, both assume that Halliday's metafunctional hypothesis can be applied to semiotic systems other than language. Halliday has recently suggested that language may be the only semiotic system to be organized metafunctionally (see Halliday, 2009).
5. Further, given how little work has been done on relating language to the parameters of context, despite it being central to the SFL paradigm, we are at this point also testing out the networks.
6. See Hasan (1996) for a detailed discussion of types of exophoric reference.
7. Talk presented at University of British Columbia, International Systemic Functional Linguistics Congress, July 2010. See www.youtube.com/watch?v=nC-blhaIUCk.
8. See for example Chaser Non-Stop News Network (www.cnnnn.com) and Onion News Network (www.theonion.com).

References

Butt, D. (2003) *Parameters of Context: On Establishing the Similarities and Differences between Contexts*. Mimeo: Centre for Language in Social Life, Macquarie University.

Cloran, C. (1994) *Rhetorical Units and Decontextualisation: An Enquiry into some Relations of Context, Meaning and Grammar*. Nottingham: Department of English Studies, University of Nottingham.

Dower, J. (2010) *Cultures of War: Pearl Harbor/Hiroshima/9-11/Iraq*. New York: W. W. Norton/The New Press.

Halliday, M. A. K. (1971) Linguistic function and literary style: an enquiry into the language of William Golding's *The Inheritors*. In S. Chatman (ed.) *Literary Style: A Symposium* 330–68. Oxford: Oxford University Press.

Halliday, M. A. K. ([1975] 2007) Language as social semiotic: towards a general sociolinguistic theory. In J. J. Webster (ed.) *Language and Society, Volume 10 in the Collected Works of M. A. K. Halliday* 169–202. London: Continuum.

Halliday, M. A. K. ([1976] 2003) Early language learning: a sociolinguistic approach. In J. J. Webster (ed.) *The Language of Early Childhood, Volume 4 in the Collected Works of M. A. K. Halliday* 60–89. London: Continuum.

Halliday, M. A. K. ([1977] 2002) Text as semantic choice in social contexts. In J. J Webster (ed.) *Linguistic Studies of Text and Discourse, Volume 2 in the Collected Works of M. A. K. Halliday* 23–81. London: Continuum.

Halliday, M. A. K. ([1982] 2002) The de-automatization of grammar: from Priestley's 'An Inspector Calls'. In J. J. Webster (ed.) *Linguistic Studies of Text and Discourse. Volume 2 in the Collected Works of M. A. K. Halliday* 126–148. London: Continuum.

Halliday, M. A. K. (1985) Part A. In M. A. K. Halliday and R. Hasan *Language, Context and Text: Aspects of Language in a Social-Semiotic Perspective*. Geelong, Vic: Deakin University Press.

Halliday, M. A. K. ([1994] 2007) Contexts of English. In J. J. Webster (ed.) *Language and Education, Volume 9 in the Collected Works of M. A. K. Halliday* 306–28. London: Continuum.

Halliday, M. A. K. ([2001] 2003) Is the grammar neutral? Is the grammarian neutral? In J. J. Webster (ed.) *On Language and Linguistics, Volume 3 in the Collected Works of M. A. K. Halliday* 271–92. London: Continuum.

Halliday, M. A. K. (2003) On the 'architecture' of human language. In J. J. Webster (ed.) *On Linguistics and Language, Volume 3 in Halliday's Collected Works* 1–29. London: Continuum.

Halliday, M. A. K. (2009) Methods – techniques – problems. In M. A. K. Halliday and J. J Webster (eds) *Continuum Companion to Systemic Functional Linguistics* 59–86. London: Continuum.

Halliday, M. A. K. and Greaves, W. (2008) *Intonation in the Grammar of English*. London: Equinox.

Halliday, M. A. K. and Hasan, R. (1976) *Cohesion in English*. London: Longman.

Halliday, M. A. K. and Matthiessen, C. M. I. M. (2004) *An Introduction to Functional Grammar* (3rd edition). London: Arnold.

Halliday, M. A. K., McIntosh, A. and Strevens, P. ([1964] 2007) The users and uses of language. In J. J. Webster (ed.) *Language and Society, Volume 10 in the Collected Works of M. A. K. Halliday* 5–37. London: Continuum.

Hartley, J. (1982) *Understanding News.* London: Metheun.

Hasan, R. ([1973] 2005) Code, register and social dialect. In J. J. Webster (ed.) *Language, Society and Consciousness, Volume 1 in the Collected Works of Ruqaiya Hasan* 160–93. London: Equinox.

Hasan, R. (1984) Coherence and cohesive harmony. In J. Flood (ed.) *Understanding Reading Comprehension* 181–221. Newark, DE: IRA.

Hasan, R. (1985) Part B. In M. A. K. Halliday and R. Hasan *Language, Context and Text: Aspects of Language in a Social-Semiotic Perspective.* Geelong, Vic: Deakin University Press.

Hasan, R. (1995) The conception of context in text. In P. H. Fries, and M. J. Gregory (eds) *Discourse in Society: Systemic Functional Perspectives. Meaning and Choice in Language: Studies for Michael Halliday* 183–283. Norwood, NJ: Ablex.

Hasan, R. (1996) Ways of saying, ways of meaning. In C. Cloran, D. G. Butt and G. Williams (eds) *Ways of Saying, Ways of Meaning* 191–242. London: Cassell.

Hasan, R. (1999) Speaking with reference to context. In M. Ghadessy (ed.) *Text and Context in Functional Linguistics: Systemic Perspectives* 219–328. Amsterdam: John Benjamins.

Hasan, R. (2004) Analysing discursive variation. In L. Young and C. Harrison (eds) *Systemic Functional Linguistics and Critical Discourse Analysis: Studies in Social Change* 15–52. London: Continuum.

Hasan, R. (2009) The place of context in a systemic functional model. In M. A. K. Halliday and J. J. Webster (eds) *Continuum Companion to Systemic Functional Linguistics* 166–89. London: Continuum.

Hasan, R. (forthcoming) *Unity in Discourse: Texture and Structure. Volume 6 in the Collected Works of Ruqaiya Hasan* (ed. J. Webster). London: Equinox.

Iedema, R., Feez, S. and White, P. R. R. (1994) *Media Literacy.* Sydney: Disadvantaged Schools Program, NSW Department of School Education.

Liu, Y. and O'Halloran, K. L. (2009) Intersemiotic texture: analyzing cohesive devices between language and images. *Social Semiotics* 19(4): 367–88.

Lukin, A. (2010) 'News' and 'register': a preliminary investigation. In A. Mahboob and N. Knight (eds) *Appliable Linguistics: Texts, Contexts and Meaning* 92–113. London: Equinox.

Lukin, A. (2013) The meanings of war: from lexis to context. *Journal of Language and Politics* 12(3): 424–444.

Martin, J. R. (1992) *English Text: System and Structure.* Amsterdam: John Benjamins.

Matthiessen, C. M. I. M. (1992) Interpreting the textual metafunction. In M. Davies and L. Ravelli (eds) *Advances in Systemic Linguistics: Recent Theory and Practice* 37–81. London: Pinter.

Matthiessen, C. M. I. M. (1993) Register in the round: diversity in a unified theory of register analysis. In M. Ghadessy (ed.) *Register Analysis: Theory and Practice* 221–92. London: Pinter.

Matthiessen, C. M. I. M. (1995) *Lexicogrammatical Cartography: English Systems.* Tokyo: International Language Sciences Publisher.

Montgomery, M. (2007) *The Discourse of Broadcast News: A Linguistic Approach.* London: Routledge.

Ricks, T. (2006) *Fiasco: The American Military Adventure in Iraq.* Harmondsworth: Penguin.

Royce, T. D. (2007) Intersemiotic complementarity: a framework for multimodal discourse analysis. In T. D. Royce and W. L. Bowcher (eds) *New Directions in the Analysis of Multimodal Discourse* 63–110. Mahwah, NJ: Lawrence Erlbaum Associates.

Smith, B. (2008) *Intonational Systems and Register: A Multidimensional Exploration.* Unpublished PhD thesis. Sydney: Macquarie University. Available at: <http://www.isfla.org/Systemics/Print/Theses/SmithBradPhD.pdf>

Van Leeuwen, T. (1992) Rhythm and social context: accent and juncture in the speech of professional radio announcers. In P. Tench (ed.) *Studies in Systemic Phonology* 231–62. London: Pinter.

Wolff, M. (2003) Groundhog's Day at CentCom's Media Centre. In B. Katovsky & T. Carlson (eds) *Embedded: The Media at War in Iraq* 39–44. Guilford, CT: Lyons Press.

Appendix: Additional tables and figures

Table 2.A1 Theme and Information Focus (IF).

IU (Information Unit) #	THEME	IF: word rank * = marked for IF	IF: clause rank
1 //4 US Com/**manders** /say	US Commanders	*Commanders	Subj/Sayer (person)
2 //4 the /battle for /**Bagh**dad has be- //	the battle for Baghdad	Baghdad	Subj/Actor (non-Head) (place)
3 //1 -**gun** //		begun	Predicator/Process
4 //13 tens of /**thous**ands of A/merican /**troops** are at- //	tens of thousands of American troops	thousands/troops	Subj/Actor [Dual: number (non-Head)/person]
5 //13 -tacking /**five** Re/publican /**Guard** Di/visions in the//		five/Guard	Compl/Goal [Dual: number (non-Head)/classifier(non-Head)]
6 //1 Coalition /push to sur/**round** the I-//		surround	Predicator/Process
7 //1 -raqi / **cap**ital The //		capital	Compl/Goal (place)
8 //4 fiercest /fighting is /taking /place about /80 /kilometers /**south** of Bagh/dad where //	The fiercest fighting	*south	Adj/Circ (place)
9 //1 US /forces have taken /control of the /city of /**Karb**ala //	US forces	Karbala	Compl/Goal (non-Head) (abstraction)
10 //4 **Else**where a //	Elsewhere	Elsewhere	Adj/Circ (place)
11 //4 Coalition /bombing /raid in /**Hilla** has left //		Hilla	Adj/Circ (place)
12 //4 dozens of ci/**vil**ians //		civilians	Compl/Carrier (person)
13 //1 **dead** //		dead	Compl/Attribute (quality)
14 //3 ^ / ^ In the /**north** there are //	In the north	north	Adj/Circ (place)

IU (Information Unit) #	Information Unit	THEME	IF: word rank * = marked for IF	IF: clause rank
15	//4 airstrikes on I/raqi /army /positions /in and a/**round** the //		around	Adj/Circ (non-Head) (place)
16	//1 oil centre of Kir/**kuk** and in//		Kirkuk	Adj/Circ (non-Head) (place)
17	//4 **Basra** the //	and in Basra	Basra	Adj/Circ (place)
18	// 4 key to con/trolling the /south /**east** //		east	Compl/Goal (non-Head=Head ellipsed) (place)
19	//4 **British** /troops are //		*British	Subj/Actor (non-Head) (person)
20	//1 waiting for rein/**forcements** be- //		reinforcements	Adj/Circ (purpose)
21	//1 -fore a final /**push** to //		push	Adj/Circ (nominal. pro.)
22	//1 take the /**city** //		city	Compl/Goal (place)
23	//4 From /Central /Command in /**Qatar**, //	–	Qatar	Adj/Circ (place)
24	//1 ABC corres/pondent / Peter /**Lloyd** re/ports//		*Lloyd	Subj/Sayer (reporter)
25	//4 These could /well be the /first /**shots** in the //	These [cross modal ref]	shots	Compl/Value (act of war)
26	//4 final /**phase** of the in- //		phase	Compl/Value (non-Head) (act of war)
27	//1 -**vasion** a //		invasion	Compl/Value (non-Head) (act of war)
28	//1 ground /battle is under /**way** be- //	a ground battle	way	Compl/Attrib (phase)
29	//4 -tween / US /**forces** and the e- //		forces	Adj/Circ (person)
30	//4 -lite Re/publican /Guard di/visions pro/tecting the /**outskirts** of //		outskirts	Compl/Goal (place)

IU (Information Unit) #	THEME	IF: word rank * = marked for IF	IF: clause rank
31 //1 southern /**Bagh**dad //		Baghdad	Compl/Goal (non-Head) (place)
32 //4 ^ The /aerial /war isn't over /**yet** there's been //	The aerial war	yet	mood Adj
33 //1 more at/tacks /in and a/round the /**cap**ital the //	be	capital	Adj/Circ (place)
34 //5 tactic of /so-called /shock and awe bom/**bard**ment has //	the tactic of so-called shock and awe bombardment	bombardment	Subj/Token (act of war)
35 //1 lasted /almost /two /**weeks** but the re- //		weeks	Compl/Value (time)
36 //1 -**gime** is //	the regime	regime	Subj/Actor (institution)
37 //1 sounding as de/fiant as /**ever** //		ever	Adj/Circ (manner)
38 // 4 Let me /say that the enemy them/**selves** are saying that//	Let me/the enemy	*themselves	Reflexive pronoun (person)
39 // 4 **their** objective is //	their objective	*their	Subj/Token (non-Head) (abstraction)
40 // 1 **Bagh**dad//		Baghdad	Compl/Token (place)
41 // 4 ^while /**our** ob/jective is [[to //	our objective	*our	Subj/Token (non-Head) (abstraction)
42 // 4 **fight** the /enemy on //		*fight	Predicator/Process
43 // 4 every /**front** //		front	Adj/Circ (place)
44 // ^in /every pos/**ition** /		position	Adj/Circ (place)
45 // 4 and we /**will** prevent the enemy	we	*will	Finite
46 // 1 ^ from ap/proaching /**Bagh**dad//		Baghdad	Compl/Range (place)

IU (Information Unit) #	THEME	IF: word rank * = marked for IF	IF: clause rank
47	//53 the A/mericans /killed thirty /**five** I/**raq**is in- //	the Americans	five/Iraqis	Dual focus: Compl/Goal number (non-Head)/person
48	// 3 -cluding Re/publican / Guard /**troops** be- //		troops	Compl/Attribute (person)
49	//4 -fore /capturing an im/portant Eu/phrates /**River** /crossing at //		River	Compl/Goal (non-Head) (place)
50	// 1 Hinde/**yah** and //		Hindeyah	Adj/Circ (place)
51	//1 during a /battle at Nasi/**riyah** //	during a battle at Nasiriyah	Nasiriyah	Adj/Circ (place)
52	//4 US /Special /**Forces** //		Forces	Subj/Actor (person)
53	//4 rescued /servicewoman /Jessica /**Lynch** //		Lynch	Compl/Goal (person)
54	// 1 captured / ten /**days** ago //		days	Circ/Adj (time)
55	// 53 Grave /**fears** are /**held** for//	Grave fears	fears/held	Dual:Range/Compl; Process/Pred emotion/process
56	// 4 these American /**sold**iers //		soldiers	Circ/Adj (person)
57	//[[4 captured /**with** /her and//]]		with	Circ/Adj (non-Head) (accompaniment)
58	//4 later /**shown** on I- //		shown	Pred/Process process
59	//1 -raqi T/**V** //		TV	Adj/Circ (place [semiotic])
60	//4 To the /**south** there've been //	To the south	south	Adj/Circ (place)
61	//1 more /**clashes** be- //		clashes	Compl/Existent (act of war)
62	//4 -tween /British /forces and I/**raq**is //		Iraqis	Compl/Existent (person)
63	//1 in and a/round the /second /city of /**Basra** //		Basra	Adj/Circ (non-Head) (location)

IU (Information Unit) #	THEME	IF: word rank * = marked for IF	IF: clause rank
64 //53 In near/**by** /**areas** //	In nearby areas	nearby/areas	Dual focus: Adj/Circ (non-Head) (place)
65 //4 more /**signs** of the re- //		signs	nominal element neither Subj nor Compl
66 //1 -gime's de/**mise** //		demise	nominal element neither Subj nor Compl (non-Head)
67 //1 British ma/**rines** have been un- //	British marines	marines	Subj/Actor (person)
68 //4 covering /caches of /arms and ammu/**nit**ion in //		ammunition	Compl/Goal (non-Head)
69 //4 this / **case** //	in this case	this	Adj/Circ (abstract)
70 //1 stashed in/side a /village /**class**room there were //		classroom	Adj/Circ (place)
71 //4 **guns** //	be	guns	Compl/Existent (weapon)
72 //4 rocket pro/pelled gre/**nades** and//		grenades	Compl/Existent (weapon)
73 //1 **mor**tar rounds //		mortar	Compl/Existent (weapon)
74 //1 ^ There's /also been /action on the /**north**ern /front just//	be	northern	Adj/Circ (non-Head) (place)
75 //4 two hours /drive from /**Bagh**dad //		Baghdad	Adj/Circ (non-Head) (place)
76 //4 Saddam's /troops around the /Kurdish /village of /**Kif**re are //	Saddam's troops	Kifre	Adj/Circ (non-Head) (place)
77 //1 taking di/rect /**hits**		hits	Compl/Scope (act of war)
78 //4 ^ what the /shelling /**does**n't a/chieve the//	[[what the shelling doesn't achieve]]	doesn't	Finite

IU (Information Unit) #	THEME	IF: word rank * = marked for IF	IF: clause rank
79 //4 bombs /dropped from B5/2s in the //		B52s	Adj/Circ (place)
80 // 4 skies a/**bove** will //		above	Adj/Circ (non-Head) (place)
81 //1 finish /**off** //		off	Predicator/Process
82 //4 Still the / prepa/**rations** //	the preparations	preparations	Subject/Actor (nominal. proc.)
83 //1 go /**on**//		on	Predicator/Pro
84 //1 30 /thousand /**men** of the //	30 thousand men of the US fourth division	men	Subject/Actor (person)
85 //3 US /fourth di/**vision** have be- //		division	Subject/Actor (non-Head) (person)
86 //1 -gun ar/**riving** with A- //		arriving	Predicator/Process
87 //4 -merican /**generals** pre- //	with American generals	generals	Adj/Circ (person)
88 //1 -dicting /there could be /many more /**casu**alties in the //	be	casualities	Compl/Existent (person)
89 //4 days a/**head** it's //		ahead	Adj/Circ (time)
90 //4 likely /these /**troops** will //	these troops	troops	Subject/Goal (person)
91 //4 soon be /drawn /**north**ward into the //		northward	Adj/Circ (place)
92 // 1 Battle for /**Bagh**dad //	these troops	Baghdad	Adj/Circ (non-Head) (act of war)
93 //4 ^ Peter / **Lloyd,** //		Lloyd	minor cls
94 //4 ABC /**news,**		news	minor cls
95 // 1 /**Qatar**//		Qatar	minor cls

Table 2.A2 Theme/Rheme analysis.

	Theme						Rheme
	'People'	'Act of war'	'Place/time'	'Be'	'Strategy'	'Emotion'	
1	US Commanders						say
2		The battle for Baghdad					has begun
3	10s of 1000s of American troops						are attacking five Republican Guard Divisions in the Coalition push to surround the Iraqi capital
4		The fiercest fighting					is taking place about 80 kilometers south of Baghdad
5	US forces						have taken control of the city of Karbala
6			Elsewhere				a Coalition bombing raid in Hilla has left dozens of civilians dead
7			In the north				there are airstrikes in and around the oil centre of Kirkuk
8			in Basra				British troops are waiting for reinforcements before a final push to take the city
9							the key to controlling the south-east
10		(these)*					could well be the first shots of the final phase of the invasion

	Theme						Rheme
	'People'	'Act of war'	'Place/time'	'Be'	'Strategy'	'Emotion'	
11		a ground battle					is under way between US forces and the elite Republican Guard divisions [[protecting the outskirts of southern Baghdad]]
12		the aerial war					isn't over yet
13				(there)'s been			more attacks in and around the capital
14		the tactic of so-called shock and awe bombardment			tactic of so-called shock and awe bombardment		has lasted almost two weeks
15	The regime						is sounding as defiant as ever
16	(Let) me						say
17	the enemy themselves						are saying
18					their objective		is Baghdad
19					our objective		is [[to fight the enemy on every front in every position]]
20	we						will prevent the enemy from [[approaching Baghdad]]
21	The Americans						killed 35 Iraqis including Republican Guard troops

	Theme						Rheme
	'People'	'Act of war'	'Place/time'	'Be'	'Strategy'	'Emotion'	
22							capturing an important Euphrates river crossing at Hindeyah
23			during a battle				US special forces rescued service woman Jessica Lynch
24							captured 10 days ago
25						Grave fears	are held for these American soldiers [[captured with her // later shown at Iraqi TV]]
26			To the south				there have been more clashes between British forces and Iraqis in and around the second city of Basra
27			In nearby areas				more signs of the regime's demise
28	British marines						have been uncovering caches of arms and ammunition
29			In this case				stashed inside a village classroom
30				(there) were			guns, rocket propelled grenades and mortar rounds
31				(there) has < > been			action on the northern front just two hours drive from Baghdad
32	Saddam's troops						are taking direct hits

	Theme						Rheme
	'People'	'Act of war'	'Place/time'	'Be'	'Strategy'	'Emotion'	
33		what the shelling doesn't achieve					the bombs [[dropped from B52s in the skies above]] will finish off
34					the preparations		go on
35	30 000 men from US 4th Division						have begun arriving
36	with American generals						predicting
37				be			many more casualties in the days ahead
38	*these troops						will soon be drawn northward into the battle for Baghdad

Table 2.A3 Deixis in nominal groups (ignoring NGs embedded).

+/−MQ		+MQ		−MQ
+/−D	M	Q	MQ	
+Deictic [specific]	the Iraqi capital the fiercest fighting the aerial war the final phase the regime's demise the northern front Saddam's troops the US 4th Division	the battle for Baghdad the city of Karbala the outskirts of southern Baghdad the key to controlling the south east the bombs [[dropped from B52s in the skies above]] the skies above the battle for Baghdad	the Coalition push [[to surround the Iraqi capital]] the oil centre of Kirkuk the first shots in the final phase of the invasion the final phase of the invasion the elite Republican Guard divisions protecting the outskirts of southern Baghdad the tactic of so-called shock and awe bombardment these American soldiers [[ ]] the second city of Basra the Kurdish village of Kifre	the north the southeast the city the invasion the capital the regime the enemy [themselves] their objectives our objectives the enemy the enemy the preparations these troops the Americans the south this case the shelling
+Deictic [nonsp]	a Coalition bombing raid in Hilla a ground battle an important Euphrates River crossing a battle at Nasiriyah a village classroom		a final push to take the city	every front every position

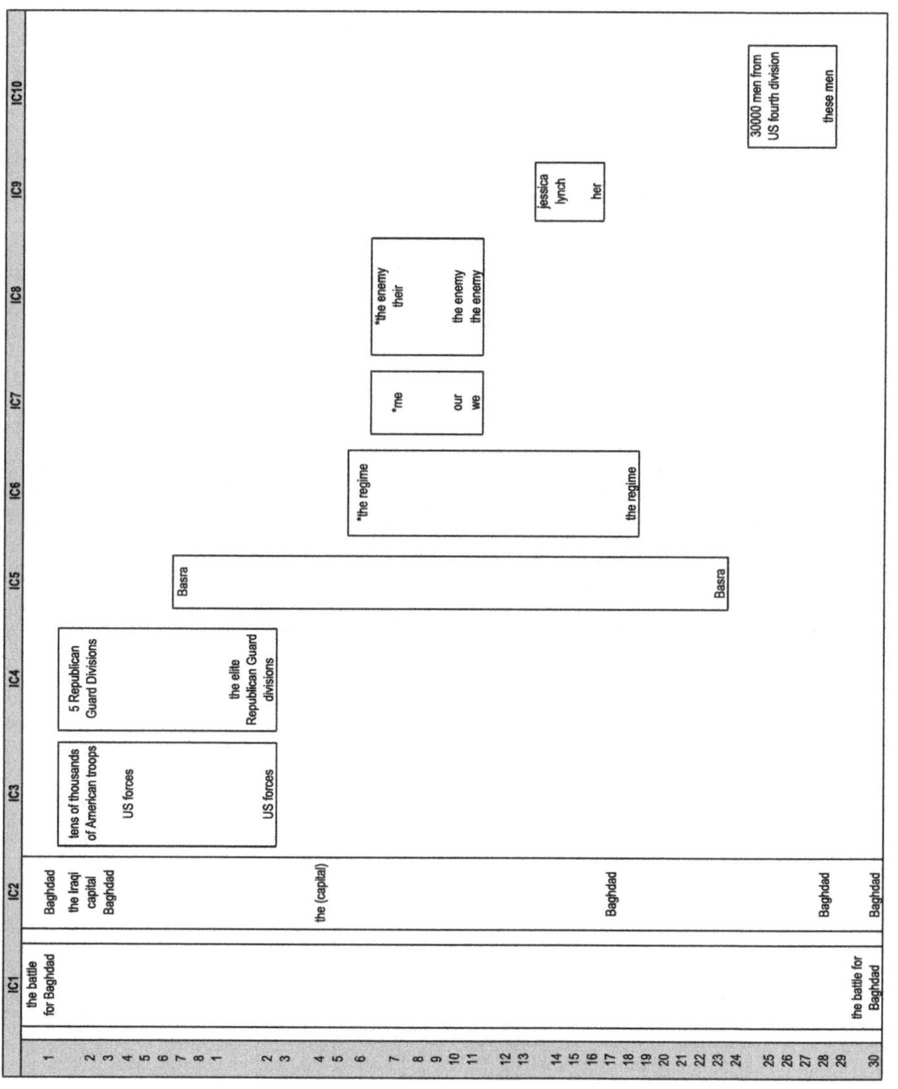

Figure 2.A1 Identity chains for example text.

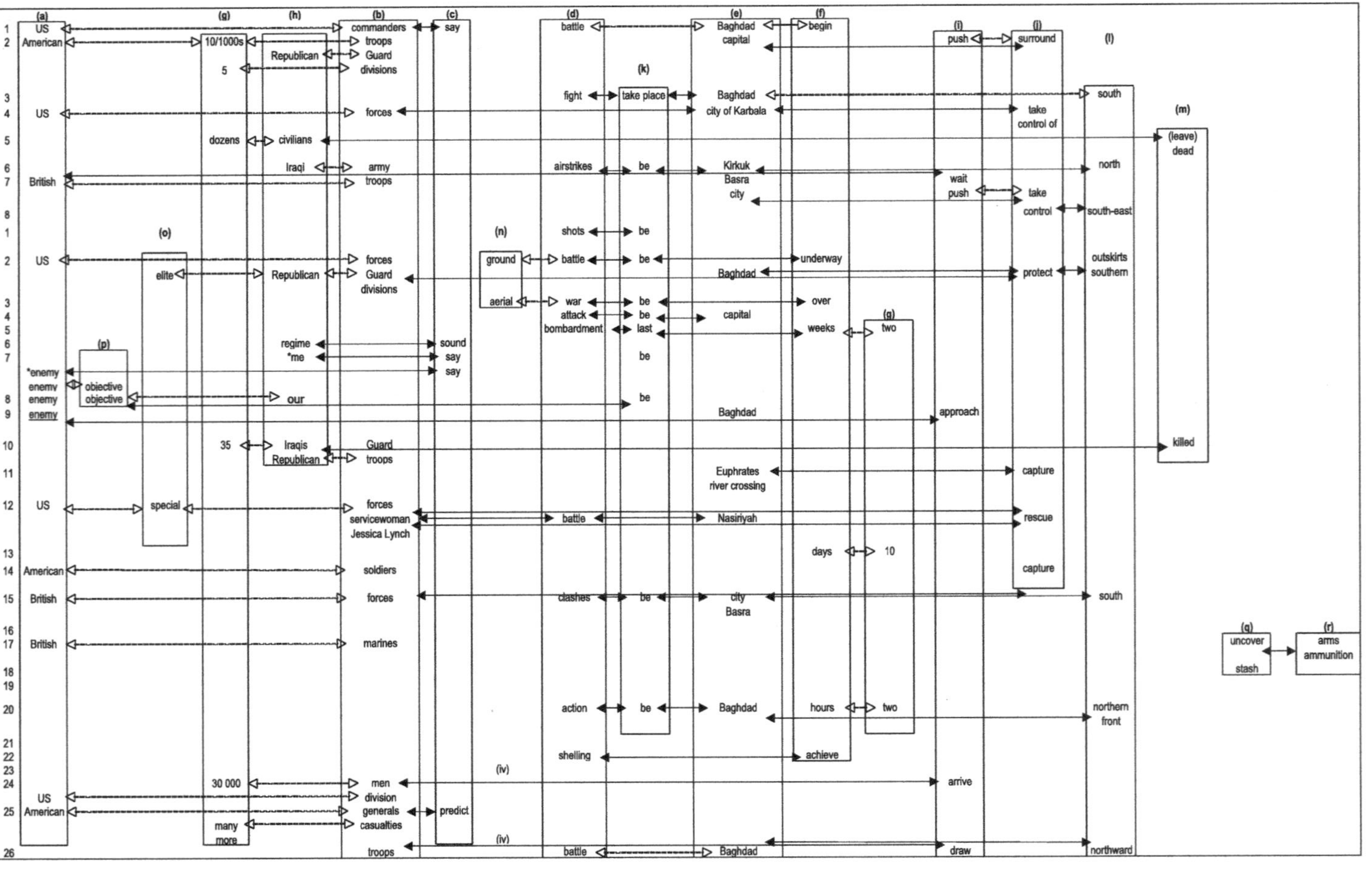

Figure 2.A2 Cohesive harmony analysis of case study text.

3

Intonation: Signal of information peaks

Shan Zhu[a]

3.1 Introduction

To communicate information, speakers have several ways of creating meaning in spoken language. They may do it through wording (the choice of words, the organization of these words into sensible utterances, etc.), and they can do it through intonation. However, in a discourse like news reading on radio, the speaker (i.e. the newsreader) does not have any choice in wording in that he or she has to read from the script, a text written to be read aloud. Tench (1996: 26) postulates three factors combining the discrete tone groups in a spoken discourse: the topic of the message, the grammatical systems of reference and conjunction, and intonation. Newsreaders have only 'intonation' at their disposal because the 'topic of the message' is already there in the script and so are the 'grammatical systems of reference and conjunction'.

Fortunately, according to the theory of English intonation systems proposed by Halliday (1963a, 1963b, 1967, 1970, [1994] 2000) and Tench (1990, 1992, 1996), the repertoire of intonational options is readily accessible to the newsreader. In the system of tonality, a speaker may choose how to break the message into tone groups to help the audience perceive each information unit; in the system of tonicity, they may choose within a tone group where to put the tonic prominence to attract the audience's attention to that highlighted new information; finally, in the system of tone, they may select one tone for each tone group to show the status of information: whether it is complete or not complete, major

a   **Shan Zhu** (family name Zhu) is a senior lecturer in the School of Foreign Languages at Sun Yat-sen University, where she received her PhD. She has been a visiting scholar at Hong Kong University and in the USA at Texas A&M University and the University of Florida. Her research interests include systemic functional linguistics, systemic phonology and discourse analysis. She is particularly interested in the functions of intonation in both English and Chinese.

or minor. Also, the newsreader can use tone concord and tone sequences to indicate the logico-semantic relation between consecutive tone groups.

There is another important prosodic feature needed to be introduced here: 'onset pitch'. Onset refers to the first accented syllable in each tone group. Based on the research findings of Brown *et al.* (1980), Tench (1990, 1996) and Wichmann (2000), in spoken discourse, especially newsreading, the combination of long pause and the following high pitch of the onset syllable of the initial tone unit is said to indicate the beginning of new ideas.

Brown *et al.* (1980: 26) suggest that pauses combined with high initial peaks indicate a change of topic. The speaker organizes his or her speech by dividing it into paratones. In other words, the use of pause and the following high pitch signals the speaker's organization of the discourse and thus, in terms of SFL, realizes the textual metafunction.

Tench (1990: 496) states that 'the combination of lengthy pause and high pitch correlate usually with a distinct change of subject matter'. Here the 'high pitch' refers to the high pitch of the onset syllable (Tench, 1996: 23). 'Onset syllable' is the 'first stressed and usually pitch-prominent syllable' (Crystal, 1969: 206) in a tone group. In a later account, Tench generalizes the pitch pattern typical in newsreading as 'high start, gradual descent and low finish' (Tench, 1996: 23).

Wichmann (2000) investigates the pitch variations of onset syllables in news summary and news reports chosen from the Spoken English Corpus (SEC). Wichmann's analysis of the onset pitch in each major tone group proves the function of the onset pitch: to signal the organization of units of discourse around a single topic.

In this chapter the onset pitch of the initial tone unit in each clause of a news commentary will be examined to check whether it is also used by the newsreader to indicate a change of topic. The news commentary under discussion in this chapter, 'China's economic boom', was downloaded from the website of BBC World Service at www.bbc.co.uk/worldservice/learnin-genglish/newsenglish/witn/archive_2005.shtml. The news commentary was published at 12:45 GMT on 18 February 2005.

The present chapter examines the ways the newsreader signals the peaks of information prominence by selecting from the system of intonation (tonality, tonicity, and tone) and the changes of onset pitch. In other words, it shall explore the ways the newsreader organizes the messages contained in the news commentary by expounding the interplay of thematic structure and information structure in the unfolding of the text.

3.2 Information flow

Halliday uses the image of a wave to describe the textual meaning of the clause:

> The textual meaning of the clause is expressed by what is put first (the Theme); by what is phonologically prominent (and tends to be put last – the New, signaled by information focus); and by conjunctions and relatives which if present must occur in initial position. Thus it forms a wave-like pattern of periodicity that is set up by peaks of prominence and boundary markers. (Halliday, [1994] 2000: 190)

When analysing the information framed in news stories in printed media, Martin and Rose use the term 'information flow' to refer to 'the way in which meanings are organized so that readers can process phases of meaning' (Martin and Rose, [2003] 2007: 20). The functions of information flow include 'giving readers some idea about what to expect, fulfilling those expectations, and then reviewing them' (*ibid.*: 175).

Information flow is a useful term applicable in analysing spoken discourse, too. In newsreading, unlike printed media, the audience does not have access to the script and therefore they cannot look back and forward to check what has already been talked about and what to expect in the next part. Signals must be provided by the newsreader through the use of intonation, leading the audience to surf smoothly on the peaks and slide through troughs on the information flow (cf. Bowcher, 2003, 2004). This chapter discusses how the information encoded in the news commentary is packaged to make it easier for the audience to follow by the newsreader's uses of intonation.

3.2.1 HyperTheme and hyperNew, macroTheme and macroNew

Halliday holds that 'Theme and information together constitute the internal resources for structuring the clause as a message – for giving it a particular status in relation to the surrounding discourse' (Halliday, [1994] 2000: 308). The messages in each clause are packaged according to what is given and what is new information and then distributed into the positions of Theme and Rheme.

In systemic functional linguistics (SFL), both thematic structure and information structure operate in the domain of the clause (where the information distribution is unmarked, i.e. one clause equals one information unit). The former is indicated by position in a clause: Theme always comes first in a clause and the rest of the clause is Rheme. The latter is signalled by the assignment of tonic prominence. The New usually carries the prominence and the Given does not have prominence since it is something recoverable in the context, in the air, or to be treated as Given for a rhetorical citation.

The two structures are semantically related in that in unmarked cases, the Given falls in Theme and the New within Rheme for the reason that whenever we communicate information we start from what is shared knowledge for both participants of the speech event. However, in some cases, for contrastive purposes, it is possible for the New to appear in the Theme and the Given in Rheme. Thus the New is highlighted by occurring at the thematic position besides the prominence already allocated to it.

By characterizing the unfolding of a text as a wave-like periodicity, we get a clear picture of how a text is organized as information flow (see Bowcher, 2004 for an analysis and discussion of the relationship between Given/New and Theme/Rheme in radio sports commentating). In newsreading, the information has already been packaged into chunks of information in the script in terms of Theme and sometimes with the help of punctuation (full stops, commas, etc.). What the newsreader can do is to provide the audience with signals that will help them process the information successfully with a minimum of effort.

According to Martin and Rose ([2003] 2007: 179), 'the recurrent choices for Theme and related choices for New work together to package discourse as phases of information'. The thematic and informational analysis of the news commentary may help reveal how the newsreader realizes the textual organization of the news commentary.

The term 'hyperTheme' refers to the Theme of a phase of discourse at a higher level, which is usually the 'topic sentence' of a paragraph. Accordingly, new information that accumulates at this higher-level phase is hyperNew. Martin and Rose (*ibid.*: 181) state that 'the hyperTheme is predictive; it establishes expectations about how the text will unfold'. They contend that 'hyperThemes tell us where we're going in a phase; hyperNews tell where we've been' (*ibid.*: 182). There will be a macroTheme at an even higher level which predicts hyperTheme. Similarly, macroNews distill hyperNews. In this way, the different layers of Theme construct the model of the development of a text, which is summarized in Figure 3.1 below.

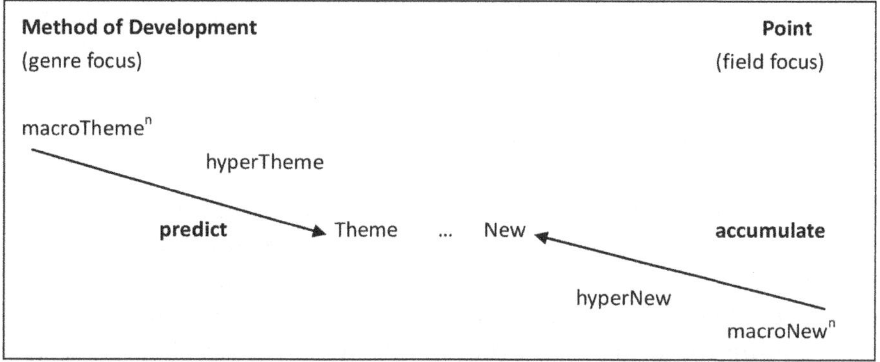

Figure 3.1 Layers of Themes and News in discourse (Martin and Rose, [2003] 2007: 186).

3.2.2   Ripples of information: Theme and New

If the information in a text is compared to waves, then the information contained in a clause is like small ripples. While the Theme forms a peak at the beginning of a clause, the New accumulates another peak at the end of the clause. In other words, in speech a clause may have two peaks of information: one peak in a thematic wave at the beginning and another at the end of the clause in the New (Halliday, [1994] 2000; Martin and Rose, [2003] 2007: 179). Generally speaking, the two peaks may overlap as text unfolds. In marked cases, the two peaks may coincide if the New falls within the Theme in a clause. This happens when the Theme is treated as new information and thus carries prominence, or spoken with a separate tone group and thus has its own tonic. In this case, the thematic wave and the news wave coincide.

3.3   Phonological analysis

This section investigates the way(s) the newsreader highlights the thematic waves and news waves intonationally. The importance of Theme can be seen from the following observation: 'The thematic organization of the clause (and clause complexes, where relevant) is the most significant factor in the development of the text' (Halliday and Matthiessen, 2004: 105). Thematic analysis may help us understand how the message in the news script is organized. Therefore, the thematic structure of the news commentary will be analysed first. A phonological transcription of the news commentary is then provided for the exploration of the ways the newsreader signals phonologically to help the audience predict the development of the news commentary and identify the location of New.

3.3.1 Highlighted Theme

The news commentary under discussion comprises seventeen clauses. Table 3.1 lists all the Themes with indications of the tone used if a separate tone group is assigned to the Theme, and the pitch height of the onset syllable in the initial tone unit of each clause. The Tonic of each tone unit is in bold type and onset pitches of significance to the analysis worth noticing are in italics.

As can be seen in Table 3.1, among the clauses with Subject as Theme, Clauses 3, 5, 11 and 14–17 have short Themes of only one or two words.

Table 3.1 Highlighted Themes in the news commentary.

Clause	Marked Theme	Tone	Subject/Theme	Tone	Onset pitch (Hz)
1			the Chinese **econ**omy	4	*271.72*
2	but even **now**	1	personal **in**comes	4	262.55
3			That (**means**)	4	256.14
4	and if		the experience of earlier Asian economic **mir**acles; Japan and South Korea	4-1	230.77
5			China		192.80
6	for **oth**er economies	4			*288.37*
7	on **one** hand	4			251.71
8			com**mod**ity producing countries	1	249.14
9	and just as im**por**tant	4			248.64
10	but on the **other** hand	4			*282.62*
11			China		168.71
12			manu**fac**turers in other places	4	*251.45*
13	though at the same **time**	1			194.17
14			the country		174.30
15			China		*257.74*
16	But		it		216.86
17			it		196.89

They are not spoken with a separate tone. Therefore, no further Thematic analysis is given to these clauses.

The Themes of the rest of the clauses are marked off for being allocated a separate tone group or falling on items other than Subject or marked off for both. This echoes Halliday's observation that in speech, Theme as the starting point of the message is frequently marked off with a separate tone group (Halliday, [1994] 2000: 39). We can see in Table 3.1 that these marked Themes are doubly highlighted by the use of a separate tone group and contrastive tone 4. In these ways the newsreader tries to attract the audience's attention, telling the audience what to expect. Therefore our analysis focuses on these highlighted Themes. By analysing the Theme structure of these clauses and their accompanying intonation, we can demonstrate how the newsreader signals the peaks of thematic waves phonologically.

Clause 1

// 4 ∧ the / Chinese e/<u>con</u>omy has // 3 been / growing / nearly / ten per / cent a / <u>**year**</u> for // 1 three / <u>de</u>cades //

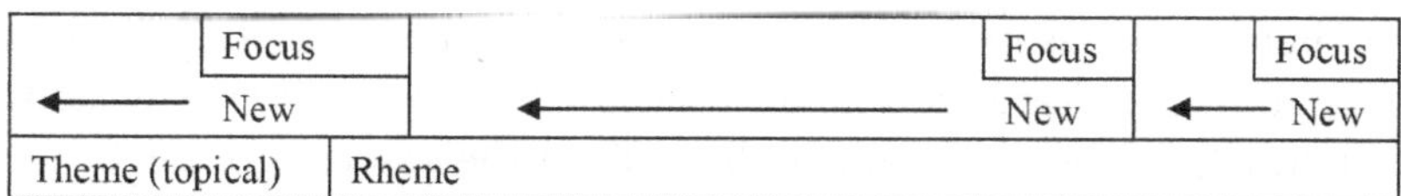

In Clause 1, the experiential Theme 'the Chinese economy' is spoken with a separate tone group on contrastive tone 4. Besides this, the onset is spoken at a high pitch (271.70 Hz). In doing so, the newsreader gives the audience a signal that this is the main topic of the news commentary thus telling the audience what is coming next. Since tone 4 conveys a meaning of reservation, the newsreader uses it to suggest that despite the information in Clause 1 – 'the Chinese economy has been growing nearly ten per cent a year for three decades', there is something unexpected coming in the following clause.

Clause 2

//1 ∧ but /even / <u>**now**</u> // 4 personal / <u>in</u>comes are //4 only at the / level of Ja/<u>**pan**</u> in the // 1 early / nineteen / <u>**fif**</u>ties //

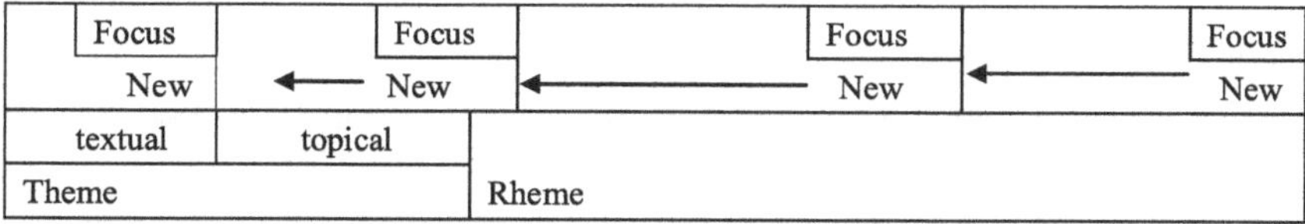

The textual Theme of Clause 2, 'but even now', introduces to the audience a fact which is disproportionate with the fast development of the economy:

'personal incomes are only at the level of Japan in the early nineteen fifties'. 'Personal incomes' is spoken on contrastive tone 4, for the newsreader wishes to compare it with China's economic development.

Compared with Clause 1, Clause 2 is more important because the fact encoded in the former is known to all but the fact encoded in the latter is something new that the newsreader wants the audience to pay particular attention to. That is why the informing tone 1 is used for the textual Theme of Clause 2, 'but even now', to emphasize the disproportion between personal incomes and China's economic development. The tonic falls on the default position, the final lexical word.

Clauses 1 and 2 form the beginning of the news commentary. As a rule, this is the place where writers usually set the overall topic of the text, the macroTheme. This is true in this news commentary. By connecting the two facts with 'but', the writer sets the key of the news commentary: though the Chinese economy grows very fast, the overall level of economic development is still low. In the reading of the news commentary, the newsreader signals the contrast by assigning a separate tone group to each Theme. Besides, the two concepts in contrast, 'Chinese economy' and 'personal incomes', are spoken on tone 4. The textual Theme to address the contrast, 'but even now', is delivered on the asserting tone 1.

Clause 3

// 4 that / **means** // 1 ₐthere's / huge po/**ten**tial for // 1 further ex/**pan**sion / ₐ //

	Focus		Focus		Focus
Given	New	⟵———— New		⟵———— New	
Theme (topical)		Rheme			

In Clause 3, the Theme 'that' refers back to what has been talked about in previous clauses. The Theme 'that' together with the unembedded Rheme, 'means', signals that this clause is an explanation of the previous clauses. The newsreader unfailingly shows this by using tone 4.

Clause 4

//4ₐand /if the ex/perience of / earlier / Asian eco/nomic / **mir**acles // 1ₐ Ja/pan and / South Ko/**re**a // 13 ₐ is / anything to / **go** / **by** //

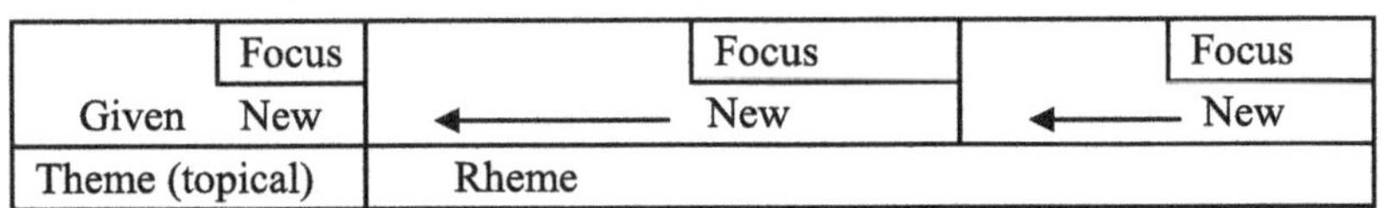

		Focus		Focus		Focus
Given	⟵———————————— New		⟵———— New		⟵———— New	
textual	topical				Rheme	
Theme						

Clause 5

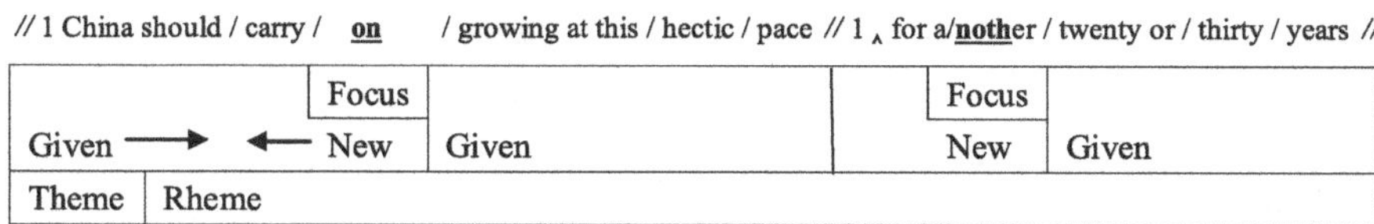

		Focus				Focus	
Given →	← New	Given				New	Given
Theme	Rheme						

Clauses 4 and 5 form a clause complex. The textual Theme of Clause 4 'and if' foreshadows the inference in the following clauses so that the audience knows a claim is coming next. The topical Theme of Clause 4 'the experience of early Asian economic miracles Japan and South Korea' is a nominal group with 'experience' as the Head and the 'of' phrase as post-modifier. Within the 'of' phrase there are two nominal groups. The logico-semantic relation between them is exemplification: 'Japan and South Korea' explains what 'the earlier Asian economic miracles' refer to. The first nominal group is assigned a tone 4, indicating the information is non-final. The second one is spoken on tone 1 and with obviously lower pitch. Though tone 1 may suggest the second nominal group contains the major information, the low pitch presents it as something less important than the previous one.

Clause 6

// 4 ∧ for / **oth**er e/conomies // 1 China is / seen as / both an oppor/tunity and a / **threat** //

	Focus					Focus
	New	Given	Given	←		New
textual		topical				
Theme			Rheme			

The textual Theme of Clause 6 serves as a signpost of a new wave of information, spoken with a high onset pitch (288.37 Hz). The previous clauses describe the economic development of China. The textual Theme of Clause 6 and the accompanied contrastive tone 4 imply that what follows is something in contrast with what has just been talked about. It tells the audience a shift of perspective is happening: 'we are going to analyse the effects of the Chinese economic development from the perspective of other economies.'

Clause 7

// 4 ᴧ on / **one** / hand // 1 it 's cre/ated a / vast new / **mark**et // 1 ᴧ for sup/pliers of / ... //

Focus				Focus	
New	Given	Given	←———————	New	
textual		topical			
Theme			Rheme		

Clause 7 starts with a marked textual Theme 'on one hand', spoken on tone 4. It is a clear indicator that the information contained in this clause is just a ripple of the big wave of information introduced by the textual Theme of Clause 6 ('for other economies'): Clause 7 about 'suppliers of basic commodities', Clause 8 'commodity producing countries', and Clause 9 'world prices for basic products'. The textual Theme of Clause 7, 'on one hand', encodes one aspect of the analysis. It initiates the analysis of the effects of Chinese economic development on 'commodity producing countries' (Theme of Clause 8).

Clause 8

//1 ᴧ com/modity pro/ducing /**coun**tries like Aus// 1tralia Bra/zil and / Argen/**ti**na // 1 have / seen ...//

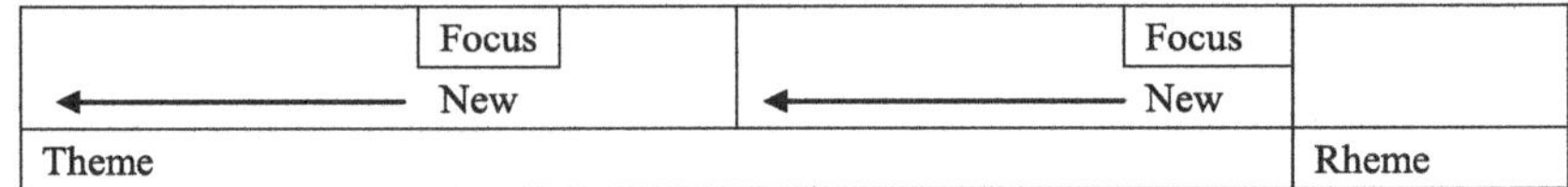

	Focus			Focus	
←——————— New			←——————— New		
Theme					Rheme

The Theme of Clause 8 presents another aspect of the analysis. It is a long nominal group, spoken as two tone groups: one for the Head ('commodity producing countries') and the other for the Post-modifier ('like Australia, Brazil and Argentina'), although the boundary does not fall exactly between the two components. The tone concord between the Head and the Post-modifier (both are spoken on tone 1) shows the apposition relationship between them.

Clause 9

// 4 ᴧ and / just as im/**por**tant // 13 world / **price**s for / basic / **pro**ducts // ... // 1 ᴧ have gone up very sharply //

	Focus		Focus		Focus	
Given ←——— New			New		New	
textual		topical				
Theme						Rheme

The textual Theme of Clause 9 is marked off and spoken on contrastive tone 4. This introduces something just as important as what has been mentioned in Clause 8. That is the reason why a contrastive tone 4 is chosen. Compound tone 13 is selected for the topical Theme since the final element in it is semi-New. 'World prices' is a new topic and therefore is spoken with a falling tone. 'Basic products' has been under discussion as 'basic commodities' in Clause 7 but is still newsworthy here.

Clause 10

//4 ˌbut/on the/**other** / hand//1China's/ rise as a manu/**fac**turing / centre//5ˏis /seen as/ **worr**ying by/ many /rivals//

Focus			Focus	Focus	
New	Given	Given ←	New	← New	Given
textual		topical			
Theme				Rheme	

When the audience hear the Theme of Clause 7 'on one hand', they would expect that there might be something 'on the other hand'. The expectation is confirmed by the information contained in the following clauses. The analysis from another perspective is launched by the textual Theme of Clause 10 signalled, again, by the combination of a separate tone group, contrastive tone 4 and raised onset pitch (282.62 Hz). With these resources Clause 10 brings a totally different idea to the audience. In Clauses 7, 8 and 9, the economic development of China is seen by some countries as something good ('an opportunity'). But, as Clause 10 suggests, other countries may view it negatively ('a threat').

Clause 12

//4 manu/**fac**turers in / other places // 1 often / find it / hard to com/**pete** / ˏ //

Focus		Focus
New	←	New
topical	textual	
Theme	Rheme	

Once again, the Theme of Clause 12 is highlighted in a way that appears common to this newsreading: a combination of a separate tone group, contrastive tone 4 and raised onset pitch (251.45 Hz). After presenting the hard news in Clause 11, that China absorbs a larger amount of foreign investment than any other nation every year, the newsreader reinforces the consequence of this fact – 'manufacturers in other places find it hard to compete' – by highlighting the Theme with a separate tone group, contrastive tone 4 and raised onset pitch.

Clause 13

//1 ∧ though at the / same / **time** // 1 ∧ as / China's / popu/lation gets / indi/vidually / **rich**er / ∧ //

	Focus				Focus
Given ⟶ ⟵ New		Given ⟵			New
textual		topical			
Theme				Rheme	

Clause 14

// 1 ∧ the / country is e/merging as a / key / **mar**ket // 1∧ for the so/**phis**ticated / products and / services / ... //

		Focus		Focus	
Given ⟶ ⟵		New		New	Given
Theme	Rheme				

After the analysis of the effects of China's economic development from two different perspectives, there is still something in the script the newsreader wishes to attract the audience's attention to, which is the information conveyed in Clauses 13 and 14. In order to indicate the shift of perspective and also to reveal the importance of the information, tone 1 is chosen for the marked Theme of Clause 13.

3.3.2 Summary of thematic and phonological analysis

The thematic and phonological analysis shows that the newsreader emphasizes the information within the Theme by marking it off with a separate tone group, or assigning it contrastive tone 4, or raising the onset pitch, or using all these ways together. These overlappings of Theme, New, tonality, tonicity and onset pitch create different layers of information prominence, which are the focus of analysis in the following sections.

3.4 Highlighted new information

According to Halliday ([1994] 2000: 299), Theme is what the speaker chooses to take as the starting point of the message. To achieve a common ground between both participants of a speech act, the speaker would naturally choose to put Given information in the Theme: 'let's start from something we all know'. Therefore we could say the thematic structure is speaker-oriented. However, in most cases the purpose of speech is to communicate New information. The New, as the name implies, is something the speaker knows but the listener does not; at least the speaker supposes so. Therefore, the information structure is listener-oriented. Nevertheless, both structures are 'speaker-selected' (*ibid.*: 299). As the communication progresses, both the speaker and the listener keep expanding upon the shared information by providing/receiving New information.

The unmarked pattern of the mapping of the two structures, as mentioned earlier, is therefore the choice of Theme within the Given and New within the Rheme (*ibid.*). Nonetheless, this unmarked pattern is often overridden by local conditions created by the environment. So the speaker may exploit these circumstantially-defined potentials to achieve a great variety of rhetorical effects.

This section discusses how the newsreader guides the audience to confirm their expectations by highlighting the new information. The news commentary is phonologically transcribed as follows:

Clause 1

//4 ∧ the / Chinese e/**con**omy has//3 been / growing / nearly / ten per / cent a / **year** for//1 three / **dec**ades //

Clause 2

//1 ∧ but / even / **now**//4 personal / **in**comes are //4 only at the /level of Ja/**pan** in the//1 early / nineteen / **fif**ties //

Clause 3

//4 that / **means**//4 ∧ there's / huge po/**ten**tial for//1 further ex/**pan**sion //

Clause 4

//4 ∧ and / if the ex/perience of / earlier / Asian eco/nomic / **mir**acles//1 ∧ Ja/pan and South Ko/**rea** //3 ∧ is / anything to / go / **by** //

Clause 5

//4 China should / carry / **on** / growing at this / hectic / pace //1 ∧ for a/**noth**er / twenty or / thirty / years //

Clause 6

//4 ∧ for / **oth**er e/conomies//1 China is / seen as / both an / oppor/tunity / and a / **threat**//

Clause 7

// 4 ∧ on / **one** / hand//1 ∧ it's cre/ated a / vast new / **mar**ket// 1 ∧ for sup/pliers of / basic com/**mod**ities //1 ∧ like / oil / steel / wood / **soy**a / beans // 1 ∧ and / many / other / agri/cultural / **prod**ucts //

Clause 8

//1 ∧ com/modity pro/ducing / <u>coun</u>tries like Aus//1 tralia Bra/zil and / Argen/<u>ti</u>na//1 ∧ have / seen de/<u>mand</u> for their goods //1 <u>soar</u>//

Clause 9

//4 ∧ and / just as im/<u>por</u>tant//13 world / <u>price</u>s for / basic / <u>prod</u>ucts//1 ∧ notably / steel / many / <u>met</u>als / ∧ //1 oil and / some / <u>foods</u>//1 ∧ have / gone up / very / <u>sharp</u>ly //1 ∧ in the / last couple of / <u>years</u> //

Clause 10

//4 ∧ but / on the / <u>oth</u>er / hand//1 China's / rise as a manu/<u>fac</u>turing / centre//5 ∧ is / seen as / <u>wor</u>rying by / many / rivals //

Clause 11

//4 China / sucks in be/tween / thirty and / fifty / billion / <u>dol</u>lars of//1 foreign in/ <u>vest</u>ment//1 every / <u>year</u> //1 far / <u>more</u> than //1 any / other / <u>na</u>tion//

Clause 12

//4 manu/<u>fac</u>turers in / other places//1 often / find it / hard to com/<u>pete</u> //

Clause 13

//1 ∧ though at the / same / <u>time</u> //4 ∧ as / China's / popu/<u>la</u>tion //1 ∧gets / indi/vidually / <u>rich</u>er //

Clause 14

//1 ∧ the / country is e/merging as a / key / <u>mar</u>ket//1 ∧ for the so/<u>phis</u>ticated / products and / services / ∧ //1 typically pro/duced in the in/dustrialized / <u>West</u> //

Clause 15

//4 China / <u>is</u> on / course //1 ∧ to be/come an eco/nomic /<u>_super</u>/power//

Clause 16

//1 ∧ but it's / not / actually / there / <u>yet</u>//

Clause 17

//1 ∧ it's / currently the / <u>sixth</u> / largest e//1 conomy in the / <u>world</u> / ∧//1 still / smaller than / Britain and / <u>France</u> / ∧//1 ∧ let alone the / <u>real</u> / giants//1 ∧ Ja/pan and the United / <u>States</u> //

As the peaks of news waves most often predictably occur at the end of a clause, the clauses with marked New create additional peaks at unexpected places and thus need further exploration. As can be seen from the above phonological transcription, marked New in the news commentary occurs in Clauses 5, 6, 9–12, 14, 15 and 17. These clauses are examined one by one through looking into their information structure and the pitch contour of each tone group with marked tonicity.

Clause 5

// 1 China should / carry / **on** / growing at this / hectic / pace // 1 ∧ for a/**noth**er / twenty or / thirty / years //

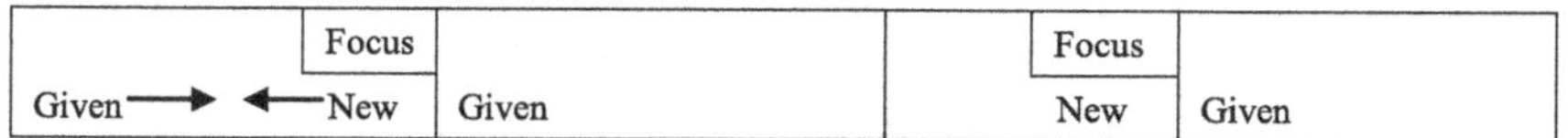

The tonic in the first tone group of Clause 5 is allocated to 'on' to indicate where the New is located. From Clause 1 we know the fact that 'the Chinese economy has been growing nearly ten per cent a year for three decades'. Therefore, in this tone group, 'growing at this hectic pace' just echoes the fact in Clause 1. What the writer wants to highlight here is not the rapid growth itself, but the inference that China will 'carry on' the tendency of rapid growth in the future if the condition in Clause 4 is present. Thus, the newsreader indicates this by assigning the prominence to 'on' rather than 'growing' or 'pace' or any other lexical items. The reason for highlighting 'another' in the second tone group is the same. From Clause 1 we know that the fast growth of the Chinese economy has been continuing for three decades, which means the same as 'twenty or thirty years' in the second tone group. What this tells the audience is that 'we have already known that the Chinese economy has been growing fast for three decades. What I want to tell you now is that the Chinese economy will keep on growing rapidly for **another** twenty or thirty years.'

Clause 6

// 4 ∧ for / **oth**er e/conomies // 1 China is / seen as / both an / oppor/tunity / and a / **threat** //

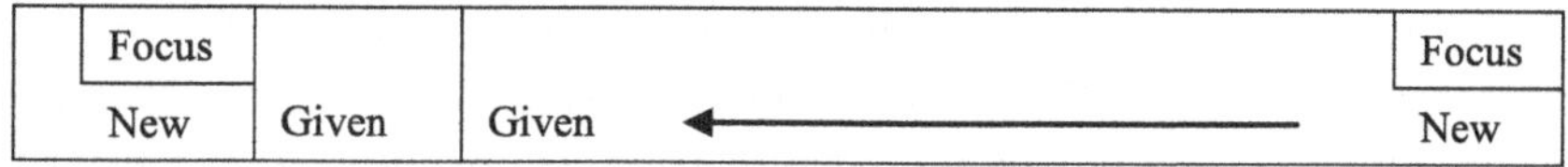

The New in the first tone group in Clause 6 falls on 'other' to form a contrast with the Subject of Clause 4, 'China', in the next tone group. More importantly, since it also signals a shift of perspective, the newsreader highlights it by not only raising its pitch height to the highest one (288.37 Hz) in the whole news commentary, but also giving it contrastive tone 4.

Clause 9

Clause 9 is divided into three tone groups. The tonic of each tone group falls on the last lexical item except that of the second one.

//4 ∧ and / just as im/**port**ant //13 world / **price**s for / basic / **prod**ucts //1 ∧ notably / steel / many / **met**als / ∧ //1 oil and some / **foods** //1 ∧ have / gone up / very / **sharp**ly //1 ∧ in the / last / couple of / **years** //

Here only the tonicity of the second tone group is analysed.

//13 world / **price**s for / basic / **prod**ucts //

	Focus		Focus
	New		New

As mentioned in the Thematic analysis of Clause 9 in Section 3.3.1, compound tone 13 is chosen for the second tone group because it contains some semi-New information. 'Prices' forms the major tonic which carries the principal new information. Though the minor tonic 'products' appears in Clause 7, it is still a significant part of the message, hence its status as minor focus. What the writer wants to focus on is 'world prices' of 'the basic products', not just 'the basic products' themselves.

Clause 10

//4 ˌbut/on the/**oth**er / hand //1China's/ rise as a manu/**fac**turing / centre//5ˌis /seen as/ **worr**ying by/many /rivals//

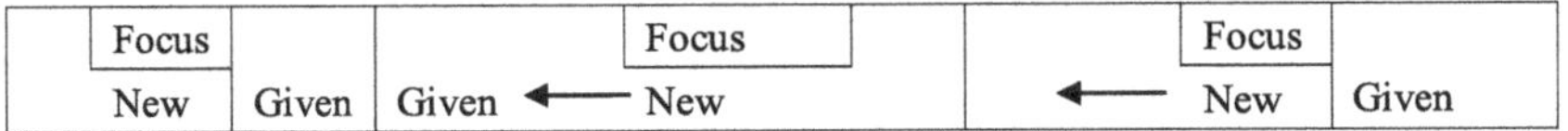

Focus			Focus		Focus	
New	Given	Given	← New	←	New	Given

The tonic of the first tone group in Clause 10 is allocated to 'other' in order to make a contrast with the conjunctive adjuncts //4 ∧ on / **one** / hand // in Clause 7. In English the conjunctives 'on one hand' and 'on the other hand' have their preferred intonation patterns, spoken on tone 4 with tonics on 'one' and 'other' (Halliday, 1970: 40). Like Clause 6, Clause 10 is a place where a shift of perspective happens. So the pitch height of the onset is the second highest (282.62 Hz) in the whole news commentary. The tonic of the second tone group falls on the classifier of the nominal group 'manufacturers' according to the common rule that the tonic usually falls on the first word of true compound (*ibid.*: 45). The tonic of the last tone group in Clause 10 is on 'worrying', spoken with an assertive tone 5. Compared with 'worrying', the final lexical item 'rivals' is less important since its existence is predictable judging from the word 'worrying': only rivals would worry about their competitors' rapid growth. The interpersonal commitment of the tone 5 reveals that this is what the newsreader thinks about China: an additional assertion of interpersonal certainty.

Clause 11

The tonic in the first three tone groups in Clause 11 falls on the final lexical items in each tone group, hence there is unmarked tonicity. In the last tone group of this clause, the tonic is on 'more', emphasizing the comparison between China and other nations:

//1 far **more** than / 1 any other / **na**tion //

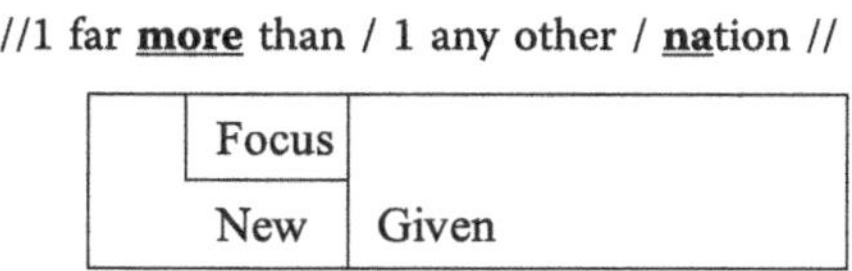

The final lexical items are predictable from the context and therefore lose the status of newness.

Clause 12

//4 manu/**fac**turers in / other places // 1 often / find it / hard to com/**pete** / ∧ //

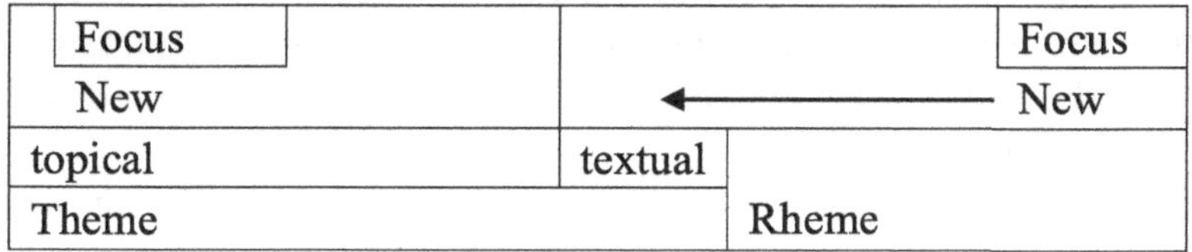

In Clause 12, the tonic of the first tone group falls on 'manufacturers'. The newsreader narrows the pitch range of the phrase 'in other places' and keeps the average pitch height low. We could say the Post-modifier of the nominal group 'in other places' functions as parenthesis in this tone group. Therefore, it carries no informational prominence.

Clause 14

//1 ∧ the country is e/merging as a / key / **mar**ket //1 ∧ for the so/**phis**ticated / products and / services / ∧ //1 typically pro/duced in the in/dustrialized / **West** //

The adjective 'sophisticated' in the second tone group is spoken with the highest pitch among the three tone groups in the whole clause:

// 1 ∧ for the so/**phis**ticated / products and / services / ∧ //

	Focus	
	New	Given

This indicates that the newsreader assigns the tonic on 'sophisticated' in order to put it in a contrastive position against another adjective 'basic' appearing previously in Clauses 7 and 9: 'sophisticated products and services' vs. 'basic commodities/products'.

Clause 15

// 4 China / **is** on / course // 1 ∧ to be/come an eco/nomic / **su**per/power //

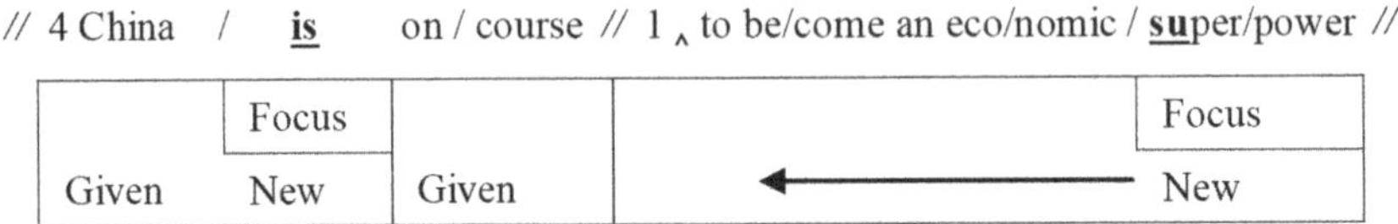

Clauses 15 and 16 reinforce the thesis of the news commentary expressed in Clauses 1 and 2. Therefore, in Clause 15, the fact that 'China is on course to become an economic superpower' is not something new because the audience may infer this from Clauses 1 and 2. What the newsreader highlights here is the emphatic meaning of 'is', the Finite of the clause: the writer emphasizes the proposition stated in Clauses 1 and 2 by confirming its validity. The newsreader interprets the writer's macro-textual emphasis by putting the tonic on 'is' and using contrastive tone 4. Thus the interpersonal aspect of the message is highlighted as being informationally important.

Clauses 1 and 2 may be considered as a higher-level Theme, which is the 'topic sentence' of the news commentary as a whole. Clauses 15 and 16 are higher-level New. They not only rephrase the meaning of Clauses 1 and 2 but also put it forward to a new point. The importance of higher-level Theme and New is discussed in 3.5 in more detail.

Clause 17

// 1 ∧ it's / currently the / **sixth** largest e/conomy in the / world / ∧ // 1 still / smaller than / Britain and / **France** / ∧ // 1∧ let alone the / **real** / giants // 1 ∧ Ja/pan and the U/nited / **States** //

There are four tone groups in Clause 17. The second and the fourth tone groups have unmarked tonicity, hence not discussed here. The first tone group is analyzed as follows:

// 1 ∧ it's / currently the / **sixth** largest e/conomy in the / world / ∧ //

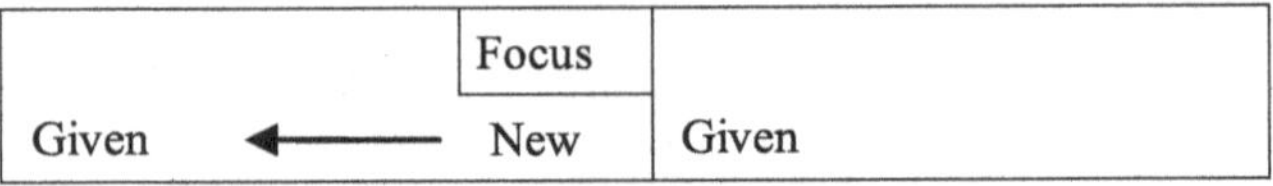

In the first tone group, the tonic falls on the rank of the Chinese economy in the world, 'sixth', the pitch of which is higher than the surrounding items. Compared with the ranking 'the sixth', the domain of the ranking 'largest economy in the world' can be surmised from previous clauses. The audience knows that China's economy is developing very fast, but they may not know exactly its ranking in the world economy.

The tonic of the third tone group falls on a marked place:

// 1ʌ let alone the / **real** / giants //

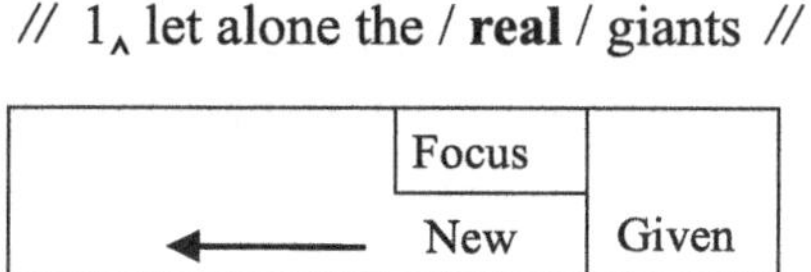

The reason for the tonic to fall on 'real' is that the writer wants to achieve a contrastive effect here: though the Chinese economy develops rapidly, China is not a real superpower yet because of its disproportionate development mentioned earlier in the news commentary. The 'real giants' are Japan and the United States, not China. The final lexical item 'giants' has no prominence because it is just another form of 'superpower' in Clause 15.

3.4.1 Summary of tonicity analysis

The tonicity analysis of the above clauses carrying marked new information shows that the newsreader highlights the new information by allocating prominence to it wherever it occurs, either initially, medially or finally. In this way, he provides clear signals for the audience to follow whenever there is something worth noting, either contrastive or unrecoverable from the context.

As mentioned earlier in §3.3.1, the highlighted/marked New in Clause 6 (//4 ʌ for / **oth**er e/conomies//), Clause 10 (//4 ʌ but / on the / **oth**er / hand //) and Clause 15 (// 4 China / **is** on / course //) also serve as a signal of a perspective shift, which indicates macro/hypertextual organization. This way of adding additional textual prominence to the New/ tonicity assignment helps the audience better understand the unfolding of a text. This issue is addressed in detail in the next section.

3.5 Waves of information: hyperTheme and hyperNew

The thematic and information structure of every clause has been examined in §3.3.1, and we have explored the tonicity of clauses with marked New in §3.3.2. If we examine the news commentary closely to find out how the ripples of information accumulate into bigger waves, we can see more clearly the interplay of the thematic structure and the information structure. This section looks at how the newsreader signals the hyperThemes and hyperNews, and macroThemes and macroNews.

3.5.1 HyperTheme and macroTheme

Since onset is the first stressed syllable in the first tone group of each clause and Theme is always at the initial position of a clause, it is not surprising to find all the onsets are within Theme. In Table 3.1, we find that the onset pitch of Clauses 1, 6, 10 and 15 are higher than the surrounding items. From the thematic analysis in §3.3.1, we know Clause 1 is the beginning of the news commentary, and Clauses 6, 10 and 15 signal a shift of perspective respectively. Therefore we may say these four clauses correspond to the peaks of the thematic waves in the news commentary and function as macroThemes and hyperThemes. They enable the listener to process the text as a totality, in terms of its macro-thematic design.

In the same way as the Theme in a clause tells what to expect in the rest of the clause, hyperTheme and macroTheme help in predicting what is to follow in the rest of the text. By examining the hyperThemes and macroThemes in a text, we may find how the text is organized at levels beyond clauses. Through studying how the newsreader leads the audience to successfully interpret the information ripples and waves intonationally, this part of the section shall observe in detail the way the newsreader signposts the hyperThemes and macroThemes. Because of limitations of space, only the hyperThemes and macroThemes of Clauses 6–10 are analysed. The description of hyperThemes and macroThemes are shown as follows:

macroTheme

(Clause 6) <u>**For other economies**</u> China is seen as both an opportunity and a threat.
(signalled by high onset pitch, long pause, and contrastive tone 4)

hyperTheme[1]

(Clause 7)   <u>**On one hand**</u> it's created a vast new market ...
             (signalled by contrastive tone 4)

hyperTheme[2]

(Clause 10) <u>**But on the other hand**</u>, China's rise as a manufacturing centre is seen as worrying by many rivals ...
             (signalled by high onset pitch, long pause, and contrastive tone 4)

At the level of clause in a written text like the news commentary, the Themes of Clauses 6, 7 and 10 are marked. The newsreader gives additional prominence to these marked Themes through assigning a separate tone group and contrastive tone 4 to each of them.

Observed from a higher level than clause, these clauses indicate the method of development of the news commentary. Clause 6 serves as a macroTheme, telling the audience that the following analysis will be conducted from two sides: on one hand, why China is seen as an opportunity and on the other hand, why it is seen as a threat. The newsreader employs high onset pitch, a long pause preceding Clause 6 and contrastive tone 4 to signal this macroTheme.

Under the macroTheme, Clause 6, there are two hyperThemes in this news commentary. Clause 7 functions as hyperTheme[1], informing the audience 'you are going to hear one side of the analysis'. Since Clause 7 occurs immediately after the macroTheme (Clause 6), the newsreader only uses contrastive tone 4 to indicate the beginning of the two-folded analysis. The analysis on one side is expanded upon by Clauses 8 and 9. Clause 10 is hyperTheme[2], indicating the coming of the analysis from another side. The newsreader signals the transition of perspective shift through the high onset pitch, a long pause before Clause 10 and contrastive tone 4.

If we take the news commentary into consideration as a whole, we find Clauses 1 and 2 are the 'Theme' of the news commentary. Here a new term may be introduced to name this Theme at a higher level than macroTheme: text-level Theme. Clauses 1 and 2 as text-level Theme generalize the content of the whole news commentary. Clauses 3–5 further explain the proposition proposed in the text-level Theme. The newsreader highlights the text-level Theme by using high onset pitch and a separate tone group on the Theme of Clauses 1 ('the Chinese economy') and 2 ('but even now'). Combined with the analysis of hyperThemes and macroThemes in Clauses 6–10, the different levels of textual organization of the news commentary can be demonstrated as follows:

text-level Theme

Clause 1   **The Chinese economy** has been growing ...
Clause 2   but even now personal incomes are only ...

> **macroTheme**
> Clause 6 <u>**For other economies**</u> China is seen as both an opportunity and a threat.
> **hyperTheme[1]**
> Clause 7 <u>**On one hand**</u> it's created a vast new market ...
> **hyperTheme[2]**
> Clause 10 <u>**But on the other hand**</u>, China's rise as a manufacturing centre is seen as worrying by many rivals ...

To recapitulate, the newsreader exploits intonation, including onset pitch, to clearly indicate the unfolding of the different levels of textual organizations. Marked Themes, hyperThemes and macroThemes are intonationally highlighted to form waves of information ripples. In doing so, the newsreader leads the audience through the thematic peaks smoothly without confusing their place within the overall organization of the text as a whole.

3.5.2 HyperNew, macroNew and text-level New

If the text-level Theme, macroThemes, hyperThemes and Themes notify the audience what to expect in the following discourse, it is the News, hyperNews, macroNews and even text-level New, that enhance what have already been stated in the Themes, hyperThemes, macroThemes and text-level Theme. The following part of this section observes how the newsreader presents the higher-level New by using intonation and other prosodic features.

The analysis of hyperNew, macroNew and text-level New can be illustrated as follows:

text-level Theme	Clause 1	**The Chinese economy** has been growing nearly ten per cent a year for three decades
	Clause 2	but even now personal incomes are only at the level of Japan in the early 1950s ...
macroTheme	Clause 6	**for other economies** China is seen as both an opportunity and a threat
hyperTheme[1]	Clause 7	**on one hand** it's created a vast new market for ...
hyperNew[1]	Clause 8	commodity producing countries like Australia, Brazil and Argentina have seen demand for their goods soar
	Clause 9	and just as important, world prices for ...
hyperTheme[2]	Clause 10	**but on the other hand**, China's rise as a manufacturing centre is seen as worrying by many rivals

hyperNew²	Clause 11	China sucks in between thirty and fifty billion dollars of foreign investment every year – far more than any other nation.
	Clause 12	Manufacturers in other places often find it hard to compete.
hyperTheme³	Clause 13	**Though at the same time,** as China's population gets individually richer,
hyperNew³	Clause 14	the country is emerging as a key market for the sophisticated products and services typically produced in the industrialized West.

text-level New (Clauses 15–17)

Clause 15	China **is** on course to become an economic superpower
Clause 16	but it's not actually there yet.
Clause 17	it's currently the sixth largest economy in the world, still smaller than Britain and France let alone the real giants Japan and the United States.

In the news commentary, the expectations provoked by hyperTheme, macroTheme and text-level Theme are confirmed by hyperNew and macroNew. According to Martin and Rose ([2003] 2007: 198), layers of Theme 'construct the method of development of a text' and layers of New 'develop the point of a text, focusing in particular on expanding the ideational meanings around a text's field'. Let's take Clauses 6–14 as an example to see how different layers of New expand the information.

In §3.3.2 it was found that the newsreader chooses to highlight the marked Themes of Clauses 6, 7 and 10, which are in turn macroTheme, hyperTheme¹ and hyperTheme², by assigning them a separate tone group, raised onset pitch and contrastive tone 4. Besides, within these marked Themes, based on the meaning he wants to emphasize, the newsreader puts the tonic on items other than the final lexical elements. Thus the interplay of thematic markedness and information markedness helps generate strong waves of information at the beginning of each of these clauses.

HyperNew is treated in similar ways. The choice of what to emphasize is mainly a decision of information status: Given or New. Whenever there is something the newsreader wishes the audience to focus on, he would use intonation to signal its prominence. This helps the audience receive further related information contained in hyperNew and thus better understand what has been mentioned in the hyperThemes.

As discussed in §3.4.1, the thesis of the news commentary stated in Clauses 1 and 2 is the text-level Theme. It tells the audience what is coming in the rest of the news commentary: it's all about the unproportional economic development of China. At the end of the news commentary, this thesis is reinforced in Clauses 15, 16 and 17: though it *is* true that the Chinese economy has been developing very fast, the country is not a real superpower. They form the last big wave of information. Therefore they are the text-level New.

To realize this higher level of textual organization, the newsreader puts the focus of Clause 15 on the Finite 'is' instead of the final lexical item in the same tone group, indicating that although this *is* mentioned at the beginning of the news commentary, it is necessary to state it again as to remind the audience of the main idea of the news commentary.

On the textual level, it is the text-level Theme and the text-level New that makes the news commentary as a coherent text. But on the phonological level, it is the newsreader's broadcasting, his exploitation of intonation, that realizes this coherence.

3.6 Summary

This chapter has explored the ways the newsreader indicates the peaks of thematic and informational ripples and waves. While the Theme of a clause tells what the rest of the clause is about, hyperThemes and macroThemes provide information of what to expect in the following discourse at higher levels. In the same way as the new information in a clause forms the peak of informational ripple, hyperNews and macroNews strengthen the News patterns in previous clauses.

The investigation of the tonality and tone of all the Themes in the news commentary (see Table 3.1) shows the ways the newsreader highlights the Themes. All the Themes except those of Clauses 5, 11, 14, 15, 16 and 17 (which are either 'China', 'the country', 'it' or 'but it'), are allocated a separate tone group to make them marked in tonality. For Themes at higher levels, the newsreader uses other ways to indicate their importance: to raise the onset pitch and give them contrastive tone 4. As can be seen in Table 3.1, high onset pitches together with tone 4 appear in Clauses 1, 4, 8, 10 and 15. These clauses are where the text-level Theme, macroTheme and hyperTheme and text-level New are located. The newsreader employs these methods to indicate the beginning of the news commentary and shifts of perspective. In doing so, the newsreader leads the audience through the thematic peaks smoothly without confusing their places in the text.

In examining how the newsreader draws attention to the New in a clause, it is found from the analysis of clauses with marked tonicity that the newsreader provides clear signals for the audience to follow whenever there is something worth noting, either contrastive or unrecoverable from the context. He gives additional prominence to marked Themes by raising the onset pitch and assigning them separate tone group and contrastive tone 4. In his broadcasting, he also chooses to allocate tonics on marked places to emphasize their prominence. The strong effects caused by the interaction of thematic markedness and intonational markedness help the audience perceive the information unfailingly.

References

Bowcher, W. L. (2003) Creating informational waves: theme and new choices in play-by-play radio sports commentary. In M. Amano (ed.) *Creation and Practical Use of Language Texts: Proceedings of the Second International Conference for the Integrated Text Science* 111–22. Nagoya: Graduate School of Letters, Nagoya University.

Bowcher, W. L. (2004) Theme and new in play-by-play radio sports commentating. In D. Banks (ed.) *Text and Texture: Systemic Functional Viewpoints on the Nature and Structure of Text* 455–93. Paris: L'Harmattan.

Brown, G., Currie, K. L. and Kenworthy, J. (1980) *Questions of Intonation*. London: Croom Helm.

Crystal, D. (1969) *Prosodic System and Intonation in English*. Cambridge: Cambridge University Press.

Halliday, M. A. K. (1963a) Intonation in English grammar. *Transactions of the Philological Society* 62(1): 143–69.

Halliday, M. A. K. (1963b) The tones of English. *Archivum Linguisticum* 15(1): 1–28.

Halliday, M. A. K. (1967) *Intonation and Grammar in British English*. The Hague: Mouton.

Halliday, M. A. K. (1970) *A Course in Spoken English: Intonation*. London: Oxford University Press.

Halliday, M. A. K. ([1994] 2000) *An Introduction to Functional Grammar* (2nd edition). Beijing: Foreign Language Teaching and Research Press.

Halliday, M. A. K. and Matthiessen, C. M. I. M. (2004) *An Introduction to Functional Grammar* (3rd edition). London: Arnold.

Martin, J. R. and Rose, D. ([2003] 2007) *Working with Discourse: Meaning Beyond the Clause*. London: Continuum.

Tench, P. (1990) *The Role of Intonation in English Discourse*. Frankfurt am Main: Peter Lang.

Tench, P. (1992) Tone and the status of information. In P. Tench (ed.) *Studies in Systemic Phonology* 161–74. London: Pinter.

Tench, P. (1996) *The Intonation Systems of English*. London: Cassell.

Wichmann, A. (2000) *Intonation in Text and Discourse: Beginnings, Middles and Ends*. London: Longman.

4

A multi-stratal approach to paragraph-like organization in lectures

Kazuyoshi Iwamoto[a]

4.1 Introduction

Brown (1977), Coulthard and Brazil (1979), Lehiste (1975, 1979, 1982), Tench (1990, 1996) and Yule (1980), among others, have proposed that spoken language is organized into paragraph-like units in the same way that written language is. Where a written paragraph is visually marked by white space and/or indentation, a spoken paragraph is said to be phonetically signalled by pitch levels, pitch movement, tempo and pauses. College composition textbooks are a rich source of received opinion about the 'proper' ideational nature of paragraphs as these occur in student essays. Each paragraph should, for example, contain one idea/topic. Tench begins with this notion: 'Paragraphs in writing usually indicate the division of the larger text into separate smaller topics', but he extends the concept to talk: 'The same kind of division is, not unnaturally, found in spoken discourse too' (Tench, 1996: 24).

Genres other than the college essay, however, reveal different organizational principles. A play script, for example, organizes on an interpersonal basis, and is normally paragraphed into the turns that characters take. This is because such a text is 'written to be performed, to be acted out on a stage before an audience' (Bain *et al.*, 1981: 935). And paragraphing has to organize the text according to the interpersonal flow in the story even more than by ideational topics with which the characters deal. If

---

a **Kazuyoshi Iwamoto** is an Associate Professor in the Faculty of Foreign Studies at Kyorin University in Tokyo, Japan. After receiving his bachelor's degree in English language from Kyorin University, he went to Central Michigan University to study TESOL for his Master's degree. There, while completing his degree, he became interested in the relationship between grammar and phonology, and he later obtained his PhD from York University, Canada. His research interests include the relationship between systemic phonology, thematic development in English texts, paragraphing from a systemic functional perspective, and human–bonobo discourse.

a spoken paragraph is parallel to a written one, it must textually weave together both of these metafunctions.

To understand what a spoken paragraph is, this chapter first reviews previous descriptions proposed for both written and spoken paragraphs, and interprets them from the perspective of systemic functional linguistics (SFL). It then presents multi-stratal analyses of monologic text segments to illustrate variations in the organization of spoken paragraphs occurring in two very different tenor contexts.

4.2   Paragraphing and paragraphs in writing

It is useful for an investigation of spoken paragraphs to understand what written paragraphs are because the idea of paragraphing in speech has been drawn from what people think a written paragraph is. Iwamoto's (2009) review of research into the nature of paragraphs includes instructive advice from college composition textbooks, e.g. Gardner (1996), Hacker (1999) and Johnson (1997); Pike and Pike (1980), Young and Becker (1966) and Longacre (1996) from the tradition of Tagmemics; Mann and Thompson (1988) from Rhetorical Structure Theory; Giora (1983) and Daneš (1995) from the Prague School; and Hoey (1983, 1997). Iwamoto interprets this research from the SFL dimensions of stratum and metafunctions (see Table 4.1).

Table 4.1 Earlier studies on written paragraphs (based on Iwamoto, 2009).

Metafunction / Stratum	Ideational		Interpersonal	Textual
	Experiential	Logical		
Context				
Semantics	Gardner Hacker Johnson Young and Becker Pike and Pike Giora	Gardner Hacker Johnson Longacre Mann and 　Thompson Hoey		Gardner Hacker Johnson Young and Becker Pike and Pike Giora Daneš Hoey
Lexicogrammar		Gardner Hacker Johnson Longacre		Gardner Hacker Johnson Young and Becker Giora Daneš
Graphology	←————————— Hoey —————————→			

Although a written paragraph is commonly said to be unified around one idea (Gardner, 1996; Giora, 1983; Hacker, 1999; Johnson, 1997; Pike and Pike, 1980; Young and Becker, 1966) scholars use different terms for an 'idea' (e.g. 'theme', 'topic', or 'discourse topic'). From an SFL perspective these represent one particular aspect of the experiential world, and sentences within the paragraph contribute to its representation. The segmental pieces of experiential meaning are in some logico-semantic relation, such as 'comparison and contrast or cause and effect' (Gardner, 1996: 15), composing a larger unit. The unity at the paragraph level, however, is created by textual phenomena: the organization of a topic sentence/hyper-theme and its development by the subsequent sentences; clause-level themes within a paragraph that show a type of progression based on the purpose of the paragraph (Daneš, 1995); and cohesive devices such as conjunctions, conjunctive adjuncts, and a 'lexical equivalence chain' (Young and Becker, 1966: 5).

While most of these scholars presuppose that a paragraph consists of more than one sentence, Hoey (1983) argues that there are units which are clearly paragraphs, but have no specific grammatical or semantic structure within themselves; his example is a paragraph which consists of one grammatical word, *So* (see Appendix 1 for the entire text):

> A few of you have a political interest in the form and function of the Institute, and a few of these few have a sincere desire for the Institute to become a stalking-horse for a form of nationalisation of a part or all of the film industry.
>
> So.
>
> To all members I would say that for some time the Governors have been examining the present identity and future role of the Institute. (Hoey, 1983: 12–13)

The paragraph *So* is marking the movement from the preceding paragraphs to the rest of the text (Figure 4.1):

> though [*So's*] meaning differs somewhat from that of the normal conjunct 'so', its function is essentially the same – to link together in a particular relationship two parts of the discourse (or rather, as we shall argue elsewhere, to make explicit a relationship and link that is already there). (Hoey, 1983: 13)

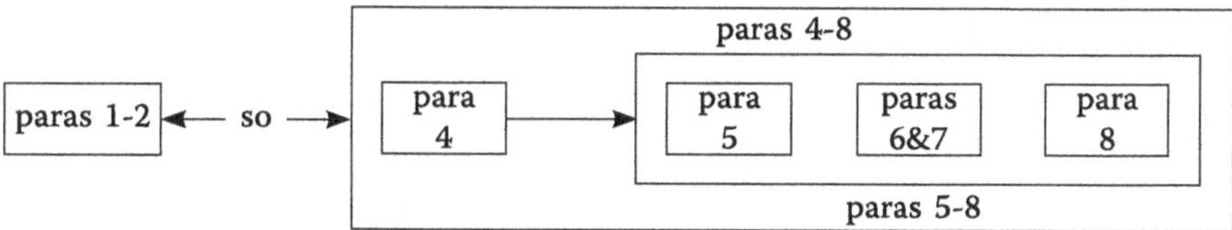

Figure 4.1 The illustration of the paragraph relations in Hoey (1983: 14).

From this example, Hoey defines a paragraph in graphological terms as 'an orthographic division in a discourse marked normally by indentation or greater space between lines' (Hoey, 1983: 14). But elsewhere he discusses it more broadly:

> paragraphing is the product of two different phenomena. On the one hand it is the marker of relationships between (rather than within) blocks of information ... The other phenomenon ... is a lexical one. (*Ibid.*: 141)

Hoey does not mean that a paragraph cannot be internally structured. Rather, he means that the internal organization is of secondary importance and the primary importance lies in the fact that a paragraph functions as part of a discourse and is related to its other paragraphs. Organizing a text as such, paragraphing marks logical relationships between paragraphs.

At least two points should be made in this review of written paragraphs. First, as Hoey points out, although a paragraph can be defined by its internal structure (e.g. begins with a topic sentence/hyper-theme and organizes one idea), such a definition applies most directly to limited registers like academic writing. Such structure is a necessary resource to realize a particular type of paragraph. But of primary importance from an SFL perspective is what a paragraph does, its function in discourse, rather than how it is structured.

Second, a paragraph tends to be described with respect to its ideational and/or textual metafunction. As in Table 4.1, none of the scholars above fully discuss the interpersonal aspect of a paragraph. Consider, however, that paragraphing in much of the literary genres is likely to organize the interpersonal semantic unit turn as a paragraph. The following is an excerpt from the children's book *Sunny Boy and his Playmates* (White, 1922):

'Get down like the Indians,' urged Sunny Boy, as Nelson took the marble. 'Shut one eye, Nelson.' [Sunny Boy's turn]

Nelson put his head down to the floor and closed one eye. He meant to aim straight at the row of beautiful new lead soldiers, but, as he afterward explained, the marble slipped before he was ready. It shot across the floor and went crash into the glass door of the bookcase. [Nelson's nonverbal turn]

'What was that, Sunny Boy? Did you break anything?' asked Grandpa Horton, coming in from the dining-room, where he had been reading the newspaper. He carried the paper in his hand and his glasses were pushed up on his forehead and he looked worried. [Grandpa Horton's turn]

'My marble hit the bookcase door, but I don't believe I broke it,' said Nelson. 'Tisn't even cracked, is it, Mr. Horton?' [Nelson's turn]

Grandpa Horton looked carefully at the glass door and said no, the marble had not been able to crack the heavy plate glass. [Grandpa Horton's turn]

If paragraphing were motivated only by ideational unity, this excerpt would have been organized into two paragraphs according to the field that the participants construe. Since the first two paragraphs construe the field: recreation: games: the lead soldiers, they would be lumped together as one unit. The other three deal with quite a different field: social behaviour: respect for property: damage to furniture. Grandpa Horton is investigating the physical condition of the glass door, and they too, would be lumped together.

There are thus two possible motivations for this paragraph organization. One is the tenor relation between the writer and the reader. The potential reader is assumed to be a juvenile, for whom it is easier to follow the story if each paragraph does not contain too much information. Another is the purpose of the text. The text is trying to represent fictional events as if they were happening in reality; the event happening in this segment is a symbolic interaction in which the characters co-construct their social reality (cf. Eggins and Slade, 1997). Therefore, the main purpose of this segment is to describe how the characters are interacting with each other to negotiate a proposition or proposal. The text being paragraphed according to the shifts in interpersonal flow (i.e. turns) unfolds the interactional aspect in the event, allowing the reader to understand the fictional world being created on a participant-by-participant basis. Note that this does not mean that these five paragraphs lack ideational unity. Each character is a participant in the story, so there is ideational unity. If there were not, the author would have failed. While maintaining the ideational unity, paragraphing of this text has segmented it in terms of its interpersonal flow by reflecting on the movement in the interactions of Sunny Boy, Nelson and Grandpa Horton.

Reviewing previous studies on paragraphs and analysing texts from different registers, I have proposed the following definitions from an SFL perspective:

> Paragraphing
> The function of paragraphing is comprehensive. Paragraphing is a [TEXTUAL] process to organize the [IDEATIONAL] and [INTERPERSONAL] choices made in the graphological, lexicogrammatical, and semantic systems as a text. Through the organization of the [NON-TEXTUAL] resources into blocks, paragraphing ultimately creates semantic movement in a text.
>
> Paragraph
> A paragraph is the product of paragraphing; most concretely, it is a semantic unit bounded in the expression plane. (Iwamoto, 2009: 199)

Paragraphing weaves the ideational and the interpersonal meaning into coherent blocks. The way it processes the two kinds of meaning, however, is not necessarily symmetrical. In some register types, paragraphing may operate mainly to create ideational unity as in academic writing, and in others it may process according to interpersonal movement as in the 'Sunny Boy' text. Further, in the process of paragraphing a text, a paragraph may carry only the textual meaning, such as *So* in Hoey (1983) does. Such a block is still a product of paragraphing; it is the result of weaving the non-textual meaning into the other blocks, among which a clear transition is required to create coherence. What differentiates paragraphing of one text from that of another is one aspect of mode (i.e. the purposes that a text is trying to achieve).

4.3 A spoken paragraph from an SFL perspective

An extensive literature review on a spoken paragraph[1] has been done by Tench (1990). In order to reduce redundancy, I will here interpret the findings in some of the studies addressed by Tench from an SFL perspective, mainly focusing on Lehiste (1975, 1979, 1982), Brazil (1975, 1978, 1985, 1997), Brown (1977), and Yule (1980) because they discuss the phonetic features of a spoken paragraph and other features in the upper strata. Table 4.2 organizes these studies in the dimensions of stratification and metafunction according to their findings.

Table 4.2 Earlier studies on spoken paragraphs.

Metafunction / Stratum	Ideational		Interpersonal	Textual
	Experiential	Logical		
Context				Yule
Semantics	Brazil Coulthard Tench Yule	Brazil		
Lexico-grammar				Brown Lehiste Sinclair Coulthard Yule
Phonology		Brazil	Brazil (only in a dialogue)	Brazil
Phonetics		Brazil	Brazil (only in a dialogue)	Brazil Brown Lehiste Yule

Let us start from the phonetic features that identify a spoken paragraph. Although there are some differences among their descriptions, the phonetic features that these studies propose in common are the following:

1. A relatively high pitch level at the first salient syllable in a spoken paragraph.
2. A low pitch level at the end of the spoken paragraph, which is followed by another high pitch level to mark the next spoken paragraph.
3. General tendency of pitch gradually lowering toward the end.
4. The deepest fall at the last tonic in the spoken paragraph.
5. The slowing down tempo toward the end.
6. Relatively longer pauses before and after the spoken paragraph.

Table 4.3 illustrates two spoken paragraphs in Brazil *et al.* (1980). Although pauses and tempos are not represented in the table, the two spoken paragraphs are segmented between 'down' with low pitch and 'fold' with high pitch. This low-high sequence of pitch is required for a spoken paragraph to be bounded. In the sense that these phonetic phenomena serve to segment or organize a spoken paragraph similarly to a certain type of pitch movement organizing a stretch of sound to realize a tone unit (i.e. tonality), they can be interpreted as part of the set of textual phenomena.

Table 4.3 Spoken paragraphs in Brazil *et al.* (1980).[2]

```
H   PUT your pens                                    FOLD your
M o                  DOWN //  PENcils       // o                       ARMS //
L                          o        DOWN

H   LOOK at the              LOOK at the            LOOK at the
M o                 WINdow // o              CEIling // o            FLOOR //
L

H
M o LOOK at the DOOR //   LOOK at    //
L                   p            ME  .
```

In SFL, however, segmentation of pitch contours to pitch levels has been rejected in theorizing the intonation systems:

> Treating tone as a sequence of pitch heights makes it analogous to the constituent-like structure that is typical of experiential meanings; and ... this is the one kind of meaning in which intonation plays no part at all.... It is not, in fact, easier to represent intonation patterns as discrete segments; it is virtually impossible to derive either the paradigmatic or the syntagmatic continuities from sequences of pitch levels. (Halliday and Greaves, 2008: 74)

Pitch levels are indeed not the best way to describe a tone unit in the SFL model because it is the melodic movement that carries all the metafunctions except the experiential one. At the paragraph level, however, a spoken paragraph could possibly be signalled by the pitch levels at the initial and final positions, rather than by the overall pitch movement, as a written paragraph is physically marked as such.

Another issue is that pauses are considered not as a systemic resource in SFL; they are a purely phonetic phenomenon, which realizes no phonological system:

> In natural speech pauses are not, on the whole, associated with
> grammatical boundaries; rather, the speaker tends to pause in the middle
> of a structure when he or she comes to an unexpected word ...
>
> [The] pause, if it does occur, is merely an optional extra. Hence what
> the punctuation is actually representing, whether grammatical or phono-
> logical in its orientation, is not any kind of pausing. (Halliday, 1985: 39)

Although pauses are often claimed to be functional (cf. Goldman-Eisler,
1968; Reich, 1980), their functions tend to be psychological ones (e.g.
hesitation and predictability of words). In non-spontaneous speech,
the occurrence of pauses may coincide with grammatical and discourse
boundaries, but it is not systematic in spontaneous spoken discourse
(cf. Krivokapić, 2007).

Abstracting pitch levels into three choices (high, mid and low), Brazil
(1975, 1978, 1985, 1997) provides a phonological system called 'key', which
seems to function logically. A key choice is realized by the pitch level on
the first salient syllable in a tone unit, and concerns the semantic relation
of a tone unit to the previous one: high, mid and low key choices imply
a contrastive, additive and equative relation, respectively. Table 4.4 is
one of Brazil's examples in which the first salient syllables and the tonics
coincide with each other.

Table 4.4 The three key choices with their communicative values (Brazil, 1978: 22).

_P_ he <u>GAM</u>bled // _P_ and <u>LOST</u>	(contrary to expectations: there is an interaction-bound opposition between the two) <u>CONTRASTIVE</u>
_P_ he <u>GAM</u>bled // _P_ and <u>LOST</u>	(he did both) <u>ADDITIVE</u>
_P_ he <u>GAM</u>bled // _P_ and <u>LOST</u>	(as you would expect: there is an interaction-bound equivalence between them <u>EQUATIVE</u>

Brazil (1978, 1985, 1997) provides another system 'termination', which
could possibly be associated with the interpersonal metafunction as
well as the logical one. Termination has the same choices as the key
system, but the choices are realized by the pitch level at the tonic
syllable, and realize different kinds of expectation that the speaker has
to the interlocutor.

Table 4.5 Examples of high and mid terminations (Brazil, 1978: 25).

1	Doctor: *p* VERY <u>IR</u>ritating you say Patient: *p* <u>VER</u>y irritating // *p* <u>YES</u>
2	Doctor: *p*+ it's <u>DRY</u> skin //p <u>IS</u>n't it Patient: *p* <u>MM</u>

Brazil argues that the doctor's high termination in example 1 expects a polar response, and the mid termination in example 2 anticipates a response of agreement as the patient does accordingly in each example. In contrast, low termination leaves the space for negotiation open without expecting any particular response. In the sense that each choice demands a different kind of reaction to the interlocutor, the system can be interpreted as an interpersonal resource. However, in the case of a monologue, these termination choices imply the further development of either the current segment (high and mid termination) or a possible closure point of the segment (low termination), and thus do not function interpersonally at all.

The key and termination systems have allowed Brazil to theorize what he calls 'pitch sequence' (Brazil, 1978). He defines a pitch sequence as 'any stretch of language which ends with low termination and has no other occurrences of low termination within it' (*ibid.*: 18), and very provisionally associates it with a sentence (*ibid.*: 19). Like sentences forming a paragraph in written language, pitch sequences can be combined into a series which can be equated with a spoken paragraph. Starting with high key, 'whose contrastive meaning serves to mark the beginning of a completely new topic unit' (Coulthard and Brazil, 1979: 45), a series of pitch sequences is closed by low termination to signal the end of the topic unit which is immediately followed by high key to begin another new topic.

These intonational systems are fundamentally different from those in systemic phonology. As implied in the descriptions above, the choices in the key and termination systems are directly related to distinctive meanings:

> intonation choices are seen as making separate and distinctive contributions to the discourse function of the utterance, capable of being described at an appropriate level of abstraction without reference to co-occurring lexical and grammatical choices. (*Ibid.*: 21)

Coulthard and Brazil view intonation as a system above phonology in parallel with lexicogrammar. They argue:

> While it is possible to discuss the meanings of contrasts that are realised
> <u>lexically and grammatically</u> in terms of a stable and publicly available
> categorisation of experience, what the speaker seems to encode intona-
> tionally is a set of distinctions that apply only at the moment of utterance
> and in the semi-private world that the parties to the interaction share.
> (*Ibid.*: 20; underlining original)

In contrast, systemic phonology requires a grammatical environment for
the phonological choices to be contextualized:

> If we regard intonation in English as meaningful ... then we should seek
> to state the place which such choices occupy relative to the total set of
> formal patterns in the language; and there are only two kinds of formal
> pattern: grammatical and lexical....
>
> English intonation contrasts are grammatical: they are exploited in
> the grammar of the language. (Halliday, 1967: 10)

Any phonological phenomenon like other linguistic phenomena is always
seen from three perspectives in SFL. For phonological phenomena this
means from above (lexicogrammar), from roundabout (phonology), and
from below (phonetics) (Halliday, 1996: 26–7; Halliday and Greaves,
2008: 79). This is because '[the] entire phonological system is a resource
– a resource for making meaning' (Halliday, 2000), and 'the energy by
which this is achieved, the source of [the] semogenic power [of language],
is grammar' (Halliday, 2005: 63).[3] If phonology contributed to meaning
independently of lexicogrammar, it would merely be semiotic, like traffic
lights, but not semogenic, and it would be as if meaning were created
by combining different parts (phenomena) together. SFL is interested in
theorizing the semogenic as well as semiotic power of language, in which
different linguistic phenomena, all of which simultaneously occur (Garrod
and Pickering, 2004), are correlated with each other by realization.

Aside from these issues at the expression plane, there seem to be
lexicogrammatical patterns at the initial and final positions of a spoken
paragraph. The unit tends to start with a discourse marker (cf. Schiffrin,
1987) and/or a hypertheme-like element (cf. Thompson, 2003). Sinclair
and Coulthard observe in their data of teacher–pupil discourse that 'a
small set of words—"right", "well", "good", "O.K.", "now", recurred frequently
in the speech of all teachers' (Sinclair and Coulthard, 1975: 21), and that
such words serve to indicate the beginning of a 'transaction', which deals
with a single topic. These are purely textual and can be thought of as a
textual theme at the spoken paragraph level.

A hypertheme-like element can be understood to be experiential. Coining the term 'major paratone' for a spoken paragraph, Yule suggests that 'a major paratone is coextensive with a single topic' (Yule, 1980: 38) and its initial position tends to contain a 'topic expression', a nominal group that describes what the major paratone is about. Exploring a number of dialogues between an interviewer and interviewees who did not previously know each other, Brown *et al.* (1980) have found that a spoken paragraph is likely to start from either the speaker's or the listener's perspective:

> The new beginning usually relates in some way to the here and now, either to the speaker: <u>I've often thought</u>, <u>I suppose</u>, <u>Jim was telling me the other day</u>..., <u>When I was</u>..., or to the hearer <u>Have you ever wondered why</u>..., <u>Was it you who was telling me</u> ... (*Ibid.*: 25–6; underlining original)

In the situation where the interactants have few experiences to share, the immediate situational materials (in these cases, the interactants themselves) are highly possible candidates to be placed at the beginning of a spoken paragraph.

Lehiste (1979, 1982) has also found significance in the word choice at the beginning of a spoken paragraph. She prepared a recording of a spontaneous monologic text and its filtered version which was unintelligible but kept the pitch of the original sound (Lehiste, 1979). She presented the filtered sound first then the original one afterwards to twenty-five subjects, and asked them to identify sentence and paragraph boundaries. In the filtered version, the subjects perceived 265 sentence boundaries and 38 paragraph boundaries, but they placed only 158 sentence boundaries and 16 paragraph boundaries in the normal version. Reviewing these results elsewhere, Lehiste states that in normal speech 'the listeners seemed to wait for the first word of the next sentence before deciding whether the preceding sentence was completed or not' (Lehiste, 1982: 122). For example, when the subjects heard a co-ordinate conjunction 'and' at the beginning of the next sentence, they decided not to indicate a boundary. These results suggest that phonetic signals that people perceive for a spoken paragraph do not necessarily mark a semantic unit; however, they become meaningful when they coincide with certain lexicogrammatical choices.

The end of a spoken paragraph too seems likely to be signalled lexico-grammatically. Associating a spoken paragraph with a topic, Brown *et al.* (1980) state that 'the end of the topic is typically marked by the repetition of lexical items already introduced (unusual – yes, I think that's true) or by a lexical tail-away on prefabricated phrases: <u>and so on</u>, <u>and things like that</u>, <u>that's how I see it</u>, etc.' (*ibid.*: 25; underlining original). Yule has come to a very similar conclusion: 'the speaker can use a summarising phrase, often repeating the topic expression' (Yule, 1980: 38).

As can be inferred from the lexicogrammatical descriptions, a spoken paragraph is considered to be a unit to develop a topic. Yule (*ibid.*) asserts a very strong, almost one-to-one relation between a major paratone and a topic:

> The motivation for organising stretches of speech into major paratones is the discourse-originated notion of topic, in particular, 'speaker's topic'. A major paratone is coextensive with a stretch of discourse presented by a speaker as forming a unit with a single topic. (*Ibid.*: 38)

Reviewing a number of researchers, Wennerstrom (2001: 101–4), too, suggests the correspondence between a 'high paratone' and a topic, although acknowledging the difficulty in dealing with the notion of topic.

These studies apparently describe a spoken paragraph in association with a written paragraph in terms of its semantic and lexicogrammatical features. This is understandable if paragraphing functions in the same way in the two distinct modes. If so, however, spoken paragraphing should be a textual process to weave the ideational and interpersonal metafunctions, and spoken paragraphs can be more than a unit for a topic. When representing one part of the experiential world, for example, a speaker possibly paragraphs a text differently if the audience changes; the speaker would create topically organized paragraphs to those who are familiar with the field, but more paragraphs to those who are novices in the field along with different choices made in all the strata. Further, while organizing the non-textual metafunctions in other paragraphs, the speaker may create a purely textual paragraph like the written paragraph *So* in Hoey (1983). Whether it is written or spoken, paragraphing should be one of the processes to enable the non-textual semantic components to become a text and to be operational in context (cf. Halliday, 1978; Halliday and Matthiessen, 1999; Matthiessen, 1992).

4.4   Paraphoning and paraphones

As we have seen so far, there are two major issues in integrating the notion of a spoken paragraph directly into the SFL framework. First, pitch levels, the essential markers of a spoken paragraph, are not systemicized as a meaningful resource in systemic phonology because its focus is on the tone unit level, at which segmental pitch levels cannot carry the logical, interpersonal, and textual meaning that pitch contours do. However, this does not mean that spoken discourse cannot be organized at the paragraph level. While there still remains a question of whether or not pitch levels realize a phonological system, the previous studies described above have illustrated a close relationship between a spoken paragraph and a topic. What is assumed is that the expression plane merely provides the boundary markers for a spoken paragraph in harmony with the choices made at the clause and tone unit levels or lower to create a kind of semantic movement.

Second, confining the function of spoken paragraphing to the organization of topics is too exclusive from an SFL perspective. Language bears three kinds of metafunctional meaning: the ideational meaning to construe human experience, the interpersonal meaning to enact the social relation between the interactants, and the textual meaning to enable the non-textual meaning to be a text. If spoken paragraphing is a textual process like written paragraphing, then it should weave both the ideational and interpersonal meanings, and operate differently in accordance with the variables of the context of situation. Then choosing one way of spoken paragraphing rather than the other(s) among distinctive choices becomes meaningful.

Instead of the term 'spoken paragraph', henceforth, I would like to use 'paraphone' that Halliday ([1961] 2002: 78) once suggested as a possible term for a paragraph-like unit in spoken language, and to preliminarily propose the following definitions of paraphoning and a paraphone from an SFL perspective:

<u>Paraphoning</u>
Paraphoning is a textual process to organize the ideational and interpersonal choices made in phonology, lexicogrammar and semantics, according to the context of situation in which a text is created. Through the organization of the non-textual metafunctions into blocks, paraphoning ultimately creates semantic movement in the text.

<u>Paraphone</u>
A paraphone is the product of paraphoning. Most concretely, it is a semantic unit bounded in the expression plane. Paraphoning in phonology, lexicogrammar and semantics creates blocks in their own strata, which are in the relation of realization. The semantic blocks are paraphones, and serve as the basic units for the semantic movement created by paraphoning.

These definitions are based on two hypotheses. One is that pitch levels, as the main phonetic marker to realize paraphone boundaries, should be part of the systematic linguistic system; that is, a unit bounded by pitch levels should necessarily realize a phonological unit which then realizes a lexicogrammatical unit. In order to prove the validity of this hypothesis, however, a vast number of spoken texts from various registers need to be analysed, which is beyond this study. Related to this, the other hypothesis is that paraphoning should be part of the semogenic activity; that is, there should be at least two ways of paraphoning to bear distinction in wording and eventually in meaning. The topical organization that the earlier studies have proposed for a spoken paragraph would be one way; if it is the only way, however, it is merely semiotic, and cannot be semogenic. If paraphoning is one aspect of the meaning creation in context, there should be multiple options for it.

4.5   Text analysis

In order to illustrate different ways of paraphoning, this section will explore two text segments from lectures (Text A and Text B) multi-stratally. Instead of starting from the phonetic analysis, this study will take a 'top-down' approach, from the context of situation down to phonetics, because the phonetic signals for spoken paragraph boundaries have not been systemicized in systemic phonology; pauses are especially considered as allophonic variation that does not realize phonological distinction. This section will illustrate how the choices made in the upper strata are related to pitch levels and their movement.

Before moving to the text analysis, let me briefly describe the system network I use to explore the semantic movement of the selected texts (Figure 4.A1 in Appendix 2). It is a modified version of the system network illustrated by Eggins and Slade (1997) as an analytical tool for an exchange structure in conversation. Although their network is for conversation, it is applicable to this study as the starting point because a monologue can be seen as a series of exchanges constructed by a single speaker, and because the network allows us to illustrate how an initially raised proposition is developed within an exchange, which can be assumed to be the typical development of a lecture.

The first major modification was made at the most general point in the network to distinguish two types of moves: negotiate and frame. A negotiating move deals with a proposition/proposal. Although the terms proposition and proposal are choices in the interpersonal semantic system, they simultaneously make choices in the ideational semantics as well to construe the field of discourse because they deal with a specific type of commodity to be exchanged. In contrast, a framing move is independent of the field of discourse: it either organizes an exchange (i.e. only textual functions) or enacts the tenor relation (i.e. only interpersonal functions), before a proposition/proposal is provided (attend), while it is negotiated (continuative), or after the negotiation is finished (coda). An attending move is further divided into three types: transition, call, and greeting. In addition to call and greeting that Eggins and Slade (1997) provide as an engaging move, a transition move has been added. This is a move to signal the beginning of a new exchange, like a discourse marker.

Second, the system of CONTINUE, which is for the same speakers to develop their preceding move, has been modified for a monologue. In Eggins and Slade's model, the system has the choices of monitor, append and prolong. The monitoring move has been changed to a continuative move under frame because its function in a monologue is for the speaker to make sure that the audience is following without developing the proposition/proposal under negotiation. The appending move has been eliminated because it occurs only 'when a speaker makes one move, loses the turn, but then as soon as they regain the turn they produce a move which represents a logical expansion of their immediately prior move' (Eggins and Slade, 1997: 199), which does not happen in a monologue. Moreover, the prolonging move has been renamed as continue, and its further choices, elaboration, extension and enhancement have been made more delicate based on the paradigm of the logico-semantic choices provided by Halliday and Matthiessen (2004: 598–600) in order to see if there is any relationship between the way of developing a proposition and paraphoning.

Each of the following two sub-sections (§§4.5.1 and 4.5.2) first presents the phonologically transcribed text with a semantic move analysis and possible paraphone boundaries indicated by double lines. Then it illustrates the context of situation of the entire segment based on Halliday and Hasan (1985) and Halliday and Matthiessen (1999). For the linguistic strata, the discussion will be presented on the basis of an exchange[4] because a lecture is assumed to generally be organized around a proposition, which is developed within an exchange. Note that the numbers for the semantic moves are also used to indicate their realizational clauses or tone units in the discussion.

4.5.1 Text A

Table 4.6 The phonological transcription of Text A with the semantic move analysis and possible paraphone boundaries shown in double horizontal lines.

Move	Phonological Transcript	Analysis
1	*//1 okay //	transition
2	//1 what will you / need for this */ class //	open
3	//3 you will / need ... /∧ the */ textbook //	open
4	//3 ∧ the */ textbook //3 either / comes as / three */ soft/cover //3 ∧ uh e/ditions like */ this //	positive
5	//1 ∧ or it / comes as / one */ hardcover / ∧uh / version //	alternation
6	//3 I don't / care / which you */ buy	clarification
7	just //3 make / sure you */ buy the //1 one with the / elephant on the */ cover //	positive
8	//1 ∧ um ... / this will be the / same / textbook that you / use in bi/ology / one fifty */ four if you go //1 on to / take / that */ course //	positive
9	*//3 ∧ um */ lab / manual //3 is */ this one //	open
10	//3 that's the / same one we've */ used //4∧ uh /∧ through/out the / year so */ far //	reason
11	*//3 so it //13∧ there / should be */ copies of /that uh /∧ in */ bookstores //	result
12	//1 ∧ uh you will / need that / starting to*/morrow when //1+ labs */ start //	time-points

// represents tone boundary, / represents foot boundary, * indicates that next syllable is tonic.

This text segment is from the data collected by the Michigan Corpus of Academic Spoken English (Simpson *et al.*, 2002),[5] and it is part of the first day of an introductory course on biology offered at the University of Michigan. Previous to this segment, the lecturer introduced himself and his graduate student instructors, and in this particular segment he explains about the course materials that the students are expected to purchase. After this segment, he describes two more materials. Here I would like to focus on the first two paraphones because the second and the third ones show similarity in terms of their function and structure.

4.5.1.1 Context of situation

Although this is a lecture on biology, the participants have not moved into the field of biology yet; the lecturer is doing administration (first-order field) for the upcoming lecture, and the current activity is about the course materials (second-order field). As the text is created, the field shifts at a more delicate level from the textbook to the lab manual. The tenor relation between the professor and the students is constantly unequal: the professor is the authority in this institutionalized situation. Their social distance is maximal because the lecturer is assumed not to know the students previously to this session. The mode is spoken, monologic, expository, and constitutive in terms of the language role. The lecturer has distributed handouts to the students, and he follows what is written on them. However, mostly he is speaking spontaneously, which can be assumed from the use of pause fillers *uh*.

4.5.1.2 Moves 1–2

The first two moves function as the framework of this entire segment. By Move 1 the lecturer only signals the shift in the second-order field from the instructors' introduction to the course materials. Then in Move 2 he raises a new proposition to develop the field of discourse, making a statement realized metaphorically through the non-polar interrogative mood ('I am going to tell you what you will need for this class'). Since the Subject (also the Possessor in the transitivity system) is *you*, which encompasses the students into the discourse, not only does the statement construe what is required for the course, but it also plays an important role in enacting the tenor relation. Note that in the sense that specific materials are introduced in Moves 3 and 9, the whole segment could be analysed as one large exchange. However, what are described in Moves 3 and 9 are semiotically distinct materials in our experiential world, and therefore, the moves are analysed as open moves for separate exchanges.

Lexicogrammatically, the minor and the major clauses serve as the macro thematic elements of this segment. This function is enabled partly by the choices made in the intonational grammar, specifically in the systems of information distribution and status (Halliday and Greaves, 2008: 58–60, 142–9). The minor and the major clauses are realized by individual tone units, which assign each of them the status of an information unit. Through the choice of tone 1 for both of them, their statuses become independent of each other (cf. *ibid.*: 130). Realized as such, Move 1 thus signals the transition from the previous 'section' to the next one, which is similar to the function of *So* in Hoey (1983) discussed earlier. The only difference from Hoey's example is that the conjunctive adjunct is followed by another clause functioning as an experiential theme of the section.

These choices made in the upper strata co-occur with some of the phonetic phenomena found in a spoken paragraph. The highest point in pitch at *okay* is 175 Hz,[6] which seems to be relatively high in the speaker's pitch range, and it falls down to about 120 Hz. Thus the semantic prominence of *okay* realized by the systemic choices discussed above seems to be intensified by this high pitch level. Then the pitch rises to about 185 Hz at the first salient syllable in the next tone unit, and gradually falls down to around 100 Hz. The deepest fall occurs at the Tonic in the second tone unit: from about 160 Hz to 100 Hz. The high pitch level at the beginning and the deep fall at the Tonic could possibly highlight the semantic prominence of this move functioning as a macroTheme. Thus the two moves constituting an exchange are at the same time paraphoned as a unit to orient the audience to the message of the entire text segment.

Note that according to Brazil's description of a series of pitch sequences, the second tone unit cannot terminate this portion. In his framework at least two tone units are required for pitch to drop from high key to low termination (Brazil, 1978: 18), because a termination choice is relative to the key choice within the same tone unit, and because low termination cannot be identified without mid key to be compared with. The termination choice here would possibly be mid rather than low. However, 100 Hz at the end of the tonic foot is relatively low in the speaker's pitch range.

4.5.1.3 Move 3–8

Moves from 3 to 8 are organized around the course textbook. In Move 3 the speaker introduces the textbook as a new proposition, which is then described in terms of its physical features (Moves 4, 5 and 7) and of its relation to a different course (Move 8). As two versions of the textbook being introduced in Moves 4 and 5, both of the versions are announced to be acceptable for the course (Move 6).

The unity of this part is realized mostly by the cohesive devices of reiteration and reference (Halliday and Hasan, 1976) and by a type of thematic progression. After *the textbook* is introduced in the N-rhematic position (Fries, 1993) in Move 3, the noun phrase and pronouns used to refer to it (*it, which, one* and *this*) appear in all the moves, and three of them in the thematic position (Moves 4, 5 and 8). This development is equivalent to what Daneš proposes as 'paragraphs with a stable [paragraph]-theme' (Daneš, 1995: 33), which tends to be found in a text describing a 'thing.'

Although these moves are all associated with the textbook, Moves 6 and 7, where the themes are not the textbook, particularly realize the asymmetrical tenor relation. The lecturer *I* as the departure point of Move 6 orients the audience to a message about the lecturer: how the lecturer internally processes the phenomenon of the students' purchasing one of the two different versions. Move 7, while providing a physical feature of the textbook, is realized by imperative mood, which here realizes authoritative advice on the purchase of a copy. Thus, in this portion both the ideational reality of the textbook and the asymmetrical interpersonal relation between the interactants unfolds.

Phonologically, this part is mostly realized by tone sequences of tone 3^(3^)1 which extend over multiple moves: from Move 3 to 5 and from Move 6 to 7. This type of tone sequence unmarkedly coincides with a paratactically related clause complex, realizing the equal status of the information units, and forming an information unit complex (Halliday and Greaves, 2008: 47). Here, the relations between the moves are not necessarily realized by co-ordinate conjunctions in the clause grammar (see Moves 3 and 4, and Moves 6 and 7). However, the choices in the intonational grammar assign equal importance to each information unit in an information unit complex, and consequently realize equal relationship between Moves 3, 4 and 5, and between Moves 6 and 7.

The beginning and the end of this portion coincide with high and low pitch levels respectively. The pitch height at the first salient syllable in Move 3 is 173 Hz, and it gradually falls down to about 85 Hz at the tonic in the last tone unit (see Figure 4.2). Although no long pause is observed before Move 3, this part generally agrees with the characteristics of a phonological paragraph that the earlier studies have proposed.

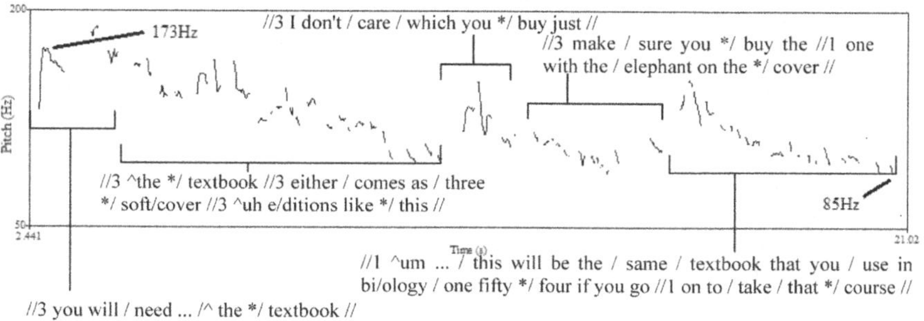

Figure 4.2 The pitch movement as a realization of Moves 3–8.

In this section, we examined two instances of paraphones. The first paraphone starts with a discourse marker to signal a shift in the field of discourse at a general level, and then a macro-theme-like move serves to provide the ideational framework for the subsequent text. Being paraphoned as such, the first two moves serve as the departure point of a larger segment, say, a 'section'. In the second paraphone, the field shifts to a specific course material, the textbook, and with Move 3 functioning as the hyper-theme-like element, the proposition is developed. This textual development is similar to the general pattern of a topic sentence followed by its development found in academic writing. While illustrating the course textbook, the lecturer integrates his perspective as the course director as well by making *I* the topical theme in Move 6 and by using an imperative mood in Move 7.

4.5.2 Text B

Table 4.7 The phonological transcription of Text B with the semantic move analysis and possible paraphone boundaries.

Move	Phonological Transcript	Analysis
1	//1+ ʌso / how do you */ do that //	open
2	//4 ʌit */ means //3 ʌyou / speak di*/rectly *//3 honestly //1 ʌand */ openly //	means
3	//2 ʌo*/kay //	continuative
4	//3 ʌso we / talked a / lot about di*/rect //1 ʌand */ indirect //	exemplificatory
5	//2 ʌo*/kay //	continuative
6	//4 so you */ speak //3 ʌdi*/rectly *//3 honestly //1 ʌand */ openly //	expository
7	//2 ʌo*/kay //	continuative
8	//1 that's my */ skateboard //1 that was di*/rect //	exemplificatory
9	//2 ʌo*/kay //	continuative
10	//3 ʌbut */ then //1 ʌhe */ stopped //	positive
11	//2 ʌo*/kay //	continuative
12	//1 that's my */ skateboard //1 ʌI / want it */ back //	positive
13	//2 ʌo*/kay //	continuative
14	//1 ʌhis */ feelings //	expository
15	//3 that's my */ skateboard //3 ʌI / want it */ back //2 ʌcould you / give it to me */ now //1 ʌwould be / very */ good //	positive
16	//2 ʌo*/kay //	continuative
17	//1 ʌin*/stead // *//1 you can / have it //	replacive
18	//2 ʌo*/kay //	continuative
19	//1 give */ up //	expository
20	//2 ʌo*/kay //	continuative
21	//1 not so */ good //	clarification
22	//3 ʌso ex/press your / feelings */ directly *//3 honestly //1 ʌ and */ openly //	expository
23	*//4 and //4 ʌit does / not */ mean //1 being ag*/gressive //	negative
24	//4 ʌag/gressive */ means //1 ʌyou at*/tack the / other / person //	clarification
25	//2 ʌo*/kay //	continuative
26	*//1 last / week //1+ ʌwe / talked about the */ lion //	exemplificatory
27	//2 ʌo*/kay //	continuative
28	//1 very ag*/gressive //	exemplificatory
29	//4 self-as*/sertiveness //4 ʌ is */ not //1 ʌag*/gressive //	expository
30	*//4 if //1 ʌyou re*/spect the other / person //	positive-condition

Text B is part of a lecture on self-assertiveness, which was delivered at a university in Japan. Previous to this segment, the lecturer showed the students a video clip, in which a big boy robbed a small boy of his skateboard and the small boy tried to be self-assertive to get his skateboard back, but failed. After watching the video, the lecturer describes self-assertiveness using a PowerPoint slide that has three points:

1. Expressing our thoughts, opinions and feelings while respecting others.
2. It means direct, honest and open communication.
3. It does NOT mean being aggressive.

In Text B the lecturer describes the second and the third points.

4.5.2.1 Context of situation

The kind of social activity that the participants are engaged in (the first-order Field) is a lecture, and it is about self-assertiveness in communication (the second-order Field). The Mode is spoken, monologic, expository, and constitutive in terms of the role of language. Although the lecturer frequently checks the students' understanding of the content, providing opportunities for her students to take a turn, the students do not respond verbally to her. Some of the students might possibly have indicated their understanding by gestural responses like a nod, but there is no way of finding out about their physical actions from the sound data. Since the lecturer does not verbally react to such an action, even if there is any, it seems fair to characterize her talk as monologic as we would expect as the default for this register of discourse.

The Tenor relation between the lecturer and the students is unequal, and even more asymmetrical than in Text A because the lecturer is a native speaker of English and the students are all Japanese with very limited English skills. This difference in their linguistic backgrounds, however, imposes on the lecturer a paradoxical power relation. On the one hand, the lecturer as the authority has the power to provide information however she likes to, as long as the particular field is correctly represented. On the other, because she is responsible to help the students understand the field in English, she is forced to limit her linguistic resources more or less to those which are available to the students in the semiotic interaction. In this respect, the participant roles in Text A are quite different from those in Text B although both the texts are from lectures.

4.5.2.2 Moves 1–30

All the moves in this segment constitute one ideationally organized unit. Previous to this segment, the lecturer defines self-assertiveness as expressing one's thoughts, opinions, and feelings while showing respect to the interlocutor. The field shifts from this theoretical definition to a rather practical aspect of self-assertiveness here. In Move 1 the lecturer introduces a proposition concerning how to be self-assertive through a rhetorical question, meaning 'I am going to tell you how to express our thoughts, opinions, and feelings while showing respect to others'. Then she provides three ways to be self-assertive, 'directly, honestly, and openly' and develops the initial proposition. From Move 4 to 21, she particularly describes and exemplifies directness, and in Move 22 she repeats almost the same meaning that is expressed in Moves 2 and 6. She then extends the assertive way of communication to aggressiveness in a negative manner (Move 23), which is the third point on the PowerPoint slide. After she explains and exemplifies the meaning of aggressiveness (Moves 26 to 28), she associates the concepts of self-assertiveness, aggressiveness and respect (Moves 29 and 30).

There are three semantic characteristics to be pointed out here. One is that this text segment demonstrates a pattern similar to the typical textual structure of a paratone that Brown *et al.* (1980) and Yule (1980) have found in their texts. Move 1 orients the listener to the subsequent message in this exchange, functioning as a hyper-theme, and the last two moves include summarizing expressions of the preceding discussion.

The second is the frequent use of the continuative move *okay* (eleven out of thirty moves) also typically known as a 'discourse marker'. This is assumed to be due to the speaker's role. Because of the students' limited English skills, the lecturer is 'obligated' to confirm their understanding frequently, as well as to make her own language use as simple and easy to follow as possible. Especially when she refers to the video clip as a bad example of self-assertiveness, she represents a small segment of the ideational reality one by one and inserts the continuative move every time she adds a small portion of description about the clip. Such development should be partly motivated by the fact that the exemplification forces the students to remove themselves from 'here and now' to the past, and the lecturer is being especially careful about adding each piece of information.

Third, the development of the proposition is mostly done with a very limited amount of new information added to it. There are seven extending or enhancing moves (2, 10, 12, 15, 17, 23 and 30) by which the speaker adds new information. However, it is only in Moves 2 and 23 that the lecturer provides new pieces of information about self-assertiveness. In

Moves 10, 12, 15 and 17 she describes the interaction between the two boys in the video clip as an example, and in Move 30 she adds conditional information to what she describes in Move 29. This semantic development is very different from that of the second exchange in Text A, where the speaker provides new information in four out of five moves; the difference is assumed to be due to the students' linguistic backgrounds. The kind of development found in Text B would be to enable the students with limited English skills to firmly understand the lecture.

These moves are lexicogrammatically realized in rather simple and segmental forms. Most of them other than the continuative moves are realized by single simplex clauses, among which Moves 14, 19 and 21 are elliptical clauses, and only Moves 8 and 12 are realized by two clauses which are not related in taxis. In Move 8, for example, the lecturer could have said something like 'the small boy in the video said "that's my skateboard", which was direct', specifying the Sayer of the Verbiage *that's my skateboard*, and forming a clause complex of 1α"2α=β.[7] Moves 12 and 14 and Moves 17, 19 and 20 could have been constructed as clause complexes as well: 'he should have added his feelings by saying "I want it back"' (α×β1×β"2) and 'instead he said "you can have it" giving up his skateboard, which was not so good' (1αα"2αα=ββ) respectively. The lecturer exemplifies self-assertiveness by representing small segments of the ideational reality, by accumulating them one by one, and by leaving out omissible elements. This is also assumed to be an adaption to the students' language skills.

Such segmental organization can be found in the choice of the intonational grammar as well. While the 30 moves are realized by 32 major and minor clauses, they are organized into 53 information units: around 1.77 information units per move on average (if ignoring the continuative moves, 2.2 information units per move). The clause in Move 2, for example, is organized by the system of information distribution into 4 information units: *it means, you speak directly, honestly* and *and openly*, which are realized by a tone sequence of tone 4^3^3^1 (see Figure 4.3 for their relationship).

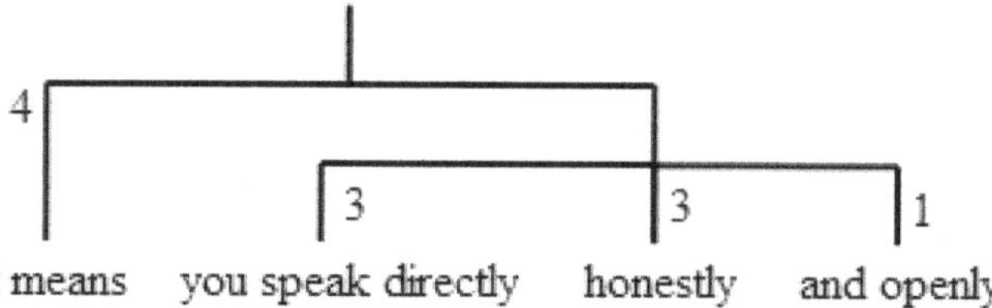

Figure 4.3 The logical relation among the information units realizing Move 2.

The first information unit marked by tone 4 indicates its subordination to what follows, which is organized as three equally prominent pieces of information by tone 3^3^1. The most prominent pieces in these tone units are the adverbs. More or less the same meaning is carried by Moves 6 and 22 with almost identical realizational structures; tone (4)^3^3^1 sequences in which the three adverbs are the culminations of New. These repeated phonological structures allow the lecturer to reinforce the significance of the three manners of speaking and to provide the students with more opportunities to understand their significance. The last two moves are also segmental in their internal organization. They are realized by two hypotactically related clauses, each of which is further segmented by intonation: the first clause is realized by three tone units, and the second one by two tone units. This phonological organization may be partly a realization of the lecturer's response to the students' language skills, and partly due to the function of the moves (i.e. the summarization of the entire text segment, which is reasonable to receive special prominence).

Although this text segment is semantically unified around self-assertive communication, this is phonetically segmented into seven paraphones. Table 4.8 presents the pitch values at the first salient syllable and those at the last salient syllable of each paraphone:[8]

Table 4.8 The pitch values at the beginning and the end of the paraphones.

Paraphone	Pitch at the first salient syllable	Pitch at the last salient syllable
1 (Moves 1–21)	530 Hz	202 Hz
2 (Move 22)	527 Hz	283 Hz
3 (Move 23)	601 Hz	285 Hz
4 (Move 24)	585 Hz	243 Hz
5 (Moves 26–28)	536 Hz	264 Hz
6 (Move 29)	638 Hz	270 Hz
7 (Move 30)	560 Hz	165 Hz

Table 4.8 indicates that these paraphones do not have commonality in terms of their internal structure. While Paraphones 1 and 5 consist of multiple moves, the others organize single moves as their own paraphones. In the case of Paraphones 6 and 7, two hypotactically related clauses are organized as separate paraphones.

Although paraphoning here does not seem to be systematic, it creates reasonable semantic movement in this text segment. First, organizing Move 22 as one paraphone can reinforce the importance of the message that has already been expressed twice in Move 2 and 6. Then, the only extending move that is directly related to the self-assertive way of communication (Move 23) is paraphoned with the second highest pitch in this text, which could clearly signal or even intensify the addition of new information along with the conjunction *and*. In Paraphones 4 and 5 the meaning of the word 'aggressive' is clarified and exemplified respectively. These paraphones would not be necessary if the students were native speakers of English, and separation of these paraphones from the neighbouring ones could highlight the fact that these paraphones are not directly related to the current negotiation but rather they are peripheral to it.[9] Finally, coming back to the current negotiation, in Paraphones 6 and 7 the lecturer summarizes the points made in this segment. These paraphones are realized by two clauses composing a clause complex; in this sense, the two paraphones together recapitulate the points made in this text segment. However, the clause complex realizes two separated moves because the clauses are intonationally organized as two independent information unit complexes by the choice of a tone $4(^4)^1$ sequence. Coinciding with these segmental choices, the organization of these two paraphones possibly intensifies the significance of each message.

It is hypothesized that this relatively short paraphoning is motivated mainly by the tenor relation, specifically the students' linguistic backgrounds and the lecturer's role to help them understand given information. This is similar to the paragraphing of the children's book we saw in §4.2; in order for the prospective reader to easily understand the interaction between the characters, each paragraph is relatively short according to the turns they take. In this text too, paraphoning organizes the text into small paraphones, within which yet smaller organizational choices are made in the clause and intonational grammar. Through such segmental organizations the lecture can describe a part of the experiential world step by step, so that the students can easily understand the description.

In Text A and B, paraphoning does serve as a textual process to weave ideational and interpersonal meanings as a text in accordance with the context of situation. In Text A, the paraphones are undoubtedly organized around ideationally distinct materials. At the same time, however, the audience is encompassed as participants in the discourse, or the speaker's perspective as the authority is included in the paraphones. In Text B, although the whole segment deals with how to be self-assertive in communication (i.e. one exchange), it is segmented into seven paraphones along with rather segmental and simple choices made at lower ranks in semantics, lexicogrammar, and phonology, all of which are assumed to be a realization of the lecturer's response to the students' limited English skills.

The organization of these texts implies that there are at least three types of paraphones. The first paraphone in Text A construes a part of the ideational world, but as a whole, it functions textually as a macro-theme. The second paraphone in Text A is organized largely around the ideational unity with some interpersonal meaning integrated into it. Most of the short paraphones in Text B are assumed to be realizations of the tenor relation between the lecturer and the students. Although paraphoning of the two texts seems non-systematic, it creates different types of semantic movement that seem rational in relation to the choices made in phonology and lexicogrammar. This means that paraphoning has semogenic power and a speaker can choose one way of paraphoning over the other to create meaning.

4.6 Summary

This study has explored paragraph-like organization in speech, in comparison with written paragraphs. Earlier works describe a spoken paragraph as a unit marked by phonetic signals such as pitch levels, pauses and tempo, and propose that it be a unit for an ideational topic like a written paragraph in academic writing. Two issues pointed out from an SFL perspective are: first, pitch levels and pauses have generally been treated as being semiotic but not semogenic in systemic phonology; second, an organizational aspect is part of the textual metafunction, and the metafunction deals with both the ideational and the interpersonal metafunctions, so that the two non-textual meanings can be operational as a text in context. Borrowing the term 'paraphone' from Halliday ([1961] 2002: 78), this study preliminarily proposed that 'paraphoning' be a textual process taking place in all the linguistic strata and a 'paraphone' a semantic unit organized by paraphoning, on the basis of the assumption that pitch levels indicate paraphone boundaries, and paraphoning is semogenic (i.e. there are multiple ways for such organization in relation to the context of situation).

In order to see if there is more than one way of paraphoning, this study selected two text segments from lectures. Text A is a lecture conducted in English to native speakers of English, and Text B is also in English but to Japanese students with very limited English skills. The analyses of the texts revealed at least three distinct ways of paraphoning. In Text A, paraphoning first organizes a conjunctive adjunct and a major clause as a paraphone, so that they serve as the macro-theme of a yet larger unit like a section. Then paraphoning groups ideationally related elements together with realizations of the asymmetrical tenor relation between the speaker and the listeners. In Text B, along with segmental choices at the clause and tone unit levels, paraphoning segments one ideationally unified exchange into seven paraphones; the small quanta of information can be understood as a realization of the lecturer's response to her students with low English proficiency. Hypothesized from the text analyses is that there are more ways of paraphoning in different registers, and that a speaker selects one way over the others according to the context of situation to create distinctions in meaning.

As Wennerstrom (2001) points out, there are several unanswered issues on the relation between prosody and discourse organization (2001: 114–16), and thus much to be investigated to understand more about paraphoning, such as the status of pitch levels and the relation between paraphoning and its register variation. This study has explored only a part of the phenomenon, focusing on the function and variation of paraphoning. Hopefully, it has made a small contribution towards our greater understanding of paraphoning.

Notes

1. I will use 'spoken paragraph' to refer to a paragraph-like unit, since people have coined different terms such as 'paratone' (Brown, 1977), 'major paratone' (Yule, 1980) and 'phonological paragraph' (Tench, 1990) for such a unit.
2. H, M and L stand for high, mid and low pitch levels respectively. Double slashes for tone unit boundaries are placed at the mid level. Capital letters indicate the first salient syllable in a tone unit, and underlined ones the tonic syllable. The italicized letters *o* and *p* are for level and falling tones respectively, and placed on the same levels as the tonic syllables.
3. Although his theory differs from systemic phonology, Crystal (1969) is hesitant to discuss a unit above the sequence of two tone units because of 'the lack of grammatical perspective' (*ibid.*: 242). He further states that '[phonological] analysis of tone-sequences of any length is clearly of limited application, without a grammatical frame of reference of some kind' (*ibid.*: 243).
4. I would like to use the term 'exchange' for a unit in a monologue that is equivalent to an exchange because a monologue in a face-to-face situation is usually part of a larger dialogue.
5. The entire transcript and the sound file are available at http://micase. elicorpora.info/sound-files-online (see 'Intro Biology First Day Lecture' under the heading of 'Large Lectures').

6. For the phonetic analysis, I used a sound analysis program called Praat (www.fon.hum.uva.nl/praat). The pitch values here are mostly from the pitch lines that the program shows; however, when a line is not clearly represented, the first harmonic and the wave form were used to identify its approximate value.
7. Greek letters denote hypotactic relations between elements. Numerals denote paratactic relations. Logico-semantic relations of expansion and projection are denoted by the symbols '=' (elaborating), '+' (extending), '×' (enhancing), '"' (locution) and ''' (ideas) (see Halliday and Matthiessen, 2004 for a full explanation).
8. The instances of *okay* are all ignored in this analysis because almost all the instances would reset a paraphone with a high pitch level of 550 Hz or higher.
9. Wennerstrom (2001) proposes a 'low paratone' for a parenthetical phrase that is signalled by a low pitch level. Although they are marked by high pitch at their beginnings, Paraphones 4 and 5 share similarity with a low paratone in terms of the function in discourse.

References

Bain, C. E., Beaty, J. and Hunter, J. P. (1981) *The Norton Introduction to Literature* (3rd edition). New York: W. W. Norton & Company.

Brazil, D. (1975) *Discourse Intonation*. Birmingham: University of Birmingham.

Brazil, D. (1978) *Discourse Intonation II*. Birmingham: University of Birmingham.

Brazil, D. (1985) *The Communicative Value of Intonation in English*. Birmingham: University of Birmingham.

Brazil, D. (1997) *The Communicative Value of Intonation in English*. Cambridge: Cambridge University Press.

Brazil, D., Coulthard, M. and Johns, C. (1980) *Discourse Intonation and Language Teaching*. London: Longman.

Brown, G. (1977) *Listening to Spoken English*. London: Longman.

Brown, G., Currie, K. L. and Kenworthy, J. (1980) *Questions of Intonation*. Baltimore, MD: University Park Press.

Coulthard, M. and Brazil, D. (1979) *Exchange Structure*. Birmingham: University of Birmingham.

Crystal, D. (1969) *Prosodic Systems and Intonation in English*. Cambridge: Cambridge University Press.

Daneš, F. (1995) The paragraph: a central unit of the thematic and compositional build-up of texts. In B. Wårvik, S. K. Tanskanen and R. Hiltunen (eds) *Organization in Discourse: Proceedings from the Turku Conference* 29–40. Turku: Anglicana Turkuensia.

Eggins, S. and Slade, D. (1997) *Analyzing Casual Conversation*. London: Cassell.

Fries, P. H. (1993) Information flow in written advertising. In J. Alatis (ed.) *Language, Communication and Social Meaning* 336–52. Washington, DC: Georgetown University Press.

Gardner, P. S. (1996) *New Directions: An Integrated Approach to Reading, Writing, and Critical Thinking*. New York: St Martin's Press.

Garrod, S. and Pickering, M. J. (2004) Why is conversation so easy? *Trends in Cognitive Sciences* 8(1): 8–11.

Giora, R. (1983) Functional paragraph perspective. In J. S. Petofi and E. Sozer (eds) *Micro and Macro Connexity of Texts* 153–82. Haburg: Buske.

Goldman-Eisler, F. (1968) *Psycholinguistics: Experiments in Spontaneous Speech*. New York: Academic Press.

Hacker, D. (1999) *A Writer's Reference* (4th edition). Boston, MA: Bedford/ St Martin's.

Halliday, M. A. K. ([1961] 2002) Categories of the theory of grammar. In J. J. Webster (ed.) *On Grammar, Volume 1 in the collected works of M. A. K. Halliday* 37–94. London: Continuum.

Halliday, M. A. K. (1967) *Intonation and Grammar in British English* (Janua Linguarum Series Practica 48). The Hague: Mouton.

Halliday, M. A. K. (1978) *Language as Social Semiotic: The Social Interpretation of Language and Meaning*. London: Arnold.

Halliday, M. A. K. (1985) *Spoken and Written Language*. Oxford: Oxford University Press.

Halliday, M. A. K. (1996) On grammar and grammatics. In C. Cloran, D. Butt, and R. Hasan (eds) *Functional Descriptions: Theory into Practice* 1–38. Amsterdam: John Benjamins.

Halliday, M. A. K. (2000) Phonology past and present: a personal retrospect. *Folia Linguistica* 34(1–2): 101–11.

Halliday, M. A. K. (2005) On matter and meaning: the two realms of human experience. *Linguistics and the Human Sciences* 1(1): 59–82.

Halliday, M. A. K. and Greaves, W. S. (2008) *Intonation in the Grammar of English*. London: Equinox.

Halliday, M. A. K. and Hasan, R. (1976) *Cohesion in English*. London: Longman.

Halliday, M. A. K. and Hasan, R. (1985) *Language, Context, and Text: Aspects of Language in a Social-Semiotic Perspective*. Oxford: Oxford University Press.

Halliday, M. A. K. and Matthiessen, C. M. I. M. (1999) *Construing Experience through Meaning: A Language-based Approach to Cognition*. London: Continuum.

Halliday, M. A. K. and Matthiessen, C. M. I. M. (2004) *An Introduction to Functional Grammar* (3rd edition). London: Arnold.

Hoey, M. (1983) *On the Surface of Discourse*. London: Allen & Unwin.

Hoey, M. (1997) The interaction of textual and lexical factors in the identification of paragraph boundaries. In M. Reinhardt and W. Thiele (eds) *Grammar and Text in Synchrony and Diachrony* 141–67. Frankfurt am Main: Veruert.

Iwamoto, K. (2009) A paragraph and paragraphing: from the perspective of Systemic Functional Linguistics. *Annual Review of the Faculty of Foreign Studies* 21: 183–211.

Johnson, J. (1997) *The Bedford Guide to the Research Process* (3rd edition). New York: St Martin's Press.

Krivokapić, J. (2007) Prosodic planning: effects of phrasal length and complexity on pause duration. *Journal of Phonetics* 35: 162–79.

Lehiste, I. (1975) The phonetic structure of paragraphs. In A. Cohen and S. G. Nooteboom (eds) *Structure and Process in Speech Perception* 195–206. Berlin: Springer-Verlag.

Lehiste, I. (1979) Perception of sentence and paragraph boundaries. In B. Lindblom and S. Ohman (eds) *Frontiers of Speech Research*. London: Academic Press.

Lehiste, I. (1982) Some phonetic characteristics of discourse. *Studia Linguistica* 36(2): 117–30.

Longacre, R. E. (1996) *The Grammar of Discourse* (2nd edition). New York: Plenum Press.

Mann, W. C. and Thompson, S. A. (1988) Rhetorical structure theory: toward a functional theory of text organization. *Text* 8: 243–81.

Matthiessen, C. M. I. M. (1992) Interpreting the textual metafunction. In M. Davies and L. Ravelli (eds) *Advances in Systemic Linguistics: Recent Theory and Practice* 37–81. London: Pinter.

Pike, K. L. and Pike, E. G. (1980) *Grammatical Analysis* (2nd edition). Arlington, TX: Summer Institute of Linguistics, University of Texas.

Reich, S. S. (1980) Significance of pauses for speech perception. *Journal of Psycholinguistic Research* 9(4): 379–89.

Schiffrin, D. (1987) *Discourse Marker*. Cambridge: Cambridge University Press.

Simpson, R. C., Briggs, S. L., Ovens, J. and Swales, J. M. (2002) *The Michigan Corpus of Academic Spoken English*. Ann Arbor, MI: The Regents of the University of Michigan.

Sinclair, J. M. and Coulthard, R. M. (1975) *Towards an Analysis of Discourse: The English Used by Teachers and Pupils*. London: Oxford University Press.

Tench, P. (1990) *The Roles of Intonation in English Discourse*. Frankfurt am Main: Peter Lang.

Tench, P. (1996) *The Intonation Systems of English*. London: Cassell.

Thompson, S. E. (2003) Text-structuring metadiscourse, intonation and the signalling of organisation in academic lectures. *Journal of English for Academic Purposes* 2: 5–20.

Wennerstrom, A. (2001) *The Music of Everyday Speech*. Oxford: Oxford University Press.

White, R. A. (1922) *Sunny Boy and His Playmates*. New York: Barse & Co.

Young, R. E. and Becker, A. L. (1966) *The Role of Lexical and Grammatical Cues in Paragraph Recognition* (Studies in Language and Language Behaviour, Progress Report No 2). Ann Arbor, MI: Center for Research on Language and Language Behaviour, University of Michigan.

Yule, G. (1980) Speakers' topics and major paratones. *Lingua* 52: 33–47.

Appendix 1: A letter cited by Hoey (1983: 2–13)

Dear Member,

At last year's AGM one view expressed (amongst many) was that the Institute should 'keep in touch more closely with its members'. At the time I had no idea that I was ever going to be anything but a member and so supported this proposal. Obviously better communication was a good idea.

Now that I am faced with the prospect of actually communicating, it doesn't seem so simple after all. To begin with, who are you? Some of you are members because of an interest in the history of the cinema. Some of you because you are professionally concerned with film study in education. Some of you want information and views about current films from the Institute's publications. Most of you hold an associate's ticket so that you can see the programmes at the NFT. A few of you have a political interest in the form and function of the Institute, and a few of these few have a sincere desire for the Institute to become a stalking-horse for a form of nationalisation of a part or all of the film industry.

So.

To all members I would say that for some time the Governors have been examining the present identity and future role of the Institute. We have now reached conclusions. A policy report is enclosed with this letter to members and is available to Associates at the NFT or through the Publications Department. [Footnote omitted.] There would be little point in pre-empting the contents of this document, but there are three things that I would like to say rather emphatically now.

First, we want to accelerate the flow of material from the fastnesses of the Archive into the light of day so that people may see what we have got. [Footnote omitted.] We are unanimous about this and have the support of Lord Eccles, the Minister responsible for the Arts. We need a lot of money for prints and viewing machines and we have asked for it with confidence.

Second, we want to give the NFT better technical facilities, better prints and better opportunities to give you the best programmes. The NFT with three auditoria and really good clubroom facilities is an achievement. (Have you visited them yet? If not, please go.) It is also a place with the most exciting potential. The programmes there are sorely afflicted by problems of film availability and film supply. As interest in our kind of film increases (which is just what we want) so more and more barricades are thrown up around material that was once there for the asking. We've got to surmount these.

What we want at the NFT is interest and attendance. This is not the same thing as 'a commercial policy'. No one puts on a string quartet at the Albert Hall, because it would not only be uncommercial, but crazy as well. We do not want NFT1 to play to audiences of a few dozen enthusiasts. It is our main arena. NFT2 can cater for the large minorities and NFT3 for the specialists. We must show what is worth while regardless of 'commercial' considerations, but we want the place full. If attendance is low (which happily is not usually the case) we are not succeeding on any level. There is not *necessarily* any antithesis between quality and popularity, and anyone who believes this about our medium of film and television should write out a list of names such as Keaton, Ford, Hancock, Fellini, Garnett, etc. ten thousand times.

Third, we want more of you. If every member and associate of the Institute persuaded one friend to join, we would double our membership and greatly strengthen our position. The financing of a public body is a delicate thing, and the more that the demand for its services can be demonstrated, the more government support it will get. Covent Garden would never get its famous million-plus pounds (whatever you think about that) unless it was booked to capacity much of the time.

Appendix 2: Semantic system network for semantic movement in a monologic text

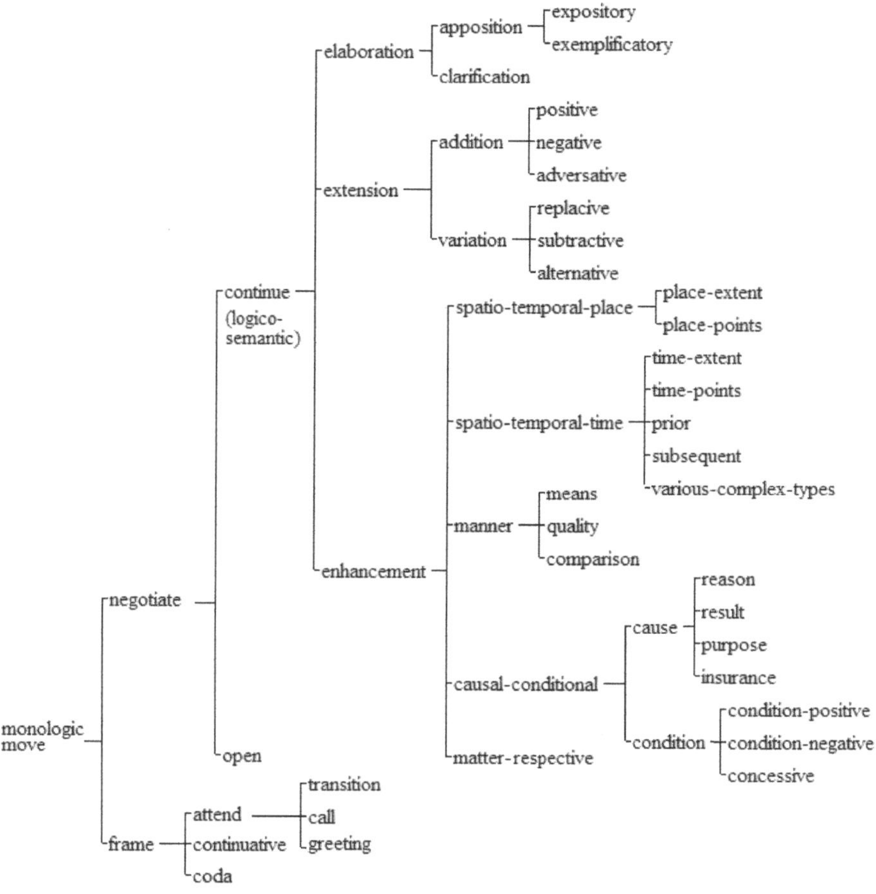

Figure 4.A1 A modified version of the system networks from Eggins and Slade (1997).

The Interface between Written and Spoken Language

<table><tr><td>5</td></tr></table>

The black hole in graphology

Martin Davies[a]

5.1 Introduction

As a secondary school English teacher in the 1950s and 1960s, I had to read numerous essays, at various levels. Most were at sixth-form level. Occasionally, I found that though I could read a sentence I could not understand it, and could not read it aloud. I could then either re-read it and try to 'make sense' of it, or if that still didn't work I could ask the writer to read it aloud for me next day in class. This they could sometimes do, and I could then suggest a rewording, not knowing why the rewording worked when the original wording had not worked. What I could not then do was answer the writer's next question, 'Why?', meaning 'Why reword it like this?', other than by saying, 'It works, whereas your wording didn't.' But the most interesting occasions were when the writer couldn't read it aloud either. I could not understand why this was so. Now, I would concentrate on encouraging students to get the Focus as well as the cohesion right, without my necessarily using those terms in the process. Later, I realized that when I hesitated over the rhythm of a line of written verse, and had to read it again to make it run properly – something which still happens – it was a closely related phenomenon.

During the same period, for a short-lived examination in the 1960s called 'The Use of English', I was reading – and teaching from – Quirk's most useful book, *The Use of English* (1962), with its very helpful first

a **Martin Davies** retired from the University of Stirling in 1996. He began his career as a secondary teacher at Canford School in Dorset, moving from there to The King's School Canterbury, then on to Loughborough College of Education, before taking up a lecturer position at the University of Stirling in 1976. Davies has long been interested in the connection between phonology and reading aloud and the educational insights that can be gained from understanding this connection. He has published widely in the area of prosodic choice in reading aloud, literacy and intonation, and theme, information and cohesion. He is co-editor with Louise Ravelli of *Advances in Systemic Linguistics* (1992). His major research interests include intonation implicit in writing, cohesion and information structure, standard English and alienation in education, and applications of systemic functional linguistics in educational contexts.

supplement, *The Transmission of Language*, by Gimson (1962a). This not only introduced me to phonetics but told me there was such a thing as intonation, and that it had been systematically studied. And soon afterwards I discovered *The Linguistic Sciences and Language Teaching* (Halliday *et al.*, 1964), with its helpful transcripts of texts in ordinary orthography showing intonation in a notation designed to be typed, without diacritics which added unwanted complexity for both typists and beginner readers. This eventually led me to produce my dissertation titled 'A comparison of prosodic features used by subjects when reading aloud a printed passage' (Davies, 1970), using the method of comparing texts in multi-line transcriptions, which has eventually paid dividends (Davies, 1973, 1984, 1986).

When asked why Halliday and Hasan's (1976) *Cohesion in English* did not give more than three pages – devoted chiefly to discussion of tone sequences – to 'The cohesive function of intonation', Halliday replied that to have done so 'would have doubled the length of the book and we chickened out. You do it!'[1] The present essay is nowhere near as long, or as full, as *Cohesion in English*, but it is all that can be achieved here and may be a short step in the direction of a full account of prosodic cohesion.

5.2 Cohesion and Information Structure in spoken text

In spoken text, cohesion (Halliday and Hasan, 1976) is realized in lexico-grammatical form, and lexicogrammatical form itself is then re-realized in segmental and prosodic phonology and phonetics. Cohesion creates texture by means of a network of cohesive ties between cohesive items and their targets; and without such ties, a text will not be well formed. It will not be a text, in fact, but word salad (or 'pseudo-text').

In spoken text, choices in the systems of INFORMATION DISTRIBUTION and INFORMATION FOCUS (Halliday, 1967a, 1970; Halliday and Greaves, 2008) are realized as a series of Given–New structures, in which the relationships between Given and contrastively New items and their antecedents are similar to, and run parallel with, those between cohesive items and their targets.

Information distribution and focus, however, are not realized in lexicogrammar but are realized directly in the prosodic phonology and phonetics, in choices in the systems of TONALITY and TONICITY.

	LINGUISTIC		SYSTEM		
meaning				**expression**	
semantic metafunctions		*lexico-grammar*		*phonology*	
semantic systems	*semantic output/ input to grammar*	*grammatical systems*	*grammatical units and structures*	*phonological systems*	*units-and-structures*
Ideational: experiential (logical)	*semantic*	TRANSITIVITY: - Material - Mental - Relational: Identifying - Relational: Attributive - *Others....*	Actor–Process-Goal Senser- Process-Phenomenon Identified-Process-Identifier Carrier-Process-Attribute *etc*	(i) segmental	tone group: (Pretonic) -Tonic - (Post-Tonic) foot: Ictus - (Remiss)
Interpersonal	*configu-*	MOOD - Mood - Modality - Modulation - *Others....*	Mood-Residue *various* *various*		syllable: (Onset) - Rhyme
		- Key		(ii) prosodic: Tone	(a) Rhythm
Textual	*rations*	THEME₁: - Information Structure - Information Focus - Cohesion (non-structural) - Theme₂	reference *etc* iteration *etc* Theme-Rheme	Tonality Tonicity (i) segmental (cont'd)	(b) Melody phoneme [no structure; constituents = (CCC)V(CCCC)]

TEXT

Figure 5.1 Realization of textual meaning in spoken text.

And again, without the meanings of information distribution and focus, a text is not well formed; and it, too, will be word salad, prosodic word salad (or prosodic pseudo-text) (see Davies, 1999). Figure 5.1 suggests how realization works in speech, the shaded area indicating the kinds of meaning, textual and interpersonal, which are realized prosodically.

5.3   Parallelism between cohesion and Information Structure

The two kinds of textual meaning run in close parallel: what is Given or contrastively New is also cohesive; and what is cohesive is Given or contrastively New. The parallelism between cohesion and intonation was noted in Davies (1989, 1992: 226), in which it was found that the relationships between Given elements and earlier items in the text closely parallel the ties set up by cohesion (see also Chapter 6 of this volume). And earlier, Halliday had noted that in the 'North Star' text, 'all the Given items, and also the New items that are contrastive, are also cohesive in the discourse' (Halliday, 1985a: 278, 1994: 299; Halliday and Matthiessen, 2004: 92). But this relationship between the cohesion and the information distribution and focus is not confined to the 'North Star' text. It is general, and the close parallelism between them creates what we might call 'cohesive redundancy'. (For a discussion of information and cohesion, see Davies, 2002.)

5.4   Redundancy and noise

In spoken text, the parallelism creates redundancy in the expression (Halliday, 1992; Shannon, 1948). Cohesive meaning is expressed in the wording, which is itself expressed in the segmental phonology, in syllables and phonemes; and Information Structure, while not expressed in the wording, is expressed in phonology, as tonality and tonicity. Both sets of meanings work in parallel, so that it might appear that one or other would create the necessary textual meanings without any need for the other, each being redundant with respect to the other. But this is not so, as in speech they are independently variable. Nevertheless, only one of them, cohesion, is realized in written text. So the absence of any representation of prosodic phonology in writing creates noise, the difficulty being that there is no way in which readers can apprehend the information distribution and focus directly from the lettering (the problem which underlay my problem in reading essays).

5.5 Cohesion and Information Structure in written text

In written text, cohesive meaning is realized in the wording, which is then re-realized in graphology, in letters and spaces. But information distribution and focus are not expressed in the letters and spaces of ordinary orthography, which do not realize tonality and tonicity (unless technical notation is used). This means that the cohesive meaning has to work to create texture without any expression of the information distribution and focus. The result is that the two are not independently variable as in speech, and any interpretation of written information and distribution in speech, when reading aloud, is not expressed independently but has to be implied in the lexicogrammatically expressed cohesion (Davies, 1970, 1989, 1992, 1994a, 1994b, 1998, 2002). So the absence of any expression of tonality and tonicity in the lettering, far from creating redundancy in the expression, as in speech, creates noise, making life more difficult for a reader than for a hearer, although at least the information distribution and focus – though not the 'key' – are implicit in the lexicogrammar of the written form, being expressed only if the written text is read aloud and a 'derived', spoken text is created. Figure 5.2 suggests how realization works in written text, the heavily shaded area, i.e. the black hole, represents the kinds of meaning, textual and interpersonal, that are not realized in graphology.

The noise in written text is considerable (*cf.* 'Too much noise' in Stoppard, 1993: 62), and causes a well-known problem in teaching reading. A teacher will say of a child that it can make the sounds but 'can't read for meaning', as though the segmental sounds themselves are not meaningful. But the teacher is not talking nonsense: the child can read parts of the sounds (the segmental parts), but can't read the prosodic elements. Why not? The reason is that, within certain limits, orthography represents the smallest segmental sounds, the phonemes, but does not represent units higher up the rank scale (i.e. syllables, feet or tone groups); and still less does the orthography represent the prosodic rhythm and melody of speech.

<table>
<tr><th colspan="11">LINGUISTIC   SYSTEM</th><th rowspan="2"></th></tr>
<tr><th colspan="10">m e a n i n g</th><th>➘ e x p r e s s i o n</th></tr>
<tr>
<th colspan="3">semantic metafunctions</th>
<th colspan="4">lexico-grammar</th>
<th colspan="3">graphology</th>
<th rowspan="2">TEXT ➘</th>
</tr>
<tr>
<th>semantic systems</th><th></th><th>semantic output/input to grammar</th>
<th>grammatical systems</th><th></th><th>grammatical units and structures</th><th></th>
<th>graphological systems</th><th></th><th>segmental units-&-structures</th>
</tr>
<tr>
<td>Ideational: experiential (logical)</td><td>➘</td><td>semantic</td>
<td>TRANSITIVITY:
- Material
- Mental

- Relational: Identifying

- Relational: Attributive
- Others....</td><td>➘</td>
<td>Actor–Process-Goal
Senser- Process-
      Phenomenon
Identified-Process-
      Identifier
Carrier-Process-Attribute
      etc</td><td>➘</td>
<td>segmental systems
sentences,
sub-sentences
words
letters</td><td>➘</td>
<td>letter "prosodies"
capitalization
punctuation &
      stops
underlining
paragraphing
indentation</td>
</tr>
<tr>
<td rowspan="2">Interpersonal</td><td rowspan="2">➘</td><td rowspan="2">configu-</td>
<td>MOOD - Mood
      - Modality
      - Modulation
      - Others....</td><td>➘</td>
<td>Mood-Residue
various
various</td><td>➘</td>
<td rowspan="2">bracketed elements are in print only

(italicization)</td><td rowspan="2"></td><td rowspan="2"></td>
</tr>
<tr>
<td>   - Key</td>
<td colspan="3">NOT REALIZED
Key, Information Structure and Information Focus are not realized explicitly in graphology and have to be inferred from Cohesion and other meanings.</td>
</tr>
<tr>
<td rowspan="2">Textual</td><td rowspan="2">➘</td><td rowspan="2">rations</td>
<td>THEME₁: - Information Structure
      - Information Focus</td>
<td colspan="6"></td>
</tr>
<tr>
<td>   - Cohesion (non-
        structural)
      - Theme₂</td><td>➘</td>
<td>reference etc
iteration etc
Theme-Rheme</td><td>➘</td>
<td>(segmental systems
continued)
sentences,
sub-sentences
words
letters</td><td>➘</td>
<td>(letter "prosodies"
continued)
(bolding)
(font ranges)
(other typography)</td>
</tr>
</table>

Figure 5.2 Partial realization of textual meaning in written text.

So there is no indication of the syllabification in the orthography, and orthography may be misleading and confusing. For instance, 'Wemyss' looks as though it may be spoken on two syllables but has only one, /wiːmz/; 'Wednesday' looks as though it may have three syllables but has only two, /wenz/+/dɪ/, with no indication of which syllable is accented and potentially tonic. And the only indication of the ends of some tone groups is sometimes given by punctuation, while there is no indication at all of the higher units on the phonological rank scale, let alone of the rhythm and melody which realize information distribution and focus in tonality and tonicity. It is these unrealized meanings, absent from written text, which constitute 'noise' in all writing. A learner has to develop the ability to exploit the cohesive redundancy to overcome the noise. This is why teachers often refer to this stage in the learning process as 'barking at print', since 'barking' in this sense does not have the rhythm or melody needed to express the Information Structure.

5.6 Redundancy

Part of the value of redundancy in a system is its potential for overcoming noise, as here: the redundancy created by the parallelism in the two strands of textual meaning in speech enables readers to overcome the noise created by the absence of any realization of the meanings in the information distribution and focus in written text. Once readers can work out the information distribution and focus choices from the cohesion, they can read the text aloud convincingly, leading teachers to say that learners can then 'read for meaning', the teachers meaning 'prosodically expressed meaning' though they don't put it like that, even though they are right. And it is possible to watch learners develop the ability to do this.[2] (Redundancy is also exploited in Cloze Tests, where every fourth or fifth word may be omitted, though these seem to be less useful for testing than as a resource for teaching, if appropriately adapted, as they can be exploited in devices such as 'Reading Invisible Words',[3] where it is not every fourth or fifth word that is omitted but any word expressing one or other type of cohesion, such as conjunction or reference.)

Redundancy also enables readers to recognize 'mistakes', as for example when an apocryphal choirboy read part of the Rite for the Solemnization of Matrimony in *The Book of Common Prayer* as '/for /richer /for /poorer /for /better /for /worse' (a '/' indicates rhythmical salience in the immediately following syllable). If the words really meant that, the statement would be morally questionable (as well as logistically tricky), and we know that he has made a mistake: he should have said 'for /richer for /poorer for /better for /worse' like everybody else. This shows that we have to understand the rhythm in written text correctly, even though it is not normally realized in graphology. Readers 'know' that the choirboy was wrong, because they 'know' – as the choirboy (even though he was apocryphal) actually did 'know' (because we all 'know', even those of us who are apocryphal) that he had been developing the system of rhythm since before birth. Rhythm is fundamental to speech, and though we are not taught the rhythm of our mother tongue, any more than we are taught TRANSITIVITY, MOOD, and THEME, we have to have it, and so we normally develop it for ourselves, in social interaction, where 'social' includes 'the society of the womb'! Halliday (1980: 7) points out that a 'baby has already started learning language before [it] was born, picking up the rhythms of speech from their source in his mother's diaphragm'.[4]

5.7 Rhythm

We do not say so (because we do not need to say it), but what we and the apocryphal choirboy all 'know' is that:

> 'Salient' and 'weak' are properties of syllables in connected speech. They are related to *word accent* in the following way. 'Word accent' is the potentiality that certain syllables, in certain words, have for being salient when put into sentences. In general, the syllables which become salient in connected speech are:
>
> (1) the one-syllable words of the 'content' class (lexical words)
> (2) the *accented* syllables of words with more than one syllable
>
> while those which become weak syllables in connected speech are
>
> (1) one-syllable words of the 'form' class (structural words)
> (2) the non-accented syllables of words with more than one syllable.
> (Halliday, 1970: 2)

In the 'Rite for the Solemnization of Marriage', 'for' is a word of the form class and is therefore weak in connected speech, and should not be salient unless it is contrastive. So if it is wrongly made salient in connected speech, without being contrastive, then it is interpreted as a one-syllable word of the 'content' class (i.e. in the choirboy's case the word normally realized in graphology as 'four'). Since reading aloud is 'connected speech' it requires readers to follow these rules. Moreover, if we are to understand the meaning correctly, we have to follow the spelling and recognize words of the form class, whether or not we read them aloud and make them weak (and salient only if the meaning is contrastive or there is no word of the content class available).

5.8   Recognizing meanings

What is true of word class and rhythm, is just as true of segmental phonology. Just as the lettering on its own can never tell us the rhythm, so it cannot tell us all we need to know about the segmental phonology. In 'Have you read$_1$ this?', 'read$_1$' is pronounced /red/, and in 'No, I'll read$_2$ it tonight', 'read$_2$' is pronounced /riːd/. So we need to know that, in context ('context' here means 'following "have" in the verbal group'), the tense form is past-in-past, and so the meaning of the lettering in 'read$_1$' includes 'past', which readers need to recognize in order to know what it means (and thus to know what sounds to make to read it aloud). Similarly, we need to recognize that the meaning of the lettering in 'read$_2$' includes 'present', in order to know what it means (and thus to know what sounds to make to read it aloud); and the lettering by itself is not 'adequate' to specify the vowel, even for barking at print. The function of lettering, like the function of phonemes, is not to notate sounds, as though it were musical notation, but to express meaning, and tense is part of the meaning and has to be expressed. So we have to have much more than an understanding of so-called grapheme-phoneme relationships in order to read, whether silently or aloud.

And grapheme-phoneme relationships have changed in numerous ways in the last thousand years; they are different in different accents around the English-speaking world; and they have been further confused in the 500 years of changes in the language since Caxton brought the first printing press to England as the spelling system settled down. We have to live with these problems, though they can't be discussed further here. But the same principle – that we have to know the meanings in order to realize in speech the words before us realized in graphemes – applies equally to segmental and to prosodic meanings.

5.9   Matching cohesion with prosody

More generally, what is surprising is that in normal reading, people don't make mistakes of this kind. They do make mistakes, and say things like, 'I'm sorry, I'll read that again' (Davies, 1994b), and misreadings and misunderstandings certainly do happen. But in general, when people read aloud, they get most of the segmental phonology right, and get a kind of fail-safe tonality and tonicity right; at least they do if they can 'read for meaning'. This means that although there is no representation of the TONALITY and TONICITY systems in written text, they can work them out. The argument here is that this is done from the cohesion, since the meanings expressed in spoken text by tonality and tonicity are not 'visible' in written text (Davies, 1994a), but can be inferred from the cohesion as a necessary part of understanding written text. Just as we infer the rhythm of written text by identifying the classes of form and content words (and from much else, of course) – otherwise, as David Abercrombie used to say, we would never be able to tell whether a line of words on the page is a line of verse or not – so we infer the tonality and tonicity by identifying the cohesion. It is not a matter of conscious analysis. Rather, we may feel the need to run through the sentence again, 'to see how it goes', silently or otherwise. But we must do it, or we can't read, still less read aloud, except by chanting it on a monotone perhaps, and even then we can't avoid giving our utterance an appropriate rhythm.

The Given elements are given either homophorically in the context of situation or context of culture, or endophorically in the environment of the text itself, the 'co-text'. 'There are a number of elements in language that are inherently 'given' in the sense that they are not interpretable except by reference to some previous mention or some feature of the situation: anaphoric elements ... and deictic elements' (Halliday and Matthiessen, 2014: 118). And in the present context, what needs to be said is that both Given and cohesive items function in this way, simultaneously and jointly. So we can expect to find cohesive items either in the Given elements or in what is contrastively New, and that is where we do find them, as will be shown below. Halliday and Matthiessen continue by making the latter point: 'Typically these items do not carry information focus; if they do, they are contrastive' (*ibid.*: 118). Thus, what is cohesive is Given, and therefore it is not New, and does not carry the information focus, unless it is contrastive.

The contrastive New elements make a contrast which, again, is either with elements in the environment of the text or with elements in the preceding co-text. Information distribution and focus thus also contribute to the creation of texture in spoken text, by means of what can be regarded as a network of prosodically engendered 'ties', parallel to the cohesive ties and similar in nature and function, but created structurally rather than non-structurally. Some of the most important of these 'prosodic ties' are displayed in the next section in a series of questions and answers, to show their links with non-prosodic cohesion.

5.10 Tonicity: The placing of the Tonic

The questions differ from each other, but the answer is always the same: *Angus has sunk the boat.* (It is usually helpful to read both the questions and answers aloud, to pre-empt any conditioning from the subsequent text.)

1.	What has Angus sunk?	Angus has sunk the boat.
2.	What has Angus done to the boat?	Angus has sunk the boat.
3.	Who has sunk the boat?	Angus has sunk the boat.

If we are presented with this series, we are able to read the answers aloud and give them an appropriate rhythm, and can also give Tonic prominence correctly to the appropriate word in each case. Leaving aside the question of how we know how many syllables a written word has when pronounced, because there are no clues in the text, this is because the 'one-syllable words of the "content" class' (i.e. lexical words) here, are 'sunk', and 'boat' and 'the accented syllable of the word with more than one syllable' is 'Ang-', so the rhythm in all the answers must, in the first instance, be '/Angus has /sunk the /boat'. Each segment beginning with a forward slash, consisting of at least one salient syllable and any weak syllables which follow it, constitutes a rhythmical 'foot'. This is a 'phonometric' foot, not a metrical one. (The metrical foot, in English, derives from the phonometric one.) The lines in English blank verse, metrically, are iambic pentameters but phonometrically these are usually trochaic hexameters, although there are different kinds of blank verse, notably the one often said to use 'four-stress' lines, as often in T. S. Eliot's verse plays (for example *The Family Reunion*), which are neither iambic nor trochaic, pentameters nor hexameters, but metrically are mixtures of various kinds of feet that are best described phonometrically.

These answers all consist of three such phonometric feet, containing three, two and one syllables respectively: '/Angus has', '/sunk the', and '/boat'. In all the questions and answers which follow, it will be assumed that such a group of one or more feet, one and only one of which contains a Tonic, constitutes one 'Tone group', the tone group boundaries being represented by double forward slashes initially and finally. It is possible for some of the utterances to be assigned more than one Tone group, such as //Angus has //sunk the /boat //, but such cases will not be considered: the regular case will be //Angus has /sunk the /boat //. Also, in some cases the choice of tone will be specified, as in Halliday (1967a, 1970), but only in quotations, because tone expresses meanings in key, which is not part of the textual metafunction, and is not discussed here. And in every Tone group there will be one and only one Tonic syllable, indicated here by underlining, the one which is made prominent in each answer. These are now shown, and at the same time the cohesion is also shown. (There is no cohesion in the questions, because they are initial. 'Lex' stands for 'lexical reiteration'. 'Ref' stands for 'reference'.)

			Lex	Lex	Ref	
1	//What has /Angus /<u>sunk</u>? //	//Angus has	/sunk	the	/<u>boat</u>. //	

			Lex		Ref	Lex
2	//What has /Angus/done to the /<u>boat</u>? //	//Angus has	/<u>sunk</u>	the	/boat. //	

				Lex	Ref	Lex
3	//Who has /sunk the /boat? //	//<u>Angus</u> has	/sunk	the	/boat. //	

Items creating cohesive ties are Given unless they are contrastive, so the focus of the New is only on words which are not cohesive unless the New is contrastive. So in the absence of any contrast, the Focus is on the non-cohesive items, the words underlined in whole or in part. Hence there is no cohesion between the words with underlined syllables and the preceding question.

The Focus is expressed by the Tonic, the placing of the tone choice on a salient syllable, indicated by underlining. Here, this means that in example (1) the Tonic is on 'boat', in (2) it is on 'sunk' and in (3) it is on 'Angus'. As before, / indicates salience on the immediately following syllable. The Focus is always on a non-cohesive word.

		Lex	Lex	Ref		
1	//What has /Angus /sunk? //	//Angus has	/sunk	the	/<u>boat</u>.	//
					Focus/New	

		Lex		Ref	Lex	
2	//What has /Angus /done to the /boat? //	//Angus has	/<u>sunk</u>	the	/boat.	//
			Focus/New			

		Lex	Ref	Lex		
3	//Who has /sunk the /boat? //	//<u>Angus</u> has	/sunk	the	/boat.	//
	Focus/New					

The Focus expresses the speaker's orientation of their message as answer to the questioner. The meaning is: 'this item is Tonic because it's what's New to you and answers your question; so focus on this.'

		Lex	Lex	Ref	
1 //What has /Angus /sunk? //	//Angus has	/sunk	the	/<u>boat</u>	//
	Given Given	Given	Given	Focus/New	

		Lex		Ref	Lex
2 //What has /Angus /done to the /boat? //	//Angus has	/<u>sunk</u>	the	/boat //	
	Given Given	Focus/New	Given	Given	

		Lex	Ref	Lex	
3 //Who has /sunk the /boat? //	//<u>Angus</u>	has	/sunk the	/boat //	
	Focus/New	Given	Given Given	Given	

The tonicity in the answers, the locating of the Tonic within one tone group, therefore varies systematically according to the form of the question: what is unmentioned in the question (because it is unknown, which is why the question is being asked) is appropriately (and politely!) made the focus of the answer. The meaning is: 'since that's what you want to know, focus on this Tonic element because it is what's New'. In each case, the word which carries the Tonic is not found in the question, and so in that sense it is 'New', while the words that are not underlined, 'words of the "content" class', having been given in the question, are treated as Given in the answers. It makes good communicative sense: what questioners want to know will be new to them, which is why they ask the question. So the respondent makes the new items 'New'.

Since the questions are initial in the dialogue, there can be no cohesion between them and the preceding text, so everything in them is New, and from now on this is represented in the same way as in the answers. The rule is that when this is so, the focus is on the last (non-anaphoric) 'content' word (lexical item), if there is one, and on the last otherwise rhythmically appropriate word if there isn't — that is, the 'last word of the "form" class (structural words)' which can be salient in the context. So also, since there is a non-anaphoric 'content' word, '/<u>boat</u>', at the end of the answer to the first question, this is the focus, and gets the Tonic. And similarly for '/<u>sunk</u>' and '/<u>Angus</u>' in (2) and (3). Again, the rule is to focus on something which is not Given and put the Tonic on that, unless there is a need to express a contrast. Thus, if the cohesion is displayed together with the Given–New structures, as in the last display above, the cohesive lexical reiteration is always in the Given elements.

The combination of cohesion and Information Structure, including that of the questions (which are initial and therefore show no cohesion, and are all New), is as follows. Having identified the individual items which are both cohesive and Given, we can display the Information Structure and focus of these sequences, using the conventional double bar boundary markers for the information groups, and noting that all the New information is fresh (and not contrastive):

```
                                            Lex        Lex    Ref
1   //What has /Angus /sunk? //            //Angus has /sunk  the    /boat. //
    ||<------------- New   ||              ||Given -------------> - New ||
               fresh                                            fresh

                                            Lex          Ref    Lex
2   //What has /Angus /done to the /boat? //  //Angus has  /sunk the    /boat. //
    ||<------------------------ New   ||      ||Given ---> - New - <---- Given ||
                      fresh                              fresh

                                            Lex   Ref Lex
3   //Who has /sunk the /boat?  //          //Angus has /sunk  the /boat. //
    || <------------- New ||                ||New - <---------- Given ||
               fresh                          fresh
```

Note that 'the' is Given in two different ways here. In (2) and (3) its reference is anaphoric: the meaning is 'the boat mentioned in the question'. In (1) it is exophoric: the speaker assumes that which boat is in question is known to the questioner from the context of situation. This variation continues through the remaining examples. (I am grateful to Margaret Berry for discussion of this point.)

5.11 Tonicity and ellipsis

The notion of 'Given' is given further substance by the elliptical answers to the questions.

```
1   //What has /Angus /sunk? //          //∧ The   /boat. //
    ||<------------- New   ||            || <---- New    ||
               fresh                             fresh

                                                 Ref
2   //What has /Angus /done to the /boat? //   // Sunk  it.    //
    ||<------------------------ New   ||        || New -  Given ||
                      fresh                        fresh

3   //Who has /sunk the /boat?  //            // Angus.  //
    ||<------------- New ||                    || New    ||
               fresh                             fresh
```

The ellipted elements in the answers are now so Given that they are omitted altogether, leaving only the New to focus on, and the cohesion is in the ellipsis (Halliday and Hasan, 1976), and so not visible in the orthography. This is particularly common in the context of questions-and-answers, as here, but ellipsis can and often does happen in other contexts, as for example, throughout Gerard Manly Hopkins's poem 'Carrion comfort' (Davies, 1998). A fourth, different question gives us the following answer, in which ellipsis is not possible so everything in the answer is New.

```
4   //What has /happened?  //              //Angus has /sunk the /boat.  //
        <-------- New       ||             ||<-------------- New   ||
                 fresh                                    fresh
```

If we compare the Information Structure here with that in the answer to the first question, the 'same' answers then display two different extents of the New, since there is cohesion in the first answer but not in the fourth.

```
                                           Lex          Lex    Ref
1   //What has /Angus /sunk?  //           //Angus has /sunk  the  /boat.  //
      ||<-------------- New   ||           ||Given ----------> - New   ||
                  fresh                                     fresh

4   //What has /happened?  //              //Angus has /sunk the  /boat.  //
      ||<------- New        ||             ||<--------------- New   ||
              fresh                                      fresh
```

The Tonic in the fourth answer is final, on 'boat', as in the first answer, but there is no reiteration, and no cohesion, so the focus being final, everything is New.

5.12 The extent of the New

The answer to a fifth question, compared with the answers to the first and fourth questions, shows the way the extent of the New in the answer varies according to the form of the question.

```
                                           Lex          Lex   Ref
1   //What has /Angus /sunk?  //           //Angus has /sunk the    /boat.  //
      ||<------------ New    ||            ||Given -----------> - New   ||
                 fresh                                    fresh

                                           Lex
5   //What has /Angus /done?  //           //Angus has /sunk the /boat.  //
      ||<------------- New    ||           ||Given - <------------ New   ||
                 fresh                                    fresh
```

```
4   //What has /happened? //          //Angus has /sunk the /boat. //
    ||<------ New        ||           ||<--------------- New  ||
            fresh                                      fresh
```

The extent of the 'New' in the answers increases as the questions decrease the amount of Given information in the answers.

This is also clear in the elliptical answer forms, where there is minimal or no Given information in the answers, all the cohesion being in the ellipses.

```
                                                     Ref
1   //What has /Angus /sunk? //       //∧ The      /boat. //
    ||<------------- New   ||         ||  Given -  New        ||
              fresh                             fresh

                                                  Ref
5   //What has /Angus /done? //       //Sunk the      /boat.  //
    ||<------------ New   ||          || <-------- - New   ||
              fresh                             fresh

                                                     Ref
4   //What has /happened? //          //Angus has /sunk the /boat. //
    ||<------- New        ||          ||<--------------- New  ||
            fresh                                      fresh
```

Though the full answers in (1), (5) and (4) are both orthographically and prosodically identical in their respective written and spoken forms, they are informationally different (i.e. they have different informational meanings). In running text, readers need to understand these different informational meanings both to understand the written text and to read it aloud.

5.13 Contrastive tonicity

We now turn to three new question–answer pairs (6–8).

```
                                       Lex            Ref Lex
6   //∧ Has /Angus /burnt the /boat? //  //Angus has  /sunk  the  boat. //
    ||<-------------- New    ||         ||Given --> - New - <-- Given ||
                  fresh                            contrastive

                                       Lex    Ref Lex
7   //∧ Has /Fraser /sunk the /boat? //  //Angus has  /sunk the  boat. //
    ||<------------ New    ||           ||New - <--------       Given ||
                  fresh                    contrastive

                                       Lex        Lex Ref Lex
8   //∧ Has /Angus /sunk the /boat? //   //Angus /has /sunk the /boat. //
    ||<--------------- New   ||          ||Given - New - <----- Given ||
                  fresh                            contrastive
```

The answers to questions six and seven illustrate contrastive focus, when the Tonic is on non-final 'content' words. The New on *sunk* in (6) is contrastive, contrasting with 'burnt' in the question, and the New on Angus in (7) contrasts with 'Fraser' in the question. Then the answer in question eight illustrates contrastive focus when the Tonic is on a non-final 'form' word. When the Tonic is on a non-final form word, that word is contrastively New and everything else in the Tone group is Given. And then, as always, all the cohesion is entirely in the Given, and the contrast on the positive polarity is with the negative polarity, the polarity being all that is in question in a polar interrogative.

If we compare (2) and (9), the New is exclusively on the Tonic word in (2), but not exclusively so in (9), varying in relation to the cohesion in the regular way, as it also was in (3). And it is not contrastive in either.

```
                                             Lex          Ref     Lex
2  //What has /Angus /done to the /boat? //  //Angus has   /sunk   the  /boat. //
   ||<--------------------- New   ||         ||Given ---> -  New - <--- Given ||
                    fresh                                 fresh

                                                    Ref     Lex
9  //What has /happened /to the /boat?  //   //Angus has /sunk  the   /boat. //
   ||<-------------------- New  ||           || <------- New - <--- Given ||
                  fresh                                 fresh

                                             Lex          Lex
3  //Who has /sunk the /boat?  //            //Angus has /sunk  the  /boat. //
   ||<------------- New  ||                  ||New - <----------- Given ||
               fresh                         fresh
```

5.14 Informational ambiguity in written text

We now have nine different interpretations of the Information Structure and Focus of the same written sentence, *Angus has sunk the boat*, showing that it is informationally ambiguous on the page, although it is not ambiguous in speech, and is not in these instances ambiguous in writing, since the co-text shows the necessary information clearly.

The sentence has been read with Focus on four different words. First, the three answers in (1), (3) and (5) place the Focus on 'boat'. As always, although the information focus is expressed on the same Tonic in all three, the information distribution differs according to the cohesive relations with the preceding text. Secondly, in the answers in (2) and (6) the New is *fresh* in (2) but *contrastive* in (6); and the extent of the New varies in

(2) and (9), being on 'has sunk' in (2) and extending to 'Angus has sunk' in (9), the Information Distribution being the same in (2) and (6) but different in (9). Thirdly, the answers in (3) and (7) both place the Focus upon 'Angus'. In these answers, the Information Distribution is the same in both cases, but one New is fresh and the other is contrastive. And fourthly, one other answer, (8), places the Focus contrastively upon 'has', everything else being Given and cohesive.

In all these cases the correct interpretation of the information distribution can be determined from the cohesion in analysis and in reading the text aloud. It is unfailingly found to have been read aloud with the consistent relationship between the cohesion and the Focus found in analysis. It cannot be the letters and spaces on the page which enable readers to know which meaning is intended. Rather, a learner has to develop the ability to work out the Information Structure from the cohesive meanings (because it is not Given in the orthography and is all New to learners!). Thus, once the Information Structure is realized, in both senses of that word, it would appear that a reader can place the Tonic on the appropriate syllable or word.

5.15 Information Structure in running text

Choosing where to put the Focus in running text, and the extent of the New are described in the first two editions of Halliday's *An Introduction to Functional Grammar* (1985a, 1994) but not in the third and fourth editions (Halliday and Matthiessen, 2004, 2014, where it is described more fully in other terms) as follows:

> The choice of information focus ... expresses the main point of the information unit, what it is that the speaker is presenting as news: the pattern of focus throughout the text likewise expresses the main point of the discourse. In speech, the focus is realized by Tonic prominence; it typically falls on the final lexical element, in the clause or in whatever unit is matched with the information unit, although it can be 'marked' and put anywhere. In writing, the principle is that (i) the information unit is the clause, unless some other unit is clearly designated by the punctuation; and (ii) the focus falls at the end of the unit, unless some positive signal to the contrary is given, either by lexical cohesion (no focus on repeated word) or by grammatical structure (predication: *it is ... that...*). (Halliday, 1985a: 315, 1994: 336; and see also Halliday and Matthiessen, 2004, 2014)

In interpreting written text, with its unexpressed information focus, and in reading it aloud, the reader seeking the Focus has to find what is cohesive, in order to avoid making it New (unless the New is also contrastive). Readers also have a third option: finding a viable contrast for what is both cohesive and New, so that if they then choose to focus on something cohesive, the contrast is meaningful.

5.16 Getting sound from written text

Another apocryphal choirboy read the words 'Truly, my lot is cast upon a fair ground' (from the Old Testament of the Bible) as //<u>tru</u>ly my //lot is /cast u/pon a /<u>fairground</u>//, when, if he had understood the archaic language, he would have said //<u>tru</u>ly my //lot is /cast u/pon a /fair /<u>ground</u>//, which is phonemically homophonous but rhythmically different – //<u>fairground</u> // and //fair /<u>ground</u> //.

Similarly, the lady who asked the priest to make the announcement, //Harold /having /gone to /<u>sea</u> his //wife re/quests the /congre/gation to /pray for his /safe re/<u>turn</u>//, was much put out when the priest, making clear that he was announcing the wife's request, actually said //Harold /having /gone to /see his /<u>wife</u> re//quests the /congre/gation to /pray for his /safe re/<u>turn</u>//; the priest appearing to be announcing a rather unseemly request from Harold, rather than the wife's perfectly decorous one.[5] Again, despite the spelling difference (*sea/see*), these utterances are phonemically homophonous, but prosodically different:

> //Harold /having /gone to /<u>sea</u> his //wife re/quests ...

and

> //Harold /having /gone to /see his /<u>wife</u> re//quests...

The focus on different words expresses different meanings, requiring *inter alia* different spellings for /si: /.

Unfortunately for the second choirboy, time had moved on, leaving the text 'frozen' in time, as written text always is, and nowadays we might say 'the house is in a very nice place' or 'is very well sited' or 'has got a lovely position', but are much less likely to use the seventeenth century usage: 'it stands upon a fair ground'. So the choirboy cannot be blamed for being insufficiently archaic and not interpreting the graphology adequately.

Equally unfortunately for Harold's wife, the minister hadn't listened to her attentively enough and hadn't expressed her meaning rightly.

More generally, 'inadequate reading' (of which the 'barking at print' mentioned earlier is one kind), is commonly heard in those learning to read, when it contrasts with 'adequate reading', achieved later, sometimes called 'reading for meaning'. What happens here is that the strong and necessary emphasis in teaching on the phonemic interpretation of the lettering ignores readers' parallel need to interpret the Information Structure. There is good reason for ignoring the latter in the early stages of teaching, and ignorance is not the reason this happens. The reason is that it is difficult enough for learners to find the phonemic constituents of a text whose meaning they have to say aloud, without having to try to find the Information Structure to be expressed in tonality and tonicity as well, usually without any explicit instruction in the matter. Furthermore, it is much easier, and more practicable, for the teacher, to deal with what is visible on the page, so far as that is possible, than with what is invisible (Davies, 1994a), even though the invisible does have to be dealt with later.

So it is for good reason that beginners are taught that letters 'stand for' noises, a necessary half-truth which ignores the facts that all letters are silent (if we hold a page to our ears we hear nothing) and that the function of lettering is to express meaning, not to symbolize noises, whether we call them 'phonemes' or not. And of course phonemes are more than language noises, and are noises which make contrasts of phonological meaning (Gimson, 1962b: 44–5).

A different pattern emerges with the place name 'Gillingham', not widely taught in primary schools, but a simple illustration of a problem. We need to know whether we are referring to a place in Kent to say /dʒɪlɪŋəm/, or to a place in Dorset to say /gɪlɪŋəm/, *i.e.* there are two 'correct' pronunciations. Place names such as 'Ratlinghope' /rætʃəp/ and 'Anstruther' /eɪnstə/ are fruitful sources of examples of this kind, but pronunciation, especially of vowels (the name of the river 'Nene' is sometimes pronounced [nen] in Northamptonshire, and [niːn] in Huntingdonshire, and class affiliations are also involved, [niːn] being a spelling pronunciation), and problems of word-accent and syllabification, are regular sources of difficulty in the classroom, of which 'Wednesday' – and 'awry', if you're reading Shakespeare – are only two examples. (It's common for a child to ask why /wenzdɪ/ is spelled 'Wednesday', and it is bewildering, for a young reader, to be laughed at for saying /ɔːrɪ/.)

5.17 Exploring relations between orthography and Information Structure

To explore relations between orthography and Information Structure, a text from Halliday (1985b: 88–9) was used in a brief experiment. Since this text was originally spoken, it is here referred to as the 'Spoken Text'. The published version is a 'derived text' (i.e. a transcription of the Spoken Text, which is a conversation between three speakers, giving the rhythm and intonation at primary delicacy). For example, the first turn appears in Halliday (1985b: 88) as follows. (Tonic syllables are indicated by bolding in the original, but this is changed here to underlining, for consistency in this chapter.)

A: //13 actually I / spent / most of last / <u>year</u> being / ill / one way and a / <u>noth</u>er //

5.17.1 The written form of the antivenene text

Converting the whole text into an orthographic one necessarily involved some intervention into the text, as readers could only be presented with ordinary orthography. Specifically, it meant removing all indications of rhythm and intonation such as forward slashes, tone numbers and bolding, and providing upper-case letters, commas, shrieks, question marks and full stops where needed, though punctuation was kept as light as possible, to minimize the intervention. Items such as B's incomplete tone group, 'Do tell us about ...', and C's false start, 'it's ...', before saying 'it attacks the respiratory system', and A's false start, 'it doesn't ...', before saying 'it's not poison in the bloodstream', were also discarded, as no intonation for them was provided in the source so there was no possibility of comparison with what a reader might do.

The resulting orthographic text was given to three readers to read aloud, with whatever preliminary preparation they wished, as though they were doing a script reading, prior to rehearsal for a play. And they were recorded. Here is the orthographic version they read.

A : Actually, I spent most of last year being ill, one way and another.
B : Do tell us about ...
A : I was bitten by a snake.
C : Ooh! What sort?
A : Well, I don't know, exactly. But it made a very deep hole in my foot ... and the antivenene made me very ill indeed. In fact I've heard since of somebody dying from antivenene, not from the snake's poison!
C : Well, it's the serum allergy, isn't it? It's usually a horse serum allergy.

A : Yes, that's right. It was a horse serum allergy.
C : Yes, I've got it too.
A : Don't be bitten by a snake then!
B : You've got it? How do you know you've got it?
C : As a result of contracting tetanus by being injected against tetanus.
A : You had tetanus!
C : Yes.
A : And what happened then?
C : Oh, I went rigid for thirty-six hours and then fortunately the effect passed off.
A : So that wasn't long enough to mean that you starved.
C : No, the danger isn't usually starvation: it's ...it attacks the respiratory system and when that happens you no longer breathe and therefore you die in a few minutes.
A : Like the effect of the bite of a mamba: you just have time to say 'Good bye!'
C : I haven't been bitten by a mamba recently!
A : No, but it does paralyse your breathing apparatus. It doesn't – it's not poison in the bloodstream in the same way as with many other snake bites. It just has a paralysing effect.
B : Where were you during those thirty-six hours, then, that you were rigid?
C : In bed!
A : At home?
B : In your own bed or in a hospital bed?
C : At home. It was a long time ago.
B : But presumably under supervision? Medical supervision?
C : Oh, yes! Supervision all the time. I fell out of a car and was therefore injected against tetanus and then a few months later I fell off my bike and ... sort of broke everything I could and they injected me again ...and you shouldn't have more than one injection every three years for tetanus. And so this, added to the fact that I was allergic to the serum – they used two different kinds of serum: the first time it was a different sort of serum which didn't hurt me – meant that I both contracted tetanus and also came out in various weals and things like that, all over my body, and lay rigid for a long time.
A : It must have been terrifying for the people around you!
C : Everybody else was given brandy, to sort of get them over it. But I didn't get any!
(Originally recorded by Afaf El-Menoufy, 1969)

The resultant recording was transcribed, and since the transcription was of a recording of a reading, it is here referred to as the 'Read Text'. ('Read' rhymes with 'Red'.) Then the information distribution of the two texts, Spoken and Read, was identified and compared.

5.17.2 Comparison of the Read Text with the Spoken Text

There were 87 complete tone groups in both the Spoken Text and the Read Text, and the Tonalities were almost entirely co-terminous but not exactly so: in 16 cases, a tone group in the Spoken Text was not exactly matched by a tone group in the Read Text, or a tone group in the Read Text was not exactly matched by a tone group in the Spoken Text, sometimes because there was more than one tone group in one text as against one in the other, but also sometimes because there were different Tonicities within each tone group. The differences were sometimes related to the punctuation provided, and sometimes not. But it was always the case that, whichever was the larger, both its boundaries matched the boundaries of one or other of the two tone groups in the other text. There were no overlapping tone groups, in either text. This meant that 80 boundaries in each text (93%) matched a boundary in the other text, and *vice versa*, leaving seven unmatched in each text.

There were arithmetical difficulties with those tone groups with either a compound tone or secondary tone <u>2</u>. In the case of the compound tones, which were all tone 13, the syllables on both tone 1 and tone 3 are bolded in the original of the Spoken Text, so both were underlined in the Read Text. Thus although the tone group has a double Tonic it is counted as a single tone group. But since it does have two Tonics, a major and a minor, it is realizing two New elements, major and minor, in the Information Structure. So it is convenient at this point to coin the term 'information group' which has no status in the theory but refers to either of the two parts of the information unit expressed on a compound tone, each part containing a major or minor Tonic. Information groups are shown separated by a double vertical bar, as though they were separate information units, but this is of no theoretical significance, being only an arithmetical convenience. It is helpful to count these separately, because in the Read Text sometimes only one is focal, sometimes neither, and sometimes both; and since there are nine tone groups with compound tones in the Spoken Text and five in the Read Text, this affects the arithmetic. It also happens that what has a compound tone in one may have two tone groups in the other, as in Spoken Text's //13∧ of / somebody / <u>dy</u>ing from anti / <u>ve</u>nene //, for which the Read Text has //1∧ of / somebody / <u>dy</u>ing from //1 anti /<u>ve</u>nene //. If these are both recognized as realizing two information groups each (i.e. || of / somebody /<u>dy</u>ing ||, and ||from / anti / <u>ve</u>nene ||), then the correspondence is clear.

```
//13 ∧ of / somebody / dying      from anti / venene //
||        <----------- New_Major  <---------New_Minor||

//1 ∧ of / somebody / dying       from //1 anti /venene //
||        <-----------New_(Major) ||  <------- New_(Major)||
```

We do not usually label single Tonics 'major' and it is only done here to point up the difference. The difference is very slight but it is there.

So taking all such patterns into account, there were 96 information groups in the 87 complete tone groups of the Spoken Text and 90 in the 87 complete tone groups of the Read Text.

In the case of secondary tone 2, in Halliday (1970: 17) a notation is used to indicate the second, rising, movement, when it begins on the salient syllable of a new foot, 'by a dot under the first letter of the foot on which the rise begins', so this may sound (and look) like an independent Tonic, even though it isn't one. But this notation is not used in the original of the Spoken Text (although both parts of the tone are underlined), so it is not used in the Read Text, and accordingly tone 2, whether in the Spoken Text or the Read Text, is only counted as one New.

The tone groups of the two texts were interpreted as Information Structures, numbered and displayed in parallel (as in Davies, 1970, and also in Davies, 1973, 1984, 1986, 1993). The tonality and tonic choices were then compared, and the information groups marked off but not additionally numbered.

Eighty information groups in both texts were exactly co-terminous with each other, and their Tonalities matched exactly the Tonalities of the corresponding words. So of the 96 information groups in the Spoken Text, 80 (83%) were exactly co-terminous with information groups in the Read Text; and of the 90 information groups in the Read Text, 80 (84%) were exactly co-terminous with information groups in the Spoken Text. Where there were mismatches, it was in most cases because the tone group was compound in the one but simple in the other. For example (with 'Con' standing for 'Conjunctive'):

$$\text{Lex} \qquad \text{Con}$$
$$\text{Spoken Text: } //13 \text{ /don't be /bitten by a /}\underline{\text{snake}} \text{ / }\underline{\text{then}} \qquad //$$
$$|| \leftarrow ------------------- \text{ New}_{\text{Major}} ||\text{New}_{\text{Minor}} ||$$
$$\textit{contr} \qquad \textit{contr}$$

$$\text{Lex} \qquad \text{Con}$$
$$\text{Read Text: } // 1 \text{ /don't be /bitten by a /}\underline{\text{snake}} \text{ / then } \quad //$$
$$|| \leftarrow ---------------- \text{ New} \qquad \text{Given } ||$$
$$\textit{contrastive}$$

and

$$\text{Ref} \qquad \text{Lex}$$
$$\text{Spoken Text: } //1\wedge \text{ the } \quad /\underline{\text{first}} \qquad \text{ time } //$$
$$|| \quad \text{Given } \quad \text{New } \leftarrow -- \text{Given } ||$$
$$\textit{contrastive}$$

```
                    Ref      Lex
Read Text: // 13 ∧ the      /first          /  time      //
           ||        Given   New_Major      ||  New_Minor ||
                             contrastive         contrastive
```

Neither of these was counted as exact matches in tonality, but in both cases they were counted as one (rather than two) matching New elements.

5.17.3 The Spoken Text and the Written Text

The boundaries in the Spoken Text owed something to the punctuation in the orthographic text. Unsurprisingly, in 100 per cent of cases an information group ended where there was a full stop, shriek, question mark, en rule or horizontal ellipsis (…) in the orthographic text. (There were two of the last in the original transcription and these were left in the orthographic text, and an information group ended at both points in the Read Text.) In 13 out of 17 cases, an information group ended where there was a comma, colon or semi-colon. The effects of commas, which have multiple functions in English punctuation, are briefly discussed below.

5.17.4 The first ten tone groups in the Spoken Text

The first two information groups of the original Spoken Text, with the corresponding three information groups of the Read Text, are shown below. The rhythm is not shown, information group boundaries are indicated by double vertical lines, and if there is no pair of lines at the beginning or end of a line, or in a large gap in the middle of a line, then there is no tone group or information group boundary at that point. Tonic segments are underlined, and the numbers of only the compound tones are given, not the simple ones, so if no tone is indicated, then the TONE choice is simple. The Spoken Text is shown first, with the cohesion above it. Below that is the orthographic text (labelled 'Written Text'), in italics, with the Read Text beneath it. Below that are the Information Structures of the Spoken and Read Texts. All the information units were compared, but we shall only display the first ten in the Spoken Text here. ('IGN' stands for 'information group number'.)

Cohesion: IGN   Conjunctive   IGN   Reference
Spoken Text: (1)   //   13   actually   I   spent most of last year
Written Text: *Actually*   ,   *I*   *spent most of last year*
Read Text: (1)   //   <u>actually</u>   //   (2)   //13   I   spent most of last <u>year</u>
Information Structure || Given -->   <------------ New[1]
of Spoken Text: contr.
Information Structure || New || || Given   <------------ New[1]
of Read Text: contrastive   contr

Cohesion: Lexical   IGN   Ref
Spoken Text: being ill   one way and <u>another</u>   //   (2)   // I   was bitten by a <u>snake</u>   //
Written Text: *being ill*   ,   *one way and another*   .   *I*   *was bitten by a snake*   .
Read Text: being ill   one way and <u>another</u>   //   (3)   // I   was bitten by a <u>snake</u>   //
Information Structure <-Given || <---------- New[2] || ||Given   <---------- New ||
of Spoken Text: *fresh*   *fresh*
Information Structure <-Given || <---------- New[2] || ||Given   <---------- New ||
of Read Text: *fresh*   *fresh*

First, the top line shows the cohesion, common both to the Spoken Text – which is shown next, immediately below it – and to the Read Text. The Spoken Text gave rise to the orthographic text, and influenced the punctuation supplied to it. The Written Text in turn gave rise to the Read Text, so that lies next, immediately below. Then below that come the two Information Structures, one above the other, to make it possible to see the relationships between them, and the relationships between either of them and the cohesion. So, column by column, item by item, it is possible to compare the Information Structures of the Spoken and Read Texts, and relate them to the cohesion which they have in common. The tone group boundaries are a linguistic fiction, in that they are displayed for the two voiced texts, not where they actually occurred but above the information group boundaries they realize, which, for rhythmical reasons, do not exactly match the tone group boundaries. This is done in order to distinguish between the tone groups in the transcription and the information groups in the analysis, and also to relate them to each other in the display. It does not seem possible or desirable, and makes no sense, to do otherwise.

In the first tone group in the Spoken Text, //13 actually I / spent / most of last / <u>year</u> being / ill / one way and a / <u>no</u>ther //, which is spoken on a compound tone, gives rise to two tone groups in the Read Text, //4 <u>ac</u>tually I // and // 13 spent / most of last / <u>year</u> being / ill / one way and a / <u>no</u>ther //. So the Spoken Text has two information groups, ||13 actually I spent most of last <u>year</u> being ill || and || one way and <u>a</u>nother ||, and the Read Text has three information groups, ||4 <u>ac</u>tually ||, ||1 I spent most of last <u>year</u> being ill ||, and ||3 one way and a <u>no</u>ther ||; and the second information group in the Spoken Text and the third in the Read Text match each other exactly. The fact that '*Actually,*' was awarded a comma in the orthographic text may have prompted the reader to take the comma as a signal to give the word its own marked tone group in the first tone group of the Read Text. It is contrastive, when in the Spoken Text it isn't, but it is also conjunctively cohesive, and so it follows the rule.

As the text is an excerpt from a longer conversation, we don't know what it is being contrasted with, but we do know that it is contrastive, not so much because it is an adversative conjunctive, as because of the way conjunctives are either maximally or minimally prominent; and here, being Tonic, it is maximally prominent. Halliday and Hasan point out that

> there is a general tendency in spoken English for conjunctive elements as a whole to be, phonologically, either Tonic (maximally prominent) or reduced (minimally prominent), rather than anything in between. This

can be explained, very simply, by reference to the function of intonation in English grammar. Cohesive elements relate the sentence to something that has gone before it; they are normally anaphoric – there is no new content in them. Now, anaphoric items in English are phonologically non-prominent … and this usually extends to their syllabic structure: in other words they are 'reduced'. But if the cohesive relation itself is to be brought into focus of attention, this is marked in the usual way by Tonic prominence. This takes the form of the Tonic either of tone 1 (falling), if the general sense is CUMULATIVE, or (perhaps more frequently) of tone 4 (falling-rising), if the general sense is CONTRASTIVE…. The fall-rise intonation pattern in English, tone 4, has in many contexts a sense of reservation, 'there's a *but* about it'. This is not necessarily a cohesive factor, since the nature of the reservation may not be made explicit. But in many instances the fall-rise intonation pattern provides a clear indication, and often the only indication, that the item on which it falls is to be interpreted as contrasting with a preceding item; and in such instances, the function of the tone is specifically cohesive.
(Halliday and Hasan, 1976: 271)

Here, the tone on 'actually' is tone 4, and the general sense is 'CONTRASTIVE', although it is not 'the only indication' of a reservation: the adversative sense of there 'being a *but* about it' is clear in it, *but* being probably the most common adversative conjunctive element there is. The probability is that the speaker's experience is being contrasted with a previous speaker's experience.

In the Spoken Text, 'actually' forms the first element in the Given, which is completed by the second element, the homophoric reference item 'I', the end of which matches the Given in the second information group in the Read Text. The New elements in both texts then match exactly, the Focus seemingly being non-final and therefore marked. If so, then 'year' must contrast with something in the preceding text, perhaps a shorter period of time being discussed in connection with a previous speaker's period of illness. But this is not entirely clear-cut, again because the text is an excerpt.

It is likely that 'being ill' is lexically cohesive with the preceding text in some way, and so is (post-Tonic and) Given in the first information group of the second tone group in the Read Text, and keeps to the rule, since it cannot be a pre-Tonic Given in the following minor Tonic, since minor Tonics never have a pre-Tonic (Halliday, 1970: 12). Halliday and Matthiessen (2004: 91) point out that 'it is possible to have Given material following the New; and any accented matter that follows the tonic foot is thereby signalled as being Given'. Here, this applies to 'being ill', indicating that if the excerpt were preceded by any discussion of illness, these words would be Given (and probably lexically reiterative).

The two last information groups of this set are identical, both being realized as the major Tonic in their respective compound tones. They set the pattern for the whole text: the utterances are identical, the Themes, with or without a conjunctive, are cohesive and Given, and the remainder of the clause is New and fresh. More than 80 per cent of the information groups are like this.

Here are the next two information groups.

Cohesion:	IGN			IGN		
Spoken Text:	(3)	// ooh //		(4)	// what sort	//
Written Text:		Ooh	!		What sort	?
Read Text:	(4)	// ooh //		(5)	// what sort	//
Information Structure of Spoken Text:		|| New || *fresh*			||<--- New *fresh*	||
Information Structure of Read Text:		|| New || *fresh*			||<--- New *fresh*	||

There are no differences between the two texts here, though there is a pseudo-question about the ellipted 'of snake' after 'sort'. Is it part of the New or isn't it? If so, the New must be contrastive, but it isn't. The point is that ellipted matter is so Given that it is not expressed (see section 5.11), so it is Given and not part of the New.

Here are the next two information groups, from both transcriptions (as before).

Cohesion:	IGN		C	R			IGN		
Spoken Text:	(5)	//	well	I	don't know	// (6) //		exactly	//
Written Text:			Well	, I	don't know	,		exactly	.
Read Text:	(6)	//13	well	I	don't know			exactly	//
Information Structure of Spoken Text:		||	Given --->	<---New[1] *fresh*	||		|| New[2] *fresh*	||
Information Structure of Read Text:		||	Given --->	<---New[1] *fresh*	||		|| New[2] *fresh*	||

So far as the tonality is concerned, the Spoken Text here uses two tone groups, as against the Read Text's one, but the latter uses a compound tone, so there are two information groups in both, and exactly the same items are Given (and cohesive) and New, respectively, in both. The tonicity is the standard pattern, and all cohesive items are Given, and New elements are non-cohesive and fresh. As has already been said, conjunctive elements such as the continuative 'well', are always Given, unless contrastive (Halliday and Hasan, 1976: 271).

```
        Cohesion: IGN    C  R                              IGN
     Spoken Text: (7) // but it made a very deep hole // (8) // in my foot //
     Written Text:        but it made a very deep hole         in my foot ...*
       Read Text: (7) // but it made a very deep hole         in my foot //
Information Structure     || Given <-------------- New ||     <--- New ||
   of Spoken Text:                               contr           fresh
Information Structure     || Given <------------------------------ New ||
     of Read Text:                                                 fresh
```

The Given-plus-cohesive pattern in these information groups follows the standard pattern, but the Tonalities differ: the Spoken Text using marked tonality and making 'hole' New and contrastive. The Read Text also makes it New, but not contrastive. The Spoken Text seems to have a slight flavour of indignation about it (perhaps the speaker thought snakes were supposed to poison you, not make holes in you) but there is no reason why a speaker should or should not use two quanta rather than one, here, and no reason why a reader should or should not do the same or different, and the reader recognizes it as New so it works.[6]

```
        Cohesion: IGN    C   Ref                     IGN    Lex  Ref
     Spoken Text: (9)     and the antivenene // (10) // made me very ill indeed //
     Written Text:        and the antivenene           made me very ill indeed .
       Read Text: (8) //  and the antivenene // (9) //  made me very ill indeed //
Information Structure     || Given -> <--- New ||    || Given -> <--- New    ||
   of Spoken Text:                        fresh                        fresh
Information Structure     || Given -> <--- New ||    || Given -> <--- New    ||
     of Read Text:                        fresh                        fresh
```

The Tonalities and Tonicities in the next and last pair of the first ten information groups of the Spoken Text, too, follow the standard pattern.

5.17.5 The arithmetic

In the 87 tone groups in the Spoken Text, 9 had compound tones, and so there are 96 information groups and 96 New elements. In the 87 tone groups of the Read text, there were three compound tones, so there are 90 information groups and 90 New elements. Of these, 80 of the 96 New elements in the Spoken Text, i.e. 83 per cent, were also New in the Read Text; and therefore the same number, (80), of the 90 New elements in the Read Text (i.e. 88%), had also been New in the Spoken Text.

What these figures amount to is that the Tonalities in both transcriptions are almost identical. This was no surprise because one feature common to the multiple readings reported in Davies (1970, 1973, 1984, 1986) was the high degree of agreement in tonality among different readers. This text is different from the others, in which all the readers in each experiment were reading the same text; here the speakers of the Spoken Text were not reading, and the speakers of the Read Text were all reading from the same script but each reader was reading their own part and not the parts of the other readers. So we cannot compare the different readers, and are not doing so. Thus, the finding is new, in a minor way, although not unexpected. However, it is not the case that the Tonalities were all mapped onto clauses and so all had unmarked tonality. What is the case is that both when the tonality is marked and when it is not, there is still a very high degree of agreement.

Work going on at the 'Survey of English Usage' at University College London, at the same time as Davies (1970) was being prepared there, had shown that in a corpus of 1880 tone groups of spoken English, the overall average length of a tone group was 5.3 words, 61 per cent being between 2 and 7 orthographic words, though 'the highest number of occurrences were between 4 and 7 words' (Quirk *et al.*, [1962] 1968). In the texts here, most frequently a tone group consisted of 4 orthographic words, the average being 4.74, although one information group (number 49) in the Spoken Text has 18 orthographic words and one information group (number 72) has 11; and it is striking that the first of these, (number 49) in the Spoken Text is given two tone groups of 6 and 12 words respectively, in the Read Text, and no other tone group in the Read Text has more than 12 words in it, whereas three in the Spoken Text have 13 words and four have 16. This was also the case in Davies (1970 and 1986), since many readers do like to keep their tone groups relatively short, especially in unstudied reading aloud, while speakers vary greatly and their tone groups can and do have as many as 20 words in them.

Although these figures are too small to have much significance, one factor which does not arise here is the relative sophistication or otherwise of the readers in relation to the subject matter of the text. In Davies (1986), it was found that a teacher and a schoolboy, reading an introductory paragraph from a mathematics textbook, which was about a topic new to the schoolboy, used tone groups of different lengths: the teacher, familiar with the material, unsurprisingly chunked the paragraph into considerably longer groups than the pupil. But the speakers in the results reported in this chapter seem to be of much the same relative sophistication in the matter of snake venom and antivenene serums, and no such variation seems to obtain.

5.17.6 Punctuation

It may be worth pointing out that L1 teachers in training find it a very useful exercise to be given transcribed spoken text to punctuate, which gives them valuable insight into the problems of meaning involved, and the difficult problems writers have to deal with in punctuating their writing. William Wordsworth found it so difficult that he gave up entirely, and asked Dorothy, his sister, to punctuate his writing, leaving modern editors major problems in finding out what he (and Dorothy!) mean. Halliday points out the relevant issue:

> It is noticeable that in modern English there are two fairly distinct tendencies in punctuation: some writers tend to punctuate according to the information structure, others more according to the sentence structure. The distinction is sometimes referred to as 'phonological' (or 'phonetic') versus 'grammatical' punctuation; but this is perhaps misleading since the two represent rather different aspects of the grammatical structure, the former being 'phonological' in the sense that, since information structure is realized directly in the phonological organization, it can be interpreted as a marking off of phonological units. (Halliday, 1967b: 220–21)

Wordsworth was caught between these two ways of punctuating, as we all are, and probably tried to lean towards the Information Structure. (He hated the education he endured at Cambridge, which probably followed the traditional pattern of punctuating according to the sentence structure.) Whether or not he did so, he consciously aimed at using 'language really used by men'[7] rather than any elevated style favoured by the Augustan poets in the preceding period of literary history. Wordsworth also favoured writing long sentences in a sequence of progressively dependent clauses, some ending with progressively dependent groups, which may or may not be embedded, the required absence of punctuation being the problem. (This is quoting from memory – accurately, I hope – of an illuminating lecture on Wordsworth given by Professor John Sinclair at Nottingham University in the 1960s. It has not, so far as I know, been published.) Wordsworth knew what he wanted, presumably, but even with the help of verse, wasn't always able to convey precisely the meanings he wanted on paper; and punctuation seemed to be no use to him, because it remains difficult to be sure what he meant.[8]

So that if we mean

//4∧ the au/<u>thor</u>ity to whom the //13 minister /<u>de</u>legated the /<u>iss</u>ue //4∧ in a /moment of /fair-/<u>mind</u>edness de//1 cided in /favour of the / private /<u>op</u>erators //,

meaning (among other things) that the authority was fair-minded, we write

The authority, to whom the minister delegated the issue, in a moment of fair-mindedness decided in favour of the private operators.

But if we mean

//4∧ the au/<u>thor</u>ity //13∧ to /whom the /minister /<u>de</u>legated the /<u>iss</u>ue in a //4 moment of /fair-/<u>mind</u>edness //1∧ de/cided in /favour of the / private /<u>op</u>erators //,

meaning (among other things) that it was the minister who was fair-minded, we write

The authority, to whom the minister delegated the issue in a moment of fair-mindedness, decided in favour of the private operators.

Similarly, if we mean

//1∧ he /said /<u>spare</u> them //2 not /<u>kill</u> them //,

we write

He said, 'Spare them!' not 'Kill them!'

And if we mean

//1∧ he /said /spare them /<u>not</u> //1 <u>kill</u> them //,

we write

He said, 'Spare them not. Kill them!'

It is not difficult to see how, in these cases, the punctuation clarifies the different meanings. And so when we write, part of our task is to devise punctuation which suggests the right information distribution that we want to mean.

However, we're not always aware, when we write, of the ambiguity we may create, and we may have difficulty in framing what we want to say in terms which offer no ambiguity. In the first linguistics lecture I attended, given by Margaret Berry, we were told that nearly everything we say or write is ambiguous, and I was somewhat sceptical, until driving home afterwards I passed two shops nearly next door to each other. One was labelled 'PORK BUTCHER' and the other 'FAMILY BUTCHER' and I was horrified to realize both were ambiguous, obviously disambiguated contextually but ambiguous nonetheless. And even when we are aware, we may not see how to disambiguate more extended texts. So we may not be able to disambiguate the wordings by punctuation. And nothing alerts L1 trainee teachers, or in-service teachers, better to the problems we all have in learning how to write than the exercise of punctuating transcripts of conversation. What matters generally is that we realize the problems we all face when writing, and which learners may be unable to articulate.

There is no once-and-for-all-time rule or set of rules for punctuation. There are only some very general principles, as Halliday (1967b: 200) implies in the words 'fairly distinct tendencies', and they do not always combine very well. Attempts to state the rules are generally inadequate, and only take us a little way into the problems, though this can be quite useful, as many teachers (and writers!) know, if not pressed too far. Anyone who has watched trainee teachers give practice lessons on punctuation, knows only too painfully how inadequate the rules generally stated are. In *Paradise Lost*, Milton writes of Satan, travelling from Hell through Chaos to come and subvert the Earth, that he found Chaos too insubstantial to row through, and too thin for his sails alone to drive him through (like the many rivers that are too thin to plough but too thick to drink). So, Milton says, 'behoves him now both oar and sail'. So it 'behoves' us, too, with our unavoidably inadequate graphology, to use both Information Structure and sentence structure to punctuate. (All graphologies are inadequate, but we cope. See Parkes (1992) for a history of numerous attempts in the last two thousand years, in both Latin and English, to improve the situation.) We sometimes fail, of course, and write unreadable sentences.[9] But we learn how to use the redundancy in the system well enough to create redundancy in our texts, and, mostly, we manage as well as or perhaps better than might be expected if we are aware of the difficulties. We may even 'fail again, fail better', as Samuel Beckett says (Beckett, 1938); that is, we may improve our punctuation and writing. Nevertheless, telling people 'how to punctuate' rarely works. This is the problem with Truss (2003), which is entertaining and enjoyable, but most of what it says has been said many times before, and frequently does not work, as pointed out by Roberts (1956: 15), who says, 'I have come to think that it is only the very good student, or at least the advanced student, who can profit much from having his papers copiously corrected and from being required to revise them', a view I came to myself, in the same L1 context, a few years later. What is certainly true is that there is a strong tendency, shown in these texts, for a punctuation mark of some kind to prompt a Tonic before it, usually immediately before it: 16 out of 19 such marks did so here, although in many cases another factor – such as the end of a group or a clause – was also influential. This being so, a student who is writing may well come to believe that something New should be followed by a punctuation mark. Very soon afterwards. If not immediately afterwards. So the teacher criticizes him. Or her. For writing sentence fragments.

Again, Shakespeare is helpful. The following is all about Tonality (and can also be given to students and teachers to re-punctuate).

> If we offend, it is with our good will.
> That you should think, we come not to offend,
> But with good will. To show our simple skill,
> That is the true beginning of our end.
> Consider then, we come but in despite.
> We do not come, as minding to content you,
> Our true intent is. All for your delight
> We are not here. That you should here repent you,
> The actors are at hand: and, by their show,
> You shall know all, that you are like to know.
> (*A Midsummer Night's Dream*, act 5, scene 1, 108–117)

5.17.7 Commas

The Read Text preserves the relationship between the Information Structure and the cohesion, taking account of the punctuation as best it can. In the Spoken Text, the opening conjunctive, 'actually', like all conjunctives (unless contrastive) is Given; in the orthographic text, it is followed by a comma, and this has prompted the closure of the information unit in the Read Text, making it Tonic, so the conjunctive is New but is contrastive, as discussed above. There are three other initial conjunctives or continuatives which also were followed by a comma in the orthographic text.

The continuative 'well', in sentence (5), is salient, cohesive and Given in both the Spoken Text and the Read Text. The second 'well', in sentence (14) in the Spoken Text, is //ʌ well it's the /<u>se</u>rum /allergy //. Here it is weak, but still Given and cohesive. The comma has not prompted the reader to make 'well' Tonic and close the information group immediately after it. But though it is not Tonic, it is salient, and the result in the Read Text is //13 well it's the /serum /allergy //, with 'well' and 'it' Given; so the relationship between the cohesion and information distribution has been correctly maintained.

In contrast, in the Spoken Text, //13 yes /that's /right //, it's not clear whether 'yes' is elliptical (meaning 'it *is* a serum allergy') or a continuative ('I take your point') or both (though my guess is it's the first); but either way it is cohesive. It gets a comma after it in the orthographic text, which appears to prompt the reader to make it Tonic and close the information unit immediately: //1 yes //2 that's /right//. 'Yes' is thus cohesive and Tonic, so the Tonic should be contrastive, and if so the contrast should be apparent. But there is nothing else in the tone group on which the Tonic can fall and there is no contrast, so informationally it is a puzzle. Perhaps the reader made a mistake or, more probably, the present writer made a mistake in mechanically putting a comma after 'yes' in the Written Text from force of habit. (But I would have found it impossible to write '*Yes that's right...*'.)

Finally, in the Spoken Text, // oh I /went /rigid//, begins with the continuative 'oh'. This is given a comma in the orthographic text, but it remains non-Tonic and therefore non-contrastive and Given, and the comma doesn't prompt the end of a tone group. (And again, as with all these four instances, I would have found it impossible to write without the comma.)

Thus, of the four commas after an initial conjunctive or continuative in the Spoken Text, two – (1) and (17) – prompt individual tone groups for the continuative or conjunctive, and two do not. This is a normal feature of the consequence of punctuation: the widespread myth that it indicates pauses, reflecting some kind of structural boundary, has a faint element of truth but it is very faint. The myth has its origins in descriptions of one kind of classical Latin texts.

> The culture of the ancient world was dominated by the ideal of the *vir eloquentissimus*. ... Texts were mostly read aloud. A reader might murmur the sounds of the words to himself, but the ideal was a kind of expressive declamation with well modulated pronunciation, in which the text was carefully phrased (*distincta*) by means of appropriate pauses. Ausonius, a fourth-century poet and grammarian, advised his grandson 'bring out the "measureless measures" [i.e. the measures of comedy] with practised accents, by modulation and subtlety of tone, and infuse

expression as you read: phrasing (*distinctio*) enhances meaning, and pauses give force to dull passages'. (Parkes, 1992: 9)

The idea that punctuation indicates pauses has persisted, and lies behind Dover Wilson's ground-breaking essay, 'A note on punctuation' in Quiller-Couch and Dover Wilson (1921: lvii–lx). It was 'ground-breaking' in the field of Shakespeare studies in 1921, and it led to extensive further study of Shakespeare's punctuation. Dover Wilson opens by making the same distinction as Halliday (in 1967b) quoted above, between what he calls 'dramatic' punctuation and what he calls 'syntax', meaning 'punctuating according to clause and sentence boundaries'. He writes,

> the punctuation is Shakespeare's. This punctuation is dramatic, that is to say it is a question of pause, emphasis and intonation. A comma indicates a short pause, a semicolon a longer one, a colon a longer one still, and a full stop—a *full* stop, which sometimes occurs in the middle of a sentence. Further, absence of punctuation, where a modern reader would expect to find it, implies rapid delivery. (Quiller-Couch and Dover Wilson, 1921: lvii)

Parkes writes (1992: 65):

> Ancient discussions of the process of reading (written at a time when the attitude towards a text was dominated by the ideal of the orator) indicate that, when a reader was declaiming or reading aloud, he was expected to introduce pauses at the ends of larger structures and certain shorter ones within the paragraph. According to the grammarians these pauses were assigned arbitrary time values, the main feature of which is that they were graded in relation to each other. Different time values would produce a minor medial pause when the sense is incomplete, a major medial pause when the sense is complete but the independent idea or *sententia* is not, and a final pause when the idea or *sententia* is complete.

An old method of teaching reading, deriving from this, requires pupils to count, aloud, up to four for a full stop, three for a colon, two for a semi-colon, and one for a comma. This allegedly still occurs (and is said to be robustly defended as a method by those who use it), so the teacher may hear, and wants to hear, 'the cat, one, sat on the mat, one, two, three, four'. (I heard this sort of thing happen in a village primary school in the 1930s, and I've met others in this millennium who have known of it happening today.)

All we can say of this smidgeon of data is that the effect of the comma is variable (an observation which is hardly new, or New), and that this variation extends to the relationship between the cohesion and the distribution of the information. But it does seem to be the case that writing a comma after an initial continuative or other conjunctive, like 'well' or 'oh' in the antivenene text, can be a graphological habit more than anything else, reminding readers of the option of making it weak, as we might if there is no comma, or salient (with optional Tonic) if there is a comma. A reader also has the option of making it Tonic and contrastive, sometimes sounding a bit heavy in the process, but in general there is no inevitability about doing so.

5.18 Realization for written and spoken text

In the next four diagrams of realizations (and only in these) we will in part follow the convention in Halliday and Hasan (1976) that when representations of meanings are put into words on the page, they are put 'between single inverted commas' to distinguish them from the normal orthographic words in the rest of the text. Additionally, when we represent the forms in which those meanings are realized in the wording (i.e. in the forms of the words), then we represent them on the page in SMALL CAPITALS. Then finally, for written text, we represent the letterings of words on the page "between double inverted commas". So the convention is that 'meanings' are realized as FORMS and FORMS are realized as phonic or graphic substance, in the first case graphic substance; so 'read' ➘ READ ➘ "read" means that the meaning 'read', is realized in the form READ, which is re-realized in the spelling "read", whether it's present or past tense. And in parallel fashion, in phonic substance, 'read₁' ➘ READ ➘ /riːd/ ➘ [riːd] means that the meanings 'read' + 'present', are realized in the form READ, which is re-realized phonologically as /riːd/ which is re-realized phonetically as [riːd]. Then in this way the processes of realization in written text and spoken text may be summarized diagrammatically.

5.18.1 Realizing written text

For written text, meanings (including cohesion and Information Structure, as well as tense), are realized in form and then re-realized as graphic substance.

	'meaning of *read* (including tense)'	FORM	graphic substance
Have you read this?	'read$_1$'	↘ READ ↘	"read"
No, I'll read it tonight.	'read$_2$'	↘ READ ↘	"read"

The two words printed as 'read', whose two different meanings are realized by the same graphic substance, are given subscripts, to distinguish between the two meanings and to draw attention to the fact that the same graphic substance realizes two different meanings. This is obvious enough, but it needs to be made explicit in discussing realization as it shows another way in which substance is ambiguous and 'noisy', and is a problem for some learners.

5.18.2 Realizing spoken text

For spoken text, meanings (including cohesion and Information Structure, as well as tense) are realized in form, as in written text, and then re-realized in phonic substance, in the usual two stages, phonological and phonetic, though in the present context we need to remember, *en passant*, that Information Structure is the one kind of meaning which is not realized in form but directly in phonology. Phonological and phonetic representations are between forward slashes and square brackets in the usual way.

	'meaning (including tense)'	form	phonic substance (1) phonology	(2) phonetics
Have you read this?	'read$_1$'	↘ read ↘	/red/	[red], [rɛd], ...
No, I'll read it tonight.	'read$_2$'	↘ read ↘	/riːd/	[riːd], [rəɪd], ...

Phonetic variants here are taken from Wells (1982: 129, 140).

Although the distinction between phonology and phonetics is not always made, it is essential to make it here, to understand the processes of realization as that is understood here. The phonetic representations are token ones only, as accent variation is the norm, and any attempt at completeness would involve listing several hundred, at least. For example, McIntosh (1961) suggests that a full survey of the dialects of Edinburgh, with a population now somewhat more than 500,000, would need to recognize between 200 and 300 accents. The Leeds Dialect Survey lists the pronunciations of more than 300 areas of England, and some in Wales and some in the Isle of Man, including 26 pronunciations for the word 'cow', only ever written in one spelling since the seventeenth century, reflecting the direct relation between graphology and phonology (not phonetics, because pronunciations have continued to vary) which makes a standard spelling possible. There is only one phonological representation of all these – /kaʊ/ – but there are 26 phonetic representations in the Survey list:

1. [kɛa], 2. [kɛʊ], 3. [kjɛʊ], 4. [kɛuː], 5. [kɛə], 6. [kœɣ], 7. [kœː],
8. [kœ.a], 9. [kœɣ], 10. [kœʊ], 11. [kˈœʊ], 12. [kjœʊ], 13. [kœ.ə],
14. [kaː], 15. [kaʊ], 16. [kauː], 17. [kɑʊ], 18. [kɒʊ], 19. [kɔʊ],
20. [kʌuː], 21. [kᵒuː], 22. [kᵛuː], 23. [kuː], 24. [kjuː], 25. [kəʊ], 26.
[kəuː].

More are listed in *The Linguistic Atlas of Scotland* (Mather and Speitel, 1975, 1977, 1986).

Within RP, too, there is wide variation, and not only between 'advanced' (younger) speakers and 'conservative' (older) speakers (see Upton *et al.*, 1994; Wells, 1982).

L1 teachers take such phonetic variation in their stride, and not only because we have to. There is no way in which we can enforce a phonetic uniformity, even if it were desirable. We settle for the practicable, and get on with it, only quibbling over word accent or vowel quality if, to our ears, they lead to ambiguity. This is unavoidably but usefully reductive. Over time, a large measure of uniformity develops in a school community as pupils pass through the school (only to diversify again, often, when they go off into the rest of the world).

5.18.3 Realizing written text asoft

In reading written text silently to oneself, the direction of realization is reversed. Graphic substance has to be realized as form, and form re-realized as meaning, if we are to read for meaning, as we all do. For example:

	graphic substance	FORM	'meaning (including tense)'
Have you read this?	"read"	↘ READ ↘	'read$_1$'
No, I'll read it tonight.	"read"	↘ READ ↘	'read$_2$'

The two different meanings of the two words printed identically in graphic substance as "read" are given subscripts here, i.e. 'read$_1$' and 'read$_2$', to identify the two different meanings, and to draw attention to the fact that the same graphic substance realizes two different meanings. This is obvious enough, but it needs to be made explicit in discussing realization as it shows another way in which substance is ambiguous and 'noisy', and can be a problem for learners

5.18.4 Realizing written text aloud

This involves realizing written text asoft and then re-realizing the meaning aloud. That is, when we come to realizing written text aloud, we have the most complex realization process of all, maintaining the reversed realization process in reading the text asoft, and then reversing it back to the first direction, as in ordinary speaking. For example:

	graphic substance	FORM	'meaning'	FORM	phonic substance		
						(1) phonology	(2) phonetics
Have you read this?	"read"	⬊ READ ⬊	'read$_1$'	⬊ READ ⬊	/red/	⬊	[red], [rɛd],
No, I'll read it tonight.	"read"	⬊ READ ⬊	'read$_2$'	⬊ READ ⬊	/riːd/	⬊	[riːd], [rəɪd],

Thus learners have to develop the ability to get meaning from graphic substance before they can realize it as phonic substance, although, for practical reasons, teachers cannot do other than talk to learners about the 'sounds' of letters, sounds which in actual fact letters do not have. Of course, we say 'but they know what we mean', which may be true although it may not, and certainly isn't always, as teachers often recognize. But whatever we say, what learners actually have to do is both to find out 'what we mean' and to develop the ability to cope with written text in the same way as they have to cope with spoken text. They have to be able to realize what a written text means, in both senses of 'realize' and in both realizational directions, that is, whether 'read' in any given instance realizes 'read$_1$' or 'read$_2$', in order to realize it as /red/ or /riːd/ in spoken text. Of course, we cannot talk to learners about these matters in these terms, and do not need to, but it is useful to conceptualize them in this way in order to appreciate the complexity, and the magnitude, of their task, if only to realize what they, like us, have to realize, both in reading asoft and in reading aloud. L1 teachers, at least, need to hear the learner's realization in phonic substance in order to judge whether the learner has realized – in both senses and in both realizational directions – the meaning of the graphic substance.

For these reasons, although in the classroom we may have to say letters 'mean' sounds, outside the classroom it is more realistic to say that a written text does not 'mean' a set of sounds; it means a set of meanings, ideational, interpersonal and textual, and only if a reader can use the system to realize those meanings asoft can they re-realize them aloud and make the meaningful sounds. The creators of the Read Text used

the language system to do exactly this, including the textual meanings –
cohesion and Information Structure. And they did so in almost exactly
the same way as the original speakers had done it.

5.19 Conclusion

Throughout the Read Text, readers unfailingly used Tonalities and
Tonicities consistent with the cohesion, and used rhythm, and Information
Distribution and Focus almost identical with those of the Spoken Text.
So it seems that there is nothing to be gained by grinding through the
remaining 70 Tone groups here. Instead, it is perhaps of interest to
quote Crystal (1975: 297) where he gives a set of rules for assigning
prosodic features to a plain transcription of spoken English, supplied
without prosodic notation. He writes: 'Out of the 12,000 tone units
examined, about 100 were incapable of prediction from the above rules.'
In a footnote, he adds:

> To avoid the charge that the transcription was biased by an awareness
> of the grammatical constraints outlined in this chapter, I should make it
> clear that the prosodic transcription of the data used here was carried
> out between 1963 and 1970, the transcription being checked by at least
> two analysts, the sole criterion they were given to work with being
> auditory agreement as to the prosodic variables involved (see Crystal,
> 1969: Ch. 1). The above analysis was prepared for a conference in 1973.
> It is of course possible that we were all of us being unconsciously
> influenced in our transcription by some innate knowledge of the rules!
> (Crystal, 1975: 297 n10)

The last sentence is the present concern. Not that I could presume to
agree that the scholars concerned were being unconsciously influenced
in any way at all by anything at all, but that it seems to be the case that
those of us who can read aloud must 'know' the rules in order to be able
to do so. So in Davies (1970 *et seq.*), what people do when they read
aloud has been investigated, and the present study concludes the series.
No claims are made about the psychology involved because realization
doesn't happen in real time. It is a concept used in modelling what
happens in language, not of what happens in real time in our heads.
But the modelling does seem to lead to insights into what we seem to
do as we read silently in order to read aloud, and it does seem to be
the case that we 'know' the rule that enables us to detect the rhythm of

the words on the page, and that we 'know' the rule that maps cohesion on to what is Given or contrastively New, and that we apply these rules when reading, cohesive redundancy overcoming noise in the 'black hole', whether we read aloud or not.

Notes

1. Personal communication.
2. I am very grateful to Mrs Mary Paterson, head teacher of St Mary's Primary School, Dunblane, and her colleagues, for allowing me for several years to take small groups of children, some with reading difficulties, to listen to them read, and to observe and try to help them. I am very grateful, too, to Derek Davy, who supervised me for Davies (1970), and indeed made it possible for me to complete it, and has provided me with much critical support over the years since then. I am also very grateful to Caroline Walmsley, Stuart Lucas and Paul Sludden, for encouraging me to continue. Last and most certainly not least, I am very grateful to Michael Halliday, whose insights inform every page of this essay, for encouraging me to study this text in this way. None of these are in any way responsible for what I have committed, but I am very grateful to them all.
3. This is an exercise which I developed for use with the groups of children mentioned in note 2 above. Reference items such as the definite article in an appropriate story from a reading book were replaced by short lines of a standard length, making it look like a Cloze Test. At eight years of age, they were always able to supply the definite article, and could usually supply conjunctives. They were encouraged to count their successes and score 100 per cent which they nearly always did. Their success encouraged them and increased their motivation markedly. And also, on one occasion, a child was able to correct the focus of a sentence because there was final lexical reiteration and she had mis-read it with unmarked tonicity. When she was asked if she knew why she had to say it differently (i.e. with the necessary marked tonicity), she was able to say, correctly, 'Because of the repetition'.
4. I am grateful to the late Mr Guy Randle, Fellow of the Royal College of Obstetricians and Gynaecologists of London, whose field of research was foetal intra-uterine perception, for describing some of his experiments to me, and confirming *viva voce* that this is both possible and probable, although the meaning of 'picking up' in Halliday's observation remains unclear. But it happens.
5. I am grateful to Professor Prabukhar Babu, of the Central Institute for English and Foreign Languages, Hyderabad (Deccan), for this example.
6. Asterisked graphological items differ from all others in the orthographic text in that they were reproduced in the orthographic text as and when they

occurred in the original transcription in Halliday (1985b), partly in order to remain faithful to the source but mostly because they had effects on the Read Text (see §5.17.3 'The Spoken Text and the Written Text').

7. From Wordsworth's 'Preface to Lyrical Ballads, 1802' in *Lyrical Ballads with Other Poems, Vol. 2* (see www.gutenberg.org or www.english.upenn. edu/~mgamer/Etexts/lbprose.html#preface).

8. I am grateful to Dr Frances Austin for this information. She experienced the difficulty in writing Austin (1989).

9. Such informationally confused sentences in sixth-formers' essays prompted the present research.

References

Austin, F. (1989) *The Language of Wordsworth and Coleridge.* New York: St Martin's Press.

Beckett, S. (1938) *Murphy.* New York: Grove Press.

Crystal, D. (1969) *Prosodic Systems and Intonation in English.* Cambridge: Cambridge University Press.

Crystal, D. (1975) *The English Tone of Voice: Essays in Intonation, Prosody and Paralanguage.* London: Arnold.

Davies, M. (1970) A comparison of prosodic features used by subjects when reading aloud a printed passage. Unpublished MA dissertation. London: University College.

Davies, M. (1973) A comparison of two readings of a paragraph of a mathematics textbook. In A. G. Howson (ed.) *Proceedings of the Second International Congress on Mathematical Education.* Cambridge: Cambridge University Press.

Davies, M. (1984) A comparison of the intonations of seven readings of free verse. Presentation, 11th International Systemic Workshop, Stirling.

Davies, M. (1986) Literacy and intonation. In B. Couture (ed.) *Functional Approaches to Writing: Research Perspectives* 199–220. London: Pinter.

Davies, M. (1989) Prosodic and non-prosodic cohesion in speech and writing. *WORD* 40(1–2; special issue: papers from the 15th International Systemic Congress): 255–62.

Davies, M. (1992) Prosodic cohesion in a systemic perspective: Philip Larkin reading Toads Revisited. In P. Tench (ed.) *Studies in Systemic Phonology* 206-30. London: Pinter.

Davies, M. (1993) Theme, Tonality and lineation in Shakespeare's 'Sonnets'. Paper given at the Second European Society for the Study of English Conference, Bordeaux, 4–8 September.

Davies, M. (1994a) Intonation IS visible in written English. In S. Cmejrková, F. Daneš and E. Havlová (eds) *Writing vs Speaking: Language, Text, Discourse, Communication. Proceedings of Conference Held at the Czech Language Institute of the Academy of Sciences of the Czech Republic* 199–204. Tübingen: Gunter Narr Verlag.

Davies, M. (1994b) 'I'm sorry, I'll read that again': information structure in writing. In S. Čmejrková and F. Štícha (eds) *The Syntax of Sentence and Text, A Festschrift for František Daneš* 75–89. Amsterdam: John Benjamins.

Davies, M. (1998) Cohesion in Three Poems. In A. D. Rothwell, A. J. M. Guijarro and J. I. A. Hernández (eds) *Patterns in Discourse and Text: Essayos De Análisis Del Discurso En Lengua Inglesa* 177–204. Cuenca: Ediciones de la Universidad de Castilla-La Mancha.

Davies, M. (1999) Unfolding text. *Seminários de Linguistica 3*. Faro: Universidade do Algarve, Unidade de Ciências Exactas e Humanas.

Davies, M. (2002) Theme, information and cohesion. In J. Hladký (ed.) *Language and Function: To the Memory of Jan Firbas* 89–110. Amsterdam: John Benjamins.

El-Menoufy, A. (1969) A study of intonation in the grammar of English. Vol 1: Theory and description. Vol 2: Texts. Unpublished PhD thesis, London University.

Gimson, A. C. (1962a) The Transmission of Language (Supplement). In R. Quirk *The Use of English* 257–311. London: Longmans.

Gimson, A. C. (1962b) *An Introduction to the Pronunciation of English*. London: Edward Arnold.

Halliday, M. A. K. (1967a) *Intonation and Grammar in British English*. The Hague: Mouton.

Halliday, M. A. K. (1967b) Notes on transitivity and theme, part 2. *Journal of Linguistics* 3(2): 199–244.

Halliday, M. A. K. (1970) *A Course in Spoken English: Intonation*. Oxford: Oxford University Press.

Halliday, M. A. K. (1980) Three aspects of children's language development: learning language, learning through language, learning about language. In Y. M. Goodman, M. M. Hausler and D. A. Strickland (eds) *Oral and Written Language Development: Impact on Schools, Proceedings from the 1979 and 1980 IMPACT conferences* 7–19. Urbana, IL: International Reading Association and National Council of Teachers of English.

Halliday, M. A. K. (1985a) *An Introduction to Functional Grammar*. London: Arnold.

Halliday, M. A. K. (1985b) *Spoken and Written Language*. Geelong, Vic: Deakin University Press.

Halliday, M. A. K. (1992) How do you mean? In M. Davies and L. Ravelli (eds) *Advances in Systemic Linguistics: Recent Theory and Practice* 20–35. London: Pinter.

Halliday, M. A. K. (1994) *An Introduction to Functional Grammar* (2nd edition). London: Arnold.

Halliday, M. A. K. and Greaves, W. S. (2008) *Intonation in the Grammar of English*. London: Equinox.

Halliday, M. A. K. and Hasan, R. (1976) *Cohesion in English*. London: Longman.

Halliday, M. A. K., McIntosh, A. and Strevens, P. (1964) *The Linguistic Sciences and Language Teaching*. London: Longman.

Halliday, M. A. K and Matthiessen, C. M. I. M. (2004) *An Introduction to Functional Grammar* (3rd edition). London: Arnold.

Halliday, M. A. K. and Matthiessen, C. M. I. M. (2014) *Halliday's Introduction to Functional Grammar* (4th edition). London: Routledge.

Mather, J. Y. and Speitel, H. H. (1975, 1977, 1986) *The Linguistic Atlas of Scotland* (3 volumes). London: Croom Helm.

McIntosh, A. (1961) *An Introduction to a Survey of Scottish Dialects*. Edinburgh: Thomas Nelson.

Parkes, M. B. (1992) *Pause and Effect: An Introduction to the History of Punctuation in the West*. Aldershot: Scolar Press.

Quiller-Couch, A and Wilson, J. D. (eds) (1921) *William Shakespeare: The Tempest*. Cambridge: University Press.

Quirk, R. (1962) *The Use of English*. London: Longmans.

Quirk, R., Duckworth, A. P., Svartvik, J., Rusiecki, J. P. L. and Colin, A. J. T. ([1962] 1968) Studies in the correspondence of prosodic to grammatical features in English. In R. Quirk (ed.) (1968) *Essays on the English Language* 120–35. London: Longman.

Roberts, P. (1956) *Teacher's Guide to Patterns of English*. New York: Harcourt, Brace & World.

Shannon, C. E. (1948) A mathematical theory of communication. *The Bell System Technical Journal* 27: 379–423, 623–56.

Stoppard, T. (1993) *Arcadia*. London: Faber & Faber.

Truss, L. (2003) *Eats, Shoots and Leaves*. London: Profile Books.

Upton, C. S., Parry, D. and Widdowson, J. D. A. (1994) *Survey of English Dialects: the Dictionary and Grammar*. London: Routledge.

Wells, J. C. (1982) *Accents of English, Volumes 1, 2, 3*. Cambridge: Cambridge University Press.

6

The spoken interpretation of written text

Michael Cummings[a]

6.1 Introduction

Systemic functional analysis of suprasegmental phonology for English links it to various aspects of clause grammar, particularly the Given/New distinction within information structure.[1] Description of this phonology and its relationship to grammar can be found in Halliday's 1967–8 articles in *Word*, in his *Intonation and Grammar in British English* (1967), in his *A Course in Spoken English: Intonation* (1970), in Halliday and Matthiessen's *Halliday's Introduction to Functional Grammar* (2014) and in Halliday and Greaves's *Intonation in the Grammar of English* (2008). The description in these treatments takes as its basis spontaneous spoken English; and the linkage with the grammar of Given and New elements within the information structure of clauses is based on the realization of the focus of New information within the clause element which includes the tonic syllable. This chapter, however, takes its departure from written English, specifically, texts of written English prose designed to be read as written English which are nevertheless being recited aloud. It poses the problem, how does a reciter of such a written English prose text decide, just on the basis of the text, how to distribute and realize the focus or foci of information in each clause? Instead of moving from phonology as phenomenon to the lexicogrammar of the clause, we are trying to move

---

a **Michael Cummings** teaches as Professor Emeritus at York University, Toronto. He has taught graduate or undergraduate courses in systemic functional grammar, discourse analysis, stylistics, the history of English, and Old English. He is co-author or co-editor of *The Language of Literature: A Stylistic Introduction to the Study of Literature* (Oxford: Pergamon Press, 1983), *Linguistics in a Systemic Perspective* (Amsterdam: John Benjamins, 1988) and *Relations and Functions Within and Around Language* (London and New York: Continuum, 2002). His most recent book is *An Introduction to the Grammar of Old English: A Systemic Functional Approach* (London: Equinox, 2010). He has also published a number of articles and book chapters on the systemic functional description of both modern and historical dialects of English and of French.

in the opposite direction, from the lexicogrammar of the written clause to a hypothetical realization of intonation that is appropriate to its text.

6.2 Hallidayan principles of information focus

I now want to summarize Halliday's theory of information focus in English. The clause as a unit of grammar has a special relationship to intonational phonology. The clause is realized with an intonation curve, an extended pitch variation or melody, which culminates in a distinctive rise or fall. Normally the grammatical boundaries of the clause and the beginning and distinctive ending of the intonation curve correspond. However, there may be more than one intonation curve per clause, or more than one clause per intonation curve, hence marked rather than unmarked tonality. The clause also has a rhythmic aspect, since it is realized by a succession of stressed and unstressed syllables. The unit which combines the melody and the rhythm is called the tone group. This unit is divided into feet, each foot having an initial salience, meaning strong stress (sometimes silent) and possibly one or more unstressed syllables. The syllable carrying the distinctive rise or fall in pitch which most distinguishes one melody from another is called the tonic syllable, always salient, and its foot is called the tonic foot. Thus we may say that in the unmarked situation, the clause is mapped together with its single tone group consisting of a series of rhythmic feet culminating in the tonic foot carrying the distinctive rise or fall tone. In Example 1 below, the boundaries of the tone group have double slants (//), those of the foot have single slants (/), the tonic syllable is bolded and the silent stress or ictus is represented with a 'ʌ'. The subscript number which begins the tone group represents the type of tone on the tonic syllable (Halliday, [1967] 2005: 57–8; Halliday and Greaves, 2008: 53–60, 98–101, 108; Halliday and Matthiessen, 2014: 11–17).

(1)   // $_1$ That / $_\wedge$ could be / just the / **an** swer. //

When the tonic syllable belongs to the final lexical item in the clause, or occurs as the stressed syllable in a non-lexical final item which is normally stressed, the clause is said to have unmarked tonicity. This is the case in Example 1. In the case of marked tonicity, the tonic syllable may belong to some normally unstressed form word which ends the clause; or it may belong to some item, lexical or not, which is not the final stressed item. The tones on the tonic syllable may belong to any one of five different categories. These may be briefly described as (1) fall, (2) rise, (3) low rise, (4) fall–rise and (5) rise–fall. Compound tones are also possible (Halliday, [1967] 2005: 66–7; Halliday and Greaves, 2008: 44–6, 101–108).

Within the perspective afforded by the textual metafunction (Halliday and Matthiessen, 2014: 30–31), the clause can be seen as divided between a Theme stretch and a Rheme stretch, and again as divided between Given information and New information. The Theme stretch conveys 'the point of departure of the message' (*ibid.*: 89), and is usually only one or more initial elements; the Rheme is the remainder. Given information is the content projected by the speaker as being recoverable by the hearer from the discourse. New information accordingly is what the speaker purports to add to the flow of information.

Looking at the clause as a grammatical unit in terms of its information structure is to see it as an information unit. The tone group and the information unit always coincide; thus in marked tonality, there may be more than one tone group/information unit per clause, or more than one clause in the tone group/information unit. The Given/New distinction then belongs to the information unit, by default mapped together with a ranking clause, in unmarked tonality.[2]

The stretch of New information ends with the focus of information (i.e. the culmination of New information, the newest information). This is realized as the clause element which carries the tonic syllable of the tone group. Just where the stretch of New information begins is more difficult to determine. A whole clause may be New information, hence Given is optional. When it does occur, its status as Given may be determined only from context, particularly its cohesive relation with prior elements in the discourse (Halliday, [1967] 2005: 57–70; Halliday and Greaves, 2008: 101–8; Halliday and Matthiessen, 2014: 114–121; Martin, 1992: 450–51). In Example 2, the tone group boundaries indicate that the clause has marked tonality, tonic syllables are again bolded, and the Given information stretch is underlined.

(2) // ₄After / five or / six / **days** of it, // ₁ ∧ <u>we</u> / finally / got a / **res** pite. //

The terms 'unmarked tonicity' and 'marked tonicity' were introduced above in relation to the clause. Tonicity more properly is a characteristic of the tone group/information unit, so that a clause mapped together with more than one tone group/information unit could show a marked tonicity in one and unmarked tonicity in the other, or even marked tonicity in both.

The clause in Example 3 thus has two tone groups/information units of which one shows marked tonicity.

(3)   // ₁ ∧ <u>He</u> a / **ddressed** this // ₄ only to the / **youn** gest of <u>the / three /</u> <u>children</u>. //

6.3   Applying the principles of information focus backwards

In this description of information focus, information structure is realized by and partly identified from intonation. That is, we begin with the spoken aspect of spoken text. The description, however, contains a principle of indeterminacy: the beginning of the stretch of new information in the clause is indeterminate with respect to phonology, and the auditor of an information unit must turn to the cohesive relationship between elements of the clause and the context to interpret the information structure fully. However, the description makes the intonational information its point of departure, and only turns to the grammar of cohesion when it must.

To explain the recitation of the written text, however, it is necessary to turn all this around and move in the opposite direction. We begin from a text which has no spoken aspect, and map onto it an appropriate phonology. Crucially, we want to take the cohesive aspects of the text as a guide to givenness of information in clause grammar, and move from there to the identification of the focus of information, and its appropriate realization in intonation. Example 4 is the beginning of a sentence from the opening paragraph of John Bunyan's *Pilgrim's Progress*.

(4)   // ₁ ∧ <u>I</u> / **looked,** // ₁ ∧ <u>and / saw him</u> / **o** pen <u>the / book,</u> // ₁ ∧ and / **read** <u>therein;</u> //

The first-person narrator is relating a dream in which he sees a man with 'a book in his hand, and a great burden upon his back'. The narrative continues with three ranking clauses: 'I looked, and saw him open the book, and read therein' (Bunyan, 1957: 9). What seems a reasonable recitation of the text is analysed in Example 4 in the standard notation. In the analysis, the three clauses are mapped together with three tone groups/ information units. The argument for the recitation and its analysis is based on the perception that the only elements in these clauses which are not significantly cohesive are the Predicators 'looked', 'open' and 'read', which are then perceived as focus of information in their respective information units. In effect, the analysis predicts how the text should reasonably be read. (The argument of course has no bearing on the choices of tone 1 from the system of tone; the motive for the choice here is just to register the sense of solemnity in the text.) A further articulation of the principles for such an analysis will now be developed.

6.4 Previous treatments

In previous approaches to this problem, I have based the intonational interpretation of clauses on their grammatical and lexical cohesion identified from a computerized analysis of the whole text. The algorithm organizes the lexis of the text, including the lexical references of proforms, into a graph. Then it measures relative distances through the graph between some lexical item or equivalent proform in the text and its preceding lexis, to derive a value for its relative degree of lexical cohesion (Cummings, 1995, 1996, 1999, 2000a, 2000b, 2001). This method, although providing an objective and principled means of identifying significant cohesion, has limits. In the present study I am using a more intuitive method, based on the identification of anaphoric reference, including reminding, relevance and redundancy reference as defined by Jim Martin in *English Text* (1992: 98–153). For a related approach, see Davies (1986, 1994).

6.5 The 'classical' text

The principles of analysis will be developed and applied in reference to the following text, a segment of an exposition about the history of music from the *Encyclopaedia Britannica* (Britannica, 1977: 710). Up to this point the article has covered Antiquity, the Middle Ages, the Renaissance and the Baroque as distinct periods. As the headline indicates, the segment selected now begins the treatment of the classical period, but refers explicitly or implicitly to earlier parts of the article. These first two paragraphs are apparently intended to be an introduction to a series of subunits, each with its own headline subordinate to 'The Classical Period'. (The following analysis is an extension of the discussions of this text in Cummings, 2000a: 343–52 and 2000b: 344–51, and is in some instances a re-evaluation of their results.)

The Classical Period

As in the case of the Renaissance, difficulties with terminology again arise with the label classical. Does it refer to a period of time, a distinctive musical style, an aesthetic attitude, an ideal standard, or an established norm? Again, the term was borrowed from the visual arts of the same epoch and is awkward when applied to music in that there were no known models from classical antiquity for composers to imitate. A full understanding of the term depends on a clear conception of the term romantic, for the two stand at opposite poles. Each represents a set of artistic ideals that has been in opposition to the other since both were recognized by early Grecian writers. As has been noted, the ancient Greek followers of Apollo established the ideal of classicism, whereas the cult of Dionysus produced the prototype of romanticism. A mixture of the two qualities has prevailed throughout recorded history, with first one and then the other in the ascendancy. Thus, there have been many 'classic' and many 'romantic' eras, but the labels have come to refer most specifically to the last half of the 18th century and the 19th century, respectively, because those periods represent most vividly the two tempers.

The social and political scene during the late 18th century was hardly a setting for a quiet, composed 'classical' age in view of the prevailing revolutionary spirit and colonial rivalry. The revolutionary movement did have a direct effect on music in that 'music for the masses' became a new ideal – music directly appealing to a large number of unsophisticated people who had previously been excluded from courtly entertainments.

This text segment is analysed below in numbered lines, each of which represents the interpretation of a separate tone group/information unit. Wording that represents the basis of givenness of information – anaphoric reference, lexical identity[3] and superordination[4] – is bolded. This method limits reminding anaphora reference to the direct presumption type, thus excluding the bridging type (Martin, 1992: 123–5). The bridging type is excluded from consideration as too weak to imply givenness. To avoid confusion, instances of bridging anaphora here and in a later diagram are shaded.

1. The / $_1$ Classical / **Period**
2. As in the case of the / $_3$ Renaissance /,
3. difficulties with terminology | again arise with the label / $_1$ **classical**/.
4. <u>Does **it**</u> | refer to a **period** of time, a distinctive **musical** style, an aesthetic attitude, an ideal standard, or an established / $_1$ norm /?
5. <u>Again, **the term**</u> | was borrowed from the / $_4$ visual / **arts of the same epoch**
6. and | is awkward when | ap / $_1$ plied <u>to / **music**</u>

7.   in that there | were no known models from **classical** antiquity for composers to / $_1$ imitate /.
8.   A full under / $_1$ standing of the / term |
9.   depends on a clear conception of the **term** ro / $_1$ mantic /,
10. for the two | stand at opposite / $_1$ poles /.
11. Each | represents a set of artistic ideals that has been in oppo / $_1$ sition to the / other
12. since both | were recognized by early Grecian / $_1$ writers /.
13. As | has been / $_1$ noted /,
14. the **ancient Greek** followers of Apollo | established the **ideal** of / $_1$ classicism /,
15. whereas the cult of Dionysus | produced the prototype of ro / $_1$ manticism /.
16. A / $_1$ mixture of the / two qualities |
17. has prevailed throughout recorded / $_1$ history /,
18. with first one and then the other | in the as / $_1$ cendancy /.
19. Thus, there | have been many 'classic' and many 'ro / $_4$ mantic' / **eras,**
20. but the labels | have come to refer most specifically to the last half of the 18th century and the 19th century, re / $_1$ spectively /,
21. because **those periods** | represent most / $_1$ vividly / the two tempers.
22. The social and political scene during the / $_1$ late / 18th century|
23. was hardly a setting for a quiet, com / $_4$ posed / 'classical' age
24. in view of the prevailing revolutionary spirit and colonial / $_1$ rivalry /.
25. The **revolutionary** movement | did have a direct e / $_1$ ffect on / music
26. in that 'music for the masses' | became a / $_4$ new i / deal
27. — **music** directly appealing to a large number of unsophisticated people who had previously been excluded from / $_4$ courtly enter / tainments.

To keep track of these categories through this text, Table 6.1 itemizes each instance of reminding, relevance and redundancy reference, the latter including 'tonicity' reference based on lexical identity (Martin, 1992: 101). The last column tracks lexical identity and superordination.

In the analysis of the 'classical' text, just less than half of the 27 numbered tone groups/information units are also integral ranking (unembedded) clauses, thus with unmarked tonality. Marked tonality is possessed by the two clauses in a single tone group/information unit of

Table 6.1 Anaphoric reference and lexical identity in the 'classical' text.

Line	Reminding reference	Relevance reference	Redundancy reference	Identity & superordination
1				Period
3				classical
4	it			period
				musical
5	the term	the same epoch	the visual arts of the same epoch	arts
6				music
7				classical
8	the term		A full understanding of the term	term
9				term
10	the two		the two	
11	Each		Each	
	the other	the other		
12	both		both	
14				ancient
				Greek
				ideal
16	the two qualities		A mixture of the two qualities	
18			one	
	the other	the other	the other	
19			many "classic" and many "romantic" eras	eras
20	the labels			
21	those periods			
	the two tempers			
22			the late 18th century	18th century
23			a quiet, composed "classical" age	classical
				age
25			a direct effect on music	revolutionary
				music
26				music
			a new ideal	ideal
27				music
			courtly entertainments	entertainments

line 6; by the two tone groups/information units mapped together with a single clause in lines 2–3, and again in 8–9, 11–12, 16–17 and 26–7; and by the three tone groups/information units mapped together with a single clause in lines 22–4.

An interpretation of the bolded items is also made to determine which stretches of text containing them are likely to be considered Given in the grammatical sense. The Given stretches in the clauses are denoted here by underlining, and any stretch which is not underlined represents the realization of New information. Theme stretches are terminated by a vertical line. Thus in line 4, pronoun 'it' refers back to 'the label classical' and is located in the Theme: an obvious candidate for Given information, which is seen to include the clause-initial auxiliary. In line 5 similarly, 'the term' is an anaphoric reminding reference in the Theme stretch, and therefore Given information along with the initial Adjunct 'Again'. The item 'arts' is a superordinate to music and the implicit other arts, and 'the same epoch' is anaphoric reference. This makes for their interpretation as a return to Given information after New information, implying that 'visual' is the focus of information: a typical pattern for marked tonicity.

The only foot which is annotated in this interpretation is the tonic foot. It begins and ends with the conventional slants, and after the opening slant is the subscript tone number. Although the location of the tonic is through interpretation of anaphora and lexical identity, the choice of tone is from an interpretation of the discourse context.

The methodology of the interpretation rests on some principles or rules of interpretation which are consistently applied after the interpretation of anaphoric reference and lexical identity as Given. To begin with, the division of the text into tone groups depends first on the application of the principle that the unmarked tonality of the ranking clause makes the boundaries of the tone group/information unit coincident with its boundaries, and second the principle that unmarked tonicity locates the tonic syllable at the last item having a normally stressed syllable (hereafter just 'stressed item'), which is usually also a lexical item.[5] These two principles can be mitigated by the occurrence of items that must be evaluated as part of the Given after the New stretch has already begun (i.e. the return of Given information). Thus the default reading of line 5 would be a single clause, single tone group/information unit, with tonic syllable in 'epoch'. The evaluation of 'Again the term' as Given is typical. However the givenness of 'arts of the same epoch' looks like a return to Given after a preceding focus of information, as already noted. The tonality remains unmarked but the tonicity is now marked. This makes perfect sense from a discourse point of view: 'visual' is contrastive with the type of arts which 'music' implies. The same thing happens in the following line (6), where the New information stretch starts at the beginning of its clause, but ends with the lexical item 'applied' because the final lexical item in the clause is the Given, yielding another instance of marked tonicity. The discourse contrast implied is between 'borrow' and 'apply'.

However, in line 7, the one item with givenness through lexical identity falls in the middle of the clause rather than at either the beginning or the end. This would seem to suggest that the clause starts with the New, as in the previous clause, and that the return of the New after a Given stretch makes for a new tone group/information unit, and thus marked tonality. However this would make just 'no known models' the focus of information in the first of the two units, which is highly counterintuitive. Another principle comes into play, based on observation: items with givenness by reference or lexical identity often occur as premodifiers ('classical' in 'classical antiquity', line 7) or head elements with appositionally specifying postmodifiers ('term' in 'the term romantic', line 9).[6] Interpreting these as part of the Given is usually counterintuitive. A reasonable interpretation of line 7 is then as a single tone group/information unit, all New information, with tonic syllable in the last lexical item 'imitate'. The same principle applies to the New information of line 4, where 'period of' and 'musical' serve as premodifiers in their respective nominal groups.

Marked tonality does occur in lines 8–9, where the single clause does have two tone groups/information units. Anaphoric reference makes 'the term' in line 8 Given, and the lexical item 'term' is a lexical identity in line 9. The focus of information just on 'A full understanding' implied by the onset of Given in 'of the term' is intuitively correct; it contrasts with the theme of classificational 'difficulties'. New information returns in the line 9 part of the clause. The principle now to be applied is that a return to New information after a New–Given stretch implies a new tone group/information unit. The repetition 'term' in line 9 does not imply another return of Given, on the principle specified above. The focus of information on 'on a clear conception of the term romantic' is of course perfectly intuitive since there is both a contrast with 'understanding' and a contrast with 'classical'. These principles of interpretation are set out in order in Table 6.2.

Table 6.2 Principles of interpretation.

---

1. In the default situation – unmarked tonality – the boundaries of the ranking clause and the tone group/information unit coincide.
2. In the default situation – unmarked tonicity – the tonic syllable is carried by the last stressed item (usually lexical) in the tone group/information unit.
3. One or more given stressed items (usually lexical) at the end of the tone group/information unit imply that the tonic syllable falls in the stressed item (usually lexical) just before them – marked tonicity.
4. Given items occurring as premodifiers, or as head elements with appositionally specifying postmodifiers do not affect tonicity.
5. A return to New information after a New–Given stretch implies a new tone group/information unit.
6. The structure of the discourse will sometimes override any pattern suggested by its lexicogrammar.

Application of the same principles accounts equally well for almost all of the rest of the text, except for the special case of lines 2–3. The title in line 1 is a minor clause with unmarked tonality. However, the givenness of the stressed Head element 'Period' suggests a focus of information on the Modifier 'Classical', giving it marked tonicity. Line 2 is a markedly thematic preposed Adjunct, which typically has its own intonation contour, making it an information unit, and giving its containing clause marked tonality. In line 3 'classical' is a lexical identity. However, a focus of information on 'label' would be highly counterintuitive because of the lack of contrast. The whole clause is New information. This suggests a final principle: that the structure of the discourse will sometimes override any pattern suggested by lexicogrammar (no. 6 in Table 6.2).

The end result, the SFL interpretation of the 'classical' text taken as a whole, constitutes a guide to a recitation of the text which is plausible, although rather more oriented to its lexical and grammatical cohesion than some readers might prefer. That is, it tends assiduously to take its cohesive properties as a guide to assigning the contrasts implicit in choices of the focus of information. Even at that, we have found that the assignment of contrasts cannot be exclusively rooted in lexis and grammar – at one point the discourse semantics seems not to be construed by reference or lexical cohesion.

6.6   A narrative text

The same analytical principles can be applied and extended through the examination of a text representing a contrasting genre, narrative. The following selection is taken from the Katherine Mansfield short story 'At the Bay' (Mansfield, 1922: 23–5). The text segment begins a chapter midway through a narrative which has continuously shifted focus from one character to another. This is the beginning of the focus on Linda. The setting is the front garden of her seaside New Zealand bungalow. A preliminary discussion of this text segment and its analysis by Jan Firbas (1992) on the principles of functional sentence perspective is in Cummings (1999: 191–200).

> In a steamer chair, under a manuka tree that grew in the middle of the front grass patch, Linda Burnell dreamed the morning away. She did nothing. She looked up at the dark, close, dry leaves of the manuka, at the chinks of blue between, and now and again a tiny yellowish flower

dropped on her. Pretty – yes, if you held one of those flowers on the palm of your hand and looked at it closely, it was an exquisite small thing. Each pale yellow petal shone as if each was the careful work of a loving hand. The tiny tongue in the centre gave it the shape of a bell. And when you turned it over the outside was a deep bronze colour. But as soon as they flowered, they fell and scattered. You brushed them off your frock as you talked; the horrid little things got caught in one's hair. Why, then, flower at all? Who takes the trouble – or the joy – to make all these things that are wasted, wasted ... It was uncanny.

On the grass beside her, lying between two pillows, was the boy. Sound asleep he lay, his head turned away from his mother. His fine dark hair looked more like a shadow than like real hair, but his ear was a bright, deep coral. Linda clasped her hands above her head and crossed her feet. It was very pleasant to know that all these bungalows were empty, that everybody was down on the beach, out of sight, out of hearing. She had the garden to herself; she was alone.

Dazzling white the picotees shone; the golden-eyed marigold glittered; the nasturtiums wreathed the veranda poles in green and gold flame. If only one had time to look at these flowers long enough, time to get over the sense of novelty and strangeness, time to know them! But as soon as one paused to part the petals, to discover the underside of the leaf, along came Life and one was swept away. And, lying in her cane chair, Linda felt so light; she felt like a leaf. Along came Life like a wind and she was seized and shaken; she had to go. Oh dear, would it always be so? was there no escape?

Like the 'classical' text, this text segment is analysed below in numbered lines, each representing separate tone groups/information units. Bolding represents the basis of givenness of information – anaphoric reference, lexical identity and superordination. Again, bridging anaphora (shaded) is excluded from consideration as too weak to imply givenness. Themes are marked off with a vertical line, and the Given information stretches are underlined.

1. In a /₁ steamer chair /,
2. under a manuka tree that grew in the middle of the front /₁ grass patch /,
3. **Linda Burnell** | dreamed the morning a /₁ way /.
4. **She** | did /₁ nothing /.
5. **She** | looked up at the dark, close, dry /₁ leaves **of the / manuka,**
6. at the chinks of blue be /₁ tween /,
7. and now and again a tiny yellowish flower | /₁ dropped on **her** /.
8. /₁ Pretty / —
9. yes, if you | /₁ held **one of those / flowers**

10. on the palm of **your** /₁ hand /
11. and | looked at **it** /₁ closely /,
12. **it** | was an ex /₁ quisite / **small thing**.
13. Each pale yellow petal | /₁ shone /
14. as if **each** | was the careful work of a loving /₁ hand /.
15. The tiny tongue in the centre | gave **it** the shape of a /₁ bell /.
16. And when **you** | turned **it** /₁ over /
17. the outside | was a deep /₁ bronze **colour** /.
18. But as soon as **they** | /₁ flowered /,
19. **they** | fell and /₁ scattered /.
20. **You** | brushed **them** off **your** /₁ frock /
21. as **you** | /₁ talked /;
22. **the horrid little things** | got caught in one's /₁ hair /.
23. /₄ Why, | then, / **flower**
24. at /₅ all /?
25. Who | takes the trouble - or the joy - to /₁ make **all these / things**
26. that | are /₁ wasted, /
27. /₁ wasted /...
28. **It** | was un /₁ canny /.
29. ¶ On the grass be /₁ side **her** /, |
30. lying between two /₁ pillows /,
31. was the /₁ boy /.
32. Sound a /₁ sleep **he | lay** /,
33. **his** head turned away from **his** /₁ mother /.
34. **His** fine dark hair | looked more like a shadow than like /₁ real **hair** /,
35. but **his** ear | was a bright, deep /₁ coral /.
36. **Linda** | clasped **her** hands above **her** /₁ head /
37. and | crossed **her** /₁ feet /.
38. It | was very pleasant to know that all these bungalows | were /₁ empty /,
39. that **everybody** | was down on the /₁ beach /,
40. out of /₁ sight /,
41. out of /₁ hearing /.
42. **She** | had the garden to **her** /₁ self /;
43. **she** | was a /₁ lone /.
44. ¶ Dazzling /₁ white the / picotees | shone;
45. the golden-eyed marigold | /₁ glittered /;
46. the nasturtiums | wreathed the veranda poles in green and gold /₁ flame /.
47. If only one | had time to /₄ look **at these / flowers**

48. /₁ long e / nough,
49. **time** to get over the sense of novelty and /₁ strangeness /,
50. **time** to /₄ know **them** /!
51. But as soon as **one** | / ₄ paused /
52. to part the /₁ petals /,
53. to discover the underside of the /₁ leaf /,
54. along | came /₁ Life /
55. and **one** | was swept /₁ away /.
56. And, lying in **her** /₁ cane **chair** /,
57. **Linda** | felt so /₁ light /;
58. she | felt /₁ like a / **leaf**.
59. **Along | came Life** like a /₁ wind /
60. and **she** | was seized and /₁ shaken /;
61. **she** | had to /₁ go /.
62. Oh dear, would **it** | /₂ always be **so** /?
63. was there | no es /₂ cape /?

Like Table 6.1, Table 6.3 itemizes reminding, relevance and redundancy reference in the text segment in its first three columns; and the last column tracks lexical identity and superordination.

The two texts show numerous stylistic differences, some of which are of course related to the difference in genre. An examination of Table 6.1 and Table 6.3 shows that the Mansfield text (allowing for its greater length at 385 words as opposed to the 275 words of the 'classical' text) has a much lower density of lexical identities and superordinates than that of the 'classical' text. The same is true for nearly all forms of anaphoric reference. A significant exception to this is the large number of pronouns in the Mansfield narrative text which realize reminding anaphoric reference. Another difference is the much greater use in the Mansfield text of bridging anaphoric reference.

Still another difference from the 'classical' text is that the Mansfield text has a much higher proportion of tone groups/information units which are also integral ranking (unembedded) clauses, thus with unmarked tonality – about two-thirds as opposed to just less than half. Marked tonality is shown in the two tone groups/information units mapped together with a single clause in lines 5–6, and again in 9–10, 23–4, and 29 plus 31. Marked tonality is also shown in the three tone groups/information units mapped together with a single clause in lines 1–3, and again in 25–7; and in the four tone groups/information units mapped together with a single clause in lines 38–41, and again in 47–50.

Table 6.3 Anaphoric reference and lexical identity in the Mansfield text.

Line	Reminding reference	Relevance reference	Redundancy reference	Identity and superordination
3	Linda Burnell			
4	She			
5	She			
	the manuka		…leaves of the manuka	manuka
7	her			
9	those flowers		one of those flowers	flowers
10	your			
11	it			
12	it		an exquisite small thing	small thing
14	each		each	
15	it			
16	you			
	it			
17			a deep bronze colour	colour
18	they			
19	thcy			
20	you			
	them			
	your			
21	you			
22	the horrid little things			little things
23				flower
25	all these things			things
28	It			
29	the grass			
	her			
32	he			lay
33	his			
	his			
34	his			hair
35	his			
36	Linda			
	her			
	her			
37	her			
39	everybody			
42	she			
	her			
43	she			
47	these flowers			
49				time
50	them			time

Line	Reminding reference	Relevance reference	Redundancy reference	Identity and superordination
51	one			
55	one			
56	her		her cane chair	chair
57	Linda			
58				leaf
59				Along came life
60	she			
61	she			
62	it		so	

A reasonable recitation of most of this text can be predicted just from the principles already applied to the expository text. The first clause in lines 1–3 is interpreted as three tone groups/information units because it begins with two markedly preposed circumstantial Adjuncts, a typical pattern. Principle 2 in Table 6.2 accounts for the unmarked tonicity of each of these units, and that of the next clause in line 4 as well. In line 5, the givenness of 'the manuka' signals the falling of the tonic on 'leaves' with marked tonicity, from Principle 3; and Principle 5 calls for a new tone group/information unit in line 6. The clauses of lines 7–8 are unmarked in tonality and tonicity. The interpretation of the clause in lines 9–10 is like that of the clause in lines 5–6, for the same reasons. Principle 4 from Table 6.2 applies to the deictic premodifier in 'your hand'.

Line 11 presents a new problem. The reminding anaphoric reference of 'it' would suggest that the tonic should fall on 'looked' and that the return of New information in 'closely' should distinguish it as its own tone group/information unit, similar to the patterning in lines 5–6 and 9–10. Unlike 5–6, where 'leaves' contrasts both with the tree itself and the next object of scrutiny, the 'chinks of blue', and unlike 9–10, where 'held' contrasts with the passivity of doing nothing, looking up and being dropped on, placing the tonic on 'looked' would be rather counterintuitive. A similar predicament is presented in lines 15, 16 and 20. What is required is an additional principle: given items occurring as unstressed pronouns or demonstratives in the Rheme before the last stressed lexical item do not affect tonicity. Table 6.2 can now be revised as Table 6.4.

Table 6.4 Revised principles of interpretation.

1. In the default situation – unmarked tonality – the boundaries of the ranking clause and the tone group/information unit coincide.
2. In the default situation – unmarked tonicity – the tonic syllable is carried by the last stressed item (usually lexical) in the tone group/information unit.
3. One or more given stressed items (usually lexical) at the end of the tone group/ information unit imply that the tonic syllable falls in the stressed item (usually lexical) just before them – marked tonicity.
4. Given items occurring as premodifiers, or as head elements with appositionally specifying postmodifiers do not affect tonicity.
5. Given items occurring as unstressed pronouns or demonstratives in the Rheme before the last stressed lexical item do not affect tonicity.
6. A return to New information after a New–Given stretch implies a new tone group/ information unit.
7. The structure of the discourse will sometimes override any pattern suggested by its lexicogrammar.

The spoken interpretation of the rest of the text is consistent with these principles. A few clauses require further explanation. Line 29 contains a preposed thematic circumstantial Adjunct, like those of lines 1–2, and is therefore its own tone group/information unit. The Subject 'the boy' in fact does not come until the end of the clause in line 31. Despite the definite article, it does not represent reminding anaphoric reference. The child has already been referred to three times in the course of the story as 'the boy', so that the reference has ironically come to seem a form of homophora (Martin, 1992: 121–2) within the culture of the family. Similarly in lines 38–9, 'all these bungalows' and 'the beach' belong to the indirect speech of Linda's mind, and are therefore also exophoric reference. The marked tonicity of the clause in line 44 is factored by the preposed Complement, a condition which also reinforces the interpretation of the clause in line 32.

Finally, it should be noted that Mansfield's rhetoric sometimes employs an asyndetic series of parallel Rheme elements heavy with embedded clauses or prepositional phrases. The most complex example is the clause in lines 38–41. The interpretation of this clause as four separate tone groups/information units follows only from this condition. In lines 47–50, the clause shows an asyndetic series of parallel Complements, each realized by a nominal group with embedded clause at Qualifier element. This type of structure also reinforces the interpretation of the clause in lines 5–6.

6.7   Summary and conclusion

The analysis of these two texts has tried to show that the location of the tonic in the recitation of a text written originally to be read as written may proceed mainly from principles of lexicogrammar. The patterns of discourse relevant to this process tend to be realized by a relatively limited set of lexicogrammatical potentials. Contrast and parallelism in the discourse structure, however, sometimes make it necessary for the interpreter to invoke principles of discourse semantics directly.

Notes

1. The systemic functional convention of capitalizing names of elements of grammatical structure will be followed throughout.
2. Here 'ranking clause' means not embedded.
3. Lexical identity, including close synonymy, in the case of nouns implies having the very same referent in the context of situation. In the case of verbs and adjectives, it necessarily means being the same process or quality – but not necessarily predicated of the same referent.
4. Superordination is actually the basis of a form of direct reminding anaphoric reference (Martin 1992: 124–5), but it is itemized separately here for clarity.
5. For the exception of 'inherently given' items see Halliday and Matthiessen (2014: 118).
6. The lexical identity of 'term' in line 9 is not with 'term' in lines 5 and 8, which are specifically in reference to 'classical', but rather with its synonym 'label' in line 3.

References

Britannica (1977) Music, western. In *The New Encyclopaedia Britannica: Micropaedia* (15th edition) 12: 710. Chicago, IL: Encyclopaedia Britannica, Inc.

Bunyan, J. (1957) *The Pilgrim's Progress.* New York: Pocket Books.

Cummings, M. (1995) Structural semantics as the basis for Theme/Rheme. In M. J. Powell (ed.) *The Twenty-first LACUS Forum 1994* 443–59. Chapel Hill, NC: Linguistic Association of Canada and the United States.

Cummings, M. (1996) Computational analysis of old English lexical cohesion. In B. Hoffer (ed.) *The Twenty-Second LACUS Forum 1995* 293–303. Chapel Hill, NC: Linguistic Association of Canada and the United States.

Cummings, M. (1999) Functional sentence perspective, focus of information and semantic relations. In S. J. J. Hwang and A. R. Lommel (eds) *LACUS Forum XXV* 191–200. Fullerton, CA: Linguistic Association of Canada and the United States.

Cummings, M. (2000a) A cognitive-spatial model for lexical semantics. In A. K. Melby and A. R. Lommel (eds) *LACUS Forum XXVI* 343–52. Fullerton, CA: Linguistic Association of Canada and the United States.

Cummings, M. (2000b) The inference of given information in written text. In E. Ventola (ed.) *Discourse and Community: Doing Functional Linguistics* 331–53. Tübingen: Gunter Narr Verlag.

Cummings, M. (2001) Intuitive and quantitative analyses of Given/New in texts. In J. de Villiers and R. J. Stainton (eds) *Communication in Linguistics: Volume 1, Papers in Honour of Michael Gregory* 61–94. Toronto: GREF Publishers.

Davies, M. (1986) Literacy and intonation. In B. Couture (ed.) *Functional Approaches to Writing: Research Perspectives* 199–230. Norwood, NJ: Ablex.

Davies, M. (1994) 'I'm sorry, I'll read that again': Information structure in writing. In S. Čmejrková and F. Štícha (eds) *The Syntax of Sentence and Text: A Festschrift for František Daneš* 75–89. Amsterdam: Benjamins.

Firbas, J. (1992) *Functional Sentence Perspective in Written and Spoken Communication.* Cambridge: Cambridge University Press.

Halliday, M. A. K. (1967) *Intonation and Grammar in British English* (Janua Linguarum Series Practica 48). The Hague: Mouton.

Halliday, M. A. K. ([1967] 2005) Notes on transitivity and theme in English, part 2. In J. Webster (ed.) *Studies in English Language (Volume 7 in the Collected Works of M. A. K. Halliday)* 55–109. London: Continuum.

Halliday, M. A. K. (1970) *A Course in Spoken English: Intonation.* London: Oxford University Press.

Halliday, M. A. K. and Greaves, W. S. (2008) *Intonation in the Grammar of English.* London: Equinox.

Halliday, M. A. K. and Matthiessen, C. M. I. M. (2014) *Halliday's Introduction to Functional Grammar* (4th edition). London: Routledge.

Mansfield, K. (1922) At the Bay. *The Garden Party* 1–58. New York: Modern Library.

Martin, J. R. (1992) *English Text: System and Structure.* Amsterdam: Benjamins.

Part C

The Interface between Music and Language

7 | A note for *-ed*: Comments on the treatment of *-ed* in Handel's *Messiah*

David Banks[a]

7.1 Anecdotal introduction

The origins of this paper are to be found in a personal anecdote. For many years I have been living and working in France, and one of my non-university activities is singing in a choir, whose repertoire is made up mainly of major baroque and classical sacred choral works, including, naturally, Handel's *Messiah*. My French-speaking colleagues in the choir have frequently asked me why they should have to sing the *-ed* ending of the simple past verb form, and the past participle as a separate syllable; they of course remember being taught at school that this was not to be pronounced as a separate syllable except when, in its written form, it followed the letters *t* or *d*. The question is an interesting and valid one, since pronunciation of the *-ed* ending as a separate syllable was already obsolete by Handel's time, and indeed the letter *e* was frequently omitted in writing and replaced by an apostrophe, so that the ending was represented by *'d*. This paper is therefore an attempt to see the extent of this phenomenon in Handel's *Messiah* and to speculate on why he should have used what was, for him, an old-fashioned form. The *Messiah* was written in 1741 and first performed in Dublin in the following year.

---

a **David Banks** is Emeritus Professor of English Linguistics at the Université de Bretagne Occidentale, Brest, France. He is Director of ERLA (Equipe de Recherche en Linguistique Appliquée) and Chairman of AFLSF (Association Française de la Linguistique Systémique Fonctionnelle). His research interests include the synchronic and diachronic analysis of scientific text, and the application of systemic functional linguistics to French. He has published over 80 academic articles and authored or edited over 20 books. His book *The Development of Scientific Writing* (2008) won the ESSE (European Society for the Study of English) Language and Linguistics Book Award in 2010. His non-university activities include ocean rowing and choral singing.

7.2   George Frideric Handel

George Frideric Handel was born in Halle, Germany in 1685, and died in London in 1759. He became cathedral organist in Halle in 1702, but the following year he went to Hamburg where he joined the Hamburg Opera as a violinist. He went to Italy in 1706, returned to Hanover in 1710, and visited England later that year. Although employed by the Elector of Hanover, he came on leave to England again in 1710, but failed to return. In 1714, Handel's former employer, the Elector of Hanover became King George I of England, and after settling their differences, Handel became the favoured composer of the monarchy. In London, he built his reputation on the composition of Italian operas, which appealed to the social elite of the capital. However, towards the end of the 1720s dwindling taste for this type of entertainment, as well as the competition of a rival opera company, meant that Italian opera was becoming less and less profitable. Faced with this financial problem, Handel developed a new form, the English oratorio, which was a public success and attracted a much wider audience than his Italian operas had. Thus from the highly static Italian *opera seria*, which was undramatic, but staged, he passed to the English oratorio, which was dramatic, but unstaged. The *Messiah* belongs to the latter, although it is less dramatic, in the sense of telling a story, than most of the other oratorios (cf. e.g. Blom, 1947; Raynor, 1980; Schonberg, 1971).

7.3   The *-ed* ending

In present-day English the *-ed* ending of the simple past tense and the past participle are pronounced simply as a consonant, either the voiced consonant /d/, when the ending follows a voiced consonant or a vowel, or the unvoiced consonant /t/, when the ending follows an unvoiced consonant. It is only when the ending follows either /d/ or /t/ that a vowel is maintained, and the ending is pronounced /əd/, or, in some varieties, /ɪd/ (cf. e.g. Banks, 2005; Garcia *et al.*, 2000; Gimson, 1970). This had not been the case in Middle English, where the *-ed* ending was pronounced as a distinct separate syllable, but this changed in the course of the Early Modern English period. The division of language development into various periods is obviously to a certain extent artificial, since all language change is more or less gradual; nevertheless the periods provide a useful tool, and the Early Modern period is generally taken to be roughly 1500 to 1700. The change in the pronunciation of the *-ed* ending is said to have occurred during the first half of this period. According to Nevalainen, 'the vowel sound in the suffix [of past tense and past participle] was usually deleted in colloquial language especially in the second half of the period' (Nevalainen, 2006: 92), and Barber (1997: 174) claims that 'by 1600 the present-day regulation was well established in speech'. Of course, there were many spelling variations, but, there seems to be no doubt that spoken language had more or less adopted the present-day system by the beginning of the seventeenth century, well over half a century before Handel's birth, and not far off a century and a half before the time when he was to write the *Messiah*. This must then have been the form he encountered first as a foreign visitor, and then as a permanent resident in England. Some have tried to account for his treatment of the *-ed* ending by pointing out that Handel himself was a non-native speaker of English, and it is said that he himself spoke English with a strong foreign accent, but it is highly unlikely that this would have led him to adopt a form which had already been obsolete for some time before he arrived (Degott, 2001).

7.4   The extent of the phenomenon

If we exclude those examples of *-ed* endings that occur following /d/ or /t/, since these are still pronounced with a separate syllable anyway, the text of Handel's *Messiah* provides twenty examples of *-ed* endings, either in simple past tense or past participles, including those that occur in compound tenses. Of course, the listener hears much more than this, since the baroque style involves the multiple repetition of phrases in vocal and choral composition, so that a single example in the written text will be heard many times by the listening audience. For example, in the aria 'The people that walked in darkness', there are two phrases that interest us:

> The people that **walked** in darkness …
> … upon them hath the light **shined**

Through repetitions, the word *walked* actually occurs ten times in the score, while *shined* occurs three times. In the aria 'He was despised and rejected', there are again two relevant phrases:

> He was **despised** …
> … that **plucked** off the hair

This is a *da capo* aria, which means that it has an ABA structure, where the second A is simply a repetition of the first. The word *despised* occurs five times in the first section, so that with the *da capo* repetition, it is heard a total of ten times. The word *plucked*, which is in the second section, is heard three times. This can be multiplied again in choral movements, where the effects of counterpoint are such that the different voices will be pronouncing the word at different moments as the music progresses. Thus for example in the chorus 'And with his stripes we are healed', the word *healed* can be heard no less than 25 times.

Of the twenty examples of *-ed* endings, twelve are very clearly intended to be sung as a separate syllable: Handel provides the syllable with a separate note, without any phrase mark or ligature binding it to the preceding notes. For example, in the extract shown in Figure 7.1, which is the first four bars of the aria 'The people that walked in darkness', it can be seen that for each of the two occurrences of the word *walked*, the first syllable has two linked notes, but the second has a single separate note.

Figure 7.1 Extract from 'The people that walked in darkness' (Pitman, Hart & Co., early twentieth century).

In Figure 7.2, bars 46 to 49 of the chorus 'All we like sheep have gone astray', there are nine occurrences of the word *turned*.

Figure 7.2 Extract from 'All we like sheep have gone astray' (Pitman, Hart & Co., early twentieth century).

It can be seen that for each occurrence of the word *turned* in this extract, two notes are provided one for each of the syllables; the notes are never linked by a phrase mark.

There are two examples, both in the first recitative 'Comfort ye, my people', which are to some extent ambiguous. The two phrases in question are:

...that her warfare is **accomplished**, that her iniquity is **pardoned**.

In my own second-hand score, which is fairly old and undated, but probably early twentieth century,[1] these are printed as if they were to be sung as separate syllables.

Figure 7.3 Extract from 'Comfort ye, my people' (Pitman, Hart & Co., early twentieth century).

Here (Figure 7.3) it can be seen that for *accomplished* and the first instance of *pardoned* there are three notes with no phrase mark; for the second instance of pardoned there are four notes of which the first two are linked by a phrase mark; hence, the first syllable has two notes leaving two separate notes, so it would seem that the word is to be sung as three syllables. However, modern scores print this slightly differently.[2]

Figure 7.4 Extract from 'Comfort ye, my people' (www.free-scores.com).

Here (Figure 7.4) it can be seen that there are two double crochets for the second syllable of *accomplish'd*, leaving only one for the final syllable, and that there are only two notes for each occurrence of *pardon'd*. It will also be noted that the words are printed with an apostrophe indicating the ellipse of the *e* of the *-ed* ending. Moreover, this is the way it is usually sung, at least today.

The remaining six examples are cases where, even in my old score, the *-ed* ending does not constitute a separate syllable. Thus in the first line of the aria 'The Trumpet shall sound' (Figure 7.5) we find a single minim for the word *rais'd*.

Figure 7.5 Extract from 'The trumpet shall sound' (Pitman, Hart & Co., early twentieth century).

There are three other cases like this where the word is spelt, like *rais'd*, with an apostrophe:

    ... but we shall all be **chang'd**
    ... and we shall be **chang'd**
    Death is **swallow'd** up in victory

There are also two cases, where although the apostrophe is not used, the *-ed* ending does not constitute a separate syllable. This is the case in the line 'Then shall the eyes of the blind be opened' (Figure 7.6).

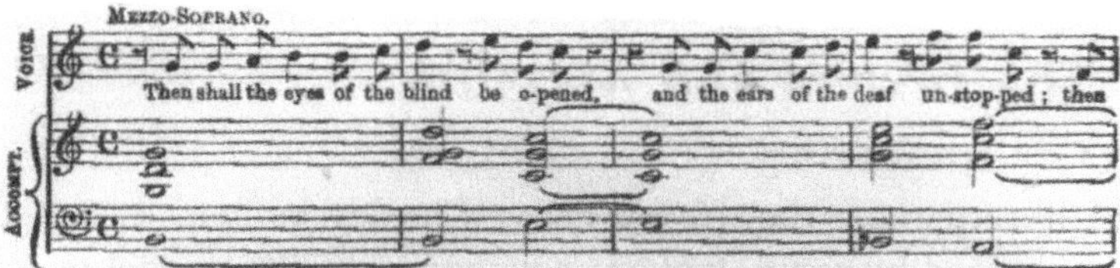

Figure 7.6 Extract from 'Then shall the eyes of the blind be opened' (Pitman, Hart & Co., early twentieth century).

In the modern score, this word is indeed spelt *open'd*. However, it will be noticed, that curiously, the next line contains the word *unstopped*, where the *-ed* is to be pronounced, and this is the case in the modern score too. The same is true for the line 'Surely he hath borne our griefs and carried our sorrows', where *carried* counts for two syllables, whereas two lines later, in 'he was bruised for our iniquities', *bruised* has *-ed* as a separate syllable.

There is one anomalous case, which occurs in the chorus 'And the glory of the Lord'. In this chorus, the phrase *shall be revealed* occurs three times in each of the four voices. On each occasion the *-ed* ending is to be sung as a separate note, with one exception, which is the second occurrence of the word in the soprano line (Figure 7.7).

Figure 7.7 Extract from 'And the glory of the Lord' (Pitman, Hart & Co., early twentieth century).

If we count the example *revealed* as having a separate syllable (as it has most of the time), and *accomplished* and *pardoned* as not having a separate *-ed* syllable, then it can be said that where there is an appropriate

-ed ending, Handel chooses to have it sung as a separate note in 12 cases out of 20, that is in 60 per cent of the cases.

7.5   The text of the *Messiah*

Handel's librettist for the *Messiah* was Charles Jennens (1700–1774). Although decried by some, Jennens collaborated with Handel on several of his oratorios. The text is a compilation or collage of extracts from the Bible. The extracts used come from fourteen different books of the Bible, but only four of these are relevant for our twenty examples of *-ed* endings; they are Isaiah, the Psalms, the Epistle to the Romans and the First Epistle to the Corinthians. In Jennens' collage the order of extracts is not respected and extracts from different books are sometimes used together. For example, in the aria 'I know that my Redeemer liveth', an extract from Job is inserted in the middle of an extract from 1 Corinthians. All of the extracts are taken from the 1611 King James Bible, and are used as they occur in that text with only a very few minor alterations. There are two that have some significance and may concern us here. Jennens uses Isaiah 53:3, 'He is despised and rejected of men', but changes the present to a past tense: 'He was despised'. And he uses Isaiah 50:6, 'I gave my back to the smiters', but changing the first-person pronoun to third-person: 'He gave his back to the smiters'. This means that the Isaian prophecies have been altered to become comments about Christ, which fits in with the general programme of the *Messiah*.

7.6   By way of comparison: *Alexander's Feast*

Handel's oratorio *Alexander's Feast* provides a useful comparison. This oratorio pre-dates the *Messiah* by half a dozen years. It is a secular, not a sacred work, and has words by John Dryden. However, Dryden did not write the words especially for Handel. They were written in 1697 for the composer Jeremiah Clark, who first set them to music. They were subsequently set a second time by Thomas Clayton in 1711. The text was prepared for Handel by Newburgh Hamilton, but his role was limited to dividing the work up into recitatives, arias and choruses, apart from the addition of an extra chorus of nine lines from his own work 'The power of musick' at the end (Degott, 2001).

In the text of *Alexander's Feast*, there are 32 examples of *-ed* simple past forms or past participles. However they are systematically spelt with an apostrophe and a separate note is never provided. There is not a single example in the whole work where the *-ed* ending is to be sung as a separate syllable.

7.7   Differences in the source text

As has been pointed out, the twenty examples which are being considered are drawn from four different books of the Bible: Isaiah, Psalms, Romans and 1 Corinthians. Isaiah is the most common, being used in fourteen of the examples; 1 Corinthians occurs in a further four, with Psalms and Romans accounting for one each. Of the fourteen extracts from Isaiah, ten use the separate *-ed* syllable and four do not. None of the four extracts from 1 Corinthians have a separate *-ed* syllable. The two extracts from Psalms and Romans both have a separate *-ed* syllable. Thus it can be said that of fifteen Old Testament (Isaiah and Psalms) examples eleven have separate *-ed* syllables, so that use of an Old Testament example gives a 73 per cent chance of a separate *-ed* syllable being used. On the other hand, of the five New Testament (Romans and 1 Corinthians) extracts only one has a separate *-ed* syllable, so that where a New Testament extract is used there is only a 20 per cent chance of the separate syllable being used. Thus, use of the Old Testament, as opposed to the New Testament, seems to favour the separate *-ed* syllable.

7.8   Differences in musical genre

There are two purely orchestral movements in Handel's *Messiah*: the Overture and a Pastoral Symphony. These do not concern us here. Otherwise there are three types of vocal and choral movements: recitative, aria and chorus. Of our twenty examples, six occur in recitatives, eight in arias, and six in choruses. In the case of recitative, only one of the six examples has a separate *–ed* syllable; on the other hand, of the eight aria examples, six have a separate syllable, and of the six chorus examples, five do so. Thus recitative examples have only a 17 per cent chance of having a separate syllable, while arias and choruses taken together have a 79 per cent chance of being treated this way. So recitative favours the choice of not having a separate *-ed* syllable. The specificity of recitative, as opposed to arias and choruses, lies mainly in two features. First, particularly in opera, recitative serves to carry the drama forward; it is there that the story is told. It can also be born in mind that Handel's reputation had originally been built on the composition of Italian operas. It is true that the *Messiah* is not, like many of his other oratorios, a dramatic work; nevertheless, it does have a distinct structure. It has three parts: the first deals with the prophecy and the birth of Christ; the second with the redemption in the passion and death of Christ; the third with the resurrection and Christ in glory. So although it does not have a narrative storyline, the recitatives serve to situate the various arias and choruses within the general structure. Recitative is also thought of as being more 'speech-like'. From a musical point of view, the recitatives usually only have a simple continuo accompaniment. There are relatively few recitatives with full orchestral accompaniment.

7.9   Context and register

It is useful to try to situate Handel's *Messiah* in terms of its context. This approach discusses context in terms of three functions: field, tenor and mode. Field relates to the ongoing activity and the subject matter of the discourse which constitutes part of that activity; tenor is concerned with the relationships set up between those taking part in the act of communication; mode concerns the means of communication and its rhetorical function. In terms of field, Handel's *Messiah* is, as has been said, a musical setting of biblical texts for public performance. The texts themselves are a collage or compilation from different books of the Bible. They do not have a narrative structure, but move through the prophecy and birth of Christ to his passion and death, followed by resurrection and heavenly glory. The tenor relates to the fact that the *Messiah* is written by a composer, abetted by a librettist, for performance to a paying audience, but necessarily filtered through the performance of musicians. It should be noted that in Handel's time, oratorios, even those of a sacred nature, were performed in theatres, not in churches as they frequently are today. In fact Handel's *Messiah* was performed only once in a church, in Handel's lifetime, and that was for a charity performance. And this was the only one of his oratorios to have even one church performance (Degott, 2001). It should also be remembered that audiences of Handel's time had extensive knowledge of the Bible. They probably knew by heart the texts used, and would be able to place them in their original contexts. Thus they would be able to recognize, for example, the relevant extracts from Isaiah in the first part of the *Messiah* as prophecies of the coming of Christ. The text, words and music, is written to be sung, and listened to in linear fashion, and in which the audience play no part. As a piece of music, its rhetorical objectives are obviously aesthetic, but as a sacred oratorio, it is presumably intended also to be inspirational.

7.10 An *-ed* hypopthesis

The extracts from the Bible used in Handel's *Messiah* are taken from the King James version of 1611; that is, from a text published 140 years earlier. Moreover, while the King James Bible is one of the most frequently cited texts in studies of the English of that period (e.g. Partridge, 1969), that version itself owes much to earlier translations. Barber (1997) describes the King James Bible as being the culmination of a whole series of trans-lations, as successive translators tried to improve on previous attempts. Tyndale is often cited as having had a particular influence on the language of the King James version (Nevalainen, 2006). For example, the King James translation of 1 Corinthians 51–52, used with only very minor changes by Handel is:

> 51. Behold, I shew you a mystery; we shall not all sleep, but we shall be changed
> 52. In a moment, in the twinkling of an eye, at the last trump: for the trumpet shall sound, and the dead shall be raised, incorruptible, and we shall be changed.

Tyndale's version[3] of these two verses, which first appeared in 1525, roughly 85 years before the King James Bible and 215 years before the *Messiah*, runs as follows:

> 51. Beholde I shewe you a mystery. We shall not all slepe: but we shall all be chaunged
> 52. and that in a moment and in the twinclinge of an eye at the sounde of the last trompe. For the trompe shall blowe and ye deed shall ryse incorruptible and we shalbe chaunged.

So, the language that Handel was setting was already, for him, the language of a previous age. It had already acquired the patina and aura of time. As an older form, it probably seemed more appropriate for sacred texts, giving them an inspirational value. It can be hypothesized that his treatment of the *-ed* ending falls into this pattern. It is highly unlikely that Handel was aware that the loss of *-ed* as a separate syllable was in progress at Tyndale's time, and would more or less have been complete by the time the King James Bible was produced, but it is probable that he was aware of the older pronunciation as one that could give extra weight and gravitas to the text of his sacred oratorio. This could therefore account for the fact that he treats the *-ed* ending as a separate syllable in the majority of cases in the arias and choruses. On the other hand in the recitatives, where Handel is, as it were, talking more directly to his audience, guiding them through the work, he, again in the majority of cases, reverts to the practice of his own day, of not treating the *-ed* as a separate syllable. It can also be hypothesized that he saw the New Testament extracts as having less of that ancient aura than the Old Testament extracts, leading him to use the *-ed* ending in the latter much more than in the former.

7.11 Value and valuation

So, it would seem that what this amounts to, is that in using the *-ed* ending as a separate syllable, Handel is giving added value to his texts. They are ancient, sacred, revered, and thus have a standing beyond that of other texts that might deal with the same subjects. In saying that Handel is giving added value to these texts, we seem to be making a statement that might be made within the terms of the Appraisal (Martin 2000; Martin and White, 2005). In introducing the Appraisal framework, Martin and White (2005: 1) say that it is concerned 'with the subjective presence of writers/speakers in texts as they adopt stances towards both the material they present and those with whom they communicate'. This seems to correspond at least to part of what Handel is doing, in that he does seem to be expressing his stance towards the texts he is using. Within the Appraisal framework, appraisal is construed in terms of engagement, attitude and graduation. Attitude is further construed as affect, judgement and appreciation, and appreciation itself in terms of reaction, composition and valuation. This last function is where we might possibly situate Handel's treatment of the *-ed* ending. The terms 'valuable' and 'priceless' are among the terms Martin and White suggest for inscribed positive valuation (*ibid.*: 56).

This tentative suggestion, that Handel's treatment of the *-ed* ending can be conceived of in terms of the Appraisal framework, is novel in two respects. Previous applications of Appraisal have dealt with the speaker's stance towards the content of his discourse, and usually to specific elements within that discourse; here we are dealing with Handel's attitude to his text as such, to his text *qua* text. This may well be taking Appraisal to a level of abstraction where it has not been used before. Second, to the best of my knowledge, previous applications of the Appraisal framework have not gone below the rank of word; this suggestion relates to the rank of morpheme, the *-ed* ending. So here again we would be going beyond previous applications of the framework.

7.12 By way of conclusion

In his sacred oratorio, the *Messiah*, Handel treats the *-ed* ending as a separate syllable in twelve cases out of twenty, despite the fact that this pronunciation was already obsolete at the time. By comparison his work *Alexander's Feast* has 32 examples of *-ed* endings, but they are never treated as separate syllables. In the *Messiah*, treating the *-ed* ending as a separate syllable is favoured by its occurrence in an Old Testament, as opposed to a New Testament, extract, and by its being in an aria or chorus, as opposed to a recitative. It can be hypothesized that using a pronunciation that belonged to a former age was a way of giving extra gravitas to a text, considered as sacred, because it was made up of extracts from the Bible. It can be tentatively suggested that this can be conceived in terms of Appraisal. However, this involves accepting that the Appraisal framework can be extended to encompass stance towards the text *qua* text, and applying it to the rank of morpheme.

Notes

1. This edition was published by Pitman, Hart & Co., London. Some indication of its date can be gleaned from a price sticker, which indicates that the price has been raised to 7/6 (seven shillings and six pence). A back cover advertisement seems to indicate that the original price was 2/– (two shillings).
2. The one printed here is freely available on the internet site www.free-scores.com.

3.   Tyndale's translation can be found online at
     http://wesley.nnu.edu/biblical_studies/tynedale.

References

Banks, D. (2005) *Writing the Sounds of English: A Précis of English Phonetics with Exercises in Phonemic Transcription* (2nd edition). Paris: L'Harmattan.

Barber, C. (1997) *Early Modern English* (2nd edition). Edinburgh: Edinburgh University Press.

Blom, E. (1947) *Music in England* (2nd edition). Harmondsworth: Penguin.

Degott, P. (2001) *Haendel et ses Oratorios: des Mots pour Les notes*. Paris: L'Harmattan.

Garcia, L., Luisa, M. and Maidment, J. A. (2000) *English Transcription Course*. London: Arnold.

Gimson, A. C. (1970) *An Introduction to the Pronunciation of English* (2nd edition). London: Arnold.

Martin, J. R. (2000) Beyond exhange: APPRAISAL systems in English. In S. Hunston and G. Thompson (eds) *Evaluation in Text: Authorial Stance and the Construction of Discourse* 142–75. Oxford: Oxford University Press.

Martin, J. R. and White, P. R. R. (2005) *The Language of Evaluation: Appraisal in English*. Basingstoke: Palgrave Macmillan.

Nevalainen, T. (2006) *An Introduction to Early Modern English*. Edinburgh: Edinburgh University Press.

Partridge, A. C. (1969) *Tudor to Augustan English: A Study in Syntax and Style from Caxton to Johnson*. London: André Deutsch.

Raynor, H. (1980) *Music in England*. London: Robert Hale.

Schonberg, H. C. (1971) *The Lives of the Great Composers*. London: Davis-Poynter.

8

A comparative analysis of the rap and the sung voice: Perspectives from systemic phonology, social semiotics and music studies

David Caldwell[a]

8.1 Introduction

This chapter presents a comparative, semiotic analysis of two distinct vocal performances: rapping and singing. While scholars have investigated the differences between speech and singing in a performance context (e.g. Titze, 1995; Callaghan and McDonald, 2007), no research to date has compared the rap voice with the sung voice. Moreover, with the exception of Caldwell (2010a, 2010b), very little research has applied van Leeuwen's (1999, 2009) socially oriented sound semiotics to a performance voice. Following in that tradition, this chapter is especially interdisciplinary. It integrates principles from phonetics (Clark and Yallop, 1995) and systemic phonology (e.g. Halliday and Greaves, 2008) with music studies (e.g. Callaghan and McDonald, 2007) and systemic functional linguistics (SFL) theory (e.g. Martin, 2010). The chapter begins by locating paralanguage within the SFL model of language stratification (e.g. Halliday and Matthiessen, 2004; Martin, 2010). It then compares the paralinguistic features of the rap voice with the 'soulful' sung voice.[1] The data analysed is sampled from a corpus

a **David Caldwell** is an Assistant Professor at the National Institute of Education, Singapore. His major research interests include systemic functional linguistics, discourse analysis, systemic phonology and social semiotics. Within discourse analysis, David has applied appraisal theory to a range of language contexts, including post-match interviews with footballers, medical consultations with hospital patients suffering depression and popular rap music. Following in the tradition of social semiotics, he has also examined the meaning-making potential of sound, with a specific focus on the semiotics of performance voices in popular music.

of rap music from rap artist Kanye West (2004, 2005, 2007, 2008). West provides a useful case study because he samples from, and collaborates with, a range of soulful singers (see Caldwell, 2010b). In addition, West both raps and sings, thereby controlling enough variables to construct a comparative analysis. In line with the paradigmatic orientation of systemic phonology, the chapter then presents the data in the form of a system network. The aim here is to illustrate the systemic, meaningful 'choices' that distinguish the rap voice from the sung voice. In addition to the system network, the data is analysed using a novel visual representation of sound (Caldwell, 2010a). This visual representation neatly captures key sound variables such as duration and pitch movement. And importantly, for a performance context such as this, it captures the multimodal interaction between voice and musical accompaniment. The ultimate aim of this chapter is to then semioticize the distinctive set of features identified in the system network and visual representations. Following van Leeuwen's (1999, 2009) 'experiential' meaning potential, the rap and the sung voice are assigned meanings according to the physiological choices that distinguish the respective vocal performances.

8.2   Locating paralanguage

Following Halliday (1985), Matthiessen (2007, 2009), Martin (2011) and Cleirigh (in preparation), the term 'paralanguage' is used in this chapter as the superordinate term for the perceivable, meaningful variables of pitch, loudness, duration and voice quality produced by the human voice. Before proceeding, it is worth contextualizing paralanguage in terms of the SFL model of language stratification and the strata of phonetics and phonology (e.g. Halliday and Matthiessen, 2004; Martin, 2010). To begin, the paralinguistic variables analysed in this chapter are not located at the level of phonology within language. For example, pitch movement in both the rap and the sung voice is similar to intonation in language. However, as discussed in the chapter, it is not *equivalent* to the system of TONE in the English language. Moreover, following Halliday and Matthiessen's (2004) stratified expression plane, paralanguage is not located in the phonetics stratum. The analysis presented here is a *semiotic* interpretation of sound, not a biological study of 'the interfacing with the body's resources for speech and for hearing' (Halliday and Matthiessen, 2004: 25).

Having said this, it is potentially misleading to present paralanguage as always distinct from the language system – as an independent meaning-making system. While vocal noises do not have to accompany linguistic signs (e.g. interjections, wailing, or the vocal performance 'scatting') the performance voices analysed here are not simply meaningful 'sounds', articulated in isolation from the content strata of the linguistic system. They are produced by the same mode – the human voice – and therefore *simultaneously* realize a potentially distinct set of meanings. Paralanguage is therefore best conceptualized as both a distinct and interacting modality – a concurrent expression form. This is captured, somewhat crudely, in Figure 8.1.

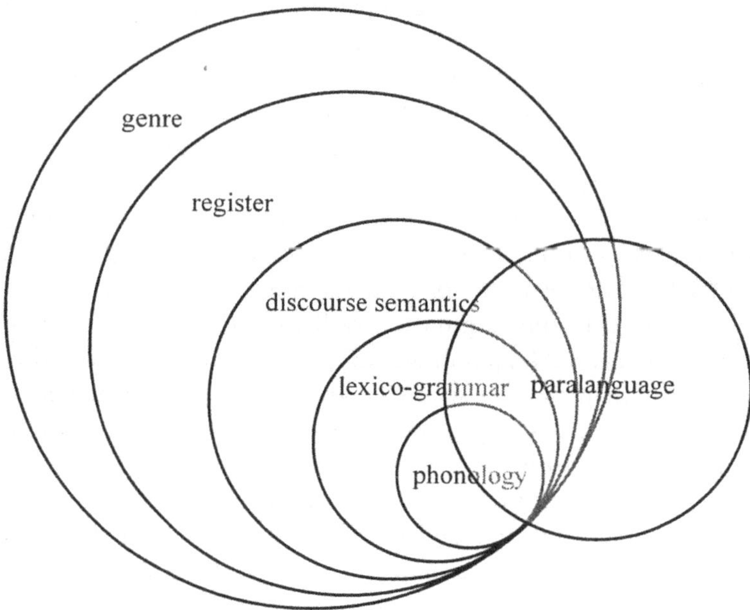

Figure 8.1 Paralanguage intersecting with the stratified language system.

While acknowledging the complex interaction between paralanguage and the language system (see also Matthiessen, 2009 for a discussion of 'semiotic integration'), this chapter nevertheless conceptualizes the aforementioned paralinguistic variables as *distinct* from the language system. In other words, the voice is considered 'meaningful', irrespective of the co-articulating meanings made in the lexicogrammar and discourse semantics. In these terms, the meaning-making potential of the voice is 'natural' or 'iconic'; there is a 'non-arbitrariness in the relation of sound to meaning' (Halliday and Greaves, 2008: 168). Or for van Leeuwen (1999), the meaning-making potential of the human voice is motivated by its inherent materiality.

8.3 The system network

A key feature of SFL (Halliday, 1985; Halliday and Matthiessen, 2004; Martin, 2010) is the foregrounding of the paradigmantic axis of language. In these terms, language is described as a set of choices from a larger system or paradigm – 'what is meant, against the background of what might have been meant but was not' (Halliday and Greaves, 2008: 94). The principle of paradigmatic organization, integral to SFL phonology, is also applicable to sound semiotics more generally. Van Leeuwen (1999), for example, offers a paradigmatic approach to the description of verbal and musical sounds in which he describes the semiotic resources of sound as sets of system networks for loudness, time, interacting sounds, melody and voice quality. For van Leeuwen, and SFL more generally, the 'choices' that comprise a semiotic resource are presented in the form of system networks. In short, a system network presents choice as: '(a) *binary opposites*, (b) *ever more 'delicate' choices* (moving from left to right in a system network one moves from the broadest headings to the finest subdivisions) and (c) in terms of their *semiotic value*' (*ibid.*: 6).

Drawing on this paradigmatic tradition, the following analysis compares the perceivable, paralinguistic features of the rap and the sung voice as a system network. To begin, the complete system network is presented, and includes a general overview of each of the systems, as well as instructions on how to read the system network. Each system is then discussed in greater detail. Where applicable, reference is made to Praat spectrograms (Boersma and Weenink, 2008) and sound representations (Caldwell, 2010a) to exemplify the various systems that comprise the system network.[2]

8.3.1 An overview

Figure 8.2 presents the complete system network for the rap and the sung voice. It comprises six main subsystems: consonant aspiration, syllable nucleus (length), rhyme, melodiousness (number of longer syllables per line), time, and voice quality: resonance. Moreover, the network comprises three distinct units: the syllable, the sound act, and the phase. The syllable systems are consonant aspiration and syllable nucleus; the sound act systems are rhyme, melodiousness and time; and the phase system is voice quality.

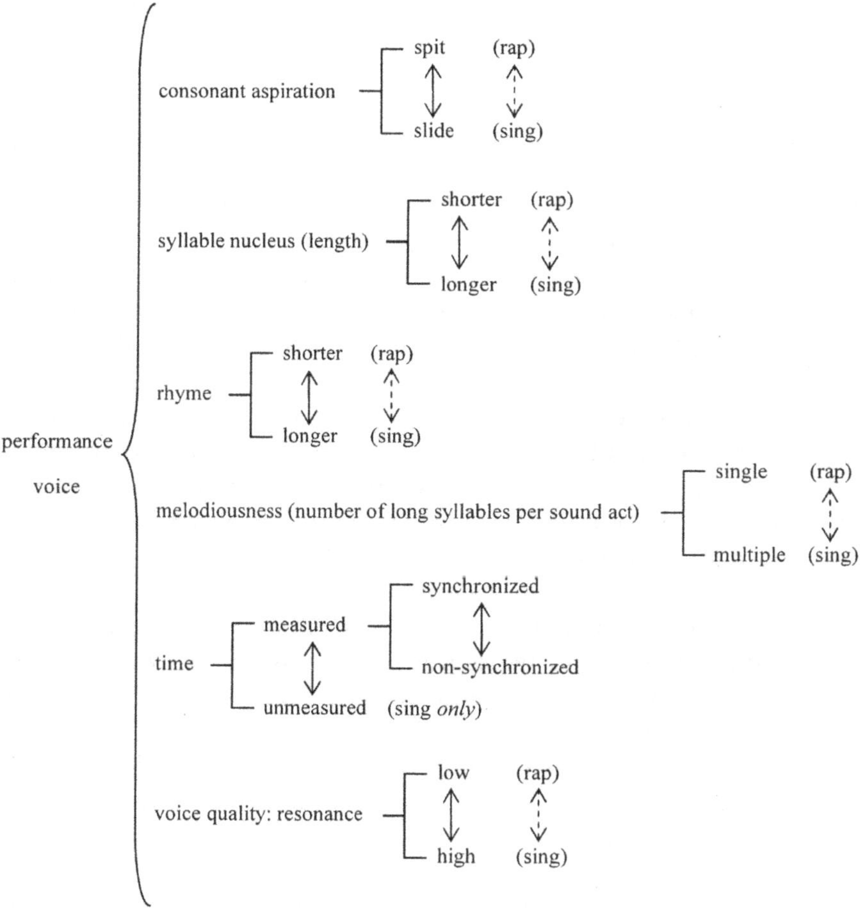

Figure 8.2 System network: the rap and the sung voice.

These systems are chosen simultaneously, as indicated by the large curly bracket for the overall system of performance voice. With the exception of melodiousness, each system comprises gradable choices, indicated by the solid double-headed arrow between each of the features. In other words, the systems do not comprise a discrete 'either-or' choice between features; it is a matter of degree. This approach aligns with van Leeuwen (1999, 2009), who argues that the systems of voice quality comprise terminal choices with gradation:

> in the case of voice quality, I found *only simultaneous* choices ... and, as the double-headed arrows indicate, these choices are not binary, not

'either/or', but graded choices, a range of intermediate positions between 'maximally low' and 'maximally high', or 'maximally loud' and 'maximally soft'. (van Leeuwen, 2009: 74–5)

So, for example, the choice between spit and slide for the system of consonant aspiration in Figure 8.2 is presented as a choice along a cline: from maximum spit to maximum slide. It is also worth noting, that alongside each of the features is a corresponding cline, illustrated with a broken double-headed arrow. This cline is especially important as it shows which performance voice, rapping or singing, corresponds to a particular paralinguistic choice. This is not applicable to the system of time.

There are two additional things to note here. First, the cline from rap to sung and its corresponding feature is a 'weighted' choice. In other words, the correlation between performance voice and paralinguistic feature presented above is not absolute; it is the more *likely*, or *probable* choice. So for example, as illustrated in Figure 8.2, there is a higher probability of the sung voice selecting to slide its consonant aspiration. That does not mean however that the sung voice can never spit its consonants. There is still that potential. Just as it is possible for the rap voice to slide its consonants, rather than spit its consonants. The point is this: there is a greater *probability* of the sung voice to slide its consonant aspiration. Conversely, the rap voice is more likely to spit its consonant aspiration. While the features presented in the system network illustrate the distinguishing features of the rap and the sung voice, they should not be read as exclusive.

Second, the system network is general in its scope and does not aim to illustrate the many different styles of rap or sung voice. It simply aims to capture the paralinguistic choices that characterize a rap voice as distinct from a soulful sung voice. It presents an 'idealized' rap voice and sung voice, as *relative* to each other. There is however the potential to capture different styles in this system network because the rap and sung voices are presented along a cline. So for example, rap styles which tend to slide more of their consonants would be located closer to the slide end of the consonant aspiration cline. In addition, there may be potential here to describe distinct vocal styles through delicacy in the system network, although, as noted by van Leeuwen (2009) above, this may not be possible with some of the paralinguistic variables.

8.3.2 The units

The system network comprises six systems, each of which can be categorized under three linguistic units: the syllable, the sound act, and the phase. Consonant aspiration and syllable nucleus correspond to the unit of syllable; rhyme, melodiousness, and time correspond to the sound act; and vocal resonance corresponds to the phase.

These units do *not* constitute a rank scale as theorized in SFL (see Zhao, 2010 for a review of rank scale in SFL). For SFL theory, rank is more than a theory of constituency. It is deeply entrenched in the paradigmatic organization of phonology and grammar, and as such, is intrinsic to the construction of system networks. The units discussed here, in contrast, are presented only as constituents: a phase is made up of sound acts, and a sound act is made up of syllables. In other words, the use of the term rank is not meant to imply system-structure cycles in the system network, just constituency.

Drawing on the phonological rank scale outlined by Halliday and Matthiessen (2004),[3] the unit of syllable for this system network is equivalent to their unit of syllable – basically defined here as a unit of sound clusters. Technically, this work follows the principles of autosegmental phonology (e.g. Goldsmith, 1990), in which the syllable is organized around a peak of high sonority, primarily consisting of onset and rhyme, realized by consonant and vowel phonemes respectively. Or as Clark and Yallop explain, 'a major peak of prominence represents the NUCLEUS of a syllable and that this nucleus will usually be a vowel or vowel-like segment; consonants will generally occur as MARGINS to these peaks, either as ONSET or CODA' (Clark and Yallop, 1995: 60).

The rank of sound act (van Leeuwen, 1999) is the most difficult of all three units to define. In terms of the phonological rank scale in SFL, a sound act is basically analogous to the tone group or tone 'unit' (Halliday and Greaves, 2008). In short, the unit of a tone group is identified by a tonic syllable – 'one particular salient syllable which stands out because of its combination of amplitude, duration (timing), and change of pitch' (*ibid.*: 54). To varying degrees, both the rap and the sung voice comprise a 'tonic-like' syllable. However, the term sound act is preferred to tone unit because the rap and the sung voice each comprises particular 'musical' qualities that spoken language does not foreground. For instance, the placement of the tonic syllable in the rap voice is much more regularized than it is in speech because it is determined by the metre of the percussive accompaniment. And in the case of the sung voice, it is sometimes difficult to even locate a tonic syllable given that most syllables are long in duration and carry an audible pitch movement. Moreover, the tonic syllable in these performance voices does not completely function as it does for the tone unit in spoken language. In contrast with spoken language, the tonic syllable identified in rap and sung voices does not always 'function directly as the realization of systems in the grammar' (*ibid.*: 47). For example, a rising pitch movement in the performance voices does not correlate with the 'yes/no' interrogative in the lexicogrammar; there is not the same systematic relationship between the TONE system in the phonology and the MOOD system in the grammar. And while the textual systems of TONALITY and TONICITY (*ibid.*) appear applicable to the rap voice, they do not appear *as* applicable to the sung voice. Without a more thorough, detailed analysis, it would be unfair to claim that any of the phonological systems identified for spoken language apply, in their *entirety*, to either performance voice.

For the purposes of this analysis then, van Leeuwen's (1999) sound act is preferred to tone unit as it distinguishes the performance voices from spoken language. Moreover, the term sound act is general enough to capture the distinct rhythms and pitch movement of the rap and the sung voice. Technically, a sound act is framed by a rhythmic phrase of up to seven measures or rhythmic feet: 'marked off from each other by breaks or changes in the regular rhythm of the pulses' (*ibid.*: 211). Moreover, much like the tone unit, the sound act carries a discernable melodic contour which van Leeuwen *likens* to the tone unit in speech (*ibid.*: 101–3). It is also worth noting that the paralinguistic unit of the sound act in both the rap and the sung voice generally equates to a clause in the lexicogrammar. This follows systemic phonology, where the tone unit, as the realization of the information unit, in the default case equates to the rank of clause in the linguistic lexicogrammar. However, as noted above, while the unit *size* may be congruent between sound act and clause, there is not necessarily the same systemic congruency between the interpersonal function of the phonology and lexicogrammar.

The term 'phase' has been adapted from discourse analysis (e.g. Martin and Rose, 2008). In terms of discourse semantics, it refers to stretches of discourse, comprising of one or more clauses, which are reasonably stable and consistent in terms of their discourse semantic composition. A shift in the paralinguistic variable of voice quality is considered analogous to this unit. In other words, a change in voice quality generally correlates with a marked shift in the discourse semantics. And in this case, this typically means a shift from the rap voice to the sung voice – from verse to chorus. Moreover, the unit of phase is applicable to the system of voice quality because it comprises one or more sound acts. In other words, a rapper or singer does not shift performance voice, and therefore vocal resonance, *within* a single sound act.

8.3.3 Consonant aspiration

The system of consonant aspiration is reproduced below in Figure 8.3. The sound bites used to produce this system were sampled from the same monosyllabic word: 'time' /taɪm/. In order to control as many variables as possible, the two instances of 'time' are produced by the same vocalist: Kanye West. Moreover, both syllables are located at the end of a sound act; they are both the rhyme syllable.

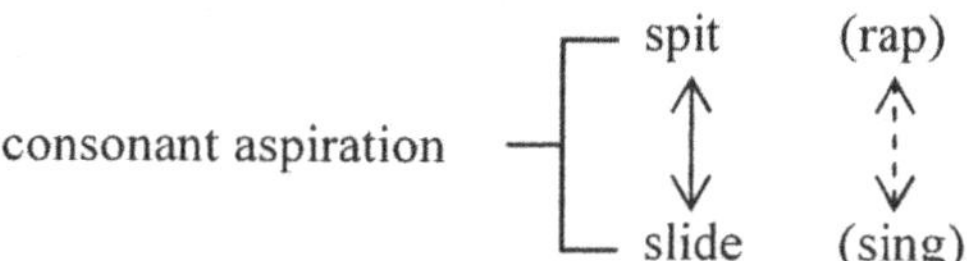

Figure 8.3 System network: consonant aspiration.

The system of consonant aspiration comprises two gradable choices: from maximum spit, to maximum slide. The term spit was chosen because it is a common term in hip-hop vernacular discourse – as a synonym for the process 'to rap' (see e.g. Smitherman, 1994). As displayed above, the rap voice is characterized by spit consonant aspiration and the sung voice by slide consonant aspiration. Consonant aspiration is applicable to the word initial voiceless plosives [p] [t] [k] and the affricate [tʃ], although there is also potential for the word initial voiced plosives [b] [d] [g] and affricate [dʒ] to articulate some aspiration (see e.g. Clark and Yallop, 1995).

There is a clear, perceivable difference between the rap voice and the sung voice in terms of the aural perception of consonant aspiration. In short, the rap voice has a longer, more audible consonant aspiration than the sung voices. Figure 8.4 and Figure 8.5 are Praat spectrograms for the syllable /taɪm/ in West's rap and sung voices. In terms of consonant aspiration, these images confirm aural perception: that the consonant aspiration is longer in duration in the rap voice than the sung voice. And as such, the exhalation sound in the rap voice is much more audible and pronounced. More specifically, the images show that the duration of the consonant /t/ in the rap voice is 0.111, compared with the sung voice 0.072 – a difference of 0.039 seconds. This is especially noteworthy given that the sung voice is significantly longer than the rap voice in terms of the overall duration of the syllable.

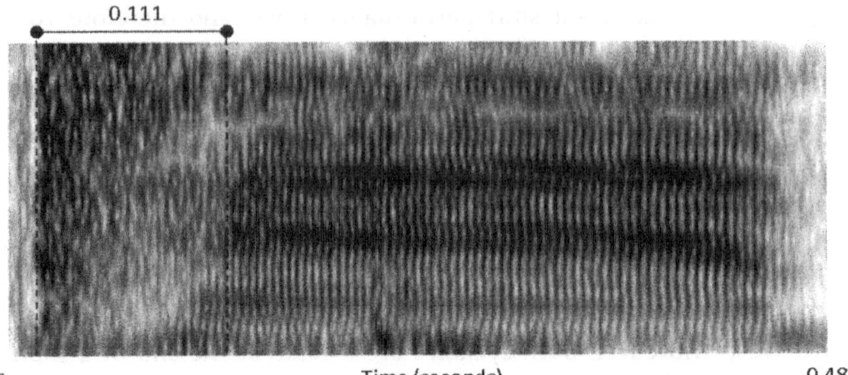

Figure 8.4 Spectrogram: spit consonant aspiration of /t/ in West's rap voice ('Gone', West, 2005).

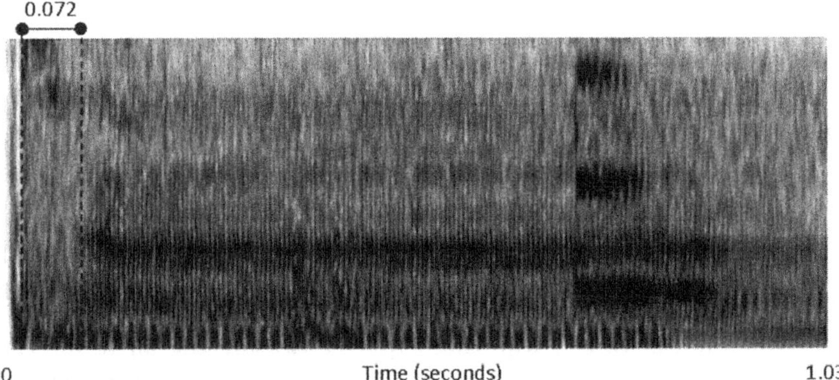

Figure 8.5 Spectrogram: slide consonant aspiration of /t/ in West's sung voice ('Say You Will', West, 2008).

In phonetics and segmental articulation, the difference in consonant aspiration described above is understood as a matter of timing, as a delay in voice onset (see e.g. Clark and Yallop, 1995). In other words, the rap voice delays the voicing of the subsequent vowel and therefore has a prolonged aspiration. In contrast, the onset of the voicing is almost immediate for the sung voice, and the aspiration reduced.

8.3.4 Syllable nucleus

The system of syllable nucleus (length) is reproduced below in Figure 8.6. The same sound bites from consonant aspiration (sound bites 3.26 and 3.27) are used to illustrate the features of this system.

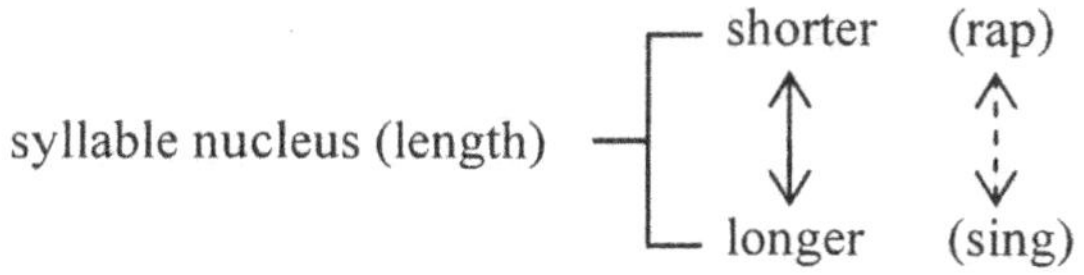

Figure 8.6 System network: syllable nucleus.

The system of syllable nucleus comprises two gradable choices: from maximally shorter to maximally longer vowel length. As discussed, syllable nucleus is a technical term from phonetics and refers to the major peak of activity or prominence of a syllable, realized by a voiced vowel, and vowel-like sounds. In short, the rap voice is characterized by a shorter syllable nucleus than the sung voice, which is characterized by a longer syllable nucleus.

The difference in vowel length between the rap and the sung voice is clearly perceivable when comparing sound bites. This perception is

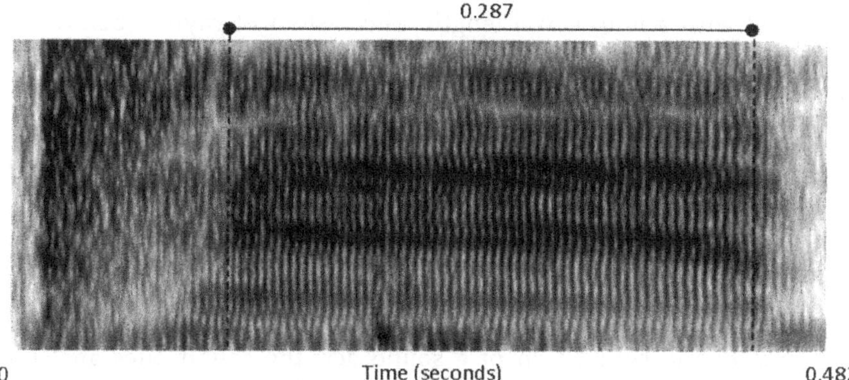

Figure 8.7 Spectrogram: shorter syllable nucleus in the phoneme /aɪ/ in the rap voice ('Gone', West, 2005).

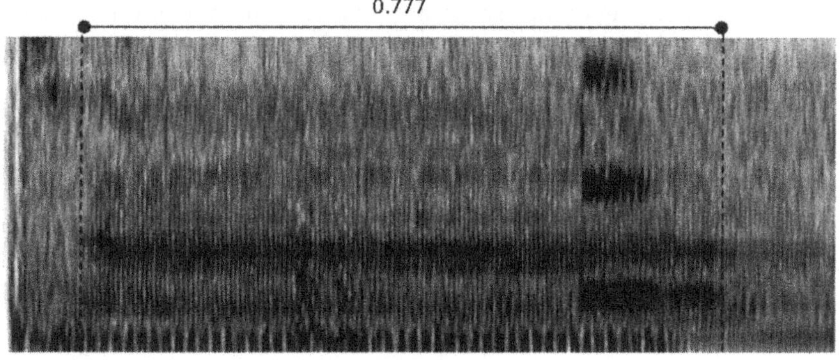

Figure 8.8 Spectrogram: longer syllable nucleus in the phoneme /aɪ/ in the sung voice ('Say you will', West, 2008).

confirmed in the following Praat images, again, of the syllable /taɪm/ (see Figures 8.7 and 8.8), which show a much longer duration for the vowel formants in the sung voice when compared with the rap voice. Specifically, the duration of the diphthong phoneme /aɪ/ in the rap voice is 0.287 seconds, compared with the sung voice of 0.777 seconds – a difference of 0.490 seconds.

From a phonetic perspective, this difference in vowel duration can be understood in terms of voice onset; the rap voice has a more delayed voice onset than the sung voice. However, this does not *completely* account for the difference in duration between syllable nuclei, and is more relevant to the system of consonant aspiration. Simply put, there is a greater duration of the syllable nucleus in the sung voice than the rap voice. The voiced sound is sustained for a longer period of time, independent of the initial consonant.

Again, this system is not meant to imply that the rap voice is never articulated with a long vowel length. The system of rhyme (below) for example shows that rappers quite systematically produce vowels that are longer in duration when compared with other syllable nuclei articulated in the same rap voice. The point is this: as a weighted choice, relative to the sung voice, the rap voice is characterized by shorter syllable nuclei.

8.3.5 Rhyme

The system of rhyme is reproduced in Figure 8.9. Because the system of rhyme marks the completion of a sound act, the sound bites analysed are complete clauses, although the features of the rhyme system itself relate specifically to the final rhyming word in each clause, in this case, the multi-syllabic 'again' /əˈgɛn/.[4]

The system of rhyme comprises two gradable choices: from maximally shorter to maximally longer syllables. Unlike the systems discussed previously, rhyme length does not separate consonant and vowel sounds; it includes all syllables in a word, including unstressed syllables. The concern here is any perceivable difference in duration between the long syllables that define the boundary of the sound act. And as discussed earlier, these

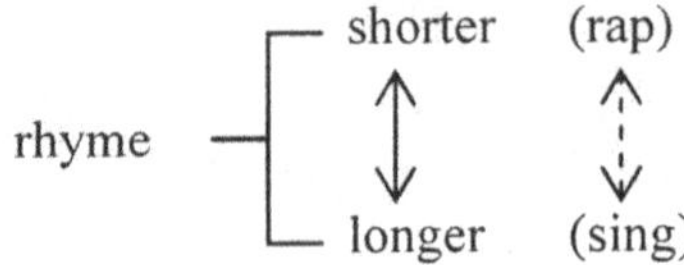

Figure 8.9 System network: rhyme.

syllables are similar in form to the tonic in spoken language, although they do not completely have the same function as they do in systemic phonology. Moreover, the syllable that realizes this system is generally the 'rhyming' syllable in poetic terms, and is not to be confused with rhyme from metrical phonology (see e.g. Clark and Yallop, 1995: 411).

Figure 8.9 shows that the rap voice is characterized by a shorter rhyme than the sung voice. The difference in syllable length between the rap and sung voices is clearly perceivable when comparing the sound bites. This perception is confirmed in the following Praat images in Figure 8.10 and Figure 8.11, which show a much longer duration for the sung voice when compared with the rap voice. Specifically, the duration of the multi-syllabic word /əˈgɛn/ in the rap voice is 0.519, and the sung voice 1.133 – a difference of 0.614 seconds.

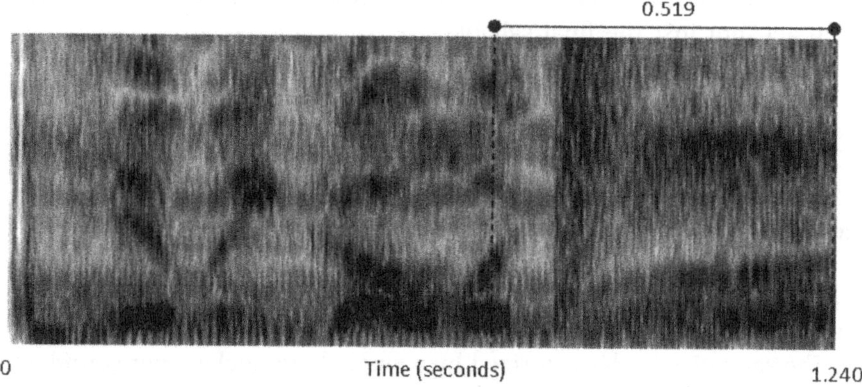

Figure 8.10 Spectrogram: shorter rhyme əˈgɛn ('Everything I am', West, 2007).

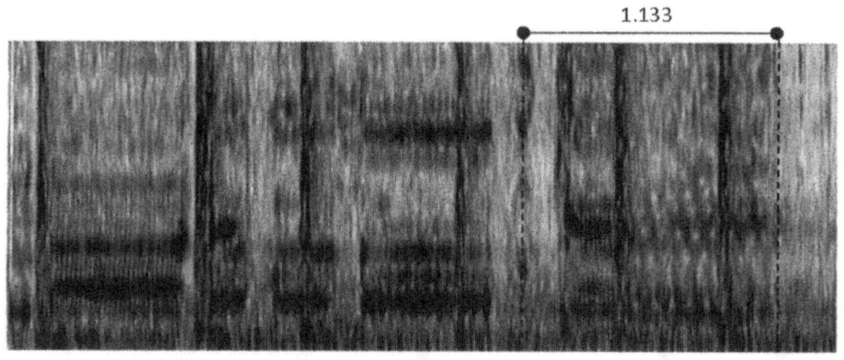

Figure 8.11 Spectrogram: longer rhyme əˈgɛn ('Coldest winter', West, 2008).

These findings are consistent with the previous analysis for the syllable; the rap syllable is shorter than the sung syllable. However, the system of rhyme is included in the complete system network to show two things. First, it shows that the paralanguage does mark the completion of a sound act. Second, it shows that the rap voice *does* include a long syllable nucleus. The point is however, that these are only long syllable nuclei with respect to the other syllable nuclei in the same sound act. And ultimately, as illustrated above, the rhymes in the rap voice are still significantly shorter than the rhymes in the sung voice.

8.3.6 Melodiousness

The system of melodiousness is reproduced in Figure 8.12. Unlike the system of rhyme, the system of melodiousness is realized by the entire sound act, not just the final syllable.

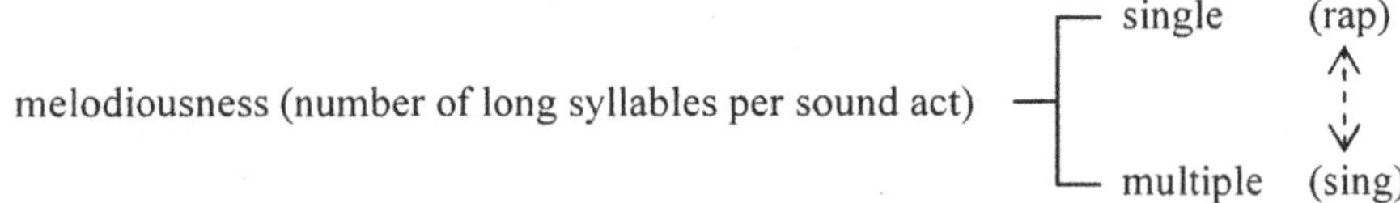

Figure 8.12 System network: melodiousness.

The system of melodiousness comprises a non-gradable choice between a single long nucleus per sound act and multiple long nuclei per sound act. The rap voice is characterized by a single long nucleus per sound act – the obligatory rhyme outlined in the previous section. The sung voice however is characterized by multiple long nuclei per sound act, including the obligatory rhyme syllable. This fundamental distinction between performance voices is captured in the following sound representations.

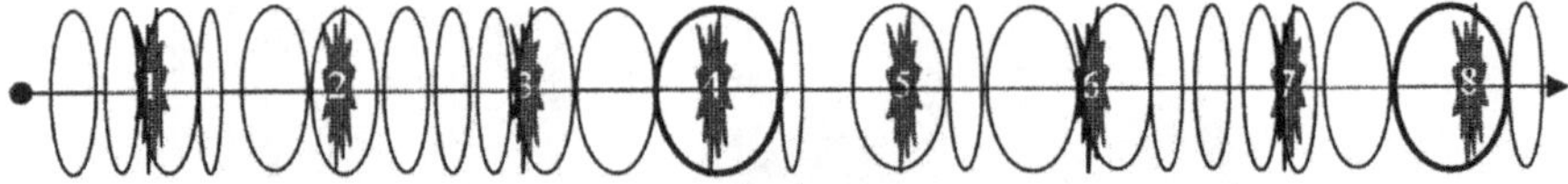

Figure 8.13 Sound representation: single long nuclei ('Family business', West, 2004: 5.172 s).

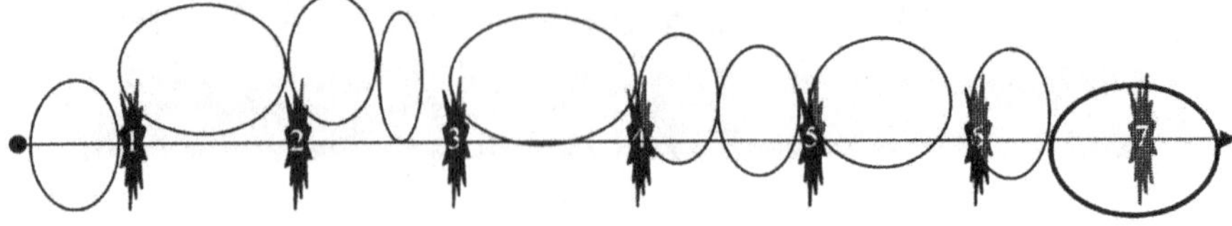

Figure 8.14 Sound representation: multiple long nuclei ('Amazing', West, 2008: 5.799 s).

The sound representations presented above are developed from Praat spectrograms (see Caldwell, 2010a for a detailed overview of the construction of these sound representations). In short, the oval symbols represent syllables expressed by a vocalist, and the shaded explosion symbols represent the rhythmic pulse of the musical accompaniment. Each sound bite is between five and six seconds in total duration (see caption for exact duration of sound bite). And this typically equates to two bars of 4/4 metred music, or eight pulses (as indicated by the numbering within the explosion symbols). This is ideal, given that most rap music, including the data analysed here, is based on quadruple time.

The first point to note here is that the contrasting sound representations presented above differ in terms of their number of sound acts. The rap voice comprises two sound acts, realized by two longer 'rhyme' syllables which articulate an audible pitch movement. These are located on pulse 4 and pulse 8, represented with a thicker line in Figure 8.13. The sung voice however presented in Figure 8.14 is one complete sound act with the rhyme syllable articulated on pulse 7.

The sound representations for the sung voice also capture pitch movement. As with traditional staff notation, this is illustrated along the vertical axis. In essence, the higher the syllable symbol is plotted on the vertical axis, the higher the pitch – the lower the syllable, the lower the pitch. The melodies are constructed from a staff transcription for pitch. Following that transcription, the syllables are plotted along the vertical axis. The horizontal line is considered 'middle C'. A single semitone movement up or down the scale is represented as four horizontal 'clicks' on the curser. In this way, the visual representation of pitch movement is accurate. However, these visual representations of sound do not include a key signature. The aim here is to simply capture the extent and direction of the pitch movement. It should also be noted that the representation of the sung voice is not meant to imply that the rap voice has *no* pitch movement. It does. However, it would be misleading to adjust the height of a rhyme syllable in the rap voice and compare it with the sung representation given that the horizontal axis is quite technically presented here as 'middle C'.

In terms of the construction of the actual system of melodiousness, the point of these sound representations is essentially to show the significantly longer syllable duration in the sung voice as compared with the rap voice. As mentioned above, there is only one longer syllable per sound act in the rap voice – the rhyme syllable located on pulse 4 and 8 respectively. For the sung voice however, there is the potential for multiple long syllables per sound act. In the representation above for example, the sung voice articulates four longer syllables per sound act, located near pulses 1, 3, 5 and 7 in Figure 8.14.

8.3.7 Time

The system of time is reproduced in Figure 8.15. Time varies from the other simultaneous systems presented here in two ways. First, the system of time comprises a level of delicacy; measured time involves an additional graded choice between synchronized and non-synchronized time. Second, in terms of the rap and sung voices, the features of time are not weighted towards one particular performance voice. The rap voice only selects from measured time. The sung voice can select from either measured or unmeasured time.

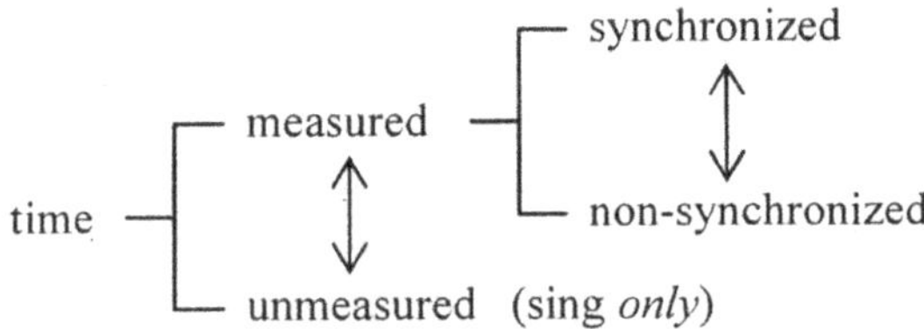

Figure 8.15 System network: time.

The system of time comprises an initial, fundamental distinction between two gradable choices: measured time and unmeasured time. According to van Leeuwen (1999: 207), measured time has a regular pulse: 'time you can tap your feet to'. In contrast, unmeasured time has no discernable regular pulse, and as such, is not a form of time to 'tap your feet to'. With unmeasured time, 'you might at best sway your body to and fro' (*ibid.*: 51). The choice between measured and unmeasured time is integral to a comparative analysis of the rap voice and the sung voice. As the system network shows in Figure 8.15, only the sung voice has the potential to articulate unmeasured time.

According to van Leeuwen, there are two kinds of unmeasured time:

> *continuous time*, which lacks any form of phrasing and either does not vary in pitch at all, or wavers in pitch in slight and irregular ways, and *fluctuating time*, which also lacks phrasing, but does shift between pitches, at more or less regular intervals which are, however, too long to produce a clear sense of regular pulse or periodicity, a rhythm listeners could tap their feet to. (van Leeuwen, 1999: 54)[5]

Following these definitions, it is reasonable to conclude that only the sung voice has the potential to be unmeasured. The syllables articulated in the rap voice are simply too short, and too bound to the time of the percussive instrumentation to be classified as unmeasured. The syllables in the sung voice however are *potentially* long enough in duration to be unmeasured – to *not* articulate a discernable pulse. This is illustrated below in Figure 8.16 with an extract from the singing voice of the Harlem Boys Choir. In this case, the single syllable is *so* long in duration that it does not articulate any kind of pulse; it is an example of unmeasured, continuous time.

Figure 8.16 Sound representation: unmeasured time (The Harlem Boys Choir in 'Two Words', West, 2004: 5.276 s).

There is a clear contrast then between the rap and the sung voice in terms of time; the sung voice has the potential to be unmeasured, the rap voice does not. However, with the exception of the segment above, there are very few other examples in the West corpus at least of an unmeasured sung voice in van Leeuwen's (1999) technical terms, that is, without rhythmic phrasing. And yet, excluding the coinciding percussive sounds, the sung voice is still very much distinguishable from the rap voice in terms of the way in which a listener physically engages with the sound. In other words, the sung voice does not articulate time to the same extent as the rap voice. As such, it does not afford the same kinds of movements to its listeners. In van Leeuwen's terms, the sung voice is *harder* to tap one's feet to. There is a pulse by virtue of the phrasing and its adherence to the beat of the percussive sounds. However, that pulse is generally *less* articulated in the sung voice. In order to capture this lack of rhythmic articulation, the system network therefore construes the choice between measured and unmeasured along a cline; it is gradable. As mentioned, the rap voice is always measured, always articulating a pulse. And as illustrated above, the sung voice has the potential to lack phrasing and therefore be unmeasured. As a modification of van Leeuwen (1999), and following van Leeuwen (2009), the sung voice is also considered here to have the potential to be *less* measured.

A sung voice is considered less measured when it does not articulate many of the key rhythmic pulses in a sound act. This is neatly captured in the sound representation in Figure 8.17.

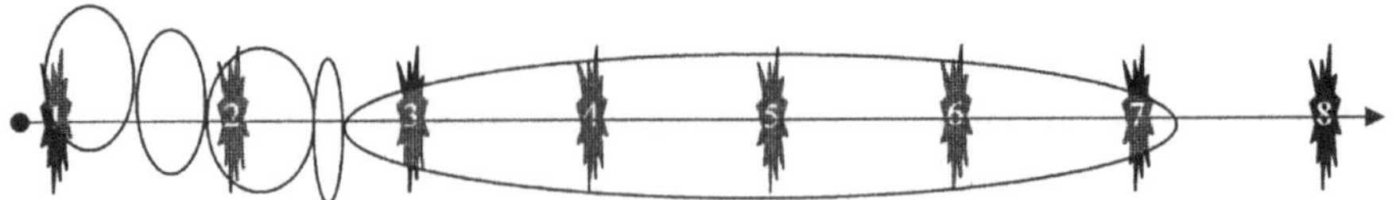

Figure 8.17 Sound representation: unmeasured time (Kahn in 'Through the Wire', West, 2004: 5.355 s).

The representation in Figure 8.17 shows that the sung voice does not articulate pulses 4–6. Technically the voice is still measured because it is synchronized with the meter of the musical sounds; the syllables coincide with pulses 1, 2 and 3, concluding the longest syllable on pulse 7. However, because this sung voice does not articulate every pulse, in terms of physical engagement at least, it is considered *less* measured. In other words, a listener has fewer sung pulses to physically engage with – to 'tap their feet' to. Of course this interpretation is applicable to the voice only. In many cases, such as the segment above, there *are* sounds aside from the voice which articulate the pulse. Listeners would still be able to 'tap their feet' to the above segment, although they would be engaging with the musical sounds, rather than the vocal performance.

The system network shows that the rap and the sung voice both express measured time; they can articulate a discernable pulse. It is important then for the system network to account for the way in which the measured voice engages with the regular, metred 4/4 pulse of the musical accompaniment. Accordingly, there is an additional level of delicacy for the system of measured time: a choice between degrees of synchronization. The system of synchronization is analogous to van Leeuwen's (1999) system of metronomic and non-metronomic time, where synchronization is metronomic and non-synchronization is non-metronomic time. According to van Leeuwen, measured time is precise and unwavering, whereas non-metronomic timing subverts measured time by anticipating or delaying the beat, or 'syncopation' in traditional music terminology. The term synchronization is distinguished from metronomic time for two reasons.

First, synchronization is strictly considered here a multimodal phenomenon – an example of semiotic integration (Matthiessen, 2009). In essence, this system captures the extent to which the salient syllables of the vocal performance actually 'map onto' or synchronize with the 4/4 pulse of the musical accompaniment. Occasionally the West corpus will involve rap or sung voice without a musical accompaniment. In those rare instances however, the pulse has already been established by the musical accompaniment and is soon reintroduced. In short, the performance voice analysed here is always interacting with a regular pulse determined by the musical accompaniment.

Second, in contrast to van Leeuwen's (1999) system of metronomic timing, the choice between synchronization and non-synchronization is gradable. This is because the system is conceptualized as a unit of sound act. It comprises multiple pulses. As such, this system is gradable in terms of the extent to which the voice synchronizes with all of the musical pulses in a sound act. A voice is classified as having a high degree of synchronization when all the salient syllables synchronize with all pulses in the sound act. When the voice mostly synchronizes with the pulses it is considered to have a moderate degree of synchronization. And when the voice synchronizes with none, or at least very few of the pulses in the sound act, it is considered non-synchronized. The following sound representations capture degrees of synchronization in the rap voice.

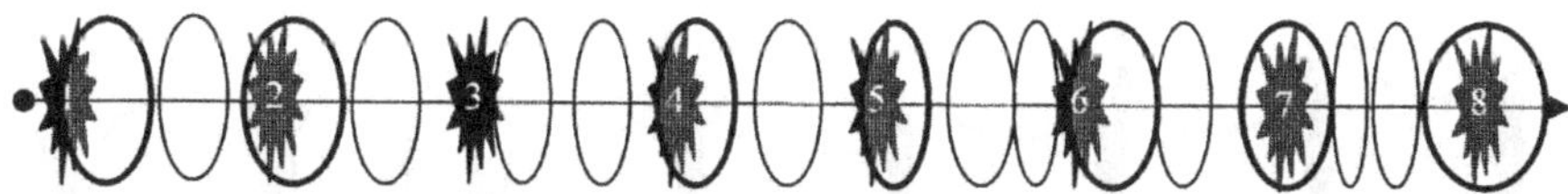

Figure 8.18 Sound representation: synchronized time ('Two words', West, 2004: 5.407 s).

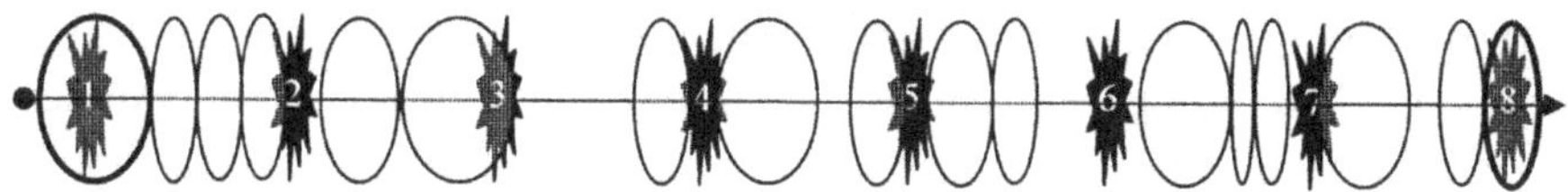

Figure 8.19 Sound representation: non-synchronized time ('Common, get em high', West, 2004: 5.093 s).

Figure 8.18 shows most of the syllables of the rap voice synchronizing with the pulse of the music – seven of a possible eight synchronizations (represented by a thicker line). In contrast, Figure 8.19 shows far fewer salient syllables synchronizing with the pulse of the instrumental support. In total, the vocalist only synchronizes two syllables with the pulse of the music. It is also worth noting that in several instances, such as pulse 7, the rapper is close to synchronizing his syllables with the musical pulse. However, these are not considered examples of true synchronization. The syllable symbol must overlap with at least half of the percussive explosion symbol for it to be classified as an instance of synchronicity. This appears to be the threshold of synchronization – where the vocals are perceived as either anticipating or delaying the beat. Furthermore, pulse 3 is not considered an instance of synchronization. Synchronization occurs when the onset of the syllable coincides with the onset of the musical sound. The point here is that the extract in Figure 8.19 is not an instance of unmeasured time. The pulse is still being realized. It is simply subverted. Moreover, the vocal performances are only ever subverted for a short period of time. In the segment represented in Figure 8.19 for example, the vocalist clearly, and quite explicitly, re-synchronizes at pulse eight.

While the rap voice is characterized by measured time, the sung voice also expresses measured time, although in the terms discussed above, it is generally *less* measured than the rap voice. And although the sung voice is less measured, it still selects from the system of synchronization. In fact, the unmarked choice for the sung voice in the West corpus is synchronized time, albeit less measured time. An example of a less measured, synchronized sung voice is presented below in Figure 8.20.

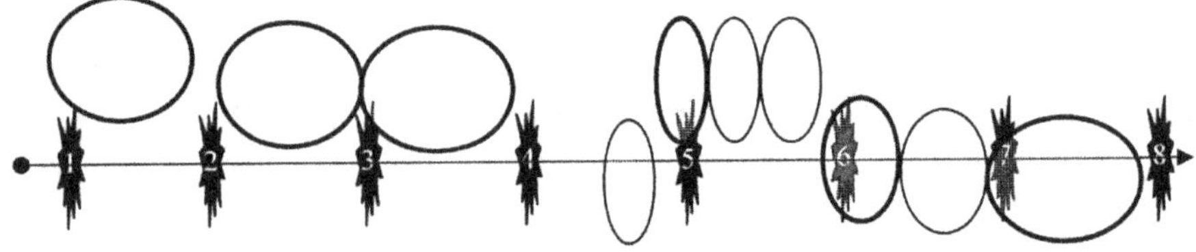

Figure 8.20 Sound representation: synchronization ('Last call', from West, 2004: 5.015 s).

In the sound representation above, the voice synchronizes with almost every pulse, excluding pulses 4 and 8. It is therefore considered an instance of synchronized time. Again, non-synchronization in the sung voice should not be confused with unmeasured time. In those terms, the rap and the sung voice are distinguishable in terms of the extent to which the voice itself articulates time. In this case, the sung voice is less measured because it does not articulate pulses 4 and 8. However it is still synchronized to the regular 4/4 metre articulated by the percussive, musical sounds.

8.3.8 Resonance

The system of resonance is reproduced in Figure 8.21. The system was constructed with the syllable /taɪm/, the same sound bites used to illustrate consonant aspiration and syllable nucleus.

The system of resonance comprises two gradable choices: from maximum resonance to minimal resonance. The rap voice is characterized by reduced or minimal resonance. The sung voice in contrast is characterized by maximum vocal resonance. As a perceptual category, resonance

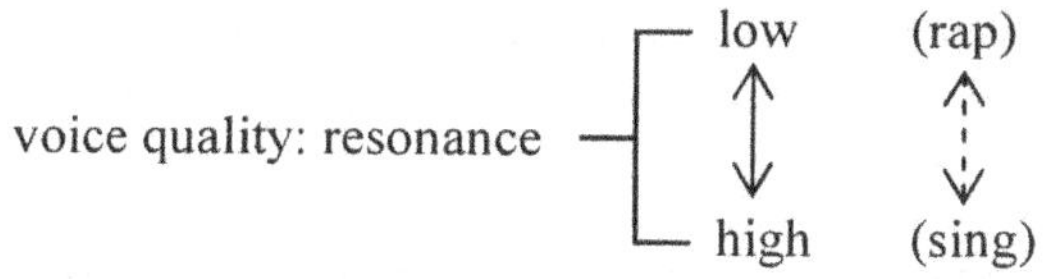

voice quality: resonance
— low   (rap)
— high   (sing)

Figure 8.21 System network: voice quality: resonance.

has to do with the extent to which a sound reverberates. For van Leeuwen (1999: 176), resonance is conceptualized in terms of absorption range: 'from the completely "dry" to the maximally spacious, reverberating and resonating sound'. And according to Callaghan (2000), vocal resonance is predominately produced through the articulation of vowels. As such, the sung voice is more resonant than the rap voice simply by virtue of its longer syllable nuclei. However, this does not necessarily mean that the vowel quality for the rap voice lacks resonance. It simply means that any perceivable resonance is substantially reduced because of its shorter syllable nucleus.

8.4   The meanings

The following semiotic interpretation of the system network draws on van Leeuwen's (1999, 2009) 'experiential' or 'embodied'[6] approach to sound semiotics. In essence, van Leeuwen argues that the meaning-making potential of sound is afforded by its materiality; meaning derives from the actual, physical experience of producing and perceiving a sound.[7] Following Lakoff and Johnson's (1980) theory of metaphor, the materiality of the voice is semioticized:

> our experience of what we physically have to do to produce a particular sound creates a meaning potential for that sound. For instance, we know that we can create tense sounds by tensing our articulatory musculature. We also know that we tend to do this in certain kinds of situations (when we are tense or 'charged up', or want to appear that way). Hence tense sound quality can come to be associated with aggression, repression, nervousness, excitement and so on. (van Leeuwen, 1999: 205)

From an embodied perspective then, the rap and the sung voice can each be assigned specific meaning potentials according to what is occurring physically in their respective vocal performances. In other words, what physiological choices do the rappers make compared with singers? And what do those choices mean? How do the embodied meaning potentials of the rap voice compare with the soulful sung voice?

8.4.1 Comparing embodied articulation

The system network presented in Figure 8.2 shows that the rap voice and the soulful sung voice are articulated, or 'experienced', in distinct ways. Of particular relevance here is the unit of the syllable, and the systems of consonant aspiration and syllable nucleus.

The first meaningful dimension of the rap and the sung voice concerns the system of consonant aspiration, which is applicable to all plosive sounds, particularly the word initial voiceless plosives [p], [t] and [k] and the affricate [tʃ]. In short, the system of consonant aspiration shows that the rap voice has a much greater, audible aspiration than the sung voice. And as discussed above, this is technically understood as a delay in voice onset. From articulatory phonetics (e.g. Clark and Yallop, 1995), the aspirated consonants have a greater duration of unobstructed air flow through the open, abducted vocal folds, prior to their eventual vibration.

Unfortunately, this explanation is not completely satisfactory for rapped consonants since it does not capture the distinctive aspiration of the rap voice. The concern here is the manner of articulation that produces a clearly audible, 'spat' aspiration in the rap voice, compared with the sung voice. It is therefore worth considering the manner of articulation of the plosive consonant, or 'stop':

> A stop is produced by the formation and rapid release of a complete closure at any point in the vocal tract from the glottis to the lips. The velum is raised to prevent airflow through the nasal cavity, and the oral airflow is thus interrupted... At the release of a stop, there is a very short sharp pulse of turbulent airflow through the (momentarily) narrow aperture of the parting articulators. During this pulse – known as the 'release burst' – the peak airflow rate can exceed 1.5 litres per second. (Clark and Yallop, 1995: 44–5)

In these terms, the 'release burst' in the rap voice is much more audible and salient than for the equivalent plosives in the sung voice. As mentioned, this can be conceptualized in terms of voice onset; the sung voice articulates a short release burst in order to foreground its vowels. However, the specific concern of the system of consonant aspiration is the articulation of the plosive consonants: what manner of articulation results in a longer, more audible, more *explosive* aspiration in the rap voice?

The concept of 'fortis' articulation from phonetics offers a useful alternative to voice onset. The term fortis articulation basically refers to relatively strong or forceful articulation, as opposed to lenis or weak articulation. And according to Clark and Yallop (1995), fortis articulation is sometimes used to account for the aspiration of stops:

> fortis articulation is probably mainly a matter of greater subglottal pressure (and the term 'heightened subglottal pressure' has been used in some descriptions) but higher airflow and stronger and more definite supraglottal articulatory gestures are likely to accompany an increase in subglottal pressure. (*Ibid.*: 51)

In summary then, the perceivable aspiration in the rap voice is the result of a greater force or intensity in the eggressive airstream. As the higher intensity of airflow is held behind the articulators, it is then released in an extremely turbulent pulse of airflow, resulting in a perceivable spitting sound in the rap voice, as distinct from the sung voice.

The other meaningful distinction between the articulation of the rap and the sung voice involves the system of syllable nucleus. In short, the rap voice has shorter syllable nuclei than the sung voice, whereas vowel sounds are foregrounded in the soulful sung voice. Following van Leeuwen's (1999: 151) system network for speech sounds, the articulation of the rap voice is therefore classified as more vocally constrained than the sung voice. There is a greater and more frequent blockage of airflow in the rap voice because it articulates a shorter syllable nucleus than the sung voice. The sung voice in contrast is classified as more unconstrained because it foregrounds vowel sounds which do not involve blocking or constricting the airflow.

In addition, the lengthy syllable nucleus in the sung voice results in a reduction in the number of syllables articulated per sound act, and therefore a reduction in the number of consonants articulated per sound act. This means an *overall* reduction in the extent to which the sung voice constricts the vocal tract, and therefore the air stream. In contrast, the rap voice is more constricted over the duration of a sound act. It reduces the length of its vowels and articulates more consonant sounds. The image in Figure 8.22 captures the typical vocal posture of the rap voice, compared with the soulful sung voice.

Figure 8.22 compares Kanye West's rap aperture with Shirley Bassey's soulful sung aperture. The image reveals a more constrained or closed aperture in the rap voice; there is very little space between West's teeth and lips for the eggressive airstream to escape. This is comparable with

Figure 8.22 Comparing rap (left, Kanye West) and sung aperture (right, Shirley Bassey). Drawing by Inneke Taalman based on images from Getty Images.[8]

Bassey's extremely open aperture. In order to articulate a lengthy syllable nucleus, Bassey's jaw is lowered, and her aperture is open, enabling the eggressive airstream to escape with minimal obstruction.

It should be noted that Figure 8.22 only captures a particular moment in time during the respective vocal performances. A soulful singer does not always have an open aperture, and a rapper's aperture is not always constrained. The point is, that *relative* to the rap voice, the soulful singer is more likely to have an open aperture, and for longer periods of time. Conversely, the rapper less often has an open aperture. Moreover, it is highly unlikely that a rapper would ever produce an 'open' aperture to the extent illustrated by Bassey in Figure 8.22.

8.4.2 Comparing embodied meanings

The comparable embodied meaning potentials of the rap and sung voice are presented below in Table 8.1. Each feature from the syllable systems

Table 8.1 Embodied meanings of rap and sung voices.

Rap feature	Meaning potential	Sung feature	Meaning potential
+spit	spat, forced, pushed...	+slide	slide, glide, skim...
+shorter	short, closed, obstructed...	+longer	long, open, unobstructed...

of consonant aspiration and syllable nucleus are aligned with a corresponding set of meaning potentials.

The designation of embodied meaning potentials outlined in Table 8.1 is straightforward: the meaning *is* the feature, by virtue of what it is not. So, in the case of spit consonant aspiration, the meaning potential is 'spat', as well as any attributes that are synonymous with spitting, such as 'forced' or 'pushed'. In contrast, slide consonant aspiration has the meaning potential of 'slide', as well as any other near synonyms such as 'to glide' or 'to skim'. For the system of syllable nucleus, a slightly different set of meaning potentials are assigned. The aim here is to capture the physical aperture of the vocalist in terms of the degree of obstruction to their airstream. As such, the rap voice is not only short, but it is physically closed and obstructed, and therefore has the meaning potential of 'closed', 'obstructed' and the like. The sung voice in contrast is long, and therefore has the meaning potential of 'open' and 'unobstructed'.

The remaining systems of rhyme, melodiousness, time and voice quality (resonance) can also be conceptualized semiotically. The rap and the sung voices can be assigned meanings according to the features identified in the system network. For instance, following the system of time, the rap voice is more regular and explicit in its execution of time than the sung voice. Accordingly, it can be assigned meaning potentials such as 'fixed' and 'predictable'. The sung voice in contrast has the potential at least to be more unmeasured, and as such, construes a set of comparative meanings, such as 'free' and 'unpredictable'. Table 8.2 provides a short list of meaning potentials for all three ranks in the system network. Again, these meanings are not meant to be exhaustive. Moreover, they are to be read as a set of *relative* meaning potentials. In other words, the rap voice is considered short, monotone and predictable, *relative* to the long, melodic, unpredictable soulful sung voice.

Table 8.2 Embodied meanings of rap and sung voices (more choices).

Rap feature	Meaning potential	Sung feature	Meaning potential
+spit	spat, forced, pushed...	+slide	slide, glide, skim...
+shorter	short, closed, obstructed...	+longer	long, open, unobstructed...
+single	atonal, measured...	+multiple	melodic, tuneful
+measured	fixed, predictable...	+un/measured	free, unpredictable
+low resonance	non-resonant, finite	+high resonance	resonant, reverberating

8.5   Some directions

This chapter has employed principles from phonetics, systemic phonology, music studies and SFL theory with an aim to describe and compare the embodied meaning potentials of the rap and the sung performance voices. While this approach has proved useful in describing and assigning meanings to the respective performance voices, there is certainly scope to develop this research further.

To begin, it would be worthwhile applying these same principles and methods of analysis to other performance voices, such as country, rock and jazz, as well as rap agnates such as toasting and declamatory speech. The aim here is not only to describe the distinct meaning potentials of those particular performance voices, but to test the robustness of the analysis presented in this chapter. From a more theoretical perspective, there is much work to be done in integrating paralanguage within SFL theory. And this has implications for the systemic phonology of language. In particular, it is important to begin to investigate the extent to which the paralinguistic systems identified in this chapter are relatable to the kinds of phonological systems described by Halliday and Greaves (2008) and explored in this current volume. It is argued in this chapter for example that the intonation systems of rap and sung voices, in interpersonal terms at least, do not have the same functions as speech. Future research needs to examine the *exact* similarities and differences between the deployment of pitch and rhythm in the performance voice compared with speech phonology. For example, what kind of pitch movement *is* possible for the tonic-like syllable in the rap voice? And importantly, how is this different than, or similar to, the TONE system in English phonology?

Returning to the data presented in this chapter, there is also much to develop. Having established a distinguishable set of paralinguistic features, there is now scope to develop the embodied meaning potentials assigned to the rap and the soulful sung voice. Caldwell (in preparation) outlines two such approaches – discourse semantic and protolinguistic. The first approach analogizes from the interpersonal discourse semantic system of APPRAISAL (e.g. Martin and White, 2005) to assign meanings to the rap and the sung voice. The protolinguistic approach follows Cleirigh (in preparation), and applies Halliday's 'micro-functions' to the respective features of rap and sung voices.

As a final comment, this author would like to encourage those scholars working in systemic phonology to consider integrating their insights with the sound semiotics pioneered by van Leeuwen (1999, 2009). Hopefully, this chapter has demonstrated that systemic phonology has implications for those scholars seeking to examine the meaning potential of the many and varied vocal sounds that comprise our contemporary soundscape.

Notes

1. The 'soulful' sung voice is distinguishable from other styles of Western sung voice, such as 'rock' and 'country' (see e.g. Bogdanov *et al.*, 2001). It is characterized by long notes, 'melisma' (the singing of a single syllable while moving between notes), an extensive pitch range and an intensity of feeling.
2. For copyright reasons the sound bites used to construct this system network cannot be reproduced in this publication. The original sound bites are cited throughout the chapter and listed in a discography.
3. In contrast with the phonological rank scale in SFL (Halliday and Matthiessen, 2004), the network presented here does not include the units of phoneme and rhythmic foot. These units are included at the rank of syllable and sound act respectively.
4. Again, for copyright reasons, the song lyrics cannot be reproduced here.
5. The term 'phrasing', or 'rhythmic phrasing', is the marking of boundaries between the sound act via 'breaks or changes in the regular rhythm of the pulses' (van Leeuwen, 1999: 211).
6. The term embodiment is used synonymously with van Leeuwen's (1999) 'experiential' meaning potential. The term 'experiential' is not to be confused with the experiential component of the ideational metafunction (Halliday and Matthiessen, 2004).
7. See also Halliday and Greaves (2008: 168–9) for a relatable discussion of 'phonaesthesia' and 'sound symbolism' more generally.
8. The original Kanye West image is from www.gettyimages.com/detail/news-photo/recording-artist-kanye-west-appears-on-bets-106-park-at-bet-news-photo/76678093, and the original Shirley Bassey image is from www.gettyimages.com/detail/news-photo/welsh-pop-singer-shirley-bassey-in-concert-in-paris-news-photo/3261898 (both accessed 10 April 2012).

References

Boersma, P. and Weenink, D. (2008) Praat: doing phonetics by computer version 5.0.32. Available at www.fon.hum.uva.nl/praat (accessed 1 December 2008).

Bogdanov, V., Woodstra, C. and Erlewine, S. T. (eds) (2001) *All Music Guide: The Definitive Guide to Popular Music.* San Francisco, CA: Backbeat Books.

Caldwell, D. (2010a) Making metre mean: identity and affiliation in the rap music of Kanye West. In M. Bednarek and J. R. Martin (eds) *New Discourse on Language: Functional Perspectives on Multimodality, Identity, and Affiliation* 59–80. London: Continuum.

Caldwell, D. (2010b) Making many meanings in popular rap music. In A. Mahboob and N. Knight (eds) *Appliable Linguistics* 234–51. London: Continuum.

Caldwell, D. (in preparation) The interpersonal voice: applying appraisal to the rap and sung voice.

Callaghan, J. (2000) *Singing and Voice Science*. San Diego, CA: Singular.

Callaghan, J. and McDonald, E. (2007) A comparative study of spoken and sung voice in performance. In K. Maimets-Volk, R. Parncutt, M. Marin and J. Ross (eds) *Proceedings of the Third Conference on Interdisciplinary Musicology (CIM07)*. Available at www-gewi.uni-graz.at/cim07 (accessed 20 November 2009).

Clark, J. and Yallop, C. (1995) *An Introduction to Phonetics and Phonology* (2nd edition). Oxford: Blackwell.

Cleirigh, C. (in preparation) *Gestural and Postural Semiosis: A Systemic-Functional Linguistic Approach to 'Body Language'*.

Goldsmith, J. A. (1990) *Autosegmental and Metrical Phonology*. Oxford: Blackwell.

Halliday, M. A. K. (1985) *Spoken and Written Language*. Geelong, Vic: Deakin University Press.

Halliday, M. A. K. and Greaves, W. S. (2008) *Intonation in the Grammar of English*. London: Equinox.

Halliday, M. A. K. and Matthiessen, C. M. I. M. (2004) *Introduction to Functional Grammar* (3rd edition). London: Arnold.

Lakoff, G. and Johnson, M. (1980) *Metaphors We Live By*. Chicago, IL: University of Chicago Press.

Martin, J. R. (2010) Semantic variation: modelling realization, instantiation and individuation in social semiosis. In M. Bednarek and J. R. Martin (eds) *New Discourse on Language: Functional Perspectives on Multimodality, Identity and Affiliation* 1–35. London: Continuum.

Martin, J. R. (2011) Multimodal semiotics: theoretical challenges. In S. Dreyfus, S. Hood and M. Stenglin (eds) *Semiotic Margins: Meaning in Multimodalities* 243–270. London: Continuum.

Martin, J. R. and Rose, D. (2008) *Genre Relations: Mapping Culture*. London: Equinox.

Martin, J. R. and White, P. R. R. (2005) *The Language of Evaluation: Appraisal in English*. Basingstoke: Palgrave Macmillan.

Matthiessen, C. M. I. M. (2007) The multimodal page: a systemic functional exploration. In T. D. Royce and W. L. Bowcher (eds) *New Directions in the Analysis of Multimodal Discourse* 1–62. London: Lawrence Erlbaum Associates.

Matthiessen, C. M. I. M. (2009) Multisemiosis and context-based register typology. In E. Ventola and A. J. M. Guijarro (eds) *The World Told and the World Shown* 11–38. Basingstoke: Palgrave Macmillan.

Smitherman, G. (1994) *Black Talk: Words and Phrases from the Hood to the Amen Corner*. New York: Mariner Books.

Titze, I. (1995) Voice research: speaking vowels versus singing vowels. *Journal of Singing* 52(1): 41–2.

Van Leeuwen, T. (1999) *Speech, Music, Sound*. Basingstoke: Palgrave Macmillan.

Van Leeuwen, T. (2009) Parametric systems: the case of voice quality. In C. Jewitt (ed.) *The Routledge Handbook of Multimodal Analysis* 68–77. New York: Routledge.

Zhao, S. (2010) Rank in visual grammar: some implications for multimodal discourse analysis. In A. Mahboob and N. K. Knight (eds) *Appliable Linguistics* 251–67. London: Continuum.

Discography

West, K. (2004) *The College Dropout*. New York: Roc-A-Fella/Island Def Jam.

West, K. (2005) *Late Registration*. New York: Roc-A-Fella/Island Def Jam.

West, K. (2007) *Graduation*. New York: Roc-A-Fella/Island Def Jam.

West, K. (2008) *808s and Heartbreak*. New York: Roc-A-Fella/Island Def Jam.

Part D

Modelling Intonation

9

Towards a systemic presentation of the word phonology of English

Paul Tench[a]

9.1 Phonology and lexicogrammar

There can be no lexicogrammar without phonology. Phonology specifies the distinctive 'shapes' of all the discrete lexicogrammatical units that participate in the systems of a given language. Phonology 'moulds' phonetic substance into all the distinctive forms of words, phrases/groups, clauses, sentences and texts (discourse structure and genres) of each language. Thus the function of phonology is to provide the means for identifying and differentiating the units of lexicogrammar and to provide the forms for those units for spoken communication. A parallel statement can be made for orthography for written communication, whether the script base is alphabetic, syllabic, rebus, iconic or ideographic; there could be no written form of a language's lexicogrammar without some form of orthography.

Phonology is not so much the 'indispensible foundation' of language as Sweet described it (see Henderson, 1971). It is certainly indispensible, but 'foundation' does not seem to be the best analogy. It is not as if lexicogrammar is 'built' upon it. It is true that in many displays of the 'levels of language', phonetics is placed at the bottom of the display, with

a   **Paul Tench** is an Associate Researcher (retired) in the Centre for Language and Communication Research at Cardiff University, Wales. He frequently presents at Systemic Functional Linguistic conferences and meetings. His main research interests include the study of English pronunciation and intonation, linguistics applied to language teaching, and the application of linguistics to the development of orthographies for minority languages, and he has published in all these fields. His major publications include *Pronunciation Skills* (1981), *The Roles of Intonation in English Discourse* (1990), *The Intonation Systems of English* (1996), and *Transcribing the Sound of English* (2011). He edited the first collection on systemic phonology, entitled *Studies in Systemic Phonology* (1992).

phonology linked to it. But lexicogrammar is 'made' of different 'material', not the material of phonetic substance. Lexicogrammar is in the mind; phonology shapes all its units (in the mind) and prepares them for use in real, physical, communication.

Thus phonology is rather the auditory shaping of units. Think of Saussure's linguistic sign: the *signe* consists of two elements, the *signifié* ('content', or 'meaning') and the *signifiant* ('expression', or sound). Think also of his analogy with the game of chess: the rules are in the mind and so are the moves planned by the players, but craftsmanship shaped the distinctive pieces and designed the playing board, providing the physical expression and thus the procedural means of an actual game (Saussure, [1916] 1974).

Other metaphors could also be used: phonology as a 'vehicle' for conveying lexicogrammatical units in discourse; as a 'servant' for performing the task of communication; it is like the performance of a piece of music; or the 'built form' of an architectural plan, the physical expression of an architect's design – this is not the same as the 'indispensible foundation' metaphor, since the assumption in that analogy is that the building was in fact the lexicogrammar. No metaphor will do adequate justice to the relationship that exists between phonology and lexicogrammar, if only on account of its sheer complexity and immensity.

This complexity and immensity of lexicogrammar is to be found not only in the huge scale of the lexicon and its morphological shapings, but also in the construction of phrases and groups, the syntax of clauses and sentences, the construction of paragraphing and discourse genres. The phonology of a language is not simply the *signifiants* of the thousands of lexical items and their morphological variations, but also the physical expression given to the higher units – phrases and groups, clauses and sentences, and discourse, by means of articulation and prosody, principally rhythm and intonation.

To illustrate this latter point before homing in on word phonology, consider the following points. First, there is a phonology that operates at the level of groups and phrases. A group is a sequence of words with a head; a phrase is a sequence of words with a preposition; they both add greater specificity to the *signe*. Thus, a person who wishes to talk about *cooks* may wish to be more specific: not all cooks, but *good cooks*, or *cooks in the kitchen*.

The relevant phonology is in part articulatory and in part prosodic. In terms of articulation, there are 'processes' of simplification that bind words together, for example assimilation, elision, liaison and, to a certain extent, epenthesis. Assimilation ensures that a change in articulation leads to transitions ('junctures') of words that are smooth and economic in effort, as when, in English, for instance, word-final /n/ accommodates to the point of articulation of the immediately following consonant, as in *ten pin bowling* /tɛm pɪm bəʊlɪŋ/; or when word-final /s, z/ adjusts to an alveopalatal position before /ʃ, ʒ, tʃ, dʒ, j/, as in *this year* /ðɪʃ jɜː/; and so on. Elision ensures a smooth transition by the omission of a phoneme; in English, typically /d/ is lost in word-final position if it is preceded by a consonant and followed immediately by another, as in *cold feet* /kəʊl fiːt/; this happens to word-final /t/ too, if it is preceded immediately by a voiceless consonant, as in *best man* /bɛs mæn/. Liaison provides a transition by means of an additional sound between certain vowel phonemes at word junctures; a well known example is the 'intrusive' /r/ in *law and order* /lɔːr ən ɔːdə/ in non-rhotic British accents; an advert for a bank formerly known as TSB played on the 'intrusive' /j/, as in *T Yes B – the bank that likes to say Yes.* The phonological rules of assimilation, elision and liaison are particular to given languages; Welsh, German, French, Italian, Greek, Turkish, Yoruba and others all have their own distinctive patterns of simplification for binding words together into groups and phrases. There is thus such a thing as group/phrase phonology.

As it happens, these articulatory processes often manifest themselves *within* words as well. /n/ 'becomes' bilabial in *unpleasant*; /s/ 'becomes' /ʃ/ in *misuse*; /d/ is lost in *windmill*, and /t/ in *postman*; /r/ creeps into *drawing* for many speakers in Britain, and also /j/ in *higher*. In the same way, epenthesis emerges as a means of smooth transition between word parts, as when /k/ is inserted in *youngster* /jʌŋkstə/ and, historically, /p/ was inserted in *Hampton, Thompson*, and so on. The epenthetic consonant is a 'compromise' articulation, combining a selection of phonetic features of the two consonants that it joins together. However, epenthesis only happens in English if the following syllable is weak, which restricts its potential effect in groups and phrases. Again, the rules of epenthesis are language-specific; they belong to the phonological system of a given language.

Additionally, phonology at the level of the group and phrase is prosodic. Groups and phrases are realized as rhythmic units with at least one stressed syllable and with the potential boundary of a pause or silent beat. For instance, *too many cooks spoil the broth* has three groups: *too many cooks* (two, possibly three, stressed syllables, followed potentially by a silent beat); *spoil* (one stressed syllable, followed potentially by a silent beat); and *the broth* (one stressed syllable, followed by silence). Rhythm ties *cooks* with the preceding *too many* and not with the following *spoil*; it ties *the* with the following, and not the preceding, word. Rhythmic units organize the string of words into the syntactic structure of the clause (it also organizes strings of numbers in telephone numbers, such as 07793 619 109, and in arithmetic, mathematical formulae, etc.).

But rhythm can also distinguish between two possible renderings of a string of words; in the string *old men and women*, it is possible to mean either that *old* 'restricts' both men and women, or just the men! Consider the semantic contrast between the two: 'First, we'll help the old men and women'. With /./ indicating a silent beat, we can render that string as either the former: *old men and women* (i.e. restricting *men and women* to just the old ones), or the latter *old men . and women* (i.e. just the men who are old, but all the women). Here is another example with prepositional phrases: 'Put the plates on the table in the middle'; the final phrase *in the middle* might be 'restrictive', identifying which table is meant ('not one of the ones on the side'), or it could provide additional 'locative' information, if a silent beat is introduced: *on the table . in the middle*, identifying where on the table the plates are to be put ('in the middle of the table'). Thus rhythm and pausing, as well as simplification processes, 'signify' units of lexicogrammar at a higher level than words.

Also, just as there are processes that bind words together into groups/phrases, there is a phonological structure that gathers the groups and phrases into a higher unit, the clause. One function of clauses is to express 'happenings' and states in terms of Processes, Participants and Circumstances. The phonological structure for clauses is the intonation unit (also known as the 'tone unit', the 'tone group' and the 'intonational phrase'). An intonation unit has to consist of at least one rhythm unit, which of necessity contains a stressed syllable, but it is also accompanied by a recognizable pitch pattern. Each language has a set of such patterns marking intonation units; these patterns are known as tones (not to be confused with 'lexical' tones) and indicate either the status or the communicative function of the intonation unit in the developing discourse. Intonation units usually consist of more than one rhythmic unit, and so it is necessary to identify which rhythmic unit carries the tone and which does not. The tone-bearing unit is known as tonic (or nuclear); the system for identifying the tonic from the non-tonic rhythmic units is thus known as tonicity. The intonation unit itself therefore consists of an obligatory tonic and, optionally, of other, non-tonic, rhythmic units. In the example mentioned above, *too many cooks spoil the broth*, the final unit will typically become tonic with a falling tone, and the preceding two units are non-tonic. Such an utterance would be transcribed as:

'too many 'cooks . 'spoil . the \broth

where /'/ indicates a stressed syllable, / \ / a falling tone, and <u>underlining</u> the tonic, in addition to / . / indicating the boundaries of the rhythmic units.

English has its system of tones, including not only falling, but also rising /ˌ/, mid / - / and falling-rising / ⱽ /, with additional low and high options and a rising-falling / ⌃ /; it also has a system of choices of pitch levels and movements accompanying the non-tonic rhythmic units that precede the tonic. Each language has its own set of tones.

English also has its own system of tonicity, distinguishing between tonic and non-tonic rhythmic units. There is high expectation in English that the tonic will come in the final rhythmic unit in an intonation unit (a phenomenon known as 'neutral tonicity') and identify new information.

Clauses may be independent ('main') as our example above, or dependent ('subordinate', 'bound'), making up sentences. There is a strong tendency for individual clauses, whether dependent or independent, to be each accompanied by a single intonation unit, as in:

> | since 'too 'many 'cooks . 'spoil . the ˌ<u>broth</u> | we 'won't ap'point . a\<u>noth</u>er one |

where /|/ indicates the boundaries of the two intonation units. The system that identifies the number of intonation units is known as tonality; 'neutral tonality' refers to the typical case of one whole clause intoned as one whole intonation unit.

Thus the phonological expression of the lexicogrammatical unit 'clause' is the intonation unit with its systems of tones and tonicity, and tonality. Clauses usually belong to 'clause complexes' or sentences, and to larger texts. To bind clauses together, English makes further use of the tone system, but also of 'marked' cases of tonicity, where the tonic occurs elsewhere instead of final position, and 'marked' cases of tonality, where intonation units do not coincide with single whole clauses.

Consider these variations to the example above:

> 'too many 'cooks . \<u>spoil</u> . the broth
> 'too many \<u>cooks</u> . 'spoil . the \broth
> 'too \<u>ma</u>ny 'cooks . 'spoil . the \broth
> \<u>too</u> many 'cooks . 'spoil . the \broth

These cases of marked tonicity each require a different set of circumstances for them to become appropriate choices, displaying variations in new information and what is 'given', or understood. However, languages vary in the extent to which marked cases are allowed; Hausa, for instance, does not seem to allow for any position for the tonic other than final, in which case there is no system, since there is no choice – Hausa has an intonational tone system (in addition to its 'lexical' tone system), but no tonicity system, since it relies on purely grammatical means to indicate new and given (Tench and Miller, 1980, 1982). Its phonology at the level of the clause is thus quite different from that of English.

English also allows its speakers to choose a different tonality configuration, such that a single clause can be intoned as two (or more) pieces of information or, less frequently, that two clauses can be contained within a single intonation unit; these are instances of 'marked tonality'. Consider our example as two pieces of information in 'marked tonality':

> ('We've now got enough cooks; you know what happens when you have too many')
> | ᵛ<u>too</u> many 'cooks | \<u>spoil</u> . the 'broth |

where the theme (*too many cooks*) is highlighted with a contrast and thus treated as a separate piece of information from the rheme (*spoil the broth*). Finally, consider this example of two clauses intoned as one intonation unit:

> | as you said 'too 'many 'cooks . \<u>spoil</u> . the 'broth |

where the first clause would typically be spoken quickly and at low pitch, indicating that it does not contain any new information. English allows for choices in tonality, as most languages seem to, between neutral and marked.

Phonology at the level of clauses and sentences is expressed as intonation in systems of tone, neutral and marked tonicity (where applicable) and neutral and marked tonality, but intonation has a role too in larger texts again. Just as written text is divided into paragraphs and sections/chapters, spoken 'text' also displays similar kinds of divisions. The information of a number of intonation units bundled together in sequence might well display an integrity which is recognizable as a phonological paragraph, otherwise known as a 'paratone', or 'pitch sequence' (see Chapter 4 of this volume). The phonological system involved is called 'key': 'high key' refers to a relatively high baseline of an intonation unit, with options for 'mid key' and 'low key'. This use of the term 'key' is taken from Brazil (1975, 1978, 1997); Halliday's notion of 'key' refers to variations in the degree and level of pitch movement in the tones, which has already been mentioned (see Halliday, 1967). A phonological paragraph is typically realized with high key in its initial intonation unit, mid key in intermediate units and low key in its final one. However, the 'key' system is available for exploitation to mark contrastive information, equivalent information and expected information within the paragraph. The key system of phonological paragraphs can even work across turns in a conversation (Brazil, 1975, 1978, 1997; O'Grady, 2010).

The point in this connection is that there is a phonological system operating as a kind of 'staging' within a spoken text. Phonological paragraphs are also bundled together to form larger units which have longer pauses at their boundaries; in this way, for instance, the sections in an extended monologue can be perceived. These sections are often marked by special discourse markers like *now, right then, OK,* and so on (cf. Iwamoto in Chapter 4 of this volume).

But phonology also provides the evidence for different types, or 'genres', of spoken discourse (Tench, 1990: 476–514). A simple example is that of calling over a distance, where the tone system is replaced entirely by level tones in a sequence of pitches:

| ˉdinner s –ready |

Another example is the kind of chanting heard in the playground with syllable timed rhythm, rather than stress-timing:

| jon . ny . is . a . sil . ly \boy |

Ghost stories in British culture have a very distinctive 'sound', with a series of low pitched intonation units intended to create a frightening atmosphere:

| _there was a dark dark ˏstreet | _and in the dark dark ˏstreet | _there was a dark dark \house |

On the other hand, public prayer also has a distinctive 'sound', with a series of mid level tones replacing rises for incomplete information:

| our –Father | which art in –heaven | hallowed be Thy –name | ...

We can detect a wide range of discourse genres by their particular 'prosodic composition'. Prosodic composition refers to the choices, preferences, proportions and omissions of specific features of prosodic substance, including voice quality, pace of utterance, rhythmicality and loudness, that play an essential role in the distinctive 'sound' of a particular genre. A speaker chooses a particular configuration to realize their choice of discourse genre; that phonological choice constitutes the 'prosodic composition system'. Prosodic composition systems vary from one language (and culture) to another, and since they are specific to a language (and culture) and not universal, they belong to the discourse phonology of that language (*ibid.*).

The roles of phonology can be displayed as in Table 9.1.

Table 9.1 Roles of phonology.

Lexicogrammar	words + affixes	groups/ phrases	clauses/ sentences	texts
Semantics	things + details actions qualities relationships	specificities	happenings States	discourse 'staging' genres
Phonology	word phonology + morphophonology	simplifications rhythmic units	intonation: Tone Tonicity Tonality	key prosodic composition

9.2   Word phonology

After this brief overview of phonological expression of the higher units of lexicogrammar, we return to look at the detail of the phonology of words in English. Although we will consider just one accent of English, Southern England Standard Pronunciation (SESP), traditionally known as Received Pronunciation (RP), the principles of description will apply to any accent. We will consider the phonology of words in citation form without extending attention to the kinds of variations that occur through the simplification processes mentioned above; such details would be reserved for a full study of phrase phonology. We will also confine our attention in this paper to monomorphemic words and will have to leave to another occasion an examination of the morphophonology of inflexions and derivations in English words.

System in word phonology is not like system in lexicogrammar or intonation, a set of options from which a speaker chooses to create meaning; system at the level of word (and also at the level of groups/ phrases) is rather the specifications of what the speakers of a language recognize as having been established in, or 'chosen' by, the language to represent its words (cf. Young, 1992).

9.2.1 Syllable count

The phonological expression of words in English embraces consonants and vowels in syllables that are either stressed to some degree or not. There are very few five-syllabled monomorphemic words; examples include *abracadabra, mulligatawny* and probably *hippopotamus* – although it is a compound in Greek and may even be treated popularly as a compound in English. Otherwise, the maximum number of syllables for a monomorphemic word is four, but the majority of words in English consist of either one, two or three syllables. (Please note that from this point, 'word' will be used for 'monomorphemic word', to reduce undue repetition.)

Four-syllabled words are relatively rare and, apart from the word *caterpillar*, appear to be, like *abracadabra, mulligatawny* and *hippopotamus*, obviously foreign in origin; examples include *catamaran* (from Tamil), *hullabaloo* (possibly from Scottish Gaelic), *shenanigans* (apparently from Irish), *Hallelujah* (from Hebrew), and names like *Abednego, Madagascar*. The largest number of four-syllabled words in fact derive from Greek, such as *apocalypse, apostrophe, catastrophe, cataclysm* (although linguists will point out that these words are in fact polymorphemic in Greek, they do not operate as such in English). Most English speakers will not readily be able to deconstruct the composition of such words as they might words like their derived forms *apocalyptic, catastrophic, cataclysmic*, or other sets of words like *befriend, friendship, friendly, unfriendly, unfriendliness* and *comprehend, apprehend, comprehension, apprehension*. These latter words are not included in this particular study because they are all polymorphemic; morphophonology will remain a separate study.

Most words that are native to English consist of just one, two or three syllables. A monosyllabic word spoken in isolation must contain a 'strong' vowel and be stressed. (The distinction between 'strong' and 'weak' vowels will be presented below in §9.2.3.) Even if a monosyllabic word is normally unstressed in context, such as a determiner, preposition, etc, it will contain a 'strong' vowel when stressed, in citation form. *Of* is /ˈɒv/ in citation form; *a* is /ˈæ/ or /ˈeɪ/, *an* is /ˈæn/, and so on.

Disyllabic words have one syllable stressed as primary (containing a strong vowel) and the other must either be less so (secondary, but still containing a strong vowel) or unstressed (containing a weak vowel).

There are four possible patterns:

ˈs s
s ˈs
ˈs ˌs
ˌs ˈs

where 'ˈs' represents a stressed syllable, 's' an unstressed and 'ˌs' a secondarily stressed syllable. A secondarily stressed syllable contains a strong vowel, but the syllable itself is less stressed than the other. The difference between primary, secondary and no stress can be illustrated with the words:

canter	ˈs s	/ˈkæntə/
contain	s ˈs	/kənˈteɪn/
protein	ˈs ˌs	/ˈprəʊˌtiːn/
canteen	ˌs ˈs	/ˌkænˈtiːn/

The potential range of three-syllabled stress patterns is much greater, but a number of patterns are unattested (indicated by *; see Guierre, 1970: 13, which still seems valid).

ˈs s s	*benefit*	/ˈbɛnɪfɪt/
*ˈs ˌs s		
ˈs s ˌs	*appetite*	/ˈapɪˌtaɪt/
*ˈs ˌs ˌs		
ˌs ˈs s	*angina*	/ˌænˈdʒaɪnə/
*ˌs ˈs ˌs		
ˌs s ˈs	*kangaroo*	/ˌkæŋɡəˈruː/
*ˌs ˌs ˈs		
s ˈs s	*eleven*	/ɪˈlɛvən/
s ˈs ˌs	*potato*	/pəˈteɪˌtəʊ/
*s s ˈs		
*s ˌs ˈs		

The potential range of stress patterns in four- and five-syllabled words would be enormous if it were not for the observation already made that they are relatively rare; in the system network below, we simply present the range of attested stress patterns. A system network for the syllable count of words in English might look like that shown in Figure 9.1.

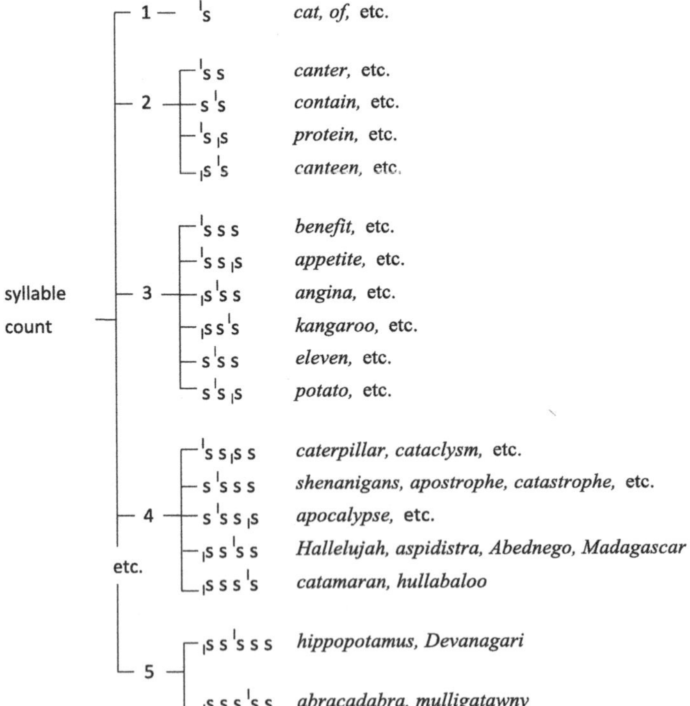

Figure 9.1 System network of the syllable count of words in English.

9.2.2 Syllable structure

The phonology of English words also specifies the permissible structures of syllables. Some languages have a very limited range of structures, such as V and CV, where 'V' represents vowels and 'C' consonants. English has 'open syllables' like these, with no final C, and it also permits 'closed syllables' (or 'checked syllables') with a final C. Furthermore, English permits up to three consonants in initial position in strong syllables and also up to three consonants in final position. (It even permits a sequence of four consonants in polymorphemic inflected forms, e.g. *glimpsed* /ˈɡlɪmpst/.) In weak syllables, English permits up to two consonants in initial position as a rule, but rare cases of three do exist; in final position, up to two consonants. In addition, the consonants /l, n, m/ can function alone syllabically.

There are thus the following possible patterns in strong syllables:

V	*awe*
CV	*law*
CCV	*flaw*
CCCV	*straw*
VC	*it*
CVC	*sit*
CCVC	*slit*
CCCVC	*split*
VCC	*ask*
CVCC	*task*
CCVCC	*flask*
CCCVCC	*splint*
VCCC	(*Alps* possibly; also *oomps!*; but otherwise unattested)
CVCCC	*waltz*
CCVCCC	*glimpse*
CCCVCCC	(*strength* for some speakers with epenthetic /k/: /strɛŋkθ/, but otherwise unattested)

In weak syllables, the possible patterns are:

V	*a(long)*
C	*(litt)le*
CV	*la(ment)*
CCV	*fla(mingo)*
CCCV	*scle(rosis)* (rare, confined to a few words of Greek origin)
VC	*(tick)et*
CVC	*(pub)lic*
CCVC	*(cul)prit*
(CCCVC)	(unattested)

VCC   *(cli)ent*
CVCC   *(li)cence*
CCVCC   *(in)stance*
(CCCVCC)   (unattested)

A system network for syllable structure in English might then look as in Figure 9.2.

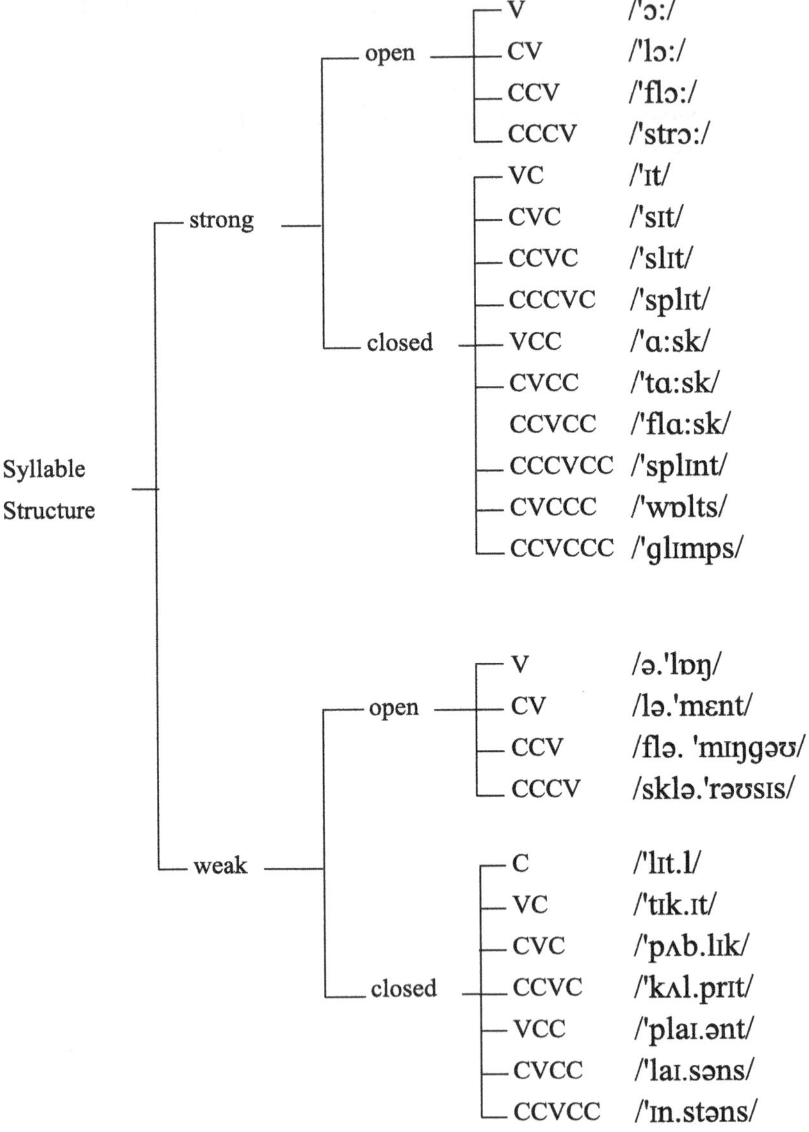

Figure 9.2 System network for syllable structure in English.

9.2.3 Syllable peaks

The peak (or 'nucleus') of a strong syllable is a strong vowel. There is an inventory of vowel articulations that only occur in syllables with primary or secondary stresses, hence the term 'strong vowel'. There is also a very much smaller inventory of vowel and consonant articulations that can only occur in unstressed syllables, and they are referred to as either 'weak vowel' or 'syllabic consonant'. Word phonology specifies what a language has 'chosen' in these respects.

There are two vowel articulations that occur in both stressed and unstressed syllables: /ɪ, ʊ/; in unstressed syllables they may only be followed by a single consonant, but there is no restriction in the number of consonants that follow them in stressed syllables (apart from the permissible number in the syllable structure network).

Strong vowels are classified by whether they may function in closed syllables only or also in open syllables. The so-called 'short vowels' are restricted to closed syllables, i.e. they must be followed by a consonant; the 'long vowels', on the other hand, function in both closed and open syllables, i.e. they need not be followed by a consonant. The short vowels of SESP are: /ɪ, ɛ, a, ɒ, ʊ, ʌ/; the long vowels of SESP are: /iː, ɑː, ɔː, uː, ɜː, eɪ, aɪ, ɔɪ, aʊ, əʊ, ɪə, ɛə, ʊə/. (The vowel /ʊə/ does not feature in all SESP speakers' speech.)

The weak vowels /ɪ, ʊ/ only function in closed syllables; there are two weak vowels that only function in open syllables: /i, u/; and there is one weak vowel that functions in both: /ə/. True 'syllabic consonants' are confined to a set of so-called 'resonant consonants' that are articulated homorganically with the final consonant of the preceding syllable with no intervening vowel articulation; in the case of /l̩/ and /n̩/, they occur in both open and closed syllables, as in *little* /ˈlɪtl̩/, *basalt* /ˈbæzl̩t/, *sudden* /ˈsʌdn̩/, *patent* /ˈpeɪtn̩t/, *tunnel* /ˈtʌnl̩/, *Arnold* /ˈɑːnl̩d/; /m̩/ occasionally occurs in the words *happen* /ˈhapm̩/ and *open* /ˈəʊpm̩/. Other so-called 'syllabic consonants' do not fulfil these precise requirements, such as *apple* /ˈapᵊl/, *quarrel* /ˈkwɒrᵊl/, *kitchen* /ˈkɪtʃᵊn/, *autumn* /ˈɔːtᵊm/.

The system network for syllable peaks might thus be presented as in Figure 9.3.

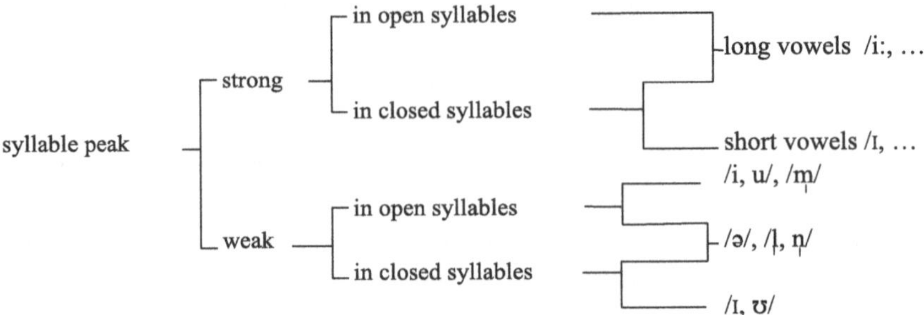

Figure 9.3 System network for syllable peaks in English.

9.2.4 Syllable margins

Syllable margins are the consonants that occur at the beginning of a syllable (often termed the 'onset') and also, in the case of closed syllables, the consonants that occur after the peak/nucleus (often termed the 'coda'); margins are thus either syllable-initial or syllable-final. Word phonology specifies what the two systems are in English, which are both a good deal more complex than those of many other languages on account of the permissible syllable structures. The syllable structure network specifies in general terms what the size of the syllable-initial and -final margins may be; the syllable margin networks specify what consonants actually figure in the two systems.

The syllable-initial margin system allows for single consonants and clusters of two and three consonants. Single consonants may be one of the following: /p, t, k, b, d, g, m, n, f, v, θ, ð, s, z, ʃ, h, tʃ, dʒ, l, r, j, w/ and in a very limited number of cases /ʒ/ (e.g. *genre*, (*force ma*) *jeure*).

The system for double-consonant clusters is complicated by the fact that if the second of the two consonants is /j/ then the vowel following is limited to /uː, ʊ, ʊə, u/. It seems appropriate therefore to separate that cluster potential from the others where there is no restriction on following vowels; the latter is known as the primary syllable-initial margin system, and the former, with /j/, as the secondary.

The regular pattern of consonants in the primary syllable-initial margin consists of an initial 'obstruent' consonant followed by a 'resonant' consonant; there are three exceptions to this rule: /ts/, /sf/ and /sv/, sequences of two obstruents; /ts/ is limited to a few loan words, each of which has a regular alternative pronunciation in SESP (*tsar* as /zɑː/, *tsetse* as /ˈtɛtsi/ and *tsunami* as /suˈnɑːmi/; /sf/ is limited to a small number of words from Greek (e.g. *sphere*) and Italian (e.g. *sforzando*), and because there is no alternative pronunciation in SESP, it is accepted as a permissible cluster; whereas /sv/ has a regular alternative as /sf/, e.g. *svelte* as /sfɛlt/. The full list of permissible double-consonant clusters is therefore as follows:

/pl/	*ply*	
/pr/	*pry*	
/pw/	*pois*	(rare, confined to a few loan words from French and Spanish)
/bl/	*blight*	
/br/	*bright*	
/bw/	*bwana*	(rare, confined to a few loan words from Swahili, French and Spanish)
/tr/	*try*	
/tw/	*twin*	
/dr/	*dry*	
/dw/	*dwindle*	
/kl/	*climb*	
/kr/	*crime*	
/kw/	*quite*	
/gl/	*glide*	
/gr/	*grime*	
/gw/	*(lan)guish*	
/fl/	*fly*	
/fr/	*fry*	
/fw/	*fois*	(rare, confined to a few loan words from French and Spanish)
/vw/	*(reser)voir*	(rare, confined to a few loan words from French)
/θr/	*thrive*	
/θw/	*thwart*	
/sf/	*sphere*	(rare, confined to words of Greek origin and loan words from Italian)
/sm/	*smile*	
/sn/	*snide*	
/sl/	*sly*	
/sw/	*swipe*	
/ʃm/	*shmuck*	(rare, confined to a few loan words from German and Yiddish)
/ʃn/	*schnapps*	(rare, confined to a few loan words from German and Yiddish)
/ʃl/	*schlock*	(rare, confined to a few loan words from German and Yiddish)
/ʃr/	*shrine*	
/ʃw/	*schwa*	(rare, confined to a few loan words from German and Dutch)

The regular pattern of consonants in the secondary syllable-initial margin consists of an obstruent or nasal consonant followed by /j/; the only possible exception is that for some speakers, the initial consonant system may include /l/, e.g. *allure*. The regular secondary system is as follows:

/pj/	*pew*
/bj/	*beauty*
/tj/	*tune*
/dj/	*due, dew*
/kj/	*cue*
/ɡj/	*gules* (rare)
/fj/	*few*
/vj/	*view*
/θj/	*(en)thuse*
/sj/	*(as)sume*
/zj/	*(pre)sume*
/hj/	*hue, hew*
/mj/	*mute*
/nj/	*new*

The pattern of consonants in both primary and secondary triple-consonant clusters must consist exclusively of initial /s/ followed by a selection of permissible double-consonant clusters. Since there is no choice of initial consonant, there is actually no system at that point. The triple primary system consists of the following clusters:

/spl/	*splint*	
/spr/	*sprint*	
/str/	*stray*	
/skl/	*sclera*	(rare, confined to a few words of Greek origin)
/skr/	*scream*	
/skw/	*squint*	
/sfr/	*sphragistics*	(rare, confined to a few words of Greek origin)

and the secondary:

/spj/	*spew*	
/stj/	*stew*	
/skj/	*skewer*	
/smj/	*smew*	(rare)

The system network for syllable-initial margins might be presented as in Figure 9.4.

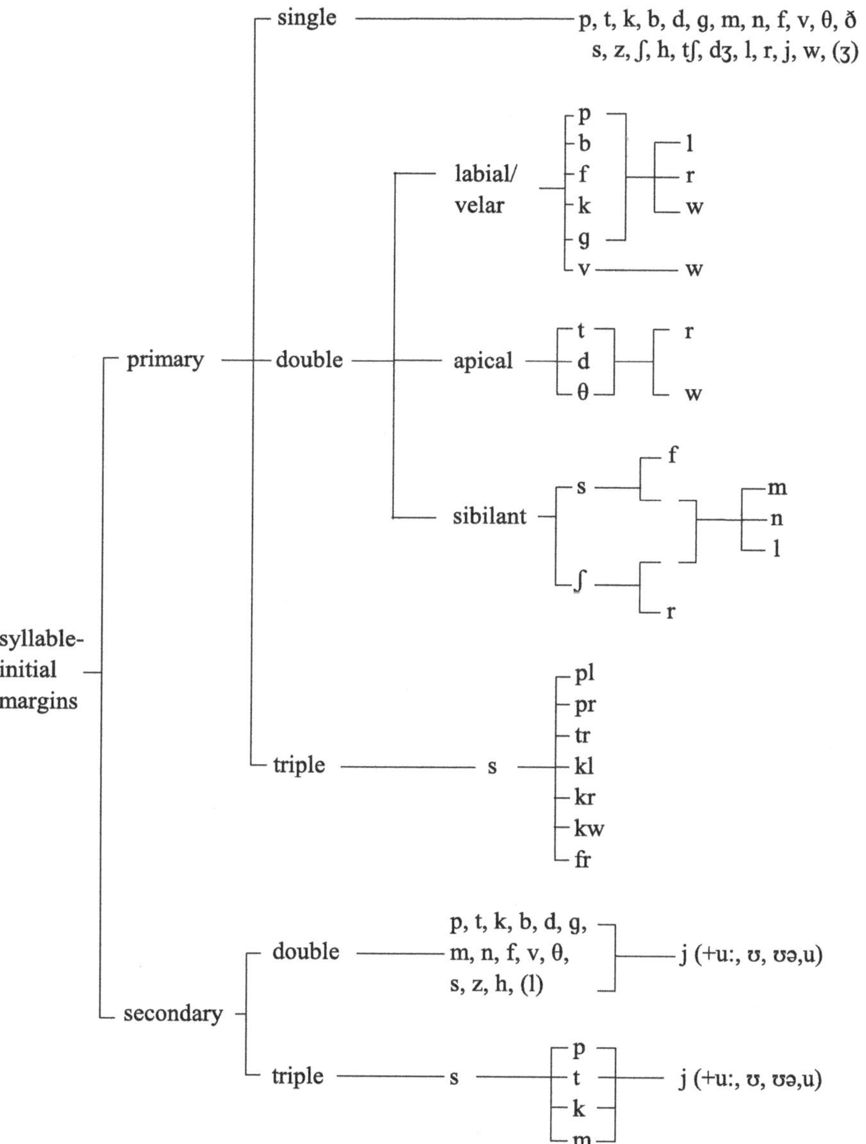

Figure 9.4 System network for syllable-initial margins in English.

The syllable-final margin system allows for single consonants and clusters of two and three consonants. Single consonants may be one of the following: /p, t, k, b, d, g, m, n, ŋ, f, v, θ, ð, s, z, ʃ, ʒ, tʃ, dʒ, l/. This syllable-final inventory differs from the syllable-initial by excluding /h, j, w/ and /r/ (in non-rhotic SESP) and including /ŋ/.

The system for double-consonant final clusters allows any of the final singletons to be preceded by /l/, except /g, ð, z, ʒ, ŋ/; it also allows the following sequences of voiceless obstruents, and nasals followed by an obstruent:

pt   *apt*
ps   *lapse*
ts   *blitz*
kt   *act*
ks   *axe*
ft   *lift*
sp   *lisp*
st   *list*
sk   *ask*
mp   *ramp*
mf   *triumph*
nt   *ant*
nd   *and*
ns   *tense*
nz   *lens*
ntʃ   *tench*
ndʒ   *hinge*
ŋk   *ink*

There is one other cluster: /dz/, which only now occurs in the one word *adze*, which itself is almost obsolete.

The system for triple-consonant clusters allows for three of the double clusters to be preceded by /l/:

lpt   *sculpt*
lts   *waltz*
lkt   *mulct*

also four 'nasal' clusters to be followed by an obstruent:

mpt   *tempt*
mps   *glimpse*
ŋkt   *instinct*
ŋks   *lynx*

and one combination of /ks/ and /t/:

kst   *text*

It is debatable whether also to include /-lst, -dst, -ŋst/ as in *whilst, midst, amidst* and *amongst*, because although the /-st/ is clearly an addition to a monomorphemic word, it is an 'unproductive' inflexion, whereas the very same /-st/ in *next* /nɛkst/ cannot be separated – at least, not in modern English. However, in the permissible triple clusters above, there is a pattern of maintaining the voice selection of the first plosive, but that is not the case in *(a)midst*. It is thus perhaps more appropriate to treat those four words as bimorphemic words and so exclude them from this present (monomorphemic) network.

The system network for syllable-final margins might be presented as in Figure 9.5.

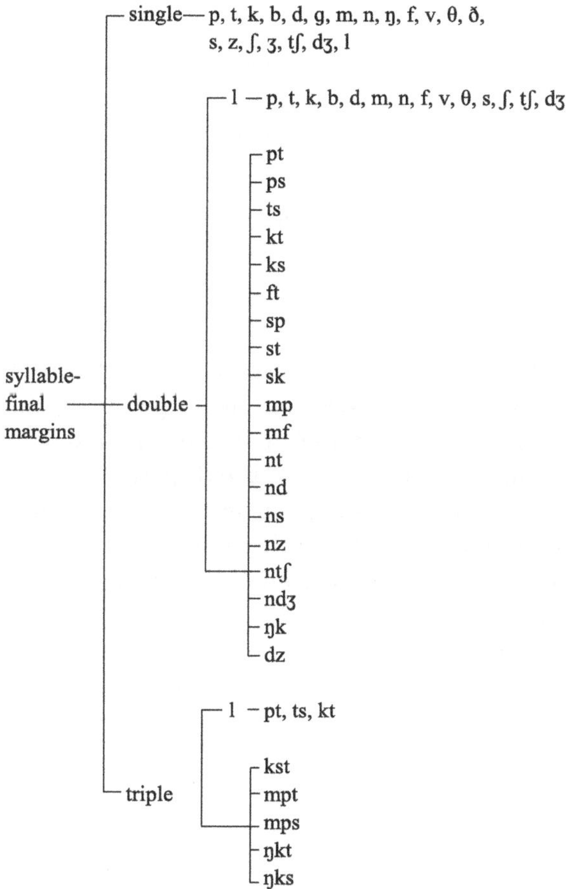

Figure 9.5 System network for syllable-final margins in English.

9.2.5 Phoneme inventories

The inventory of vowels has already been introduced under syllable peaks above. There are two systems in English: strong vowels for strong syllables and weak vowels for weak syllables. Word phonology specifies their classification criteria for a given language. The criteria for the strong vowels of SESP are well known and may be presented in a system network as in Figure 9.6.

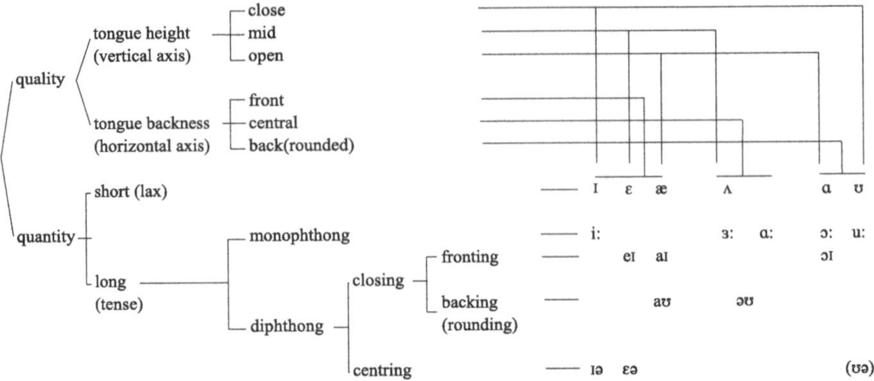

Figure 9.6 A system network of the strong vowels of Southern England Standard Pronunciation.

The incidental advantage of this display is that it not only separates the two systems, strong and weak, but also separates within the strong vowel system short vowels with their particular phonological constraint in distribution from long vowels. Also, the display integrates diphthongs with monophthongs into one single strong vowel system. The brackets around /ʊə/ are intended to indicate that not all SESP speakers have this vowel in their speech, it being replaced either by /ɔː/, as in *poor* /pɔː/, or by /uː + ə/, as in *dour* /ˈduːə/.

The network for weak vowels is very much more simple: that for closed syllables is shown on the left, and that for open syllables on the right of Figure 9.7.

Figure 9.7 A system network of the weak vowels of Southern England Standard Pronunction.

The inventory of consonants has already been introduced under syllable margins above. The classification criteria, again well-known, may be presented in a system network for syllable-initial consonants as in Figure 9.8; that for syllable-final consonants would require the addition of /ŋ/ 'nasal velar flat' and the deletion of /h/ and the 'articulator' row 'glottal', and also the 'manner' row 'approximant'.

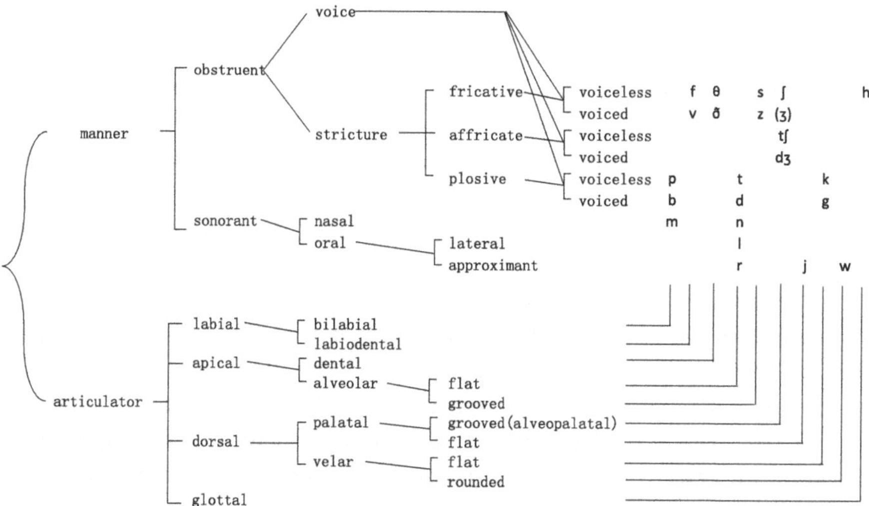

Figure 9.8 A system network of the syllable-initial consonants of Southern England Standard Pronunction.

The incidental advantages of this display over traditional consonant charts include the close link between affricates and both fricatives and plosives, the close link between nasals and both plosives (in points of articulation) and approximants (as 'fellow' sonorants), the labelling of grooved articulations and the close links between them, and the avoidance of redundant 'cells' for voicelessness for sonorants. (There is, however, a redundant voiced 'cell' accompanying /h/.) The brackets around /ʒ/ indicate its marginal status in the syllable-initial system; brackets would not be required in the network for the syllable-final system.

9.2.6 Other dimensions of word phonology

There are three other dimensions to word phonology that deserve at least a mention: allophonic variation, phonotactics and sound symbolism.

It is frequently maintained that *allophonic variation* does not belong to phonology as such, but rather to phonetics. However, allophonic features of phonemes vary according to the specifications of a given language. For instance, English and French both have a phoneme that is symbolized by /p/, but although they have much in common ('bilabial', 'voiceless', 'fortis', 'plosive' and a number of contrastive and distributional characteristics) they have nevertheless quite a different set of allophones: English /p/ is most often 'aspirated' whereas the French /p/ is not; English /p/ has glottal reinforcement in some environments whereas the French does not. The word phonology of a language specifies what allophonic variation is permissible; it is as if a language has selected certain phonetic realizations for its phonemes, and not others which another language might have selected. So having specified that within the permitted consonant inventory English has /p/, we can then specify what allophonic variation is permitted; this amounts to specifying what forms the phonetic realization of /p/ may take.

English consonant phoneme /p/ has the following phonetic realizations: it is 'aspirated' in most environments, except after /s/ in syllable-initial position; it has 'glottal reinforcement' in syllable-final position before a consonant or silence, and it is 'unreleased' in syllable-final position before a consonant; there is also regular assimilation to following labiodental fricatives. Its system network might be presented as in Figure 9.9.

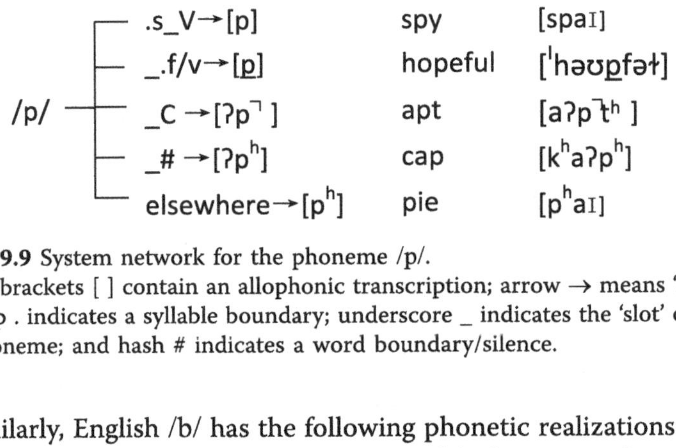

$$
/p/\quad
\begin{cases}
.s\_V \rightarrow [p] & \text{spy} & [\text{spaɪ}]\\
\_.f/v \rightarrow [\underline{p}] & \text{hopeful} & [\text{ˈhəʊ}\underline{p}\text{fəɫ}]\\
\_C \rightarrow [\text{ʔp}^\lnot] & \text{apt} & [\text{aʔp}^\lnot\text{t}^h]\\
\_\# \rightarrow [\text{ʔp}^h] & \text{cap} & [\text{k}^h\text{aʔp}^h]\\
\text{elsewhere} \rightarrow [\text{p}^h] & \text{pie} & [\text{p}^h\text{aɪ}]
\end{cases}
$$

Figure 9.9 System network for the phoneme /p/.
Square brackets [ ] contain an allophonic transcription; arrow → means 'realized as'; full stop . indicates a syllable boundary; underscore _ indicates the 'slot' occupied by the phoneme; and hash # indicates a word boundary/silence.

Similarly, English /b/ has the following phonetic realizations. It is fully voiced in most environments, but 'devoiced' before a voiceless consonant or silence; there is also regular assimilation to following labiodental fricatives. (It is also, like /p/, 'unreleased' in syllable-final position before a consonant, but in the case of /b/ the following consonant must be an affix; since that constitutes more than a 'monomorphemic' word, it will not be included in this particular study.) The system network for /b/ might simply be presented as in Figure 9.10.

$$/b/ \rightarrow \begin{cases} \_C^{vl} \rightarrow [\d{b}] & \textit{absent} \quad [a\d{b}sənt^h] \\ \_.f/v \rightarrow [\underline{b}] & \textit{obvious} \quad ['ɒ\underline{b}viəs] \\ \text{elsewhere} \rightarrow & \textit{buy} \quad [baɪ] \end{cases}$$

Figure 9.10 System network for the phoneme /b/.

It would then be possible to present such networks for each consonant and vowel phoneme of English as part of a full presentation of English word phonology.

9.2.6.1 Phonotactics

Phonotactics refers to the specification of permissible distributions and combinations of vowels and consonants in a language. A number of such features have already been noted in the descriptions of vowel peaks and margins above. For instance, there is a restriction on the distribution of short strong vowels to closed syllables; there are restrictions also on which consonants appear as syllable-initial and -final margins. Phonotactics as a term is often employed to refer specifically to the permissible combinations of consonants in clusters in syllable-initial and -final margins. In addition, there are restrictions to permissible combinations *between* syllable peaks and margins; one such restriction has also already been noted above: that the secondary syllable-initial margins can only be followed by back close vowels.

There does not appear to be any other pattern of restrictions between syllable-initial margins and following vowels. It might however be noted that a word initial /ʊ/ is relatively rare in SESP, being confined to exclamations like *oops!*, a couple of colloquialisms *oomph, oompah*, and occasional loan words like *umlaut*. (/ʊ/ does, of course, appear regularly in word initial position in other accents like North of England Standard Pronunciation: *up* as /ʊp/.)

There are, on the other hand, some cases of significant restrictions between vowels and following syllable-final margins. There is, for instance, a restriction on long vowels preceding /ŋ/ — apart from the onomatopoeic *boing* and *oink* — and /mp/, but not preceding /nt/, /nd/, /ntʃ/ and /ndʒ/, such as *pint* /paɪnt/, *fiend* /fiːnd/, *branch* /brɑːntʃ/, *range* /reɪndʒ/. Similarly, long vowels do not precede final /l-/ clusters, apart from /ld/, such as *field* /fiːld/, and occasionally /lt/, such as *bolt* /bəʊlt/, and /ls/, such as one pronunciation of *false* as /fɔːls/. Long vowels do not precede /sp/ and /sk/ apart from the /ɑː/ possibilities in SESP, such as *clasp* /klɑːsp/, *ask* /ɑːsk/, but they regularly occur before /st/: *feast* /fiːst/, *burst* /bɜːst/, *waste/waist* /weɪst/. Note that these restrictions apply to both double and triple final clusters; thus the restriction on final /ŋ/ applies equally to final /ŋk, ŋkt, ŋks/, that on /mp/ equally also on /mpt, mps/, that on /l-/ also to /lpt, lkt/. Whereas final /ks/ can be preceded by a long vowel, such as *coax* /kəʊks/, final /kst/ cannot.

Full phonotactic charts appear in Gimson (1989: 241–56), but it should be noted that they do include inflected forms of words and hence are not strictly monomorphemic. Gimson points out (*ibid.*: 256) that not all possible combinations that conform to general patterns are utilized; thus there happen to be no words like /faʊd/, /saɪdʒ/, /mɒmp/, /bruːtʃ/, /pliːk/, /splʌk/, /strɛdʒ/. This under-utilization of all possible combinations is not, it should be noted, subject to specifications in English word phonology, but rather to the specifications of the lexicon itself. More new words with permissible phonotactics may well yet enter the lexicon.

9.2.6.2 Sound symbolism

Sound symbolism refers to the significant, meaningful, associations within a given culture between certain phonemes and a range of qualities. Whereas phonemes are generally understood to have no meaning, and the relationship therefore between the meaning of a word and its pronunciation is purely arbitrary, there is in British culture a frequent association between certain vowels and qualities like small or large size, bright or dull timbre, light or heavy weight; there is equally an association between the articulation processes of consonants and actions like snapping, creaking, shaking and so on. Sound symbolism is distinct from 'primary onomatopoeia' which refers to the linguistic replication of natural sounds like *oink, meow, buzz, cuckoo, whoosh, bang, sizzle* and the like; sound symbolism is sometimes called 'secondary onomatopoeia', because the 'meaning' is not natural sound, but other natural qualities. In all these cases, the relationship between lexical meaning and pronunciation is not arbitrary, but directly linked.

Perhaps the most well-known case of sound symbolism in British culture is the linked relationship between /ɪ/ and smallness in size, movement, action, time, sound, light and sense. The relationship is not absolute, but there is nevertheless a high level of consistency. For instance, the words *pip, pick, pin, ping, piss* (a thin stream of water!), *pill, pimple, pinch* all suggest a quality of smallness, but the words *pit, pith, pitch, pink* do not. Similarly, the words *tip, tit* (a small bird), *tick, ting, tiff, titch, tint, tinker* ('do small jobs'), *tinkle, tingle, tinge, tilt* again all suggest a notion of smallness in some way, but *tin* does not, though *till* might in the sense of turning soil over to a small depth. A full set of monosyllabic (and some disyllabic) /ɪ/ words appears in the Appendix, where words in bold seem to suggest smallness of some kind, words in plain like *big, thick* do not, and words in italics are borderline.

The vowels /a, ɑː/ often suggest large size and loudness; compare *splish/ splash, zip/zap*; the vowels /ɒ, ɔː/ often suggest loudness and heavy weight: consider *roar, snore* and compare *drip/drop, flip/flop, splish/splash/splosh*; the vowels /ʊ, uː/ often suggest a low-pitched, dull or distant sound like *boom, whoosh*. It is apparent from older pronunciations of words that these symbolic associations were common; consider, for instance *lightning* as ['lɪxtɪŋg], representing quick, repeated flashes of light, and *rumble* ['rʊmbəl] and *thunder* ['θʊndər], repesenting loud or low, distant, sound.

Voiceless plosives often suggest suddenness in breaking, e.g. *cut, snip, snap*; fricatives have a more extended effect, e.g. *buzz, whoosh, splash*; resonants a gentle continuous effect, e.g. *hum, lull, murmur*. Historically, *wh-* was a voiceless fricative; notice how much voicelessness used to occur in *whistle, whisper* as ['ʍɪstəl], ['ʍɪspər] with strong onomatopoeic effect; the articulated initial /k/ of *knock* similarly.

This quick presentation of the cultural potential of word phonology is far too brief to offer a full systemic network. The network could dare only be suggestive, whereas the networks for the 'arbitrary' systems are full and comprehensive; but see van Leeuwen (1999) for fuller descriptions.

A further dimension in the study of the word phonology would review the historical changes that have occurred (e.g. the loss of consonants and consonant clusters), the Great Vowel Shift and the introduction of new words either from loans from other languages (e.g. the consonant clusters /pw-, bw-, fw-, vw-, gw-/ and numerous others) or coinages like *beep, blip* that utilize regular patterns.

9.3 Conclusion

This chapter is an attempt to show how phonology operates at all levels of lexicogrammar, to display specifically the system networks of the phonology of monomorphemic words in English, and to suggest the direction of how yet other networks might be developed to cover allophonic variation within a language, phonotactics, morphophonology and, possibly, sound symbolism. It goes very much further than previous attempts within systemic functional grammar to refer to phonology at the level of the word (Berry, 1977; Butler, 1985; Halliday, 1961; Hudson 1974).

References

Berry, M. (1977) *An Introduction to Systemic Linguistics 2: Levels and links.* London: Batsford.

Brazil, D. C. (1975) *Discourse Intonation.* Birmingham: English Language Research.

Brazil, D. C. (1978) *Discourse Intonation II.* Birmingham: English Language Research.

Brazil, D. C. (1997) *The Communicative Value of Intonation in English.* Cambridge: Cambridge University Press.

Butler, C. S. (1985) *Systemic Linguistics: Theory and Applications.* London: Batsford.

Gimson, A. C. (1989) *An Introduction to the Pronunciation of English* (4th edition). London: Arnold.

Guierre, L. (1970) *Drills in English Stress-Patterns.* London: Longman.

Halliday, M. A. K. (1961) Categories of the theory of grammar. *Word* 17: 241–92.

Halliday, M. A. K. (1967) *Intonation and Grammar in British English.* The Hague: Mouton.

Henderson, E. J. A. (ed.) (1971) *The Indispensable Foundation: A Selection From the Writings of Henry Sweet.* London: Oxford University Press.

Hudson, R. A. (1974) Systemic generative grammar. *Linguistics* 139: 5–42.

O'Grady, G. (2010) *A Grammar of Spoken English Grammar.* London: Continuum.

Saussure, F. ([1916] 1974) *Course in General Linguistics* (ed. C. Bally and A. Sechehaye, tr. W. Baskin). London: Fontana.

Tench, P. (1990) *The Roles of Intonation in English Discourse.* Bern: Peter Lang.

Tench, P. (ed.) (1992) *Studies in Systemic Phonology.* London: Pinter.

Tench, P. and Miller, J. (1980) Aspects of Hausa intonation. 1: Utterances in isolation. *Journal of the International Phonetic Association* 10: 45–63.

Tench, P. and Miller, J. (1982) Aspects of Hausa intonation. 2: Continuous text. *Journal of the International Phonetic Association* 12: 78–93.

Van Leeuwen, T. (1999) *Speech, Music, Sound.* Basingstoke: Palgrave Macmillan.

Young, D. (1992) English consonant clusters: a systemic approach. In P. Tench (ed.) *Studies in Systemic Phonology* 44–69. London and New York: Pinter.

Appendix: Sound symbolism in English /ɪ/ words

onset	-ip	-it	-ick	-im	-in	-ing	-if	-ith	-iss	-is(t/k/p)
p	**pip**	pit	**pick**		**pin**	**ping**	**piffle**	pith	**piss**	
t	**tip**	tit, tilt	**tick**		tin	**ting**	**tiff**			
k	**kip**	**kitten**, bit	kick		kin	king			kiss	
d	**dip**			**dim**	din	**ding**		**dither**		disc/k
g	**gibberish**	git, mit	gym	gin		**jiffy**				**gist**
m							miff	myth	miss	
n	**nip**	**nit**	**nick**							
f	**fib**	fit			fin					
v				*vim*	**vignette**					
th			thick		**thin**	thing				
s	**sip**	sit	sick		sin	sing	sift			*cyst*
z	**zip**		**zig**			**zing**				
sh	ship	shit		**shimmy**	shin		shift			
h	**hip**/hip	hit	**hick**	him					**hiss**	
ch	**chip**	**chit**	**chick**							
l	lip	**little**	lick	limb			lift			*lisp*, list
r	rip	writ	rick	rim		*ring*				wrist, risk
w	*whip*	wit	**wick**	**whim**	win	wing	**whiff**	**wither**		**wisp**, **whisk**, **whisper**, **wilt**
bl	**blip**					bling			bliss	
pr		**prittle**	**prick**	**prim**						
br		**brittle**	**brick**	brim		bring			**brisk**	
tr	**trip**		**trick**	**trim**						
dr	**drip**						drift			**drizzle**
tw		twit, twitter, twig	twin							twist
cl	**clip**		click			cling	cliff			

onset	-ish	-itch	-ill	-imp	-int	-ink	-inker	-inkle	-ingle	-inch
p		**pitch**	**pill**	**pimple**		pink				**pinch**
t	*tish*	**titch**	till		**tint**		**tinker**	**tinkle**	**tingle**	**tinge**
k		**kitsch**	kill			**kink**		**kindle**		
d	dish	**ditch**	dill	**dimple**	dint	**dinky**		**dingle**		**dingy**
g			*gill*							
m		mitch	mill		mint	mink			**mingle**	**mingy**
n			**nil**	**nimble**						
f	fish		fill, **village**							**finch**
th				**thimble**		think				
s			sill	**simper**		sink			**single**	*sinch*
z			**zilch**			zinc				
sh									*shingle*	
h		hitch	hill, *chill*		**hint**					hinge
ch				**chimp**		**chink**				
l			*lilt*	**limp**	lint	link	**lintel**			lynch
r		rich, **rill**				**wrinkle**				
w		witch	will	**wimp**	**wind**(v)	**wink**, **whistle**		**winkle**		winch
bl				**blimp**		**blink**				
pr					**print**, *plinth*	**plink**				prince
br						**brink**			**bristle**	
tr			**trill**			**trinket**			**trickle**	
dr			**drill**			drink				
tw		**twitch**	twill			**twiddle**		**twinkle**	**twinge**	
dw								**dwindle**		
cl						**clink**, **clinker**				clinch

		crick							criss, **crisp**	**krill**		**crimp**	**crinkle**			**cringe**	
glib									**glisten**			**glimpse**	**glint**				
grip	**grit**, grid		grim	grin					**grist, gristle**	grill							
flip	**flit**	**flick**	**flimsy**		**fling**					flitch		*flint*					
frippet	**fritter**							**frisk**									*fringe*
	spit	**spick**		**spin**		spiv					**spill**		**spindle**				
		stick			**sting**	**stiff**				**stitch**	**still, stilt**			stink			**stingy**
skip	**skit**		**skim**	skin		skiff					skill		**skimp**		**skint**		
							smith, smithereens		**smidgen**								
snip		**snick**				**sniff**				**snitch**							
slip	**slit**	**slick**	**slim**		**sling**									**slink**			
		swig	swim		**swing**	**swift, swivel**				**switch**	swill				swindle	swinge	
						shrivel					**shrill**	**shrimp**		**shrink**			
	split							**splish**					**splinter**				
					spring							**sprint**		**sprinkle**			
strip		*strict*	**strim**		**string**												
scrip			scrim									**scrimp**				**scribble**	

Note: **Bold** = highly symbolic; *italics* = possibly symbolic; plain = not symbolic.

<table><tr><td>10</td><td>

Digital phonology: Systemic perspectives

</td></tr></table>

Bradley A. Smith[a], Stefano Fasciani[b] and
Kay L. O'Halloran[c]

10.1 Introduction: the present work

[M]odern computer-based techniques of analysis and representation ...
provide a much richer and more elaborate treasury of information than
was available a generation or even a decade ago. They do not replace
the human investigator; they do make the human investigator's work
more complex – but also more thorough and more revealing. (Halliday
and Greaves, 2008: 16–17)

In this chapter we discuss the study of phonology (of speech, and other
semiotic resources with sound as expression plane, such as music) within

a **Bradley A. Smith** is a Research Fellow in the School of Education at Curtin University,
Australia. He has previously worked in a learning and teaching centre at the University
of Melbourne, and in the Multimodal Analysis Lab at the National University of
Singapore. His PhD thesis (2008, Macquarie University) is entitled 'Intonation and
Register: A Multidimensional Exploration'. His major research interests are intonation,
register, communication in higher education, and multimodality, with a focus on the
roles of sound-based semiotic resources within cultures. His publications include
(with William S. Greaves) the chapter on intonation for the forthcoming *Bloomsbury
Companion to Halliday*, co-editor (with Kay L. O'Halloran) of *Multimodal Studies:
Exploring Issues and Domains* (2011), as well as several journal articles, book chapters,
two invited encyclopaedia entries in the *Wiley-Blackwell Encyclopedia of Applied
Linguistics* (2013) and an invited review for *Linguistics and the Human Sciences* 4(1)
of Halliday and Greaves (2008) *Intonation in the Grammar of English*.

b **Stefano Fasciani** is a PhD candidate at the National University of Singapore in the
field of Music Technology at the Arts and Creativity Lab, and a former Research
Associate in the Multimodal Analysis Lab. He graduated from the Università degli
Studi di Roma 'Tor Vergata' (Italy) with an MSc in Electronic Engineering in 2006,
and for several years joined the advanced digital signal processing group of Atmel
in Rome, developing multicore embedded systems and applications for audio digital
signal processing. He is also an electronic musician, releasing productions on a regular
basis over several years with independent labels.

the environments of contemporary software resources, including a software platform currently under development. These software tools enable researchers and teachers to readily access the sound signal and create a variety of annotations of such data, and to store, search, process and display the data and their analyses. Such resources thus make possible the correlation, in both the database and interface, of phonetic, phonological, lexicogrammatical, semantic and contextual analyses within different metafunctions, at different ranks and so on. The present chapter is not a review of software applications as such, but rather a discussion of some of the affordances of and issues in the development and use of digital technologies (for a review of software resources relevant to systemic scholars see O'Donnell and Bateman, 2005).

We focus our discussion around two software applications: Praat (www.fon.hum.uva.nl/praat; Boersma and Weenink, 2011), a state-of-the-art application freely available and widely used by a variety of scholars; and software currently under development at the Multimodal Analysis Lab (http://multimodal-analysis-lab.org/?page_id=187) in the Interactive and Digital Media Institute at the National University of Singapore, which has been designed for the study of multimodal communication and informed by systemic functional theory (O'Halloran *et al.*, 2010; Smith *et al.*, 2011). We also briefly discuss other software resources for the study of sound and video. We explore the usefulness of such resources for exploiting the comprehensiveness and complementarity of analytical perspectives and approaches that systemic functional theory affords, and how contemporary software makes it possible to bring into an analytical project knowledge from a variety of disciplinary and theoretical traditions, including, importantly, integrated computational (algorithmic) analyses of the sound signal.

---

c   **Kay O'Halloran** is Associate Professor in the School of Education, Curtin University, Australia. Prior to this, she was Associate Professor with tenure in the Department of English Language & Literature at the National University of Singapore. During this time, she held a joint appointment as the founding Director of the Multimodal Analysis Lab and Deputy Director of the Interactive Digital Media Institute, a university-level research institute at the National University of Singapore. Her areas of research include multimodal analysis, mathematical discourse, digital humanities and the development of digital technologies and visualization techniques for multimodal and socio-cultural analytics. Kay O'Halloran has published widely in these fields, and she is the founding editor of the Routledge Studies in Multimodality Book Series.

10.2 Technology and the study of phonology

Progress throughout the last century of language studies in general and studies of speech in particular has been intimately linked to the development and increasingly widespread availability of technological resources enabling and supporting such study. Halliday makes the following observation in this regard:

> For linguistics, the two most important advances in the latter half of the twentieth century were technological ones: the invention of the tape recorder and the evolution of the computer. The tape recorder made it possible to record natural speech. The computer made it possible to process large quantities of data ... as a bonus, the computer enables us to test our descriptive generalizations ... and to observe and represent sound waves in a wealth of complementary perspectives. (Halliday, 2002: 7–8)

Prior to the invention of recording technology scholars had to rely upon their own real-time listening capabilities and memory to make observations about the form and function of prosodic aspects of spoken language, an acute limitation identified by the eighteenth-century scholar Joshua Steele:

> What ear can be so quick, nice, and discerning, as to keep pace with, discriminate, and ascertain the rapid and evanescent musical slides of the human voice ... so as to enable the person to mark the limits of each syllable, with regard to gravity and acuteness, and to express them on paper? (Steele, 1775; reprinted in Crystal, 1969: 25)

With the availability of recording technology from the late nineteenth century onwards two distinct traditions in the study of speech emerged, each with its own concerns and approaches, and limitations: an instrumental laboratory tradition with a description of the minutiae and patterns of the physical aspects of speech as part of a 'scientific' approach, and a pedagogic purpose specifically related to the teaching and learning of English as a foreign language with the aim of providing models of 'correct' or 'desirable' pronunciation. This approach also included the use of intonation for different speech functions within naturally occurring discourse.

Works within the latter tradition have often been dismissed as 'impressionistic' and 'unscientific'. For example, Crystal (1969: 2–3) refers to 'misleading, impressionistic statements' and 'unscientific impressionism' deriving from 'the demands of English-language teaching in the early decades of this century', while Ladd (1996: 13) comments that 'because of the general lack of agreement and the notable absence of instrumental evidence for impressionistic descriptions, adherents of the instrumental approach have often felt that their work is somehow more rigorous and more scientific'. However, the appeal to the notion of scientific (instrumentally, experimentally verifiable) rigour within the instrumental tradition has resulted in a focus on the material plane of speech, both in itself and as the basis for the development of phonological description. As Crystal (1969: 18) puts it, 'a formal, as opposed to a "semantic" or "notional" approach to description, implies that, procedurally, considerations of meaning ... do not enter in until a stable basis of formerly defined features has been determined'. Data within this tradition have consisted in the main of isolated laboratory samples rather than naturally occurring discourse. In practice, this has meant that phonological descriptions derived from the instrumental science approach have been phonetics-based, adapted for laboratory samples of speech and thus in crucial ways not adapted to the study of natural spoken discourse. Semantic descriptions so derived have reflected the limitations of this 'bottom-up', instrumentally derived approach, and are thus not readily applicable in meeting the practical demands of language teaching. Meanwhile, the lack of attention by teachers of English intonation and others working within semantics-based (especially functional) approaches to the results of work within the instrumental tradition has meant that there is much of value in these phonetics-based descriptions that remains to be exploited by such scholars; while there is a reluctance in general linguistics research and teaching to venture into the forbidding, specialized realm of 'phonology' implied by consideration of intonation.

Thus, the phonological study of speech has, as elsewhere in linguistics, been divided or compartmentalized with respect to focus and approach (cf. Halliday, 1991: 39 on the twentieth century as the 'age of disciplines'). Researchers and teachers may find in the literature on intonation, for example, a specialized focus on the phonetic aspects of speech, articulatory, acoustic or auditory, prosodic or segmental, on the patterned organization of such phenomena into phonological structures and systems, or on the use of such in human communicative acts, either with or without reference to grammar, semantics and/or context (cf. a review by Halliday and Greaves, 2008). Scholars within a particular tradition are understandably hesitant to venture into an area of study without the standard expertise expected within that discipline, leading to the situation where phoneticians tend on the whole to avoid semantics and discourse analysts tend to avoid discussion of intonation and other aspects of language involving a study of phonology. Where such boundaries are crossed, the underlying theory motivating the description derives from one discipline or the other: for example, the work by Pierrehumbert and Hirschberg (1990) on the semantics of intonation remains firmly based upon a phonetics-based approach to phonological description. Yet, as Halliday and Greaves (2008) show, the various perspectives and concerns on phonology may afford complementary rather than conflicting contributions to the general understanding of speech, especially when located within the holistic framework of systemic theory, and are often appropriate to particular research and teaching tasks.

Halliday and Greaves (2008) themselves present a multidimensional integrated view on English speech, locating intonation in particular within general systemic functional theory and the specific description of English language according to stratification, metafunction, rank and other dimensions of the theory. Perhaps the most important contribution of systemic functional theory to phonology is the provision of a comprehensive and practical (that is, 'appliable', to use Halliday's term; Halliday, 2008) framework for implementing Firth's (1957, 1968) polysystemic, meaning-based conception of linguistics and solving the 'problems of synthesis' that 'Sweet himself bequeathed to the phoneticians coming after him' (Firth, 1957: 121). From Halliday's early (1961) work, as Matthiessen (2007: 1) puts it, 'the scope of the systemic functional model of the architecture of language was comprehensive from the start. The total system of language in context has always been in focus'. Halliday and Matthiessen (2004: 19–20) elaborate: 'systemic theory … is concerned with language in its entirety, so that whatever is said about one aspect is understood always with reference to the total picture … [and] also *contributes* to the total picture' (italics original).

This approach has profound consequences for the descriptions of systemic phonology so derived. The systemic description of the phonology of intonation is based upon a consideration of phonetics and semantics (sound patterns and their signifying capacities), as well as the way in which choices in intonational systems (in the grammar), as realized through intonation systems (phonology), interact with choices in MOOD, MODALITY, THEME and other grammatical systems. The systemic principle, particularly the functional integration of multiple systems across strata, metafunctions and ranks, presents both opportunities and challenges for the study of phonology within a digital environment. In the next section we discuss digital technologies as resources for the study of sound.

10.3 Digital technology as resource for the phonologist

O'Halloran (in press) traces the synergistic development of technology, semiotic systems and knowledge, such as the late fifteenth century invention of the printing press and subsequent widespread use of the Hindu-Arabic numerical system in arithmetic books as a foundation for the development of symbolic algebra. O'Halloran points to the analogous impact of digital technologies on contemporary science, especially computational visualization resources which can represent complex and dynamic phenomena as configurations and processes, interacting and unfolding over time. Such resources thus offer the means of accounting for complex phenomena, which are difficult for human capacities to perceive or conceptualize, through computational processing and visual representation. O'Halloran provides an overview of relevant research showing that, as a result, digital technology has created new paradigms of research not possible without such technological resources. The provision of such resources in the latter half of the twentieth century has been fortuitous for the developing sciences of linguistics and multimodal semiotics, dealing as they do with the immense complexities of language and other semiotic systems and their interactions.

10.3.1 Access

The value of (even very early) recording technology and the synergy of technology and associated techniques can be seen in the following quote from Jones (1909: v):

> If while a Gramophone, Phonograph, or other similar instrument, is in operation, the needle is lifted from the revolving record, the ear will retain the impression of the sound heard at the instant when the needle is lifted.

This is the first and perhaps the most important affordance of recording technology for phonologists, greatly heightened in contemporary digital platsyrms: access to the source texts as sound. The nature of sound makes its analysis difficult: what we hear as sound is a dynamic variation of the air pressure, something which seems simple but which in fact carries an immense amount of information, interacting with humans at conscious and unconscious levels (cf. Halliday and Greaves, 2008: ch. 1

for a discussion). The human brain is a very advanced 'machine' in terms of audio analysis: we are able to accurately recognize, classify, evaluate and interpret thousands of sonic phenomena, spontaneously in real time. But without the capacity to record and replay at will, the sort of close, detailed and repeated analysis available for static visual phenomena (visual art, writing, architecture, sculpture, etc.) is not possible. There is no way to check one's results or compare with the analyses of others. The advent of sound recording thus allowed us for the first time to transcend the barriers of time and space, allowing close repeated scrutiny and the capability of transmitting sound to potentially any scholar across the world and across generations.

Computational platforms have greatly improved access to the sound signal, particularly in terms of graphical user interface resources for visualization and manipulation of the data. One of the major advances that software technology has provided for audio analysis is the capability to break down the dynamic aspect of sound, transposing it into a digital representation, stored in memory, which then provides the basis for producing static visual transformations of the original sound signal, such as frequency and intensity graph (waveform representation), formant and spectrogram, fundamental frequency and intensity (decibel) graphs. Figure 10.1 shows a Praat TextGrid, the platform for listening to, viewing and annotating sounding text. Praat offers a powerful platform and tools for navigation around a text and across different scales, from the entire text to microsecond regions, and facilitates the easy replay of such regions of interest.

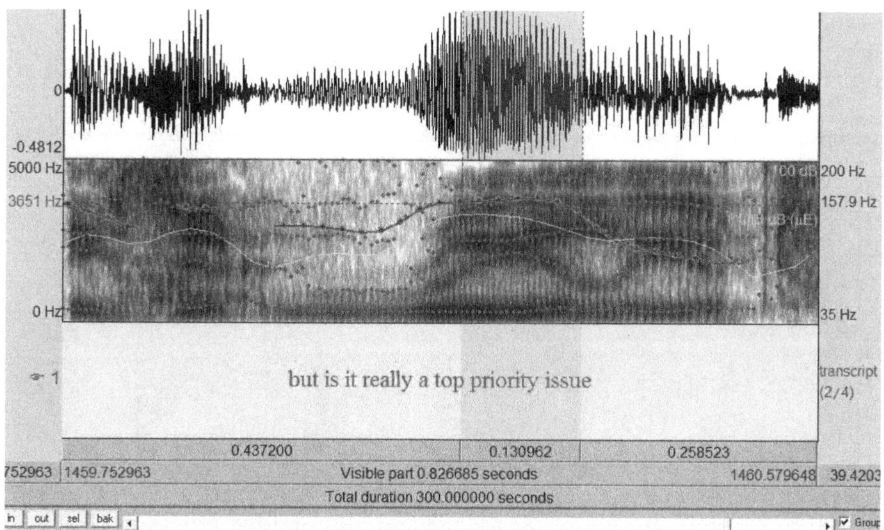

Figure 10.1 Praat interface: visual graphs and navigation tools.

Another dynamic or time-dependant resource is video. But while it is possible to freeze a video-frame, or change its reproduction speed and still retain much crucial information, freezing a sound is of course impossible, while modifying its reproduction speed (over a certain limit) completely changes its spectral features and may introduce some artefact which corrupts some of the information contained in the source signal.

For this reason, 'resemioticising' (Iedema, 2001) sound into static visualizations has great importance in sound analysis, as such visualizations give us a view of sound across a selected time window as transposed into a static spatio/temporal representation. Together with the actual sound reproduction itself, time-aligned with the visual representations, these aural and visual playback resources enable the analyst to access the sound signal as dynamic sound and as static visual representation, a powerful combination. One may play and replay a sound file, while looking at its visual representation in a variety of forms, permitting relative comparisons to be made. For example, Figure 10.2 shows a waveform view of a piece of music, 'A Day in the Life' by The Beatles (1967), using another popular software application, Audacity (http://audacity.sourceforge.net).

The waveform is a static representation in the time domain, a very simple visualization but one which offers an immediate and basic insight to one of the present authors not gained over forty years of close listening to this piece: that there are in fact three, not two, roughly identical crescendos in this song in terms of intensity (shown as vertical extent in the waveform

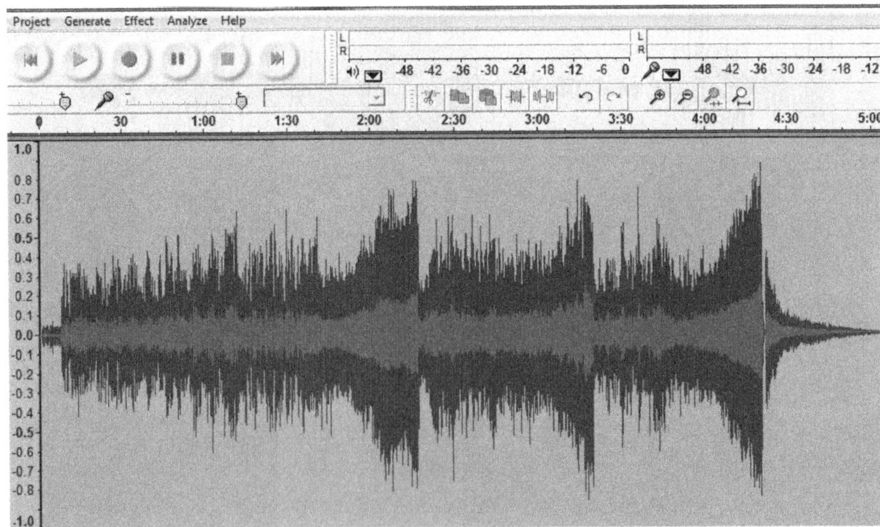

Figure 10.2 Audacity waveform of 'A Day in the Life' by The Beatles, in its entirety.

graph). The first and last are obvious, being the 'music orgasms' envisaged by John Lennon (Lewisohn, 1988); the second crescendo, only apparent when represented, not as sound, but as a visualization of intensity, is the finale to McCartney's vocal interlude, with Lennon wailing over a powerful orchestral score. These crescendos are in temporal proportion: the first coming approximately halfway through the song; the next two coming at the three-quarters and final stages of the song (not including the long decay of the final chord). It may seem trivial, yet what this visualization thus shows is the song's fundamental underlying structure in terms of its dynamics, so important to contemporary recorded (studio-based) composition, a structure comparable to Schenker's melodic 'Uberlini' (e.g. Forte and Gilbert, 1982) for score-based composition.

Visualizations of Debussy's 'Claire de Lune' and Chopin's 'Nocturne' by Stephen Malinowski's (1985) Music Animation Machine (see www.musanim.com) in Figures 10.3 and 10.4 offer dynamic visual representations of music. In Figure 10.3, the music is shown as a piano-roll style series of chromatic notes, which each light up as the video plays that timestamp; in Figure 10.4, the notes are joined by lines to show melodic intervals. As they unfold, these videos of music provide a visual articulation that

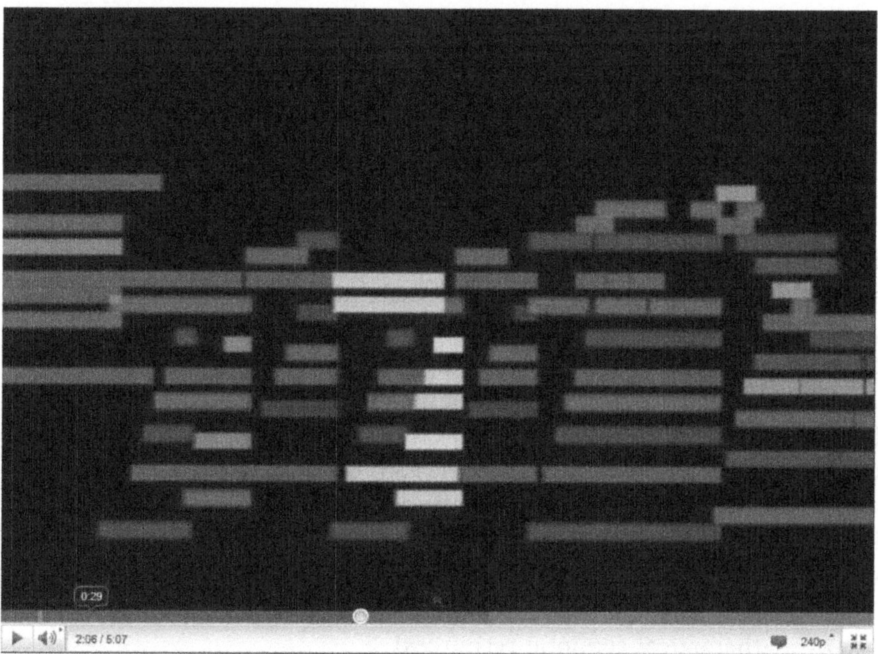

Figure 10.3 The music animation machine: excerpt from Debussy's 'Claire de lune' (www.youtube.com/watch?v=7pA8BmJ4j68).

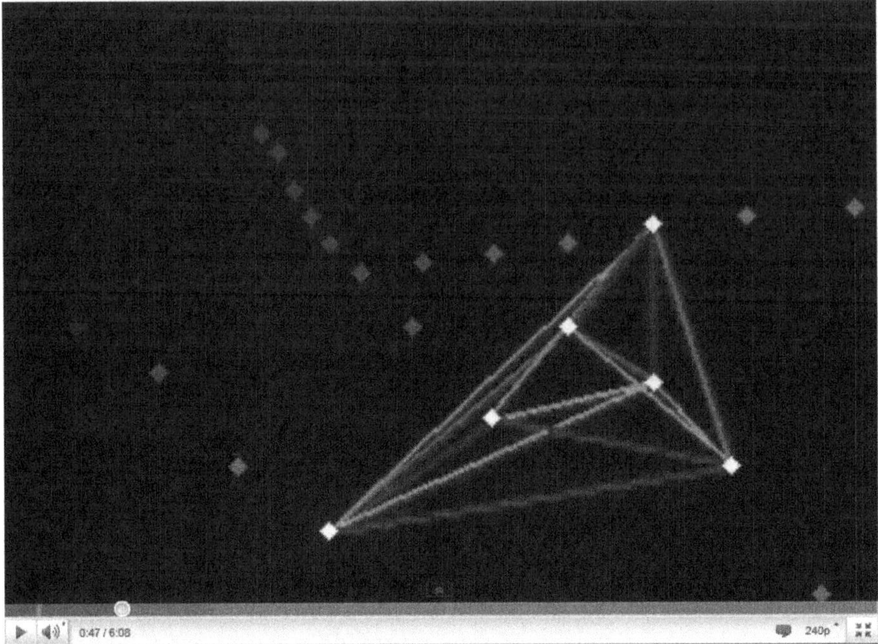

Figure 10.4 Chopin's 'Nocturne' (www.youtube.com/v/asDXpfFMKNA&rel=1).

may offer insights into a piece not easily otherwise translated from one's aural experience of that piece, especially for those not expert in music analysis but interested in multimodal studies, including multimodal studies involving musical phenomena.

These are relatively simple examples of an important principle: that different views and resemioticizations of semiotic phenomena, however simple and unsophisticated, can offer insights not readily available using our customary sensory processes. This is to foreground a multimodal approach to the analytical process itself (O'Halloran, in press; Smith *et al.*, 2011): that is, moving beyond page-based analysis to the use of multimodal (especially interactive digital) resources and techniques for the study of communication. Following Whorf's (1956) observations on language, we claim that the use of different semiotic resources in an analytical process, including digitally manifested ones, offers different views of the data, each with their own tendencies of perception and construal (cf. O'Halloran, 2005 for a discussion of this principle in relation to the development and use of mathematical semiotic resources).

In general terms, digital resources offer a powerful extension of the human capacity for perception and interaction, analogous to the invention of the telescope or microscope. For example, they offer the capacity to zoom to thousandths of a second of sound and examine and annotate phenomena at that level of magnification (via the spectrogram or by simply listening), or to view texts in their entirety (as in the example of 'A Day in the Life'); and to transpose texts across sensory modalities and media (e.g. from sound to vision). The processing of large quantities of data referred to by Halliday (2002) is another example of this extension of the human sensory capacity afforded by contemporary, particularly software, technology (cf. also Manovich, 2009).

10.3.2 Analysis

In addition to access, another important affordance of digital resources is the capacity to apply a range of annotations within the environment of the source text. In Praat, the user may insert orthographic annotations into tiers below a frequency-intensity graph, time-aligned with the source text which can be played while viewing the visual annotations. As a result of annotating in the environment of the sounding text, rather than on or with respect to a written transcription on a printed page, any analysis or transcription is readily answerable, by its proximity, to the source text, encouraging the scholar to constantly check and recheck analyses.

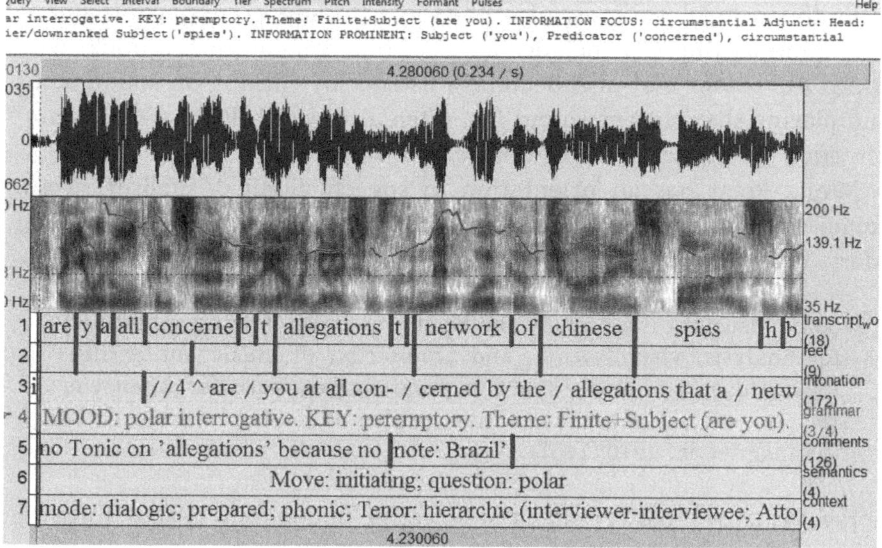

Figure 10.5 Praat picture of a multidimensional systemic analysis.

In addition, the tiers, arranged vertically, allow the systemic functional analyst to produce potentially a wide range of analyses across different strata, ranks and metafunctions. Such a platform thus encourages the application of a variety of analyses for the same text, to test and compare different frameworks and approaches, and to share and compare analyses with other scholars from the same or different theoretical traditions or disciplines. The status of any particular transcription or analysis of a source text as a faithful representation or interpretation of that original text is thus foregrounded, recalling issues of 'transcription as theory' discussed by Ochs (1979).

Figure 10.5 shows a Praat analysis of a short segment of speech analysed for various systems at different strata and ranks and in different metafunctions. Thus aligned, the multiple-tier view allows the analyst to view at a glance the various analyses, singularly and in relation to one another. One can apply analysis of varying time-scales, from the microsecond event of the onset of a syllable to the macro-perspective on a tone-group complex. Praat has proven useful for a wide variety of research and teaching tasks, being popular with mainstream phoneticians and phonologists, systemicists and discourse analysts alike, and is readily usable by those not possessing great technical competence. One interesting use has been for the study of vocalizations of bonobo apes (Benson *et al.*, 2004), involving the application of systemic perspectives over a wide range of scales of time and frequency. Halliday and Greaves (2008) is an excellent example of the usefulness of Praat for extensive multidimensional analyses of authentic naturally occurring discourse. An accompanying CD includes an electronic version of the book, with which the reader may also become a listener by clicking on sound icons and playing the relevant sound file, often also with a Praat visual representation (see Chapter 12 of this volume).

While Praat has an orientation to speech, Sonic Visualiser (www.sonicvisualiser.org), developed at the Centre for Digital Music, Queen Mary, University of London, has an orientation to music:

> Sonic Visualiser is a friendly and flexible end-user desktop application for analysis, visualisation, and annotation of music audio files. Its stated goal is to be 'the first program you reach for when you want to study a musical recording rather than simply listen to it'.
> (Cannam et al., 2010: 1467)

Sonic Visualiser, like Praat, is a powerful but readily usable software program for both accessing and analysing sound, incorporating a variety of visualizations as the product of algorithmic processing of the sound signal as well as 'editable annotation layers of various types, such as time instants (moments with no associated value, such as beat locations), time-value plots, labels, and images' (Cannam *et al.*, 2010: 1467). There are a number of valuable interactive features, such as the capacity to 'annotate points in a recording by adding a time instant layer and clicking with the mouse, or by using the keyboard to "tap" beats while the audio is playing' (*ibid.*); and the software 'supports the Vamp plugin format to provide additional analysis methods such as beat trackers, structural segmentation, key estimation and so on' (*ibid.*: 1468).

The move towards incorporating more and more capabilities within the one software and making such powerful computational resources accessible to a range of users, particularly those without technical computational skills, via well-designed graphical user interfaces and excellent supporting documentation, is a feature of recent software applications such as Praat and Sonic Visualiser. This is also evident in software designed for both sound and video analysis, such as ELAN (see Zappavigna *et al.*, 2010 for systemic work, involving phonology, using this application), ANVIL and MacVisSTA. Schmidt *et al.* (2009) discuss some of these state-of-the-art multimodal annotators and their strengths (cf. also Rohlfing *et al.*, 2006), particularly for certain tasks. Schmidt *et al.* also identify constraints and challenges which emerge when bringing together different software tools.

Such software applications and the various tools which make analysis algorithms available in software are immensely powerful resources for the study of phonology. Yet technological resources are a valuable but not self-sufficient component of the contemporary research process. At all points the use of technology remains answerable to the knowledge and skill of the analyst. Meanwhile, the analyst's purpose, theoretical framework and linguistic description will to a large extent determine the nature of focus and interpretation in any investigation (see Smith, 2011 for a discussion).

Thus the use as well as the design of such technological resources raises issues and challenges for the study of phonology and particularly for the systemic phonologist tasked with bringing to bear a holistic, polystemic functional perspective upon potentially a wide range of analyses of text and corpus. In the next section we discuss the development of a software application which is designed to address such issues, having been adapted with reference to the multidimensional systemic functional theory and derived descriptions.

10.4 Systemic phonological analysis in the digital environment

As discussed in the previous section, contemporary software applications such as Praat and Sonic Visualiser offer powerful platforms for the close study and analysis of speech, music and other sounds, including importantly the ability to add time-aligned annotations within the environment of the source text. This is particularly important for those working within the systemic functional tradition, with its emphasis on close, detailed analysis of naturally occurring text rather than relying upon introspection, discursive theorizing at a distance from actual text or on written transcriptions which then become the basis of one's analysis. The enhanced capacity for multiple analytical views afforded by interactive digital software also moves the analyst towards the comprehensive holistic vision which is a hallmark of systemic theory. However, several issues emerge from the use of such applications.

10.4.1 Issues in the use of software for analysis of sound

First, from the user's point of view, the many analyses which can be conducted may potentially produce immense complexity in terms of the interpretation and integration of the analyses in relation to one another and to the overall analytical picture upon a unitary object, the text, or corpus being studied. The challenge presented to systemic functional linguists in general is foregrounded in digital analysis: how to manage such complexity. How, considering the 'elaborate treasury of information' referred to by Halliday and Greaves in the quotation at the head of this chapter, can researchers make principled choices as to which systems and phenomena to focus on, both in conducting and interpreting one's analysis? One must, ultimately, be able to relate different analyses to one another and to the overall holistic perspective on a text or corpus so as to make sense of it; and to enable description and theory to be developed and tested through their application in analysis. The potential complexity of a typical systemic (in this case intonational) analysis is evident in the short Praat analysis of a few seconds of speech shown in Figure 10.5 and presented in Figure 10.6 in an Excel spreadsheet, where the vertical columns represent just a few of the many analytical views possible (see Smith, 2008a for a full analysis and its explanation):

2	Int	IU	TONALITY; TONICITY; TONE; RHYTHM; SALIENCE	ID	THEME	IF: lexis	IF: Grammar	IP: Lexis	IP: Grammar	MOOD: KEY/ STAT	TONE
3	J	1	//4 ^ phillip ruddock */ thanks for / joining us //	N	Phillip Ruddock	thanks	Salut	joining	Salut	sub	4
4	R	2	//1 pleasure //	N		0 pleasure	Attr/Com	0	0	D: N	1
5	J	3	//4 ^ are / you at all con- / cerned by the / allegations that a / network of / chinese */ spies has been //	M	you	spies	Phen: (dr) Act	you; concerned; allegations; network; Chinese	Sens/ Subj (addr); Proc: men/ Pred; Phen: Head; (dr) Act*2	sub	4_
6	J	4	//1_ operating in this */ country //	M	you	country	(dr) Circ: loc: spat	operating	(dr) Proc: mat	P: per: mild	1_
7	R	5	//4_ ^ well I'm / always con- / cerned about er - about alle- */ gations but er //	N	well I	allegations	Circ: matt	always; concerned	Mood Adj: us; Proc: men/ Pred	D: res	4_
8	R	6	//1 ^ one / has to es- */ tablish //	N	but one	establish	Proc: men/	has	Fin: mod: high	D: N	1
9	R	7	//-3 whether or */ not ah they are //	M	but one	not	Mood Adj: pol (neg)	whether	Mood Adj: pol (pos)	D: uncom	-3
10	R	8	//4 real or i- */ magined //	N	but one	imagined	Attr: int/ Comp	real	Attr: int/ Comp	sub	4

Figure 10.6 Intonational analysis in Excel.

Another issue for the analyst-user, particularly for systemic phonologists, is the means of annotation. Praat offers type-in orthographic annotation within its tier structure. This offers no easy way of storing information about the analysis of systemic choices within a text, for example as statistical profiles of analyses either in isolation or in relation to one another. The annotations one makes in Praat are conducted and stored as graphical user interface-based type-in text: one's own analysis remains as language-based metadiscourse only. This type of annotation misses one of the main advantages of computational technology, which is the capacity to store analytical data in a database in such a way as to retrieve, process, share and visualize one's analysis, time-aligned within the environment of the source text. In the analyses shown in Figures 10.5 and 10.6, one of the present authors, having analysed 30 minutes of speech for various intonational and other grammatical systems using Praat, had then the task of manually transporting the time-aligned information from the Praat tiers into an Excel spreadsheet and thence into the SPSS (Statistical Package for the Social Sciences) software application in order to derive statistical information about systemic choices. As a result of this cumbersome process, the valuable statistical information was no longer available within the environment of the text, the source text as sound, and bore no computational relation to the original Praat analysis.

Not only databases but also interfaces for the annotation of sound do not in general readily support analyses involving the application of analytical choices from system networks. Such interfaces do of course exist for the analysis of written text: for example, O'Halloran and Judd's *Systemics*, O'Donnell's *UAM Corpus Tool and Systemic Coder*, Wu and Matthiessen's *SysFan*, and Bateman's *Grammar Explorer* (see O'Donnell and Bateman, 2005 for a review; see also ISFLA, undated). The power of such applications for systemic analysis points to the need for such tools for the analysis of sound (and other dynamic media).

Furthermore, it is increasingly clear that analysis of the phonology of speech is, in many cases at least, impoverished if done in isolation from the analyses of other semiotic resources (e.g. Martinec, 2000; Zappavigna *et al.*, 2010). In the same way that systemic functional theory in the twentieth century has from the outset championed a holistic approach to language and meaning, so too in the early twenty-first century it is evident that it is within the framework of multimodal discourse analysis that systemic functional semiotics, as a science of meaning-in-the-round, will rightly find its fulfillment, particularly with the advent of increasingly sophisticated technical resources appropriate to such study.

10.4.2 Software for the systemic analysis of sound

10.4.2.1 Systemic analyses and their relations

The issues discussed in §10.4.1 have been important considerations for an interdisciplinary team (software engineers, linguists and multimodal semioticians, and mathematicians) developing software adapted for systemic analysis of multimodal discourse (cf. O'Halloran *et al.*, 2010). A major challenge has been to adapt both the database and the interface for systemic analysis, and to tackle the issues, both for the computer engineer and the user, that are involved in the integration of the many different types of analysis potentially relevant to the study of multimodal discourse. Building upon knowledge gained through the development of a software, *Systemics* (O'Halloran and Judd, 2002), for the systemic analysis of written text, O'Halloran's team developed a prototype interface adapted for the systemic analysis of sound and video. This interface allows for both user-generated and default system networks, displayed in a separate window with choices colour-coded so as to distinguish different options in systems, to be applied via one-click annotation across a text. These systemic annotations are displayed along a timeline which also may include other information such as time, visualizations such as spectrogram and waveform, as well as other user-generated or computational analyses of the text. These analyses can be played along with the source text so that

Figure 10.7 Section of a prototype graphical user interface with systemic analyses.

one can see the analysis unfolding in time while listening to and watching the source text, whether with video or sound alone (Figure 10.7).

Such an interface makes systemic analysis readily available via default and user-defined systems, such as those for TONE, MOOD, KEY, SPEECH FUNCTION and TENOR in the example shown in Figure 10.7. The annotations are then stored as values in the database, which can thus be retrieved, shared and post-processed (computationally), and are accessible in the interface as visualizations of one's analyses or of computational processing of such (e.g. visualizations of the results of statistical processing of choices in different systems, alone and in relation to one another). The prototype version uses tiers as in Praat and other software applications (which we have called 'strips'), with embedding of tiers within tiers enabled, allowing for various groupings of analyses. These different groupings (arranging systems in different relations to one another along the vertical axis, different principles of embedding, or hiding certain analyses) bring out different aspects of the text and its analysis (cf. Smith *et al.*, 2011).

For example, for the analysis shown in Figure 10.7 the interface has been set up to facilitate the analysis of interstratal relations within the interpersonal metafunction for one particular speaker, Tony Jones, in a multi-party discourse from an episode of the Australian Broadcasting Corporation's (2010) *QANDA*, a live television discussion programme. Jones is here enacting, as host, the 'hierarchic' setting in the tenor variable of context (the term is from Butt, 2003; cf. Moore, in press, for an extended application), by pointing to an audience member and indicating to that person that it is his turn to ask a question. This command is preceded by a minor clause 'okay', with its own information unit, in the neutral minor clause key (tone 1 – falling pitch contour), a typical device for signaling a transition to a new phase in the discourse. Then a multimodal command is realized, together with a pointing gesture and gaze, by two declarative clauses, each with its own information unit: the first in the 'committed' key, realized by tone 5 (rising-falling pitch contour), the latter in the 'mild' key realized by a tone 1_ (low falling pitch contour): 'Okay, there's a young man down the front, who's had his hand up for a while'. Such interstratally non-congruent and multimodal choices are common within this text for this speaker, in his role as host, as he manages the course of the dialogue as it unfolds dynamically and, in terms of the interpersonal metafunction, often somewhat chaotically (see O'Halloran, 2011 for a more extended example of this type of analysis). The visual still images of Jones show his command gesture from two perspectives, each of which may themselves become sites for further time-aligned analyses, including the use of graphic resources such as vectors and symbols to annotate gesture, facial expression etc. Such annotations may themselves become the site for the application of systemic analysis.

In the interface design in Figure 10.8, the user has grouped the analyses so as to explore choices within one particular system, TONE, for all the speakers in the dialogue. This interface configuration thus affords a view on the dialogic aspect of the text, including interrupting or overlapping discourse, as is the case here, where Tanya Plibersek (federal member of parliament and of the Cabinet) interrupts during a turn by Malcolm Turnbull (federal member of parliament and former opposition leader). Turnbull has just made the comment that 'Tanya obviously doesn't [like Tony Abbott]', at which point Plibersek interjects to say 'Oh I like him', using a tone 2_ (sharp falling-rising pitch contour) realizing the 'challenging–focusing' declarative key (the rising tone realizing the sense of challenge; the sharp fall in this variation of the tone 2 pinpointing a particular element of the information unit as the special locus of this interpersonal choice – here, the mental process 'like').

This view also shows, as in Figure 10.8, a still image of the speaker Tanya Plibersek at the point of her interjection, which, again, may become the site for time-aligned annotations of, for example, her facial expression, which here helps to realize a complex meaning of positive affect and contradiction.

One can of course also use orthographic annotation (the most common form of annotation in multimodal annotation software applications).

Figure 10.8 Interface set up for multi-party dialogue.

Orthographic description does not show in the interface as clearly as colour-coding, and thus is not effective for the representation of systemic analysis. However, it is useful for discursive explorations of non-systemic phenomena (for example, low-level phenomena such as phonetics, visual phenomena), and in general as a first pass, pre-systemic analysis of a text; and is of course essential for transcription of the verbal discourse.

The facility for grouping particular sets of analyses together in the interface means that one is encouraged to experiment with different couplings of strips. For example, in Tanya Plibersek's turn in the example above, a textual system is of potential interest to the interpersonal analysis. The speaker chooses to make both the Subject/Theme ('I') and the Finite-Predicator/mental Process of affect ('like') salient. The latter is of course the Tonic, but the choice of the preceding syllable as also salient is marked (two adjacent lexical items as both salient). More importantly, this choice in INFORMATION PROMINENCE (cf. Smith, 2008b for a discussion of this system, introduced at the rank below INFORMATION DISTRIBUTION) draws textual attention to the speaker–Subject 'I': this interpersonally charged Subject is given a raised textual status in the discourse. Thus the analyst may wish to bring the strip carrying the analysis of the textual system of INFORMATION PROMINENCE together within this interpersonal grouping to explore such inter-systemic (in fact inter-metafunctional) relations. The mapping of textual and other metafunctional choices, considering the second-order nature of the textual metafunction, is a particularly good example of the importance of grouping different analyses together in the interface view. The same may of course be said of analyses of other semiotic resources, such as gesture, which may be relevant to the interpersonal (or textual) intonational analysis here or elsewhere.

Such groupings, or configurations, of analyses in the interface may then be saved in the database as particular 'views' on one's analysis, which can then later be retrieved during the analysis process or during a conference or lecture presentation. One might wish to draw readily, at any point, upon a range of different configurations, or views, of the many different systemic and other analyses already conducted on a text or corpus (by the user or other researchers), arranged in a variety of different visual relations to one another and groupings in the interface (a process we have informally termed 'bookmarking'). This provides flexibility, in terms of performing and then later viewing multiple analyses, that suits well the complementarity of systemic functional theory's multidimensional framework. The resulting multiplicity of views moves the analyst towards a holistic view on the text as the synthesis of many systems at different strata and ranks, in different metafunctions, and so on. This resource is also valuable for developing and saving particular configurations or systemic analyses as relevant to particular research tasks or questions. Such resources have significant value for collaboration or comparison between researchers and analyses from the same or different theoretical traditions or disciplines, either by single or multiple researchers.

10.4.2.2 Other computational analyses

One may also apply a range of computational analyses which may then be represented visually along the timeline in relation to any other analyses, including user-generated (e.g. systemic) analysis. Algorithms are currently available which can perform tasks of immense sophistication, detail, scope and complexity, tasks far beyond the sensory and thinking capabilities of the unaided human faculties. However, from a software engineering point of view, there are difficulties in making available to the general phonologist-as-user the range of sophisticated software tools potentially of relevance to their study.

There are basically two ways in which to access such tools, involving two types of user. The first way requires little skill on the part of the user:

the software program runs a series of algorithmic analyses, processing raw data, producing a set of intermediate results and then interpreting those results for the user. An example would be a program to automatically analyse tone choices in a text. The user starts the program, which runs according to its own internal sequence, generating a set of final results, a tone analysis, which the user then manually post-processes, checking for and correcting errors. To take another example, human analysis of large corpora of sonic data can be time consuming. However, often we are interested only in particular regions of the audio data we are handling. Modern algorithms are able to find, with a reasonable level of accuracy, regions of interest for certain features. An example is when we are interested only in segments of speech or music. Software tools are able to isolate such segments, and can eliminate or hide all other segments, thus compiling a corpus relevant to the particular research task (including individual speaker detection algorithms, thus isolating a corpus of speech by one particular speaker).

These sorts of software tool are potentially of practical benefit to systemic phonologists. However, in general the results algorithms produce can be of questionable value in terms of their quality (as is commonly experienced, for example, with automated transcription software). The designer of the algorithms which power such applications cannot make any predictions about the nature and the quality of the data given to the machine by the user as input for processing, with the accuracy of results varying depending on this quality. Furthermore, if it is to be widely useful, such a program should be able to handle several kinds of data source. The audio stream that the user wants to analyse may be simply an audio file, or it may be the soundtrack of a video or part of a more complex media such as a website. Moreover there are many different forms of encoding and file formats. Being compatible and compliant with even the large set of major types is already quite a challenge in terms of software design and development.

For the average non-skilled user of software, such challenges clearly need to be dealt with by the developer of the software, offering little or hopefully no problems for the analyst wanting to get on with their own work. While most analysis algorithms can produce results of reasonable quality if adequately tuned or trained, such tuning requires a much higher degree of user skill. Therefore the software application must provide a set of basic tools that can be used for a range of data types and users, as well as for different research purposes and in different contexts.

The second way of accessing software technology is where the more computationally advanced user intervenes in the computational process, collecting and analysing manually the intermediate data (which can be a huge set of data and numbers, arising from the algorithmic processing of the raw data) and, based on this intermediate step, is thus in a position to draw his/her own conclusions. This user has a significantly higher degree of flexibility in and control over the analytical process: for example, in adjusting and fine-tuning the algorithm parameters to suit specific datasets, or in matching various data that the more generic algorithms have not been designed to compare. Thus, for example, this type of user can get the results of pitch, formant and spectrographic analyses and make a categorization of tones based on the integration of this intermediate information. Consequently in the long term such a user may be able to contribute to the development of new strategies to automatically detect tone choices based on many such observations of low-level computational analyses. Such experienced users will require a more complex interface, which allows the control of several internal parameters to produce high fidelity output.

To be useful for a range of research tasks, software must support such sophisticated use. At the same time, this more sophisticated affordance should not be a barrier to the basic user, who should be able to use the same software tools using predefined presets, and who may in fact have very high-quality data as input, making the generic application of such algorithms significantly more reliable. The challenge is that in general the more specific (and powerful) a software tool is, the more constraints need to be imposed on the input data. In our view, in terms of the use of software for multimodal, including phonological, analysis it is more important to have few or no constraints on the input raw data (both audio and visual). Rather, our aim is to provide generic and robust tools which, however, make allowance for more sophisticated users to intervene in the computational processes made available in the application.

10.4.2.3 Integration of analyses

Another major issue is the integration of software tools within a single application platform. There are many powerful software tools currently available for the analysis of an audio, but from the user's point of view their integration can be complex and potentially messy. Users may require several different programs to accomplish their analytical process. Moreover, it remains difficult and often impossible to join, merge, compare and collect the results produced by using different software algorithms (cf. Schmidt *et al.*, 2009). Therefore a software application able to handle many different kinds of input and which integrates a large set of analytical tools may have a great value for the user, particularly for multimodal systemicists who value the holistic view on 'meaning-in-the-round'. Such software not only facilitates and speeds up the task of analysis of many types, but may also reveal innovative investigative techniques through the integration of these many different analytical views on data and corpora.

While it is clear that the semiotics knowledge and analytical skill of the systemic functional scholar is far in advance of the average computer engineer who is able to manipulate algorithms, we cannot expect the average systemicist to develop the high degree of competency required to operate, let alone develop such algorithms. Nor can we expect the average computer engineer to become an expert in phonological analysis to the standard of the average (systemic or other) phonologist in order to develop more effective models of intonation. This problem lies at the heart of the issue of interdisciplinarity. Yet it is at the interface of computational science and the skills of the semiotics analyst that the digital world offers the most powerful resources for systemic phonologists. Software applications have the capability of being extremely precise and very fast in processing large quantities of data. However, algorithms are in general much more effective in processing lower-strata phenomena close to the material base, rather than the more abstract higher-strata phenomena (such as TONE and KEY choices), the analysis of which remains the province of the trained linguist–phonologist. Thus a software application for systemic analysis must facilitate both manual, user-generated analysis and algorithmic processing, including, importantly, computational post-processing of manual analysis, and be able to facilitate synthesis of the results of both types.

These considerations have been at the forefront in the post-prototype development stage of the software design and development. The commitment to the integration of both lower-level algorithmic and higher-level human-annotated analyses within the single computational environment, and to the integration of a diverse range of computational tools for the analysis of a range of data types, is one inspired and informed throughout by systemic functional theory, and aligned along its dimensions. The development of a series of more sophisticated database and graphical user interface designs, which is still ongoing, has evolved to take account of the immense complexity presented by multimodal, systemic analysis of sound and vision across different scales, dimensions and locations within dimensions, leading to the implementation of generic 'bands' with hierarchies of strips for different media types (text, image, video) and tools for drawing (searchable) overlays on the original media file, as displayed in Figure 10.9.

Figure 10.9 Graphical user interface design with bands and overlays.

By foregrounding, in the design of the software interface and database, resources for the integration of computational and human-generated analyses, we hope to overcome the limitations imposed by the traditional interdisciplinary gulf between computer engineering and linguistics/ semiotics – between the sciences and humanities – in a scientific, interdisciplinary 'feedback' process of potentially great productiveness for both sciences. For example, a fundamental problem in developing algorithms designed for specific linguistically relevant tasks such as tone detection is that for engineers the first and most important requirement is a systematic, precise and computationally implementable model of the linguistic phenomena in question, a requirement that offers immense challenges to phonologists and linguists in general. If, however, the engineer is able himself to draw upon time-aligned, multidimensional analyses conducted by linguists within the computational environment (that is, stored in a database), the engineer is then able to associate the raw data or intermediate data resulting from computational processing back to the analyses produced by the linguist and develop computational models of phonological phenomena accordingly.

Conversely, the phonologist can explore and thus specify for the engineer, through the use of computational resources of access and annotation discussed earlier, particular low-level features of the raw signal as being of interest in the higher-level phonological or other linguistic analyses, thereby prompting further computational exploration of the raw signal in terms of automated feature extraction. That is, the software scientist may develop tools and techniques for automated recognition of phenomena identified as significant by the linguist. Working together in this way, computer and semiotics scientists can develop and apply (in terms of the development of new algorithms) more sophisticated and useful scientific models for the analysis of phonology (cf. Wyse, 2003 on the importance of computational modeling in the study and particularly the production of designed sound).

10.5 Conclusion: digital phonology

The discussion presented in this chapter outlines some of the interactive digital resources available or under development for use by the systemic phonologist, and addresses both their actual and potential functions as well as issues arising from their use. Contemporary digital technology offers powerful platforms for the analysis of sound, which are increasingly accessible to the average non-skilled computer user. Systemicists have historically laid emphasis on the analysis of actual texts as the means for exploring, developing and applying descriptive and theoretical generalizations. Digital resources are clearly of use to such aims, particularly where sound is concerned, allowing close analytical access to such texts and an ever-widening range of techniques for analysis.

Perhaps most importantly, software offers communities of linguists and other scholars, including software scientists, a site for the sort of collaborative research which is the hallmark of the physical sciences but has tended to elude linguists trained within humanist traditions. It is the latter group of scholars who are arguably in the best position to assist in the development of more sophisticated computational models of language and who might most productively exploit software tools for the analysis of phonology and all other aspects of language and semiosis in general. Software engineering becomes informed by the purposes and knowledge of the phonologist through the language of software, via analyses stored in a database. Meanwhile the phonologist becomes more attentive to the needs and opportunities of software design and development through the application of phonological analysis and linguistic theory and description within the constraints and affordances of the digital environment. With its long and illustrious history of engagement with computer science since the early days of both disciplines (cf. Halliday, 2005), systemic functional linguistics is well placed to both help develop and exploit such interdisciplinarity and the resources which increasingly make it possible.

Meanwhile, linguists from different theoretical traditions are finding, in such digital resources, the tools with which to collaborate and communicate across such historical divides, generating new insights from the synthesis within the digital environment of analyses deriving from these different perspectives (cf. Goldman *et al.*, 2009). The same principle also applies across disciplines. Digital resources thus not only enable us, as Halliday points out in the earlier quotation, to 'test our descriptive generalizations … and to observe and represent sound waves in a wealth of complementary perspectives', but also thus encourage us to think more consciously and explicitly about our own metadiscourses through their realization in the media of software interface and database design.

Acknowledgements

This article was supported by a research grant (no. NRF2007IDM-IDM002-066; principal investigator Kay L. O'Halloran) funded by the Interactive Digital Media Programme Office (IDMPO) in Singapore. For further information, see the Multimodal Analysis Lab website (http://multimodal-analysis-lab.org).

Websites

Audacity	http://audacity.sourceforge.net
Multimodal Analysis Lab	http://multimodal-analysis-lab.org/?page_id=187
Music Animation Machine	www.musanim.com
Praat	www.fon.hum.uva.nl/praat
Sonic Visualiser	www.sonicvisualiser.org

References

Australian Broadcasting Corporation (2010) *QANDA*. Episode 3, Broadcast 22 February. Available at www.abc.net.au/tv/qanda/txt/s2820346.htm (accessed 17 May 2010).

Beatles (1967) A day in the life. Final track from *Sgt. Pepper's Lonely Hearts Club Band* album. London: Parlophone.

Benson, J., Debashish, M., Greaves, W. S., Lukas, J., Savage-Rumbaugh, S. and Taglialatela, J. (2004) Mind and brain in apes: a methodology for phonemic analysis of vocalizations of language competent bonobos. *Language Sciences* 26(6): 643–60.

Boersma, P. and Weenink, D. (2011) *Praat: Doing Phonetics by Computer* (version 5.2.20). Computer program. Available at www.praat.org (accessed 25 March 2011).

Butt, D. G. (2003) *Parameters of Context: On Establishing The Similarities and Differences Between Contexts.* Unpublished monograph, Macquarie University.

Cannam, C., Landone, C. and Sandler, M. (2010) Sonic visualiser: an open source application for viewing, analysing, and annotating music audio files. In *Proceedings of the ACM Multimedia 2010 International Conference* 1467–8. New York: ACM.

Crystal, D. (1969) *Prosodic Systems and Intonation in English.* Cambridge: Cambridge University Press.

Firth, J. R. (1957) *Papers in Linguistics: 1934–1951.* Oxford: Oxford University Press.

Firth, J. R. (1968) The language of linguistics. In F. R. Palmer (ed.) *Selected Papers of J. R. Firth: 1952–59* 27–34. London: Longman.

Forte, A. and Gilbert, S. E. (1982) *Introduction to Schenkerian Analysis.* New York: W. W. Norton & Company.

Goldman, R., Dong, C. and Lansiquot, R. (2009). Software design principles for video research in the learning sciences and CSCL: two studies use the perspectivity framework & Orion™. In *Proceedings of the 9th international Conference on Computer Supported Collaborative Learning, Rhodes, Greece, Volume 2.* Available at http://portal.acm.org/citation.cfm?id=1599503.1599548 (accessed 13 August 2009).

Halliday, M. A. K. (1961) Categories of the theory of grammar. *Word* 17: 241–92.

Halliday, M. A. K. (1991) Towards probabilistic interpretations. In E. Ventola (ed.) *Functional and Systemic Linguistics Approaches and Uses* (Trends in Linguistics Studies and Monographs 55) 39–61. Berlin: Mouton de Gruyter.

Halliday, M. A. K. (2002). Introduction: a personal perspective. In M. A. K. Halliday and J. J. Webster (eds) *On Grammar* 1–14. London: Continuum.

Halliday, M. A. K. (2005) *Collected Works of M. A. K. Halliday, Volume 6: Computational and Quantitative Studies* (ed. J. J. Webster). London: Continuum.

Halliday, M. A. K. (2008) Working with meaning: towards an applicable linguistics. In J. J. Webster (ed.) *Meaning in Context: Implementing Intelligent Applications of Language Studies* 7–23. London: Continuum.

Halliday, M. A. K. and Greaves, W. S. (2008) *Intonation in the Grammar of English*. London: Equinox.

Halliday, M. A. K. and Matthiessen, C. M. I. M. (2004) *An Introduction to Functional Grammar* (3rd edition). London: Arnold.

Iedema, R. (2001) Resemioticization. *Semiotica* 137(1/4): 23–39.

ISFLA (undated) Coding programs. Available at www.isfla.org/Systemics/Software/Coders.html (accessed 22 Janaury 2013).

Jones, D. (1909) *Intonation Curves*. Leipzig: Teubner.

Ladd, D. R. (1996) *Intonational Phonology*. Cambridge: Cambridge University Press.

Lewisohn, M. (1988) *The Beatles: Recording Sessions*. New York: Harmony.

Malinowski, S. (1985) *Music Animation Machine*. Available at www.musanim.com/index.html (accessed 26 March 2011).

Manovich, L. (2009) *How to Follow Global Digital Cultures, or Cultural Analytics for Beginners*. Available at http://manovich.net/articles (accessed 26 March 2011).

Martinec, R. (2000) Rhythm in multimodal texts. *Leonardo* 33(4): 289–97.

Matthiessen, C. M. I. M. (2007) The 'architecture' of language according to systemic functional theory: developments since the 1970s. In R. Hasan, C. M. I. M. Matthiessen and J. J. Webster (eds) *Continuing Discourse on Language, Volume Two* 505–61. London: Equinox.

Moore, A. (in press) Surgical teams in action: a contextually sensitive approach to modelling body alignment and interpersonal engagement. In A. Baldry and E. Montagna (eds) *Interdisciplinary Perspectives on Multimodality: Theory and Practice, Readings in Intersemiosis and Multimedia*. Campobasso: Palladino.

Ochs, E. (1979) Transcription as theory. In E. Ochs and B. B. Schieffelin (eds) *Developmental Pragmatics* 43–72. New York: Academic Press.

O'Donnell, M. and Bateman, J. (2005) SFL in computational contexts: a contemporary history. In J. J. Webster, R. Hasan and C. M. I. M. Matthiessen (eds) *Continuing Discourse on Language: A Functional Perspective, Volume 1* 343–82. London: Equinox.

O'Halloran, K. L. (2005) *Mathematical Discourse: Language, Symbolism and Visual Images*. London: Continuum.

O'Halloran, K. L. (2011) Multimodal discourse analysis. In K. Hyland and B. Paltridge (eds) *Companion to Discourse Analysis* 120–37. London: Continuum.

O'Halloran, K. L. (in press). Multimodal analysis and digital technology. In A. Baldry and E. Montagna (eds) *Interdisciplinary Perspectives on Multimodality: Theory and Practice, Readings in Intersemiosis and Multimedia*. Campobasso: Palladino.

O'Halloran, K. L. and Judd, K. (2002) *Systemics* (version 1.0). Computer program. Singapore: Singapore University Press.

O'Halloran, K. L., Tan, S., Smith, B. A. and Podlasov, A. (2010) Challenges in designing digital interfaces for the study of multimodal phenomena. *Information Design Journal* 18(1): 2–12.

Pierrehumbert, J. and Hirschberg, J. (1990) The meaning of intonational contours in the interpretation of discourse. In P. R Cohen, J. Morgan and M. E. Pollack (eds) *Intentions in Communication* 271–311. Cambridge, MA: MIT Press.

Rohlfing, K., Loehr, D., Duncan, S., Brown, A., Franklin, A. and Kimbarra, I., *et al.* (2006) Comparison of multimodal annotation tools – workshop report. *Online-Zeitschrift zur Verbalen Interaktion, Ausgabe* 7: 99–123.

Schmidt, T., Duncan, S., Ehmer, O., Hoyt, J., Kipp, M., Loehr, D., Magnusson, M., Rose, R. T. and Sloetjes, H. (2009) An exchange format for multimodal annotations. In M. Kipp, J-C. Martin, P. Paggio, and D. Heylen (eds) *Multimodal Corpora: From Models of Natural Interaction to Systems and Applications* 207–211. Berlin, Heidelberg: Springer-Verlag.

Smith, B. A. (2008a) *Intonational Systems and Register: A Multidimensional Exploration.* Sydney: Macquarie University. Unpublished PhD thesis. Available at www.isfla.org/Systemics/Print/Theses.html (accessed 22 January 2013).

Smith, B. A. (2008b) The language of the heart and breath: bridging strata, bridging discourses of INFORMATION systems. *Online Conference Proceedings for the 2007 ASFLA Congress: Bridging Discourses, held at Wollongong University, 29th June–1st July 2007.* Australian Systemic Functional Linguistics Association. Available at www.asfla.org.au/2008/07/31/the-language-of-the-heart-and-breath-bridging-strata-bridging-discourses-of-information-systems (accessed 22 January 2013).

Smith, B. A. (2011) Speech and writing: intonation within multimodal studies. In K. L. O'Halloran and B. A. Smith (eds) *Multimodal Studies: Exploring Issues and Domains* 39–54. London: Routledge.

Smith, B. A., Tan, S., Podlasov, A. and O'Halloran, K. L. (2011) Analyzing multimodality in an interactive digital environment: software as metasemiotic tool. *Social Semiotics* 21(3): 359–80.

Steele, J. (1775) *An Essay Towards Establishing the Melody and Measure of Speech.* Menston: Scholar Press.

Whorf, B. (1956) *Language, Thought, and Reality: Selected Writings.* Cambridge, MA: MIT Press.

Wyse, L. (2003) Free music and the discipline of sound. *Organized Sound* 8(3): 237–47.

Zappavigna, M., Cleirigh, C., Dwyer, P. and Martin, J. R. (2010) The coupling of gesture and phonology. In M. Bednarek and J. R. Martin (eds) *New Discourse on Language: Functional Perspectives on Multimodality, Identity, and Affiliation* 219–36. London: Continuum.

11 The meanings and forms of intonation and punctuation in English: The concepts required for an explicit model

Robin P. Fawcett[a]

11.1 The goals of this chapter

11.1.1 Introduction

Over the last few decades there have been several published descriptions of intonation in English from the viewpoint of systemic functional linguistics (SFL). The explicit goal of these descriptions is to provide a framework to assist those engaged in analysing the intonation of a spoken text (i.e. the intonational aspect of discourse analysis). Strictly speaking, such 'descriptions' are what we might term **descriptive frameworks**, rather than a component of a **model of language** (Fawcett 2011a). The most widely used of these descriptive frameworks are those in Halliday (1970), Halliday and Greaves (2008), the relevant sections of Halliday (1985, 1994) and Halliday and Matthiessen (2004), and in Tench (1996a).

---

a **Robin Fawcett** is Emeritus Professor of Linguistics and the former Director of the Computational Linguistics Unit in the Centre for Language and Communication Research, Cardiff University. His research interests embrace (i) SFL in a cognitive-interactive framework that also includes the social and cultural aspects of language; (ii) the computer modelling of language in use, in both generating and understanding texts (spoken and written), and (iii) the description of English and other languages for (a) these two purposes and (b) use analysing texts. Building on developments in describing language since the mid-1970s, work by Fawcett and his colleagues (Tucker, Lin, Tench, Young, Huang, Neale, Castel and others, including many research students) has led to the emergence of what is now recognized as an alternative version of SFL to that of Halliday: the 'Cardiff Grammar'. The year 2008 saw the publication of Fawcett's *Invitation to Systemic Functional Linguistics* in English, Chinese and Spanish, and his

However, these descriptions do not, as is often assumed, describe the intonation component of language itself. They are frameworks for describing the **outputs** from the use of language to generate text. Halliday makes this clear when he says 'This book ... presents the structures which are the "output" of the networks' (Halliday, 1994: xxvii).

In principle, therefore, a descriptive framework for text analysis should, if it is to be theoretically sound, be derived from what we may term the **intonation components** (at the levels of meaning and form) of a model of the language itself. And it is these two components that are the focus of this chapter. Such a model must be (i) as COMPREHENSIVE as it is possible to make it in the current state of our knowledge; (ii) fully EXPLICIT and so TESTABLE (e.g. in a computer implementation); and (iii) INTEGRATED with the rest of the lexicogrammar (i.e. with the components that generate words and morphemes, and the syntax that relates them). It is the construction of such models that is the true goal of the linguist's work as a scientist of language.

However, a complete model of a language should also include a model of the equivalent **punctuation components** (something that is missing from most descriptions of English). Since these are the equivalent, when generating written text, of the intonation components when generating spoken text, a linguist who is seeking to model intonation may well be tempted to develop, at the same time, a model of punctuation that is similarly comprehensive, explicit and integrated. In developing the description of intonation to be presented here, we have succumbed to this temptation, so illustrating the overlaps and the differences between the two channels of communication.

The model of intonation and punctuation described in this chapter is the current 'grammar' of these components, as found in the systemic functional model of English developed for the GENESYS sentence generator

---

2000 book *A Theory of Syntax for Systemic Functional Linguistics* was reissued in 2010 as a paperback. Altogether, he has published ten books, around seventy-five papers in journals or as book chapters, and around seventy research reports, reviews and interviews. He is currently working on three major books: *An Integrative Architecture for Systemic Functional Linguistics and Other Theories of Language*, and two handbooks, on analysing *Functional Syntax* and analysing *Functional Semantics*, respectively. He is a frequent speaker and lecturer at overseas conferences and universities, having lectured in 25 different countries. He was the founding Chair of what has grown to be the International Systemic Functional Linguistics Association; he is on the Editorial Board of the journals *Functions of Language* and the *Annual Review of Functional Linguistics*, and he is a series editor for Equinox Publishing. He holds honorary professorships in three universities in China, where he is a frequent visitor.

in the COMMUNAL Project at Cardiff University, in the period from the late 1980s to the early 2000s. The model of intonation is a development of the work of Tench (1996a), which in turn builds on the work of Halliday.

The ambitious goal of this chapter is therefore to describe a partly new model of intonation and punctuation, as these are used in a comprehensive, explicit and fully integrated model of how the overall 'grammar' of English is used to generate text.

11.1.2 Key innovations

This section summarizes five of the six major innovations that distinguish the present description of English intonation from the descriptions by Halliday and Tench (the sixth being described in §11.1.4).

The first difference, as already implied by the emphasis on 'explicitness', is that this model is **generative**. But this term is used in two senses: (i) in the sense of 'explicitly formalized' and (ii) in the sense that it is intended to model the 'generation' (i.e. the 'production') of text-sentences (as in the name of the sub-field of computational linguistics known as 'natural language generation'). In my view a systemic functional lexicogrammar can – and indeed should – be 'generative' in both senses. In other words, a systemic functional grammar that is 'generative' in the first sense can function, without any modification, as the mechanism for generating text-sentences (in the second sense). This principle is demonstrated in the implementation of the GENESYS generator in the COMMUNAL Project as described in Fawcett *et al.* (1993). So, while this model shares with Halliday's and Tench's descriptions of intonation the goal of being comprehensive, it differs from theirs in modelling the generation of intonation – and in both senses of the word. It was to attain this goal that we introduced the new concepts that are required to make a fully explicit description of this important component of language.

The second difference is in the unit that is assumed to be the **basic unit** of planning for intonation (and punctuation). Both Halliday (1967, 1970) and Tench (1976, 1996a: 31–2) warn their readers against the tempting assumption that the units of the two scales coincide. For instance, Halliday (1994: 295) writes: 'An intonation unit does not correspond exactly to any unit in the clause grammar. ... Furthermore, the boundaries may overlap, with one intonation unit covering, say, one clause and half of the next.' However, our work in the COMMUNAL Project has shown that, in generating the appropriate intonation for a text-sentence, it is not in fact necessary to introduce any structural units other than those required for syntax. Our starting point was the fact that human users of English are capable of successfully integrating (i) the set of meanings that are realized through intonation (and also punctuation) with (ii) the set of meanings that are realized through syntax. If we humans can do this – as we clearly can – then it is reasonable to try to build a computer model of the way in which this integrated output may be being achieved. The challenge is to identify (i) the stage (or stages) in the process of generation at which the integration of intonation with syntax takes place and (ii) the means used to achieve it: the 'when' and the 'how' of the integration. The model of intonation described in this chapter is the Cardiff Grammar's response to that challenge.

In a systemic functional model of language it is natural to try to treat the meanings that are expressed at the level of form in words, syntax and intonation or punctuation (depending on the channel of communication) as features in a single, fully integrated system network of choices in meaning (i.e. as **semantic features**). This, then, is the first stage in the process of integration (see §11.2).

In the present model, the input to the lexicogrammar is a representation in terms of a specially developed logical form known as **systemic functional logical form** (SFLF), a logical form that is rich enough to express the eight major strands of meaning that are found in natural language (the four 'metafunctions', in Halliday's terms). There must be a way to map the units of the **input** to the lexicogrammar onto both (i) the **syntactic units** (clauses and groups) and (ii) the **intonation units** that are generated at the level of form, such that these are essentially co-extensive with each other (even though there are small local adjustments to be made to facilitate the stress-based pattern of spoken delivery that is the norm for English).

From this perspective, then, the three major challenges are:

1. to discover how best to integrate, within the **semantic system network**, the meanings realized in intonation (and punctuation) with the meanings realized in syntax;
2. to discover how best to integrate their realizations in structures at the level of form; and
3. to create a model of language that is usable or easily adaptable for a range of uses, from generating text-sentences in a computer to describing texts in a systematic manner.

In the COMMUNAL Project we have succeeded in accomplishing these three tasks, and the main focus in this chapter is on the concepts that are needed in order to achieve this. It would require several large books to describe the model in full, so this chapter will give only the minimal description necessary to demonstrate that a single set of units at the level of form (i.e. units that are based on the **syntax** of the clause and the various classes of group) is adequate for the realization of all of the various types of meaning realized in syntax and items – and, as a bonus, intonation and punctuation.[1]

The **information unit** and the **clause** are typically considered to be co-extensive in SFL approaches to intonation, and Tench follows Halliday in referring to this relationship as one of 'neutral tonality'. But the fact that this co-extensiveness occurs very frequently does not necessarily mean that it should be the starting point for establishing their relationship. Here we take instead the following two starting points:

1. the concept of the text-sentence (or 'sentence', for short) is a valid one, such that it is possible to state criteria for identifying sentence boundaries for most practical purposes (while acknowledging the difficulties that arise from time to time); and
2. each text-sentence, whether spoken or written, necessarily contains at least one information unit.

In the present model, then, the starting point in modelling this aspect of intonation is the relationship between the **intonation unit** and the **sentence**. This may seem a small difference, but it is vital. It means that the part of the 'grammar' of intonation that is concerned with whether or not to introduce a new information unit (and so a new intonation unit) always works in the same direction (from a larger unit to a smaller one). So the basic question at each stage in the generation of a sentence when a new semantic unit (and so a new syntactic unit) is introduced is always: 'Should this semantic unit be given a separate information unit?'

In the approach to be described here, then, every choice in the system networks whose realization is the introduction of another intonation unit is also a choice to give the text-sentence that is currently being generated more than one intonation unit.

The third major innovation to Halliday's and Tench's descriptions is to recognize that the phenomenon of 'marked tonicity' is not just another type of Tonic, but one that realizes a meaning that is far more complex than merely marking an element as 'new information'. In the Cardiff Grammar, such an element is said to be marked as **contrastively new**, and its meaning is that the Performer is correcting a possible misapprehension by the Addressee concerning the element marked by the **Contrastive Tonic**.

Consider the three examples below, each being one possible response to Adam's statement in (1).

(1)   Adam: Fred likes Ivy (I've heard).
(2)   Paula: (No;) IKE likes her. [correction concerns referent of Subject]
(3)   (No;) he LOVES her! [correction concerns Process expounded by Main Verb]
(4)   (No;) he likes FiOna. [correction concerns referent of Complement]

In each response the syllable that receives the Contrastive Tonic is shown by the use of capital letters for the relevant syllable (so only the letter 'O' in the case of 'FiOna'). In (2) Paula is emphasizing that the person who likes Ivy is Ike, and not Fred, as Adam supposes, so that Adam's 'possible misapprehension' concerns the Subject (S) of the clause. Thus 'Ike' is presented as being both 'new information' and as being in contrast with what Adam believes (or purports to believe), and so as 'contrastive'. Hence the term **contrastive newness**. In (3) the contrast is between the Processes of 'liking' and 'loving' as the Main Verb (M), and in (4) it is between 'Ivy' and 'Fiona' as the Complement (C).

In fact, virtually any element in the clause has the potential to be presented as 'Contrastively New', since virtually every element is the realization of one or more 'elements' of the 'event' that is the input to the lexicogrammar.

The fourth major innovation is simply the fact that the model presented here handles both **intonation** and **punctuation**. Bringing these two components of language together in a generative grammar demonstrates just where these two areas of the lexicogrammar are similar, in both their meanings and their forms (and so in the structures that realize them), and where they are different. And it makes the point that punctuation, which has been largely ignored by linguists, is in fact an important part of the level of form, since it expresses meanings that are just as central to understanding a text as those expressed in syntax and items. Thus, intonation and punctuation are treated here as components of the lexico-grammar and not as parallel semiotic systems.

The fifth innovation is of a different order. It is that, in discovering a way to model the generation of intonation and punctuation, we have incidentally developed a formalism that not only represents the integrated outputs from the lexicogrammar elegantly, but also gives us a **straight-forward notation** that can be used for representing the intonation and punctuation of text-sentences in the applied linguistics task of discourse analysis. It is a notation in which (i) every symbol representing intonation or punctuation is motivated by its role in the realization rules and

(ii) these aspects of the analysis are fully integrated with the analysis of the functional syntax.

The sixth innovation challenges the traditional view of the relationships between the levels and components that are required in a model of language that includes intonation and punctuation. §11.1.3 will establish the overall architecture of a generative systemic functional grammar, and the innovation itself will be introduced in §11.1.4.

11.1.3 The main components of a systemic functional grammar

Here we assume a model of language in which the system network models what Halliday has aptly named the **meaning potential** of a language, and so constitutes its **semantics.** (See Fawcett, 2008: ch. 2 for a fuller description of the present model, and Fawcett, forthcoming 2015: ch. 3 for the essential similarity of the generative version of Halliday's model to the present model.)

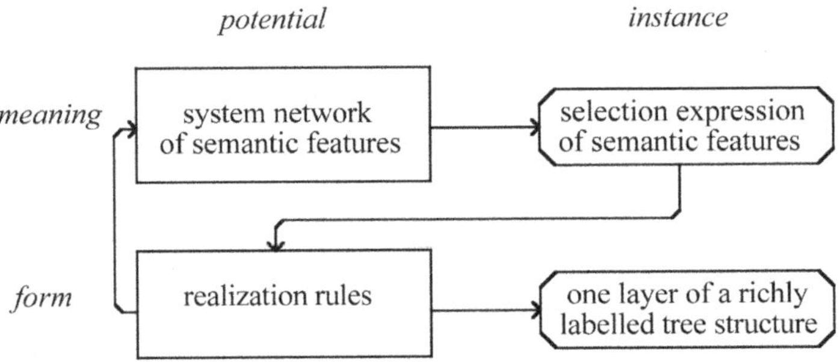

Figure 11.1 The main components of a Systemic Functional Grammar and their outputs.

Figure 11.1 shows the two main components of the grammar of a language (on the left), and their outputs (on the right). The grammar consists of two 'potentials': the **system network** of semantic features at the level of **meaning** and the **realization rules** at the level of **form**.

Figure 11.1 also shows two types of 'instance' (i.e. the outputs from each of the two components). Each traversal of the system network results in a **selection expression** of the semantic features chosen on that traversal. The realization rules take these as their input and state the ways in which they are realized at the level of form – so specifying the 'form potential'. An **output** at this level consists of a **syntactic unit**, its **elements**, and the

items that expound them – plus its intonation or punctuation. But often one or more of that unit's elements need to be **filled** by a further unit, and the type of realization rule that specifies a re-entry to the network to generate one is represented by the arrow on the left.

Thus each traversal of the network chooses features relevant to one **semantic** unit, and each generates one **syntactic** unit – and this includes, as we shall see, elements that are expounded by items of intonation and punctuation. The first traversal typically generates a clause, and later traversals generate the nominal groups (and other units) that will fill some of its elements.

Thus a 'grammar' is essentially a model of the sentence-generating component of a full model of language and its use. When the term 'grammar' is used here, it is as a short form for **lexicogrammar**, so reminding us that the model of language must cover lexis, too. However, as this chapter shows, it must also cover meanings that are realized in intonation and punctuation, i.e. two of the sub-components of the level of form.

We shall now turn briefly to these, to see precisely what their relationship to the components that surround them is in the present model of language. This is the sixth major innovation that this model makes.

11.1.4 The place of intonation and punctuation in the lexicogrammar

The traditional model of language – which has been accepted by Halliday and so most of those who work in the broad framework of SFL – is a tri-stratal model, in which it is assumed that **semantics** is realized by **form** (syntax/grammar and lexis), and that form is in turn realized by **phonology**. There are many places in Halliday's writings where he makes this assumption, and, while the alternative model to be presented here was sketched briefly in Fawcett (1980, 1983) and was the focus of Fawcett (1987), the traditional model of the relationship between 'form' and 'phonology' has barely been challenged till now.

The first problem with the traditional 'three levels' model is that intonation is clearly not the realization of either items or syntax (as it would have to be, if 'phonology' is to be the realization of form). This claim is supported by the fact that no systemic functional linguist has ever proposed realization rules that show how either syntax or items might be 'realized' by intonation, nor even discussed this possibility.

Paradoxically, supporting evidence comes from Halliday's own descriptions of intonation and its realizations. These show that, in practice, he now treats intonation as the direct realization of features in system networks that are choices in meaning – just as syntax and items are. The clear implication of his descriptions is that intonation is a sub-component of the level of form: a sub-component in which **meanings** are realized directly as **sounds**. Indeed, it is this aspect of English that most clearly exemplifies the Saussurean concept of a sign – and so the nature of language. The 'grammar' of intonation, then, illustrates the fact that human language (like every other semiotic system) consists, essentially, of two levels: meaning and form. And, just as intonation functions in parallel with syntax and items in the triple co-realization of meanings, so too does punctuation, in its role as the less rich equivalent of intonation in written discourse.

Thus the meanings that are built into a language are realized as (i) syntax, (ii) items (words and morphemes) and (iii) either intonation (in speech) or punctuation (in writing), as shown in Figure 11.2.

Now consider the place of **segmental phonology** (to use a traditional term) in an overall model of language.[2] Where does it fit in? The key to the answer is to note that it is only **items** that require this component. Syntax does not, and nor does intonation. Every language has its phonological rules, and their role is clear: it is to specify the patterns of its syllable structure and an inventory of phonemes etc. (to use the traditional terms). It is not the role of these rules to tell us how some higher representation is realized in segmental phonology. So it is unsurprising that such rules are not needed for the successful generation of a text-sentence, as all models of natural language generation that provide for a spoken output (such as COMMUNAL's GENESYS) clearly demonstrate.

So we must ask: What are the grounds for assuming that there is a third stratum of language ('phonology') when (i) there isn't one for the two other sub-components in which meanings are realized (syntax and intonation), and (ii) the 'rules' of this component are not needed in a generative model of language? I cannot think of any such grounds.

In that case, we need to ask: What concept is most appropriate for describing the relationship between items and segmental phonology? My answer is that the relationship is one of **specification**. The reason is that there is no way in which we can represent an item at the level of form other than by specifying its **segmental phonology** or its **orthography**.

So, while segmental phonology and orthography are two important components in a comprehensive description of any language, they are not 'realizations' of items at the level of form, but **specifications** of those items, i.e. they are within the level of form. They are the 'representation' of a word or morpheme at the level of form, just as the semantic features from which they have been generated are their 'representation' at the level of meaning. Segmental phonology and orthography, then, are integral parts of the level of form.

We can represent these sub-components of the 'form potential' of the language by expanding the 'realizations rules' box in Figure 11.1 in the two ways shown in Figure 11.2.

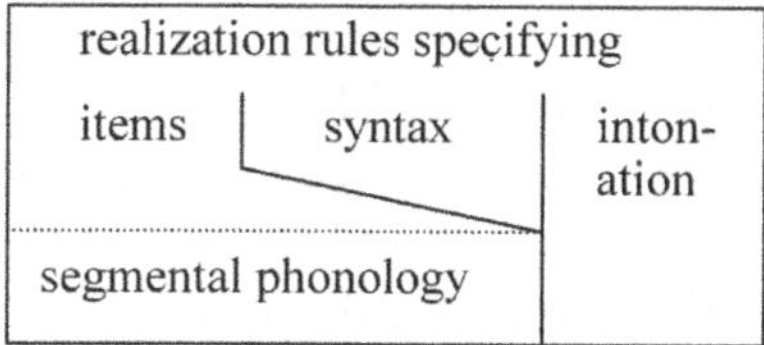

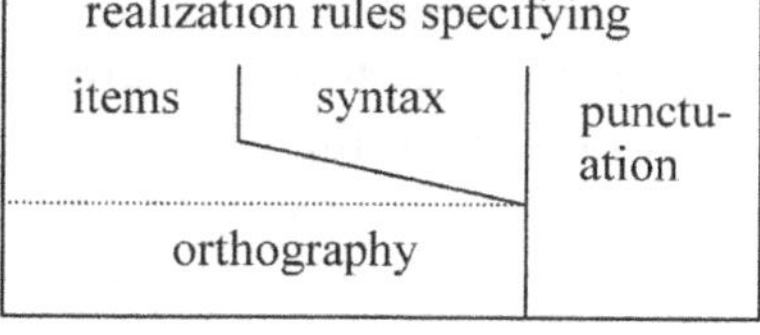

Figure 11.2 The sub-components of form in spoken and written language.

In Figure 11.2, then, the dotted line represents the relationship of **specification** between (i) items and (ii) segmental phonology or orthography. The problem of how to represent the two different sub-components that are required for the spoken medium and the written medium is resolved by showing two sets of realization rules. Of the two, it is of course the one on the left that is the more fundamental one, since all languages have a sound system (or its equivalent, e.g. in a sign language), but only some have a writing system.

In the Cardiff model of language, then, a human language is seen as a bi-stratal semiotic system, and not a tri-stratal one.

How is it that so many generations of linguists have not realized this apparently obvious fact about English? I think the answer probably lies in the history of modern Linguistics, and so the direction from which the majority of our predecessors approached the study of English and other languages. For the sound scientific reason of working from the relatively observable to the relatively unobservable, many linguists in the early part of the last century approached language 'from below'. Taking as their starting point the **sounds** of the language (i.e. (i) 'segmental phonology', including 'inherent word stress', and (ii) 'intonation'), they treated these two sub-components of language as if they both belonged within the one component of 'phonology'. This was an understandable assumption but one, in the view taken here, that is ultimately misleading. Let me explain why.

When building a model of English that will generate text-sentences, it is necessary to view language 'from above'. This entails entering the language at the level of meaning. From this viewpoint, there are three forms in which meanings are realized in the **spoken** medium: (i) items, (ii) syntax and (iii) intonation, and so three sub-components at the level of form. This is the model of form given in the left hand part of Figure 11.2.

So far we have been considering spoken English. With written language, a view from below considers (i) 'orthography' (which covers the spelling of words, apostrophes, hyphens, etc.) and (ii) 'punctuation'. These can then be put together as 'graphology'. But what you see 'from above' is, in a way that is similar to spoken language, the three forms in which meanings are realized in the **written** medium – that is, (i) items, (ii) syntax and (iii) punctuation – as in the right hand part of Figure 11.2 (see Fawcett, 1990, 2004a for the most comprehensive description and specification of this).

The preceding overview provides the theoretical model for the description of English intonation and punctuation in this chapter. The next section overviews the phenomena to be covered in the model of intonation presented here.

11.1.5 The scope of the model of intonation and punctuation: meanings and forms

In a systemic functional grammar, we can describe the scope of the area of the lexicogrammar that is to be modelled in terms of either (i) its meanings (i.e. the system networks for the parts of the meaning potential that are realized through intonation and punctuation) or (ii) its forms (i.e. the patterns of intonation or punctuation that it generates). The model itself, of course, must be a description of both levels if it is to be a truly functional model of language, so it must be like the model of language in Figures 11.1 and 11.2.

Here, I first characterize the scope of the model by describing it at the level of form. In the next section I introduce some of the main system networks for the meanings whose realizations this chapter describes, thereby presenting the first part of the grammar of intonation and punctuation. The full grammar generates all the major types of intonation and punctuation that occur within text-sentences, and its coverage is roughly the same as the description in Tench (1996a).

The phenomena described here should be thought of first as being located within the lexicogrammar, and hence as aspects of the generation of text-sentences. But these are located within the broader framework of the structure of discourse, which is itself generated from an explicit 'grammar' of discourse structure. And some aspects of discourse structure are realized in intonation, such as (i) the differences in **pitch height** associated with the place of a sentence within a 'paraphone', (ii) those that signal the end of a turn etc. (as described in Tench and Fawcett, 1988 and Tench, 1996a).

In principle, 'tone of voice' phenomena are assumed here to be part of a parallel, and often superimposed, semiotic system. Examples include those 'tones of voice' that enable the Addressee to infer that the Performer is feeling 'happy', 'sad', 'angry', 'frightened' or 'disgusted' (where the feelings may or may not be genuine). However, we also need to recognize that, in practice, there are places in the grammar where it is not possible to describe all the alternative realizations in intonation without including certain meanings that have similarities to these 'tone of voice' phenomena, such as the features 'confident' and 'deferring' (which are widely used in the present model).

The following list specifies the main phenomena that the Cardiff Grammar covers in the full description of the intonation and punctuation of text-sentences. It is expressed in a mixture of the terms of traditional grammar and specifically SFL terms.

(a) Independent (unembedded) simple clauses and final co-ordinated clauses (so 'mood-bearing' clauses).

(b) Unrestricted numbers of non-final co-ordinated clauses, with and without separate information units.

(c) Simple and co-ordinated embedded clauses, with and without separate information units.

(d) Adjuncts with and without separate information units, whether filled by clauses or any of various classes of group, and whether thematized ('initial'), integrated ('medial'), potentially new ('final') or supplementary ('final' but after the main Tonic).

(e) Semantically 'heavy' Subjects with a separate information unit.

(f) Two or more co-ordinated nominal and other classes of group (including 'lists').

(g) Qualifiers in nominal groups filled by clauses ('relative clauses'), with a separate information unit ('non-defining' or, in Cardiff Grammar terms, 'depicting' relative clauses) and ones without a separate information unit ('defining' or, in Cardiff Grammar terms, 'classifying' relative clauses).

(h) Qualifiers in nominal groups that are filled by nominal groups ('apposition'), both 'depicting' and 'classifying', so with and without separate information units.

(i)   Qualifiers in nominal groups that are filled by prepositional groups, both 'depicting' and 'classifying', so with and without separate information units.

(j)   A full range of Tones realizing meanings of MOOD (as these occur in (a) above).

(k)   A full range of Tones realizing meanings of INFORMATION STATUS for all 'non-mood-bearing' information units.

(l)   Contrastive newness ('contrastive stress') on elements of clauses expounded by items.

(m) Contrastive newness on elements of clauses filled by units.

(n)   Contrastive newness on elements of nominal and other groups expounded by items.

(o)   Contrastive newness on elements of nominal and other groups filled by units.

(p)   Giving every syntactic unit and/or item a separate information unit when required (especially in reading aloud from written text).

The description given here covers all of these (though some, such as (e) and (f) are only treated briefly, by referring to the way in which similar phenomena are handled).

11.1.6 An introduction to the concepts used in modelling intonation and punctuation

This short section provides an introduction to the key concepts used in the explicit SFL model of intonation and punctuation described here. More detailed explanations are provided in §11.3.

First, in order to generate intonation and punctuation as well as syntax and items, we need to introduce certain new **elements** to the familiar unit of the **clause**.[3] These elements are then **expounded** by **items** of intonation or punctuation (in a significant extension of the usual sense of the term 'item', so that it is not limited to words and morphemes). So, just as GENESYS (the computer model of the lexicogrammar of English) generates **elements** of syntactic units and then **expounds** them by **items** such as words or morphemes, so too it generates **intonational elements** and then **expounds** them by **intonational items** (such as a falling Tone) – and also (using some of the same elements) elements and items of **punctuation** (such as a comma). As a simple example, consider the element **Ender (E)**. This is expounded in written text by a full stop, a question mark or a comma (among others), and in spoken text by an intonation unit boundary (represented as "|" or "||").

More specifically, the model of **intonation** consists of three types of **elements of structure** and three corresponding types of **item** (each of which expounds one of those elements). These elements and items are:

1 A **New** element (with four types), each being expounded by the presence of a **Tonic** (again with four different types, corresponding to the four types of New);

2 A **Key** element (with one main type and a second occasional type), which is expounded by the presence of a **Tone** (with ten types – which can, in an over-simplified model, be seen as sub-types of three main types); and

3 A **Starter** element and an **Ender** element, both being expounded by the presence of an **intonation unit boundary marker** (with two types).

In the full grammar, other elements and items are occasionally required (e.g. in the structures of the units that realize addresses and dates).

In contrast, the model of **punctuation** presented here requires only one main element of structure, namely the **Ender**, and occasionally also a **Starter**. These are expounded by many different items of punctuation in the full grammar, quite a few of which are introduced here (see Fawcett, 2004a, 2004b for early descriptions of intonation in the Cardiff model).

11.1.7 A comment on the sections of the lexicogrammar to be presented here

The focus in this chapter is on (i) demonstrating that it is possible to integrate the generation of intonation and punctuation with the generation of syntax and items (both grammatical and lexical), and (ii) the additional concepts that meeting this goal has led us to introduce to the modelling of intonation (and punctuation).

Due to limitations on space, only representative portions of areas of the relevant system networks are presented in this chapter. However, I provide a fairly full picture of one area: the MOOD meanings that are realized in Tones, since this is the one area in which choices realized in intonation are present in every text-sentence that is generated. §§11.2 and 11.3 illustrate the degree of delicacy achieved by the model in the process of realization.

The **realization rules** will usually be presented in a fairly informal way, e.g. by giving an example of a typical realization to the right of the semantic features in the system networks. However, in §§11.3 and 11.4

some realization rules are presented in full, in order to illustrate how elegantly they capture the required facts.

11.2 Choices in meaning that are realized in intonation and punctuation

The diagrams of systems given in the rest of this chapter are taken from the full system network for the semantics of English, as represented in the GENESYS lexicogrammar (with minor simplifications). Here, the systems are represented in a form that is closer to ordinary text than the diagrams for system networks that are conventionally used, and each diagram presents just one system at a time. This method makes it easier to show clearly the complex entry conditions to systems that are required in a fully formalized lexicogrammar.

The following key explains the notations used in the network:

> → means 'enter this system'.
> / means 'or' (the notation for a system of 'x or y').
> & means 'and'.
> (1.1) etc. is the number of a realization rule.
> (....) in a complex entry condition or a realization rule means that the 'or' or 'and' relationship within the round brackets has priority over external relationships.

In English, intonation and punctuation realize choices in no fewer than four different major types of meaning, plus one choice in a very early system in the network which must be chosen if there is to be a sentence at all (which we shall term a 'forced choice'). We begin with this last type, and the rest of §11.2 will describe the choices in the four other major types of meaning that are realized in intonation and punctuation, beginning with MOOD.

11.2.1 The initial 'forced choice'

At the beginning of the procedure for generating a sentence (so near the start of the first pass through the network) the following system is entered:

situation →

100%	congruent situation (1.1) /	*She has been caught.*
0%	reified situation /	*her being caught*
0%	(other features, irrelevant to our current interests).	

Since the feature [congruent situation] has a 100 per cent probability of being selected, it is a 'forced choice'. Its main realization is stated in Realization Rule 1.1. This is that a **clause** is to be inserted in the structure that is about to be built. (For any subsequent pass through the network, however, the probabilities in this system may be changed, as the result of a realization rule that is applied after the previous pass, such that one of the other features may be chosen.)

Rule 1.1 then states that, if (i) the text is [spoken] and (ii) the 'situation' realized in the clause is [not co-ordinated with a previous situation] (both of which conditions are bound to be met if the clause is the first in a spoken text-sentence), the element **Starter (St)** is put at Place 3 in the clause, and is then expounded by the boundary marker "||" (where the double lines mark the boundary of a text-sentence).

Next, Rule 1.1 states that, if the 'situation' meets the conditions of being (i) [simplex] (i.e. it is not co-ordinated with another 'situation') and (ii) [independent], the element **Ender (E)** is added to the structure at Place 250. This section applies to every 'congruent situation' (and so to every clause) that meets these conditions, irrespective of whether it is 'spoken' or 'written'. If the text is 'spoken', the Ender is simply expounded by "||", but if it is 'written' the appropriate one of the set of sentence-final punctuation marks will be generated. (I shall give the elegantly economical section of Rule 1.1 that models these facts in §11.2.2.)

Finally (for present purposes), we should note that Rule 1.1 states that if no element anywhere in the clause is to be marked as 'contrastively new' (a complex topic that we shall come to in §11.2.5 below), a default subrule puts a **Mood-bearing New (MN)** and a **Key (K)** into the structure of the clause at two numbered **Places** near the end of the clause (but before the Ender). Features in later systems insert the items that expound them.

The fact that there are conditions on the introduction of these elements via Rule 1.1 (as described informally above) means, of course, that other rules are required to provide for those occasions when these conditions are not met, i.e. when clauses are (i) embedded and/or (ii) co-ordinated but non-final. And these rules also provide for the generation of an Ender in cases where one has not been generated by Rule 1.1. It is the main task of §11.3 to explain how the model provides for such cases.

Through one realization rule or another, then, the grammar ensures that every text-sentence has at least one **information unit** – and so, if spoken, both a **Starter** and an **Ender** to mark its beginning and its end.

At this point one could ask: Is the initial Starter and its exponent "||" really necessary? After all, in a string of text-sentences that together make up a **text**, we could regard the boundary marker at the end of the preceding sentence (so "||" in a spoken text) as also marking the initial boundary of the current one. The disadvantage of this is that it would leave unresolved the question of how to generate the initial boundary marker of the first sentence in the text. The position taken here is that GENESYS should always insert the initial Starter when generating the first clause of the text-sentence (which may be the only one), and that, if the full text contains any adjacent pairs of "||", it is a minor problem that is best tidied up by the **final adjustment rules** (to which we shall come in §11.5).[4]

Although there are three other major areas of meaning that are realized in intonation or punctuation, it is only in MOOD that a choice must be made for every text-sentence. So we shall consider MOOD first.

11.2.2 Delicate choices in MOOD

The primary choices in MOOD are realized in both syntax and items. For example, the meaning of selecting the feature [information] followed by [giver] – so creating the meaning 'information giver' – is typically realized in **syntax**. This is achieved by placing the Subject before the Operator or Main Verb, as in *She <u>does</u> love him* and *She <u>loves</u> him*. In contrast, the meaning of 'polarity seeker' is typically realized by placing the Operator before the Subject, as in *Does she love him?* And **items** such as *could you* and *please* have a role to play in realizing MOOD meanings.

But in spoken text many of the more delicate MOOD meanings are realized in variations in the **Tone**. These more delicate features offer variations on the basic meanings of MOOD, some of which reflect important aspects of the relationship between the interactants, such as the distinction between [confident] and [deferring].

In the Cardiff Grammar, as already noted, the systems realized in contrasting Tones are based quite closely on the work of Tench (especially Tench, 1996a). While Tench's work owes a considerable debt to Halliday, his description of intonation introduces many changes. Tench, for example, treats a rise-fall as a variant of a fall, and both a low rise and a low-to-high rise as variants of a rise, whereas Halliday treats each of both pairs as a primary Tone. So Tench recognizes three 'primary' Tones rather than five, and he subcategorizes them into a total of ten 'secondary' Tones. In practical terms, however, the crucial Tones are the supposedly 'secondary' Tones. A model of intonation that only introduced his 'primary' Tones would be very crude, and once we introduce the 'secondary' Tones we do not need to refer at all to the so-called 'primary' Tones.

We are now ready to look at the system network for MOOD. However, the systems for those MOOD meanings of English that are realized in intonation and punctuation are dependent on the primary systems of the MOOD network, so we must begin with these. (For a fuller version of MOOD network, see Fawcett, 2011b.)

We begin with the entry condition to the entire system network for MOOD:

> situation & congruent & independent &
> (simplex situation / final co-ordinated situation) → MOOD.

This somewhat complex entry condition states: 'If the features [situation], [congruent] and [independent] have been chosen, and also either [simplex situation] or [final co-ordinated situation], you must enter the system network for MOOD.' (Note that, by convention, in SFL the names of system networks are written in capitals and the names of features in lower case letters. And the latter are placed within square brackets, when referred to in running text, or single quotation marks, if being referred to informally.)

The key aspect of this entry condition, from the viewpoint of our interest in the Tones of English, is that it tells us that the Tones that express MOOD meanings occur in only two syntactic contexts: (i) in a simplex clause (i.e. a 'topmost' clause that is not co-ordinated with another clause), and (ii) the final clause in a string of two or more co-ordinated 'topmost' clauses. (The other types of clause, i.e. any dependent clause and any non-final clause in a string of co-ordinated clauses, receive their Tone from a feature in one of the systems for INFORMATION STATUS, as we shall see in §11.2.4.)

We come now to the first system in the network for MOOD:

MOOD →
90%	information /	
9.99%	proposal for action /	
0.01%	formal wish.	*May you live to be a hundred!*

This system states: 'In the MOOD system, there is a general probability of 90 per cent that the feature [information] will be chosen, a 9.99 per cent probability that [proposal for action] will be chosen, and only a 0.01 per cent probability that [formal wish] will be chosen.' Great efforts have been made to find labels for the semantic features that are as transparent as possible, and to the right of most semantic features a typical example of the realization of this feature at the level of form is given, as in the case of [formal wish] in this system. (Examples of the two other features will be shown to the right of the relevant features in the networks below, i.e. when we reach the points in the network where only one or two examples are needed.

With that initial guidance, it should be possible to read all of the systems set out below.

information →	
98% giver /	
1.3% seeker /	
0.2% exclamation /	*How well she read it!*
0.2% confirmation seeker /	*Hasn't she read it?*
0.1% check /	*She's read it? She's read WHAT?*
0.1% interrogator /	*Then she read what?*
0.1% proposal of entity for consideration.	*What about David Copperfield?*

giver →	
99% simple giver /	*Ivy has read it.*
1% plus confirmation seeker.	*Ivy has read it, hasn't she?*

seeker →	
60% polarity seeker /	*Has Ivy read it?*
39% new content seeker /	*What has Ivy read?*
1% choice of alternative contents seeker.	*Did she read this or this?*

proposal for action →	
90% by addressee /	*Read it! Could you read it?* etc.
5% by self and addressee /	*Let's read it, Shall we read it?* etc.
4.99% by self /	*Shall/May I read it?* etc.
0.1% by outsider.	*(Let) Ivy read it!* etc.

The semantic features in the above systems are those that constitute the entry conditions to the systems of MOOD meanings that are realized in intonation and punctuation. In other words, we have now reached the systems from which the Tones that realize MOOD meanings are generated. Here is the first:

giver & positive & spoken →	*Ivy has read it.*
60% confident /	one of five falls (see below)
30% deferring /	one of three rises (see below)
10% with reservations.	one of two fall–rises (see below)

The three features of the entry condition indicate (i) that the clause realizes the meaning 'information giver' ('information' being the feature previously chosen); (ii) that it is an 'information giver' that is 'positive' rather than 'negative'; and (iii) that the text is 'spoken'. This last feature ensures that the system can only be entered when generating spoken discourse. (There are smaller and slightly different systems for generating punctuation, most of which we omit here to save space.) Finally, note that the percentages that precede each figure again show an estimate of the general probabilities that this feature will be chosen.

But what happens if one or more of the features in the entry condition is not satisfied? The answer is that a different system is entered. If, for example, the 'information giver' were to be 'negative' rather than 'positive', the system to be entered would have the same features as the present one, but with very different probabilities. In this case, [confident] would have a probability of only 30 per cent, while the probability of selecting [deferring] would rise to 60 per cent. In this way a lexicogrammar of this type, with (i) a system network and (ii) probabilities on the features of its systems, is able to go far beyond the question of whether or not something is or is not 'grammatical', and to reflect the probabilities within language. (It even has the ability to change the probabilities on the features in the systems, where necessary.)

The same general principle applies to the other major MOOD choices. In other words, there are variants on the above system for all of the other types of MOOD, i.e. [polarity seeker], [new content seeker], [choice of alternative contents seeker], [exclamation], [confirmation seeker], [check] etc., as well as for all of the various types of [proposal for action], and we shall meet these shortly. The systems dependent on these features always include [confident] and [deferring] and sometimes [with reservations], but they may also include the features [dubious], [non-committal] and [pleading]. But even when the semantic features are shared by more than one major MOOD meaning the probabilities are in most cases markedly different.

But before introducing these other systems, let me address the fact that there are no realization rule numbers on the features in the system above. This means that those features are not terminal features in the network, and that each must therefore be the entry condition to a yet more delicate system. This brings us to an interesting point. While the features in the systems for most of the major types of MOOD are somewhat different from each other, and while the probabilities on those features are markedly different, we can use a single network to sub-categorize the differing degrees of the three features of [confident], [deferring] and [with reservations]. Thus all instances of the feature [confident], from whatever less delicate system they come, enter the system below. And the same principle applies to the two systems below it for [deferring] and [with reservations]. It is the semantic features in these more delicate systems that have the realization rule attached to them, and, while I shall not give the full technical form of each rule, I shall illustrate each by describing the shape of the Tone that realizes each feature.

confident →
2%	intensified confidence (99.61) /	high rise–fall
1%	intensified confidence with emotion (99.611) /	low rise–fall
17%	strongly confident (99.62) /	high to low fall
60%	neutrally confident (99.63) /	mid-high to low fall
20%	mildly confident (99.64).	mid-low to low fall

deferring →
2%	strongly deferring (99.66) /	low to high rise
18%	neutrally deferring (99.661) /	low to mid-high rise
80%	mildly deferring (99.662).	low to mid-low rise

with reservations →
60%	with reservations neutral (99.65) /	mid fall–rise
40%	with strong reservations (99.651).	low fall–rise

Next, I give the equivalent systems for the other primary choices in the 'information' part of the MOOD network. For some of them the probability of occurring in a 'negative' version is very low, and for others, such as [polarity seeker] and [confirmation seeker], it is zero. (The entry conditions to the system network for POLARITY ensure that the lexicogrammar models these facts.)

We begin with the type of 'information giver' that is 'plus confirmation seeker', as in *Ivy has read it, hasn't she?* This is an option that requires two Tones: one for the main clause and one for the truncated clause that fills the clause element **Confirmation Seeking Tag Adjunct (A/CSTag)**. Here is the system that applies to the main clause.

giver & positive & spoken & plus confirmation seeker → *Ivy has read it, ...*
99.98%	confident /	one of five falls (see above)
0.01%	deferring /	one of three rises (see above)
0.01%	with reservations.	one of two fall–rises (see above)

As can be seen, the probabilities make it virtually certain that the main clause will be spoken with a 'confident' Tone when it is 'plus confirmation seeker'. The system for the clause within the A/CSTag is:

plus confirmation seeker & spoken → *hasn't she?*
29%	confident /	one of five falls (see above)
70%	deferring /	one of three rises (see above)
1%	dubious (99.66).	low to high rise

Note that the Tones specified above are in fact assigned when the network is re-entered to generate the truncated clause *hasn't she*, as the unit that fills the Confirmation Seeking Tag Adjunct (A/CSTag).

Now we come to a simpler series of systems, each of which applies to one (and sometimes more) of the major 'information' options in the network.

polarity seeker & spoken →		*Has Ivy read it?*
10%	confident /	one of five falls (see above)
80%	deferring /	one of three rises (see above)
5%	dubious (99.66) /	low to high rise
5%	non-committal (99.662).	mid-low to low fall

new content seeker & spoken →		*What has Ivy read?*
75%	confident /	one of five falls (see above)
20%	deferring /	one of three rises (see above)
5%	pleading (99.65).	high rise–fall

(choice of alternative contents seeker /	*Did she drink gin or vodka?*
exclamation /	*How clever she is!*
interrogator /	*And then she ate what?*
formal wish) & spoken →	*May you live to be a hundred!*
99.98% confident /	one of five falls (see above)
0.01% deferring /	one of three rises (see above)
0.01% with reservations.	one of two fall–rises (see above)

confirmation seeker & spoken →		*Hasn't Ivy read it?*
0.1%	confident /	one of five falls (see above)
95%	deferring /	one of three rises (see above)
4.99%	pleading (99.65).	high rise–fall

(polarity check / content check) & spoken →		*Ivy has read it/WHAT?*
0.1%	confident /	one of five falls (see above)
43.9%	deferring /	one of three rises (see above)
1%	non-committal (99.662) /	mid-low to low fall
50%	dubious (99.66) /	low to high rise
5%	with reservations.	one of two fall–rises (see above)

We come finally to the 'proposals for action'. Here, as with the 'information givers', we make a distinction between the 'positive' and the 'negative' ones, and there are different subsystems for most of the 'proposals for action' that are 'positive' (see Fawcett, 2011b for a more detailed account). However, the general probability that a 'proposal for action' will be 'negative' is very low (except for a 'simple unmarked directive' such as *Don't touch that!*). Here, then, are the main types of 'proposal for action' and the meanings realized in their Tones. As you can see, the features [confident] and [deferring] occur here too, and they lead to the more delicate systems that we have already met when considering 'information givers', etc.

proposal for action & by addressee &	*Read it! / Could you read it?*
spoken & positive →	*How about reading it?* etc.
10% confident /	one of five falls (see above)
80% deferring /	one of three rises (see above)
10% pleading (99.65).	high rise–fall

proposal for action & by self and addressee &	*Let's read it!*
spoken & positive →	*Shall we read it?*
60% confident /	one of five falls (see above)
30% deferring /	one of three rises (see above)
10% pleading (99.65).	high rise–fall

proposal for action & (by self / by outsider) &	*Shall/May I read it?*
spoken & positive →	*Let Ivy read it.*
10% confident /	one of five falls (see above)
89% deferring /	one of three rises (see above)
1% pleading (99.65).	high rise–fall

Finally, here is the system for 'proposals for action' that are 'negative':

proposal for action &	*Don't read it!*
spoken & negative →	*Don't let's read it* etc.
50% confident /	one of five falls (see above)
40% deferring /	one of three rises (see above)
10% pleading (99.65)	high rise–fall

Here are the realization rules that are required to complement the above system network, by generating the Tones that realize the meanings of the semantic features (where 'K' stands for 'Key'):

99.61:	intensified confidence : K < "21+".	high rise–fall
99.611:	intensified confidence with emotion : K < "21–".	low rise–fall
99.62:	strongly confident : K < "1+".	high to low fall
99.63:	neutrally confident : K < "1".	mid-high to low fall
99.64:	mildly confident : K < "1–".	mid-low to low fall
99.65:	with reservations neutral or pleading : K < "12".	high fall–rise
99.651:	with strong reservations : K < "12–".	low fall–rise
99.66:	strongly deferring or dubious : K < "2+".	low to high rise
99.661:	neutrally deferring : K < "2".	low to mid-high rise
99.662:	mildly deferring or non-committal : K < "2–".	mid-low to low fall

Notice how economical these rules are, with one rule serving two different semantic features in several cases. Thus Rule 99.65, for example, states: 'If either the feature [with reservations neutral] or the feature [pleading] is chosen, the clause element **Key** is expounded by a Tone 12 (i.e. a high fall–rise).'

I have added a verbal description to the right (as I did in the system network) to suggest the pattern of the Tone. These brief descriptions are taken directly from Tench (1996a: 194), and they are based on a 5-level model of any Performer's pitch range (high, mid-high, mid, mid-low and low). The base of 'low' varies, naturally, from one Performer to another and from one place in the discourse structure to another (for the latter, see §11.5.1). The verbal descriptions above are insufficient on their own, however. The first one, for example, doesn't tell us that the 'high rise–fall' starts from and returns to 'mid' (rather than, say, 'low'). (For a detailed picture and a comparison with the Tones proposed by earlier scholars see Tench, 1996a: 125–8).

This concludes our overview of MOOD meanings of English that are realized in Tones. We turn next to the nearest equivalent for **written** texts.

In the vast majority of written text-sentences, the relevant realization rule is a subrule of Realization Rule 1.1, but it depends heavily on invoking features in the MOOD network above as **conditions**. The facts are summarized in the following part of Realization Rule 1.1 and its associated subrule:

> if independent and (simplex situation or final co-ordinated situation)
> then ('E' @ 250, 'Ender subrule').

> 'Ender subrule' :
> if   spoken then E < "||",
> if   written and
>   (seeker or confirmation seeker or plus confirmation seeker or
>   check or interrogator or proposal of entity for consideration or
>   request or suggestion or proposal for action by self and addressee
>   (most) or
>   proposal for action by self (most) or proposal for action by outsider
>   (some)   )
> then E < "?"
> else E < ".",
> if   written and
>   (exclamation or formal wish or directive or
>   proposal for action by self and addressee (some) or
>   fun mood or enthusiastic mood   )
> then E < "!".

Note that the condition 'else' in the eighth line of the subrule means that this part of the rule applies to many other frequent options in which E is expounded by ".", such as: (i) an 'information giver'; (ii) 'rulings' and 'statements of wish' (within 'proposal of action by addressee'); (iii) some 'proposals for action by self and addressee'; (iv) some 'by self'; and (v) some 'by outsider'. And some sub-types of all four general types of 'proposal for action' ('by addressee', 'by self and addressee', 'by self', and 'by outsider') include cases in which E < "?" and E < "!".

But where do the features [fun mood] and [enthusiastic mood] come from? The answer is that there are a few cases in which a punctuation mark does not correspond to one of the set of MOOD meanings that are realized in a Tone. I give below our attempt at characterizing the two possible meanings of an exclamation mark, each as a feature in a different system:

written & (simplex situation / final co-ordinated situation) &
simple giver →

0.1%	fun mood /	*She may like him!*
99.9%	unmarked mood.	*She may like him.*

written & (simplex situation / final co-ordinated situation) &
(simple dir / proposal for action by self and addressee) →

1%	enthusiastic mood /	*Read it! / Let's read it!*
99%	unmarked mood.	*Please read it.*

Thus [fun mood] signals that the Performer (P) is not completely serious, and [enthusiastic mood] signals that P wants very much for the event to occur (or not to occur).

11.2.3 Choices in assigning a separate Information Unit

The aspect of sentence planning that we need to consider here is the choice of whether or not to introduce an additional **information unit**. If a new information unit is introduced to a spoken text, the result is to add a new **intonation unit**, so generating a text-sentence with two or more intonation units.

This choice corresponds, in very broad terms, to Halliday's concept of 'tonality': a concept that Tench accepts and uses in his descriptive framework. Tench writes (1996a: 31) that 'tonality is the system in intonation that divides spoken discourse into its separate individual intonation units'. But this view of 'tonality' reflects the decisions that text analysts have to make when working on the transcription of a spoken text that doesn't have its intonation marked. And this is a different task from that of modelling the decisions that a Performer of a text-sentence makes when generating a text-sentence.[5]

Now consider this aspect of the task of modelling the generation of intonation. At the stage when the choices are being made in the system network, there is no string of words to be 'divided up', because the string of words has not yet been generated. The 'string of words' only appears at a relatively late stage in generation, i.e. as the output from the lexico-grammar, and not its input (as the concept of 'tonality' would require).[6]

So the challenge is: How should the model of language generate text-sentences whose representations will contain, as integral components, markers of intonation unit boundaries that are appropriate to the syntax and its meanings? And, in the case of written text, we require an equivalent model of how punctuation is generated. So, for each potential **clause** and **group** (other than the first clause in the sentence) the first step in generating intonation and punctuation is to ask: **Should this semantic unit, and so the syntactic unit that will realize it, be given its own information unit?**

If the answer is 'Yes', GENESYS will add new elements and items to the syntactic unit that will realize the semantic unit. In other words, a version of the little system introduced below for a Time Position Adjunct is found, in principle, at every point in the system network at which a new syntactic unit is introduced. I shall illustrate the principle by describing two of the more frequent types.

The first type occurs in the generation of any Adjunct, such as a **Time Position Adjunct (A/TP)**. It may be **filled** by a **clause**, as in *when he has recovered*, by a **prepositional group** such as *after his recovery* or by a **nominal group** such as *the morning after the event* – or it may even occasionally be directly **expounded** by an **item** that is a 'pro-form' such as *thereafter* or *then*. In each case there is, in principle, a choice between treating the unit as a separate information unit or treating it as part of the information unit of the clause in which it occurs. Although the probabilities differ greatly, depending on the semantic weight of the Adjunct, the choice is always there.

Let us take as our example a Time Position Adjunct that is to be filled by a 'situation' and so a clause. Some of the choices relevant to the generation of a separate information unit are made in the following system, and some in the dependent ones (one of which we shall look at in more detail shortly). As usual, a typical example of the realization of the feature is given to the right of the relevant features.

PROMINENCE OF TIME POSITION →

5%	time position thematized (20.21) /	*When he lost it, Ike cried.*
1%	time position integrated (20.22) /	*Ike, when he lost it, cried.*
90%	time position potentially new (20.23) /	*Ike cried when he lost it.*
4%	time position as supplementary information unit (20.24).	*Ike cried, when he lost it.*

These features specify the four main positions in the clause at which an Adjunct can be placed, as the examples on the right show. The realization rules (which we shall omit here) simply locate the Adjunct, and so the clause that fills it, at the designated Place in the matrix clause. It is a feature of the present grammar that it specifies the alternatives in terms of the **meaning** of placing the Adjunct in each of the four positions, as expressed in the names of the features. So each feature, in its own way, gives the Adjunct a different type of 'prominence' in the clause. For example, the effect of choosing [time position thematized] is to give it the prominence of appearing early in the clause, where it typically serves the function of 'scene-setting'.

In a moment we shall see the effect of choosing this feature. But first I should say a little about the three other choices. The feature [time position integrated] typically places the Adjunct immediately after the Operator (or, if there isn't one, after the Subject), and so putting the Adjunct at the heart of the clause. But the feature doesn't specify whether or not the clause will be assigned a separate information unit, and to get a decision on this it enters a similar system to the one that we are about to examine for [time position thematized].

In contrast, the feature [time position potentially new] does specify this. It places the Adjunct near the end of the matrix clause and, crucially, within the intonation unit associated with the matrix clause. And there is no option for it to be assigned a separate information unit. However, this does not mean that the Adjunct won't be marked as 'new information'. This is because its position at or near the end of the clause makes it very likely to receive the **Mood-bearing Tonic** (for which see §11.3) and so be marked as 'new information' (hence the word 'potentially' in the name of the feature).

This brings us to the fourth and final feature, i.e. [time position as supplementary information unit]. This feature is always realized by a separate information unit, with the Adjunct being placed after the Mood-bearing Tonic, so marking it as 'supplementary information'.

Thus two of the options in the PROMINENCE system also decide the question of whether a new information unit will be introduced for the Time Position Adjunct. (§11.3 provides a more thorough introduction to the concept of a 'Mood-bearing Tonic' and the other concepts that are required to build an explicit model of the generation of intonation.)

Now we come to the system that is entered from [time position thematized], as an example of a system that explicitly offers a choice to introduce a new information unit.

time position thematized →

50%	thematized time position as separate information unit /	*When he lost it, Ike cried.*
50%	thematized time position as part of main information unit.	*When he lost it Ike cried.*

From the viewpoint of our interest in systems with features that generate a separate **information unit**, this is the crucial system in the process of generating a thematized Adjunct, because it is here that GENESYS must make the choice between introducing a separate information unit and not doing this. (In the latter case, it will simply be treated as a part of the information unit for the matrix clause.)

Note, finally, that the choices presented here are in fact relevant to whatever unit fills the Time Position Adjunct, so also to Adjuncts that are filled by a prepositional group such as *on Friday* and nominal groups such as *next month*. But the probabilities are higher for a more semantically complex unit, such as a clause, than they are for a short form such as a group would typically be, and the grammar also provides for this. And there are similar systems for all of the other types of Adjunct.[7]

Now let us consider a different but equally frequent source of the introduction of an additional information unit. This occurs in a system near the beginning of the system network for the CO-ORDINATION OF SITUATIONS. This provides choices in adding a further co-ordinated situation, and so a further co-ordinated clause. So, if a further clause is to be generated, the following system is entered, and Rule 19.8 gives the new clause its own information unit.

another co-ordinated situation →

70%	situation is in separate information unit from following one (19.8) /
30%	following situation is in same information unit.

Sometimes a unit other than a clause may have sufficient semantic weight to be given an information unit of its own, and essentially the same systems as those described above are available for virtually all embedded and co-ordinated groups of all classes – with some, possibly, containing embedded clauses. These are modelled in essentially the same way, as we shall see in §§11.3 and 11.4. And in §11.3 we shall meet yet another frequent type of embedded clause that may be given a separate intonation unit: those that are termed 'relative clauses'.

However, the choices that we have noted in this section do only the first half of the job, because the grammar must also provide a suitable **Tone** for the new unit. And this brings us to the third type of choice that needs to be made: choices in INFORMATION STATUS. This, then, is the second source of Tones, alongside the system network for MOOD.

11.2.4 Choices in INFORMATION STATUS

While we can identify examples of this phenomenon in Halliday's description of English, it was Tench who took the vital step of recognizing it as a major area of meaning, and it was Tench who appropriately named it 'information status' (Tench, 1996a: 80).

We shall now look at the same two major sources of new clauses – and so of new intonation units – as we did in the last section, and note how the relevant systems assign an appropriate Tone for each type.

Consider the first type of clause, i.e. a **Time Position Adjunct** that is filled by a clause and is **thematized**. The system from which its Tones are generated is the following:

potentially highlighted information unit →
68%	neutral separate unit /	low to mid-high rise
30%	highlighted separate unit /	mid fall–rise
2%	with confidence separate unit.	mid-high to low fall

There are similar systems that apply to what are traditionally (but somewhat loosely) termed 'medial' and 'final' Adjuncts. These too may vary in the unit that fills them, e.g. they may be filled by (i) a clause, as in *He saw the film, after he bought the book*, (ii) a prepositional group, as in *He saw the film, after his purchase of the book*, or (iii) a nominal group, as in *He saw the film, the week after that*. In the full grammar there are system networks and realization rules for all of these different types of meaning.

Now let's look briefly at co-ordinated clauses again. We saw in §11.2.1 that 'simplex' and 'final co-ordinated' clauses must have a Tone that expresses a meaning of MOOD. But what about the co-ordinated clauses that are not the final clause?

In some cases (typically when they are short and so semantically 'light') there is no separate information unit, and so no additional Tonic and Tone. But in most cases such clauses do have their own Tonic and Tone and, as with the clauses and other units that we have been looking at, the Tone is one that realizes a meaning of **information status**. Thus a **non-final co-ordinated situation** that is to be given a separate information unit enters the following system:

situation is in separate information unit from following one & spoken →
80%	incomplete co-ord sit (99.7) /	low to mid-high rise
5%	with confidence co-ord sit (99.71) /	mid-high to low fall
15%	with reservations co-ord sit (99.72).	mid fall–rise

It is interesting to note that the forms of realization are the same for (i) a thematized Adjunct that is filled by a clause and (ii) a non-final co-ordinated clause. But the trio of semantic features that characterize their meanings are somewhat different, and so are the probabilities.

We shall see the elements and items that are required to implement these quite complex realizations in a generative model of language in §11.3. And, as in the last section, there is a third major clause type to consider: **relative clauses**.

We now turn to the fifth and final type of meaning realized in intonation.

11.2.5 Choices in INFORMATION FOCUS and so in 'contrastive newness'

So far, we have been assuming that the information unit has either a **Mood-bearing Tonic** or a **simple Tonic**. But there is a third type of Tonic. If the Performer (P) decides to present an element of the situation to the Addressee (A) as not merely 'new' but as 'contrastively new', a **Contrastive Tonic (CT)** is generated instead of a Mood-bearing Tonic or a simple Tonic.

We first met the concept of 'contrastive newness' in §11.1.2. It refers to a type of 'newness' that is presented by P as being not merely 'new information' to A, but information that P believes may be in contrast with what A currently believes. So it is not merely 'new' but 'contrastively new'. The nearest equivalent term to 'contrastive newness' that is used in descriptions of English intonation by Halliday (and so by Tench, who follows him in this matter), is 'marked tonicity'. But that is a description at the level of form rather than meaning.

In the Cardiff model the initial system for generating 'contrastive newness' for an element of the situation, and so for its realization as an element of the clause, is entered from [independent & simplex situation] (plus three other features), and is as follows:

INFORMATION FOCUS IN SITUATION →
    95%   no contrastive newness within situation /
    5%   contrastive newness within situation /
    0%   contrastive newness on role being checked (98) /
    0%   contrastive newness postponed to later co-ordinated situation (98.01).

Let me comment briefly on the meanings of the four features in the above system, starting with the first. As the percentage before it shows, [no contrastive newness within situation] is chosen with by far the greatest frequency. We have seen that every text-sentence consists of one or more information units, and that each one must consequently have at least one New element. The realization of the present feature is that the New must be one of the three types of New (which will be distinguished in due course) that is not a **Contrastive New**. Its meaning is 'This syllable, and so this word (and possibly other words that precede this word) express information that the Performer (P) is presenting to the Addressee (A) as information that is new to A.' In Halliday's words (1994: 296): 'the tonic foot (also termed "the Tonic", for short) defines the culmination of what is New; it marks where the New element ends.' The rules for the actual placement of the Tonic (typically on the last lexical item in the text-sentence) will be explained later, in §11.5.4.[8] The 'new' segment of the information unit may or may not be preceded by a segment that includes information that is presented as 'recoverable', from the preceding text, the perceivable situation, or the shared culture (cf. Halliday, 1970).

We turn now to the second feature, i.e. [contrastive newness within situation]. The meaning of this feature is that P believes the 'contrastively new' element is in direct contrast with what P thinks A may mistakenly believe it to be – and, if A does believe it, P is inviting A to correct this misapprehension. The corollary of this, of course, is that P believes that the information in the part of the information unit other than that marked as 'contrastively new' is 'common ground' between P and A. As an example, consider (1):

(1) I DIDn't take your pen.

This feature is the entry condition to many further systems, all of which carry the meaning that the Performer believes that the Addressee may be mistakenly assuming the validity of some proposition which the Performer's current utterance is designed to correct. Here is the system that underlies the example that we have just been considering:

contrastive newness within situation →
    40%   contrastive newness on polarity (98.16) /
    60%   no contrastive newness on polarity.

The realization of the first feature in this system is (i) to place the element CN by the clause element that expresses 'polarity' (which is typically the Operator but occasionally another element such as the Negator) and so (ii) to place the item "CT" that expounds it by the item that expounds the Operator (e.g. "did" in (1) above). This marks the 'polarity' as being in contrast with what P believes A to believe to be the case.

Thus the feature [no contrastive newness within situation] in the first system above is roughly equivalent to Tench's term 'broad focus', in that the newness is not focussed on one element, and the feature [contrastive newness within situation] is the equivalent of Tench's 'narrow focus' (Tench, 1996a: 57–9).

The fact that any material that follows an element marked as 'contrastively new' is to be interpreted as 'recoverable information' is merely a by-product of the explanation of the meaning of 'contrastive newness' given above. And the same applies to any material that may precede the 'contrastively new' element.

In other words, by presenting one element as 'contrastively new', all of the rest of the message is presented as being 'common ground' between P and A, and so 'recoverable' (or, to use Halliday's term, 'given'). It is because P believes that P and A share a common belief about an event, with the exception of just one (typically) of its elements, that what follows the element marked as 'contrastively new' is 'recoverable'. In this model, then, there is no element 'Given' (as there is in Halliday's); that which is 'recoverable' is merely a part of the text that is not marked as 'contrastively new'.

There are two major types of 'contrastive newness' that we need to recognize in a fully generative grammar, and two sub-types within one of them, making three in all. Since these differences are easier to understand when we see the different structures that they generate, we shall leave these distinctions till later (in §§11.3.2.3 and 11.3.3.4).

This concludes our overview of the types of semantic choice in the overall system network that are realized in intonation and punctuation. These realize five different areas of meaning: (i) the meanings that are obligatorily required in any text-sentence, such as 'boundary marker'; (ii) delicate choices in MOOD, realized in Tones; (iii) the meanings of adding one or more 'separate information units' such as [thematized time position as separate information unit]; (iv) meanings of INFORMATION STATUS such as [highlighted separate unit]; and (v) meanings of INFORMATION FOCUS such as [contrastive newness on polarity]. And the distinctions in meaning that the Tones offer vary from the considerable contrast between the 'confident' Tones and the 'deferring' Tones of MOOD to very fine distinctions, as between the five different types 'confident' Tone.

11.3 Thirteen steps in realizing intonation (and five in punctuation)

Now that we have established the nature of the five types of meaning that intonation expresses, we are ready to look at the set of concepts that is needed to make the process of generating intonation and punctuation fully explicit. These concepts are used in the **realization rules**. These are the rules that realize, in the sense of 'make real', the semantic features at the level of form. This component of a systemic functional model of intonation is one that has, surprisingly, virtually no literature. And yet these rules are as central to a complete model of the 'grammar' of intonation as they are to a complete model of how to generate syntax and items. It is this gap in our understanding, and so in the literature, that this chapter attempts to fill.

In the model presented here we can distinguish thirteen steps in the process of realizing **intonation**. These are then followed by a composite final step, namely the application of a small set of eight 'final adjustment rules'. However, these are all, as we shall see, relatively trivial, their defining characteristic being that they do not function as the realizations of choices in meaning. They are therefore grouped together as the final, fourteenth 'step'.

The thirteen main steps can be broken down into three groups. The first step concerns the generation of one or more additional information units; the next six steps concern the generation of markers of intonation that come at the end of such a unit; and the final six concern the markers of intonation that sometimes occur at the start of such a unit. The last six can be covered quite briefly because they correspond in large measure to the preceding six.

Interestingly, only five of these thirteen steps are needed when generating **punctuation**: the first one, and two for each of the start and the end of an information unit. So, since it is simpler to model punctuation than intonation, most of the rest of this chapter is about how to model the generation of intonation, rather than how to generate punctuation. Rather similarly, only a few of the final adjustment rules are required for written texts (e.g. the one that changes the initial letter of a sentence to a capital, if it is not a capital already, as in *I/Ivy did it*, and the one that changes the spelling of *an* followed by *other* to *another*).

11.3.1 Step 1: assigning, or not assigning, a separate information unit to a clause

We know from §11.2.1 that there will be at least one intonation unit for the text-sentence that we are generating (however many or however few clauses it may contain), because the grammar of English works on the assumption that each utterance presents the Addressee with at least some 'new' information. So the more specific form of the question behind the systems presented in §11.2.3 is:

Does the event or object in the mind of the Performer (represented in systemic functional logical form) that is currently being processed into text contain information that the Performer wishes to present to the Addressee as 'new' (i.e. non-recoverable) and so to be marked as 'new' by having its own information unit?

In the full grammar, this question is relevant to very many units, but in considering the thirteen steps we shall focus chiefly on examples in which the clause is

(i)   A simplex topmost clause or a final co-ordinated topmost clause.[9]

(ii) An embedded clause (the two most frequent types being illustrated here).

The key point of this sub-section is that it is only when the Performer (P) decides to give a non-final co-ordinated 'situation' or 'thing' the status of having a separate information unit that the rest of the steps described below apply to it. If P does not do this, the newly added syntactic unit is simply treated as a part of the intonation unit assigned to the matrix unit. But if P does choose to add a new information unit, the result is to activate several of a possible total of twelve further steps. And after this will come, as the final step, the application of the 'final adjustment rules'.

Thus the decision to treat a semantic unit as an information unit results in the addition of punctuation to a written text-sentence, just as it adds intonation to a spoken one.

The twelve further steps described in this section apply to all units that are to be given a separate information unit. Later in this section we shall see diagrams that show the results of the choices in the present sub-section.

11.3.2 Step 2: Generating a New (an element of structure)

For each clause with a separate information unit, GENESYS generates one of four types of intonational **element of structure** (from here on simply **element**) for introducing 'newness' to the clause. The three main types are the **Mood-bearing New**, the **Unmarked New** and the **Contrastive New**. The second step is to generate one of these. (For the **Preceding New** see § 11.3.9.)

We shall consider first the most frequent type, i.e. the Mood-bearing New. These are called 'Type A' intonation units. For the moment we shall assume that we are generating a simple clause (the unmarked type) in which there is a 'new' element that is not 'contrastively new'.

11.3.2.1 Type A: Generating the Mood-bearing New

Every text-sentence can have one, and only one, **Mood-bearing New (MN)**. (However, it may have none, if its potential MN is 'usurped' by a Contrastive New (CN), as we shall see in §11.3.2.3.) This MN can only occur in (i) a topmost simple clause or (ii) the final clause of a string of co-ordinated topmost clauses. Since these types of clause inherently have the status of containing 'new information', some or all of any such clause must be marked as 'new'. So the meaning that the MN carries is: 'This element – and very probably also earlier in the text-sentence than this – includes information that is being presented as 'new to the Addressee'. In English this rather imprecise but nonetheless important type of meaning is expressed by placing the exponent of this meaning of 'newness' on the last item with inherent word stress (to slightly oversimplify).

However, it is important to note that the rule that inserts this element applies by default; it is not the result of a positive decision by the Performer to treat the item with which the MN's exponent will be conflated as 'new'. This is why Realization Rule 1.1 will only generate a Mood-bearing New after the Performer has decided that no element in the clause is to be presented as 'contrastively new'.[10]

The problem that now arises is that GENESYS does not know, until the last of the lower units in the sentence has been generated, which item is going to be the last item with inherent word stress. So the MN cannot actually be positioned in the sentence until after that point has been reached. The mechanism used in GENESYS to provide for this is to 'park' the MN in a temporary position, close to the end of the clause (at Place 200) until the grammar is ready for it. We shall see what is entailed in being 'ready for it' in the next few sections.

After this second step in the process of generation, then, the end of the clause looks like the embryonic structure labelled 'Type A' shown below:

Type A

place   200
element   MN

11.3.2.2 Type B: Generating an Unmarked New

A clause which is assigned an **Unmarked New** element (represented as **UN**) is called 'Type B'. Thus this model recognizes the distinction between a 'Mood-bearing New' (MN) and an 'Unmarked New' (UN) as a major one.

An UN occurs in any of a wide range of types of clause or other unit which (i) has its own information unit, and (ii) does not have either a MN or a CN. Here we shall limit ourselves to the most frequent types of case in which these conditions are met, i.e. in (i) a non-final clause in a string of two or more co-ordinated clauses, (ii) a non-final nominal (or other) group in a string of two or more co-ordinated nominal (or other) groups, and (iii) several types of embedded clause. In all these cases, then, the element is 'parked' at the end of the unit, as it were, until the items with which it might be conflated have all been generated. In the case of a non-final co-ordinated clause, for example, its end, at this stage in its generation, would be as in Type B below.

> Type B
>
> place   200
> element   UN

11.3.2.3 Type C: Generating two types of Contrastive New

Some clauses contain a type of 'newness' that is 'contrastive'. This occurs when the Performer chooses to present an element of the 'event' that is the input to the lexicogrammar (and so, if it is expressed 'congruently', the corresponding element of the clause that realizes it) as being 'contrastively new' to the Addressee. This results in adding to the structure of the unit an element that we shall call the **Contrastive New (CN)**. In the full grammar a CN can be added to virtually any element of any unit, and this is a major complicating factor in the operation of the lexicogrammar as a whole.

The key point is that, when this happens, the default rule that inserts the MN or the New that would otherwise have been generated (see §§11.3.2.1 and 11.3.2.2) is not activated. It is as if the CN has usurped the role of the MN or UN – or, to put it less dramatically, it causes it not to be generated.[11]

To illustrate the way in which contrastive newness can usurp the normal patterns of intonation, here is an example of a sentence in which the first CN has usurped a UN and the second CN has usurped a MN:

First she KISSED Fred, and then she HIT him.

In the first of the two co-ordinated clauses, the CN on *KISSED* drives out an UN, and in the second the CN on *HIT* replaces what would otherwise have been a MN.[12] A CN is unlike a MN or an UN in many ways. From the viewpoint of the realization rules, its most outstanding characteristic is that it is immediately located on the appropriate element in the structure of the unit currently being generated (rather than being 'parked' temporarily at the end of the unit until more of the text-sentence has been generated, as with a MN or a UN).

There are two main types of CN, and they require significantly different treatments. Here we shall distinguish these two types (leaving a further distinction within the second type till §11.3.3.4).

The first type of CN is conflated with an element that is directly **expounded by an item**, as in the examples considered so far. We shall call intonation units with a CN 'Type C', so this is labelled as 'Type C1' in the diagram below.

But there is a second possibility. In this type the CN is conflated with an element that is **filled by a unit**, such as an Agent or another Participant Role, or any type of Adjunct that is filled by a unit. This type includes the many types of Circumstantial Role (of which there are over forty in the current Cardiff Grammar), and the thirty or so other functionally distinct types of Adjuncts (which express meanings other than experiential meaning). The way in which Type C2 differs from Type C1 is that in Type C2 we will not know till later what items will expound the element.

At this stage in generation, however, Type C1 and Type C2 have essentially the same realization, as illustrated below.

	Type C1	Type C2
place	100	33
element	M/CN	S/Ag/CN

We have seen that a MN and a UN always occur at (or very close to) the end of their unit (e.g. a clause). But the two types of CN are unlike a MN and a UN, in that they may occur on virtually any element of the unit. Thus, when the contrastive newness is on the Process, as in *She KISSED Fred*, the structure would be as shown as Type C1 – because the Main Verb (M) is located at Place 100. And we know that M will be directly expounded by a lexical verb (even though we don't know yet what it will be). In Type C2, on the other hand, we know that the clause element will not be directly expounded by an item; it will be filled by a unit. And we have no idea, at this stage in the process of generation, what the exponents of the elements of that unit will be. (In due course, however, the CN will need to be attached to an **item** within the unit that is generated to fill the clause element, and in §11.3.3.4 we shall see how this is achieved.)

Borrowing the examples used in §11.1.2, we can see that it is possible for a CN to occur on the last lexical item in its intonation unit, as in (1) below – and that when it does it looks superficially like a MN, which we represent as shown in (4).[13] But far more frequently we find that a CN is attached to an element that occurs earlier in the unit, as in (2) and (3).

> (1) Ike likes IVY (with a CN) – i.e. you're wrong if you think it's Fiona that he likes
> (2) Ike LIKES Ivy (with a CN) – i.e. you're wrong if you think he hates her
> (3) IKE likes Ivy (with a CN) – i.e. it is Ike who likes Ivy, not Fred
> (4) Ike likes Ivy (with a MN) – not correcting a misapprehension

The main distinction to be made between (1), (2) and (3) is between (2) and the other two. This is because in (2) the CN is attached to an element that is directly expounded by an **item**, i.e. a Main Verb (M). It is this that enables the grammar to generate the item that expounds the element (i.e. *LIKES*) on the same pass through the system network as the pass on which it inserts the element, and so to place the CN. But in (1) and (3) the only manifestations of 'Ivy' and 'Ike' that get generated on the current pass through the network are the insertions of the Participant Roles that are conflated with the Complement and the Subject (i.e. a Phenomenon and an Emoter respectively, in terms of the Participant Roles used in the Cardiff Grammar; see Fawcett, 2011a). And we don't know at this stage whether the Phenomenon in (1), for example, will be expounded by *Ivy*, *she*, or even *that skinny one*. So we don't know yet which item the "CT" will be conflated with.

Notice too that the item that will have the "CT" conflated with it is not necessarily the last item in the nominal group. In *that SKINNy one* the "CT" is not on the last item, because it is the inherently weak item *one*. The grammar provides for this type of variation in the **Tonic and Tone Conflation rule** (see §11.5).

Finally, consider again the difference between (1) and (4). It should now be clear why we should treat examples with a CN on a final lexical item, such as (1), as being like (2) and (3) rather than like (4). An important piece of evidence for taking this position is the nature of the **pretonic segment** of the intonation unit in each of the two cases. As Tench shows (1996a: 128–9), we need to generate a completely different pretonic segment for the intonation unit when it precedes a "CT" from the pretonic that is needed if it is a "MT". (See *ibid.* for the patterns of the pretonic segments – or, strictly speaking, in his terminology, for the 'heads' of the pretonic segments.)

11.3.3 Step 3: Generating a Tonic (an item: the exponent of an Unmarked New)

The third step is to add a **Tonic** as the exponent of the **New** element. Since it **expounds** an element, in precisely the same way that a 'noun' such as "house" may expound the head of a nominal group, it is, in the present theoretical framework, an 'item': i.e. an **intonational item**.

There are three types of Tonic. These correspond in a one-to-one manner to the three types of 'newness', so there are: a **Mood-bearing Tonic**, a **simple Tonic** and a **Contrastive Tonic**. The third step is therefore to generate one of these. We shall consider them in the order of their frequency.

11.3.3.1 Type A: Adding a Mood-bearing Tonic as the exponent of a Mood-bearing New

The most frequent type of New is a Mood-bearing New (MN), because every spoken text-sentence must have a **Mood-bearing Tonic ("MT")**. It has the name 'Mood-bearing Tonic' because the type of meaning carried by the **Tone** that will shortly be adjoined to it always realizes a meaning of MOOD.

The Mood-bearing Tonic is shown in the structure as "MT" (where the double quotation marks indicate an item). But in due course it will be conflated with a word that occurs to the left of it (see §11.5).[14]

The Mood-bearing Tonic, like other types of Tonic, has no phonological form in its own right; it only acquires this when the Tone is added to it, and so is integrated with it. So the 'adjoining' of the symbols that represent the Tonic and its Tone is a 'fusion', and not just the adjoining of one item immediately next to another (as in the case of suffixation, e.g. *did* + *n't*).

It is vital that the Tonic should be in place before the grammar tries to place the Tone in the structure (which is necessarily towards the very end of the generation process) so that the Tonic is in place to have the Tone attached to it. At this stage, the end of the clause looks like this:

Type A

```
place       200
element     MN
             |
item        "MT"
```

11.3.3.2 Type B: Adding a simple Tonic as the exponent of an Unmarked New

In the case of an UN, a simple 'Tonic', represented as "T", is similarly inserted as its exponent, resulting in:

Type B

place   200
element   UN
          |
item   "T"

11.3.3.3 Type C1: Adding a Contrastive Tonic as the exponent of a CN expounded by an item

The addition of a "CT" to a structure with a CN requires two different mechanisms, each different from the mechanism used in Types A and B. We begin with Type C1, i.e. the type in which the exponent of a CN is expounded by an **item**.

Here we assume that the clause being generated is *She didn't KISS him*, or, in the representation of the final output of the spoken equivalent:

|| she didn't kiss/CT12 him ||

In this case the developing structure would look like Type C1 below:

Type C1

place   100
elements   M/CN
           |
items   "kiss/CT"

The item "CT" and the preceding symbol for 'conflation' are inserted by a similar rule to the one that is used to add the suffix *n't* to *did* in the generation of *did+n't*, except that what is added begins with the symbol for 'conflation' '/' rather than that for suffixation, i.e. '+'. So the item that is added to "kiss" in the example above is "/CT". It is important to show the relationship of 'conflation' explicitly, with no space between the item and the "/CT", so that, at a later stage of generation, the grammar will know that the "CT" is already conflated with an item, and so cannot be moved. It cannot do this when the exponent of M is *kiss*, of course, but it could if the Main Verb was expounded by *is*, because *is* is on the list of inherently weak items. (For the description of the Tonic+Tone conflation rule, see §§11.5.3 and 11.5.4.)

11.3.3.4 Type C2: adding a Contrastive Tonic as the exponent of a CN that is filled by a unit

Matters are a little more complicated when the element is not directly expounded by an **item** (as it is in Type C1), but is instead filled by a **unit**. (Moreover, if there is co-ordination, the element may be filled by two or more units, which adds the further complication that it is necessary to specify the one in which the "CT" must be located.) A Type C2 Tonic structure, then, is one in which a Contrastive New is conflated with an element (such as an Agent, shown as "Ag") that is filled by a unit (or units), with the result that there is no item at this point in generation with which to conflate the "CT". Type C2 structures occur very frequently, i.e. whenever a nominal group fills a Participant or Circumstantial Role such as an Agent or a Time Position Adjunct.

Within Type C2 there are two important sub-types: Type C2.1 and Type C2.2. In the first, the Performer (or the grammar, when GENESYS is running in 'random generation' mode) will have selected, when generating the 'topmost' clause, a feature such as [contrastive newness on agent], and then, in the immediately dependent system, the feature [on agent as whole]. (This feature is in contrast with [on element of agent], which, if chosen, would lead to the generation of a Type C2.2 Tonic.) In the case of a Type C2.1 Tonic, the grammar is immediately able to conflate the "CT" with the Agent. And it does this even though it doesn't yet know which item within the unit or units filling the Agent the "CT" will finally be conflated with. The decision is to present the **element as a whole** as being 'contrastively new' to the Addressee. In this case, then, there is no need to make any further choices in 'contrastive newness', and the grammar will simply await the result of the generation of a unit or units to fill the Agent, after which it will conflate the "CT" with the rightmost appropriate item, using the **Tonic+Tone conflation rule** that will be described in §§11.5.3 and 11.5.4.

However, there is a second type of Type C2, i.e. Type C2.2, an example being *HIS brother made it*. Here the element marked as 'contrastively new' is not the Agent as a whole but the deictic determiner *his* within the nominal group *his brother*. In generating this structure, then, the feature [on element of agent] has been chosen in the system mentioned in the last paragraph. In such cases the grammar simply passes on the feature [contrastive newness] (by a type of realization rule termed a **preselection rule**) to ensure that 'contrastive newness' will appear at some point within the structure of the unit filling the current element. The immediate result is as shown in the diagram for Type C2.2 below, i.e. no CN is placed in the structure on the current pass through the network.

The effect of passing on the feature [contrastive newness] is that on re-entry to the network to generate a nominal group to fill the Agent, one of the various sorts of 'contrastive newness' considered here for the clause will be generated for the nominal group. Thus it could in principle result in a structure of either Type C1, Type C2.1 or Type C2.2. In the end, though, however far down the tree the feature [contrastive newness on X] is passed by the preselection rules, the point will be reached when the element that is to be contrastive is expounded by an **item**, and at that point the CN will be conflated with it, in a Type C1 structure. Usually, however, the grammar will have chosen a feature of the [on X as whole] type long before that point is reached.

Here, then, are our developing examples. For Type C1, we shall assume that we are generating the spoken equivalent of *Bill didn't KISS Ivy*. For Type C2.1 it will be the spoken equivalent of *His BROTHER made it*. And for Type C2.2 it will be the spoken equivalent of *HIS brother made it*. The words '(added later)' indicate that it will only be at a later stage in the process of generation that the "CT" is inserted into the structure, conflated with an item (i.e. a word or morpheme).

	Type C1	Type C2.1	Type C2.2
place	100	33	33
element	M/CN	S/Ag/CN	S/Ag
item	"kiss/CT"	"CT" (added later)	"CT" (added later)

Let me make a final point about the attachment of the CN to the Agent as S/Ag/CN in Type C2.1. Since the item or items that will expound the Agent have not yet been generated, the grammar handles the relationship between the "CT" and one of these items by generating the item "CT" as conflated with the Agent, not fused with it. This enables it to have a "CT" as its exponent, with which a Tone will be fused in due course.[15]

11.3.3.5 The effect of the requirements of one type of 'contrastive newness' on the overall structure of the model

From the viewpoint of the overall structure of the procedure for generating intonation, there is an even more important characteristic of Type C2.1. This is that it requires the grammar to retain at least part of the syntax tree in the representation of the text-sentence until the **Tonic+Tone**

conflation rule has been applied. (This rule is described more fully in §§11.5.3 and 11.5.4, but we shall consider some aspects of it here, because it is the Type C2.1 Tonic that requires that rule to function as it does.)

The reason why we need to retain at least some of the syntax till after the Tonic+Tone conflation rule has been applied is that, in the case of a Type C2.1 Tonic, the grammar needs to know where the start of the unit that fills the Agent (or other element) is, when it is moving the **Tonic** leftwards through the **items** of the text-sentence. If it was unable to identify the start of the unit, it would move the "CT" right through any item that was on the list of 'inherently weak' items, so that sometimes it would go past the beginning of the unit. So, if the unit were simply *he* or *it* or *you and I*, or some other item or string of items that have an inherently weak stress, the "CT" would pass through them.

Let us illustrate the problem with the following example, in which the Participant Role of Carrier, i.e. *you*, is to be marked as 'contrastively new':

Tomorrow YOU can have the car.

In a Type 2.1 Tonic, it is the Carrier as a whole that is contrastively new, so not just the head of the nominal group (ngp) that is expounded by *you* (though in this case the two possibilities coincide). The problem is that, because the item *you* is in the list of inherently weak items, the "CT", in its movement leftwards when the Tonic+Tone conflation rule is applied, would skip it and settle on *tomorrow*, unless the grammar knows that the "CT" must not move leftwards beyond the boundary of the nominal group that fills the Carrier, i.e. *you*. So, if all of the syntax were to be stripped away before the application of the Tonic+Tone conflation rule, the grammar would generate:

|| tomorrow/CT1 you can have the car ||

instead of the intended output, which is:

|| tomorrow you/CT1 can have the car ||

This is why it is essential that the generator is able to identify the start of the unit that expounds the Agent.

How can the grammar identify this unit boundary? When it is moving a Tone leftwards to find the item with which it will be conflated, it is moving through a string of both words and 'intonational items' (as we have termed them). And that is the crucial point: from the grammar's viewpoint they are items, just as words are.[16]

I shall shortly introduce a full representation of an example of Type C2.1. Figure 11.3 will show only what has been generated so far, i.e. the **places** in the clause (i.e. the numbers 3, 4, 33 and 100), the **elements** of the clause (i.e. St, &, S/Ag/CN and M) and the **items** that expound them (including the intonational item "CT"). We shall add other intonational elements and items to later versions of this diagram in due course.

I have chosen Type C2.1 because it is the most complex. Nevertheless, it is possible to infer from it what the full structure of the other types would be. The example is the real life spoken equivalent of *Then several of the ACROBATS danced,* in which it is the Participant Role of Agent that is to be marked as 'contrastively new'.[17] So the output towards which we are working is this:

|| then several of the acrobats/CT1 danced ||

The full representation of the clause (but with the Agent expounded) is at this stage in the process of generation as shown in Figure 11.3 below, with the CN conflated with the Agent (which was already conflated with the Subject):

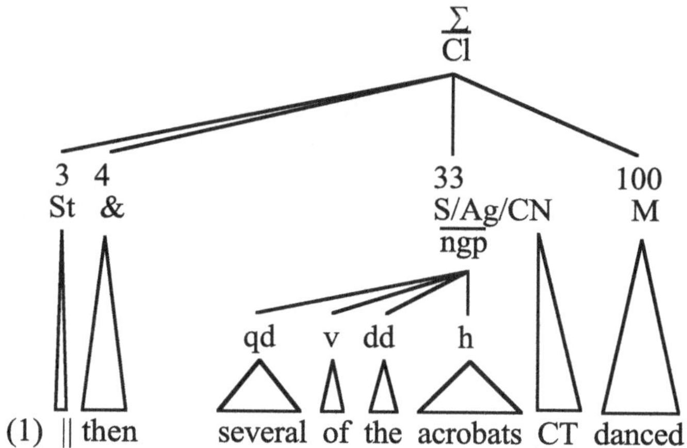

Figure 11.3 A partially completed clause with a 'contrastively new' element.

Notice that, while the CN is conflated with the element that precedes it, the item "CT" that expounds the CN is not yet conflated with the item that preceded it, i.e. "acrobats". This is because it will not necessarily be conflated with the immediately preceding word. For example, if the example had been *then the tall one danced,* where the S/Ag/CN is *the tall one,* the final output would need to be like this:

|| then the tall/CT1 one danced ||

In other words, the "CT" must be conflated with an item within the ngp that fills the Agent, but the item will not necessarily be the last word of the group. In this case it cannot be the last item because this is *one*, and *one* is inherently weak when it is the head of a nominal group. (See §11.5.)

The main difference between this example and an example of a Type A or Type B Tonic is that in those cases the Contrastive New element is placed near the end of the clause, i.e. at Place 200 (using the same Place as is used for the Mood-bearing New and the Unmarked New).

Now we are ready to look at the generation of the Key. This is the element that will be expounded by one of the Tones that we encountered in §11.2, where we noted the central role of the Tones in realizing a wide range of meanings.

11.3.4 Step 4: Generating a Key (an element of structure)

In this step we generate the element of structure that will be expounded by one of the various **Tones.** So at this point the grammar places a second intonational element in the growing structure. This element is the **Key (K)**.

Halliday uses the term 'Key' as the general label for 'a little network of choices all related to the system [network] of mood' (Halliday, 1994: 302). Here we use the term in a related sense. But here it is not the name of a system but the name of the element that is expounded by the items (i.e. the Tones) through which the delicate MOOD meanings are realized. However, it is not just MOOD meanings that are realized via the Key element. It is the element through which all meanings realized in Tones are realized, so meanings expressing INFORMATION STATUS as well as MOOD.

The same element, the Key, is used with each of the three main types of New: Mood-bearing New, Unmarked New and Contrastive New. It is always inserted at Place 201, which is towards the end of the clause. So it is immediately after the MN or the UN, and usually well after any CN. (See § 11.3.9 for the Preceding New.)

Using as our example the most frequent type (the type with a MN), the end of the clause would now look like this:

```
places       200   201
elements     MN    K
                |
items        "MT"
```

The same principle applies to other clauses (i.e. those that are not a simplex clause or a final clause in a string of co-ordinated clauses) when the element is not a MN but an UN, and when its exponent is a "T". Here are a few cases that have been assigned a separate information unit: (i) a non-final co-ordinated clause, (ii) a clause that is embedded as an Adjunct (of many functional types and at several different positions in the clause), (iii) a relative clause in a nominal group, and (iv) a non-final co-ordinated nominal group. (In the full grammar such Tonics occur at many other places in structure.) A typical example would be:

```
places        200    201
elements      UN     K
              |
items         "T"
```

But in either case a "CT" could have been generated instead of a "MT" or "T". As we have seen, a clause that typically has a MN may sometimes be given a Contrastive New instead, as also may a clause that typically has an Unmarked New. Here is an example that illustrates both – and at the same time introduces the full representation of the intonation, as it will be in the final output form:

|| Ivy did/CT12 work hard | but Ike did not/CT1 work hard ||

The insertion of the Key, however, does not vary according to what type of New it is. It is always simply a Key (K). To illustrate this, I give below the structures that would be generated by the end of this step for a spoken output. As before, I assume that for Type C1 we are generating the spoken equivalent of *Bill didn't KISS Ivy*, for Type C2.1 *His BROTHER made it*, and for Type C2.2 *HIS brother made it*.

```
              Type C1           Type C2.1           Type C2.2
place         100    201        33      201         33
element       M/CN   K          S/Ag/CN  K          S/Ag      K
              |                 |                   |
item          "kiss/CT"         "CT" (added later)  "CT" (added later)
```

It is precisely because the grammar does not know, when it is generating the Tone that expounds the Key, whether the Tone is to be adjoined to (i) a "MT", a "T" or a "CT", that it is necessary to generate the separate element of the Key to carry the Tone itself. At a later stage, when the grammar knows both (i) which type of Tonic the Tone it is to be adjoined to and (ii) which type of Tone it is to be, the grammar will adjoin the Tone to whichever it is of a "MT", "T" or "CT".

At this stage, our full example of a construction with a CN is presented in Figure 11.4.

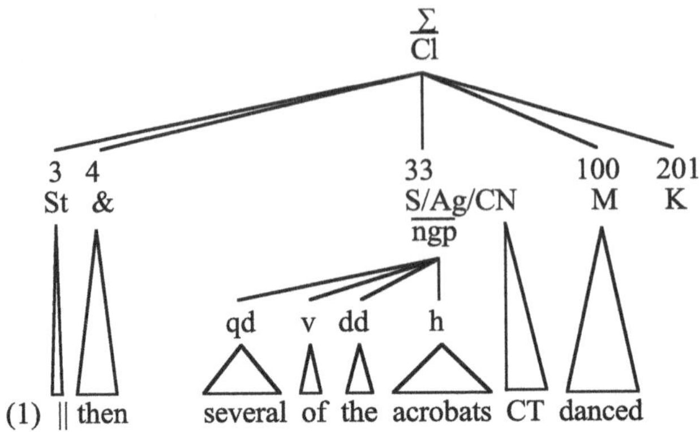

Figure 11.4 A partially completed clause with a 'contrastively new' element and a Key.

11.3.5 Step 5: Generating a Tone (an item, the exponent of a Key)

11.3.5.1 The set of Tones

The fifth step is to generate a Tone that will expound the Key. §11.2 introduced the semantic features from which the Tones are generated, and we saw that there were two main types: those that realized a meaning from the system network for MOOD and those that realize a meaning from one of the many little systems for INFORMATION STATUS.

Here, following Tench (1996a), is a list of the ten Tones that are used in the present model of English intonation, relating their representation as a number plus '+' or '-' and their verbal description:

1	= Tone 1	mid-high to low fall
1+	= High Tone 1	high to low fall
1−	= Low Tone 1	mid-low to low fall
2	= Tone 2	low to mid-high rise
2+	= High Tone 2	low to high rise
2−	= Low Tone 2	low to mid-low rise
21+	= High Tone 21	high rise–fall
21−	= Tone 21	low rise–fall
12	= Tone 12	mid fall–rise
12−	= Low Tone 12	low fall–rise

(To save space in the diagrams that illustrate their realizations, the Tones are simply represented by their numbers, i.e. "1", "1+", "1–", "2", etc.)

Interestingly, a single Tone quite often functions as the realization of two different meanings, as we saw in the realization rules for the Tones in §11.2.2.

The next section explains the three main ways in which the Tones become part of the structure (with two further variants within one of them).

11.3.5.2 With a Mood-bearing New: Adding a Tone as the exponent of K

With a clause that has a MN, the grammar adds the **exponent** of the K, i.e. a Tone, such as 'Tone 1', 'Tone 2' or 'Tone 21–'. The effect is that an item that represents the type of Tone (e.g. "1") is added immediately after an item that is a 'Tonic' (e.g. "MT"). Now the end of the clause looks like this:

places	200	201
elements	MN	K
items	"MT"	"1"

11.3.5.3 With an Unmarked New: Adding a Tone as the exponent of K

Exactly the same pattern occurs in the case of a non-final co-ordinated clause which has an Unmarked New, and so also with all the other units with an UN. Here the choice of such INFORMATION STATUS meanings is realized as one of 'Tone 1', 'Tone 2' or 'Tone 12', the choice being different in each of the various positions. This is represented simply as "1", "2" or "12". The end of the clause now looks like this:

places	200	201
elements	UN	K
items	"T"	"2"

11.3.5.4 With a Contrastive New: adding a Tone as the exponent of K

Essentially the same thing happens when a CN is generated in a clause. But in such cases the CN, and so the "CT" that expounds it, is likely to be non-final, as in the example whose final representation would be:

|| Bill didn't/CT1 kiss Ivy ||

In such cases, therefore, the K will at the present stage normally not even be adjacent to the "CT", unless the "CT" happens to be attached to the final lexical item, as in a clause such as:

|| Bill has been killed/CT21+ ||

Like the MN and the New, with their exponents as a "MT" and a "T", the K and its exponent Tone are temporarily parked at the end of the clause until it is the time to apply the 'Tonic+Tone conflation rule' (see §11.5).

In our summary diagram let us assume, as before, that in Type C1 the "CT" is on the 'Process', and so on the Main Verb, as in *Bill didn't KISS Ivy*, and that in Type C2.1 we are generating the spoken equivalent of *His BROTHER actually made it*. (As we saw in §11.3.3.4, the "CT" in Type C2.2, which has not been related to a specific element in the unit being generated on the current pass through the network, will be so related, when the 'contrastive' feature has been 'copied' down to a lower unit. At that point it will be related to an element on the pattern of Type C1 or Type C2.1.)

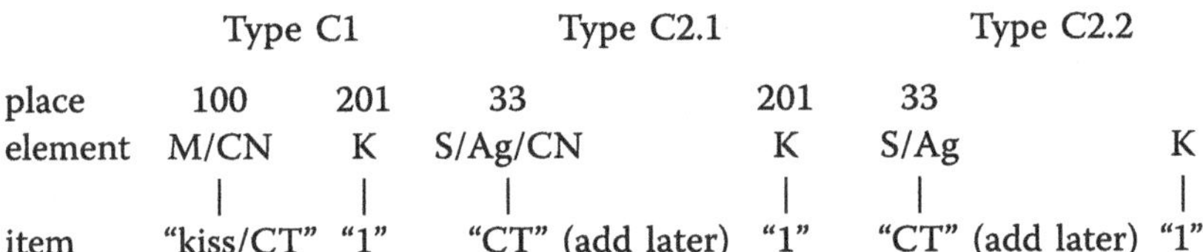

Figure 11.5 shows the stage that our developing example of Type C2 has now reached.

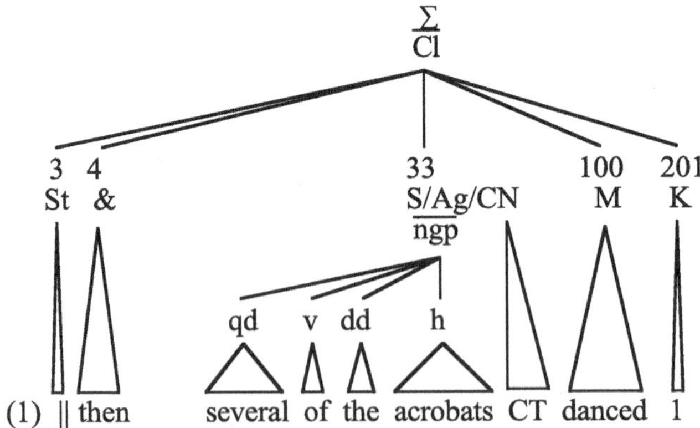

Figure 11.5 An almost completed clause with a 'contrastively new' element.

11.3.5.5 Are both elements (CN and K) and both items ("CT" and "1") really necessary?

It may appear to be an unnecessary complication to have both a New and a Key, and so to represent the Tonic as a separate item from the Tone. However, both items are needed, so that both elements are needed too. The reason is that, in the final adjustment rules (§11.6), the Tone must be able to move leftwards in the clause within each intonation unit, so as to be adjoined to either the Contrastive Tonic, if there is one, or, if there isn't, to the Mood-bearing Tonic or the simple Tonic. It is the recognition of the Tonic as an item in its own right that enables us to generalize across the three different types of Tonic. So it is important to the straightforward operation of the realization rules that the Tonic should be treated as one of the string of **items** in its own right, together with the words.[18]

In a similar way, we might ask: 'Is the distinction between the Mood-bearing Tonic, the simple Tonic and the Contrastive Tonic worth making? Couldn't they all be equally well shown as "T"?' The first part of the answer is that they do in fact behave differently from each other (especially the "CT"), so that it makes the rules easier to write if they have different names. And the second part of the answer is that, when the generator knows (i) which type of Tonic it is and (ii) which type of Tone it is, it can generate a natural-sounding **pretonic segment** for the intonation unit. This is important, because the patterns in the pretonic of an intonation unit that has a "CT", for example, are very different from those of an intonation unit with a "MT".

11.3.6 Step 6: Generating an Ender (an element of structure)

In the sixth step, the element whose exponent will mark the end of the information unit is inserted. In a spoken text it marks the end of an 'intonation unit' and in writing the end of a 'punctuation unit'. Thus the boundary markers at the level of **form**, whether spoken or written, reflect the 'information unit' boundaries at the level of **meaning**. And, as with the other elements that we have been considering, adding an element to the structure means that we must also add an item to expound it (see §11.3.7).

In §11.2.1, we saw that the **Ender** of a **text-sentence** is inserted automatically, because every text-sentence must have one. But the insertion of other Enders, such as those found in embedded clauses and in groups, is always the result of a decision taken during generation, i.e. the result of the choice in Step 1 to have a separate information unit.[19]

Inserting the information unit boundaries simply involves the placing of an Ender in the clause or group. In the case of a simple spoken clause (or the last of two or more co-ordinated clauses), we find that after applying this step the end of a spoken clause will look like this:

```
places        200    201   250
elements      MN      K     E
|              |
items         "MT"   "1"
```

In a written text the end of a typical clause would simply be like this:

```
place         250
element        E
```

The exponent of the Ender in a written text is not simply a boundary marker; it is also the written equivalent of a Tone.

11.3.7 Step 7: Inserting the final information unit boundary (an item, as the exponent of the Ender)

11.3.7.1 In spoken discourse

In this seventh step, the items that expound the elements that mark the boundaries of the information unit are inserted. In a representation of a spoken text the boundaries are shown as either "||" or "|" – where "||" signifies the end of a text-sentence, and "|" signifies the end of any other intonation unit.

Thus, in the case of Type A (a simple spoken clause or the last of two or more co-ordinated clauses), we shall find that after this step the end of a spoken clause may well look like this (with variations in the Tone):

```
Type A

places        200    201   250
elements      MN      K     E
               |       |     |
items         "MT"   "1"   "||"
```

We turn now to Types B and C. Type B has the same places, elements and items as Type A, except that "MN" and "MT" would be replaced by "UN" and "T", and "||" by "|". And with the two types of Contrastive New (Types C1 and C2) "MN" would be replaced by "CN" and the Ender ("E") would be expounded by either "||" or "|", depending on whether or not the Tonic was 'mood-bearing'

Figure 11.6 shows the stage that the overall structure of our example of a Type C2 structure has now reached. Indeed, the part that models the Ender and its exponent ("||" or "|") is the same for all three types. It represents the structure after the application of all the realization rules that apply in this case. But it is not the final representation, because the Tone ("1") has not yet been adjoined to the Tonic ("CT"), and the combined 'Tonic+Tone' has not yet been conflated with an item. For this we must await the Final Adjustment Rules, at which point we shall also discover the reason for the space in the diagram.

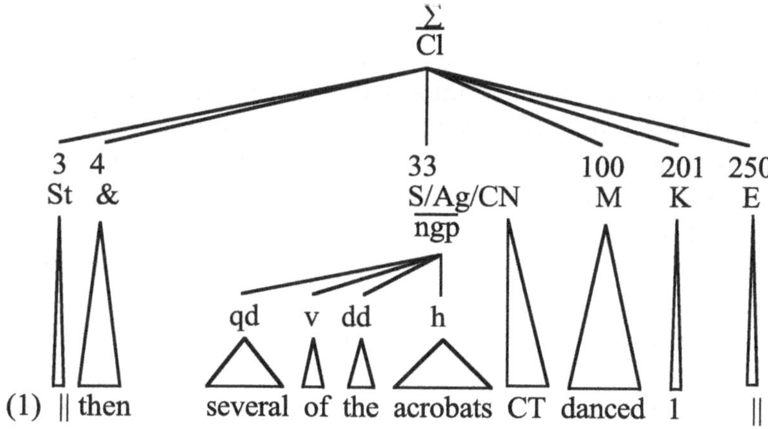

Figure 11.6 An almost completed clause with a 'contrastively new' element.

11.3.7.2 In written discourse

Up to the present point in this chapter, we have been focussing almost entirely on intonation rather than punctuation. But this is the moment to complete the generation of the punctuation that is needed for the end of a written text-sentence with an equivalent information structure. All we need is the set of items that can expound the Ender.

The representations of these are both simple and very familiar. Remembering that items are marked by being in double quotation marks (except when an example with intonation added is given a line of its own), we can say that, in the cut-down version of the model that is used for demonstration purposes, the Ender can be expounded by any of the following punctuation marks: ".", ",", "?" and "!". And in the full grammar there is also ";" and ":", as well as both (i) brackets "(" and ")", and (ii) dashes "–" and "–".

At this point we shall introduce the very simple structure that is found at the end of many clauses in a spoken text (a Type D structure):

```
Type D

places          250     or    250
element          E             E
                 |             |
item            "."           "?" etc.
```

This is the only element of structure that is needed for the end of a unit in the written mode. Indeed, the reason why we have been able to concentrate solely on intonation up to now is that the structure needed for punctuation at the end of an information unit is very simple. (But we shall find that it is a little more complicated when punctuation is needed to realize the beginning of an information unit, in the next sub-section.)

There is an interesting point about the realizations of meanings in punctuation that can now be made. This is that the choice between the meanings that are realized in the items that expound the Ender in **written** discourse (i.e. in punctuation) as described here is equivalent to both Step 5 and the present step, when generating intonation in **spoken** discourse. In other words, the choice between the meanings realized in **punctuation marks** includes the equivalent, in writing, of the choices in meanings (of MOOD or INFORMATION STATUS) realized as **Tones** in **spoken** discourse. So the use of this step in generating punctuation includes the equivalent of §11.3.5 for intonation. In a real sense, then, the Ender in a written text carries the meanings of both the Ender (expounded by an intonation unit boundary) and the Key element (expounded by a Tone) in a spoken text. Thus Steps 1, 6 and 7 are the only ones that are required, so far, in the generation of punctuation.

The next section introduces one of the most elegant innovations of the model: the Starter and the initial information unit boundary.

11.3.8 Steps 7 and 8: The Starter and the initial information unit boundary that expounds it (an element of structure and an item)

Since we have now established that inserting an element into the structure entails expounding it by an item (or items), I shall introduce at the same time, in this and the next two sections, both a new element and the item (or items) that expound it.

11.3.8.1 The Starter and the initial information unit boundary of a text-sentence

§11.2.1 explained how the element of Starter is generated automatically for the leftmost unembedded clause, as a direct consequence of the decision to generate a spoken text-sentence, thus providing every such sentence with a Starter and its exponent as "||". As an example consider the initial "||" in (1) below.

(1) || because he was feeling rather thirsty/T2 | he poured himself a glass of water/MT1 ||

How is the initial "||" generated? Is it the exponent of a Starter in the clause *because he was feeling rather thirsty*? The answer is that it is not. It is the Starter of the matrix clause (the one in which the Main Verb is *poured* and which has as one of its elements the thematized Adjunct *because he was feeling rather thirsty*). In other words, the structure is exactly the same as it would be if the initial Adjunct was not filled by a clause but by a prepositional group such as *because of this*, or even directly expounded by an item such as *consequently* or *however*.

We have now accounted for the initial boundary marker in the first 'topmost' clause, supplementing the description in §11.2.1 by explaining what happens when there is an initial embedded clause. But what about the Starter in an embedded clause that does not occur at the beginning of the text-sentence? This is the question that the next sub-section addresses.

11.3.8.2 The Starter and the initial information unit boundary of an embedded clause (or other unit)

There are two ways that the grammar marks the initial boundary of an information unit that is attached to an embedded clause. The first is simply that the Ender of an immediately preceding information unit also functions as the **initial information unit boundary** of the current information unit. So in (1) above, the "|" that expounds the Ender of the thematized clause *because he was feeling rather thirsty* also marks the beginning of the information unit *he poured himself a glass of water*. However, when an embedded clause (or indeed any unit) that is assigned its own information unit occurs anywhere within the main clause, GENESYS does need to introduce a Starter. So let us now consider the precise role of Starters in this grammar. We shall start with written texts, and then move on to spoken texts in the next section.

We have seen that there are Enders in written texts, expounded by ".", "?", etc., so it is logical to ask: 'Do written texts also have Starters?' To answer this, we need to distinguish between the concept of (i) a Starter for a text-sentence and (ii) a Starter for an embedded clause or other unit. With respect to the former, the answer is that GENESYS does not generate a Starter for a written text-sentence (as we saw in §11.2.1). However, there is a realization of the meaning of 'start of a sentence' in a written text. This is the rule that is taught to every primary school child, namely that the initial letter of the initial word is written as a capital letter. In other words, if the initial letter isn't a capital letter already (as it may be if it is *I* or a name, such as *Ivy*), it is changed into one. But this rule is applied later, as one of the final adjustment rules. See § 11.5.1.)

However, there may well be a Starter in an **embedded clause**. The easiest way to understand the way in which Starters of this type are introduced to the structure is to begin with an example from a written text. Consider an example such as (2):

(2)   Her uncle, who lives in New Zealand, is a doctor.

Here, the simple clause *Her uncle is a doctor* has been interrupted by the addition of what in the Cardiff Grammar is termed 'depictive' information. This is information about 'her uncle' which adds to our mental picture of him, but which is not necessary to enable the Addressee to identify which uncle is being referred to (in contrast with *Her uncle who lives in New Zealand is a doctor*, which implies that 'she' has at least two uncles). The key point is that the first comma in (2) is required as a result of the introduction of *who lives in New Zealand*. So, even though it is written without a gap between it and the word *uncle*, it belongs logically with *who lives in New Zealand*. In other words, what has been added is not

who lives in New Zealand

but

, who lives in New Zealand,

with a comma at the beginning and the end. Indeed, it is arguable that it is an illogicality of English orthography that the comma is attached to the last word before the embedded clause.

A similar situation occurs when a clause has a medial Adjunct that is given a separate information unit, as in (3):

(3)   At that point Fred, because he hates rows, just walked away.

The full grammar, then, sometimes requires the placing of both a Starter and an Ender in an embedded clause (or other unit) that occurs within a text-sentence. The representation of the elements at the beginning and the end of the embedded clause in ('2') or ('3') is therefore as follows:

```
place        3     ....   250
element      St    ....    E
             |             |
items       " "    ....    " "
             ,             ,
```

The full grammar provides for three types of exponents of such pairs of Starters and Enders: a pair of commas, as here, a pair of dashes, and a pair of brackets, each of which conveys a slightly different meaning. The feature names are, respectively: 'unmarked', 'downgraded' and 'afterthought'.

This takes care of the Starter and its exponent when they are used in written texts. Spoken texts require essentially the same approach, but it is considerably more complex. The Starter itself is simple, however, because the exponent is always "|".

11.3.9 Steps 9 to 12: The Preceding New and the Preceding Tonic that expounds it, and the Preceding Key and the Tone that expounds it (two elements and two items)

Here, because they are so similar to concepts already introduced, we shall introduce four new concepts in one short section. Consider first the spoken version of (2), which is presented as (4) below. The goal, then, is to generate the representation shown there.

(4) || her uncle PT2 | who lives in New Zealand T2 | is a doctor MT1 ||.

Let us assume that we have reached the point, in generating (4), when the embedded clause *who lives in New Zealand* is being generated to fill the qualifier of the nominal group that would be written as *her uncle, who lives in New Zealand,* . GENESYS now introduces to the structure both a second Starter and a second Ender, each being expounded by a "|", and each being an element of the embedded clause. The challenge is to generate an appropriate Tonic and Tone that will precede the Starter, and so be in the right position to be joined to the last word preceding it that can accept them.

To meet this challenge, the grammar introduces not only a Starter and its initial information unit boundary, but also (i) a **Preceding New (PN)** element and a **Preceding Tonic ("PT")** to expound it, and (ii) a **Preceding Key (PK)** and the **Tone "2"** to expound the PK. All three of the items are illustrated in (4) above, to the left of the word *who*, i.e. **the initial information unit boundary** ("|"), the **Preceding Tonic** ("PT") and the **Tone** ("2").

Finally, we should note that the initial "||" and the final "||" in (4) are simply the Starter and the Ender of the topmost clause, and that they are generated as part of it – as also are the Mood-bearing Tonic ("MT") and the Tone "1" that expounds it.

This description accounts for all of the intonational elements and items in (4). In the final adjustment rules, the gap between (i) 'uncle' and "PT2", (ii) 'Zealand' and "T2" and (iii) 'doctor' and "MT1" are replaced by a forward slash (the symbol for 'conflation') so signalling to the speech synthesizer to which (4) is the input that these words are to be spoken with these Tones.

The spoken equivalent of (3) from the previous section, here presented as (5), is generated in a similar way, and the result is:

(5) || Then Fred PT2 | because he couldn't stand rows T2 | simply walked out MT1 ||

So the full representation of the first three elements and the last three elements of the embedded clause in each of (4) and (5), together with the intonational items that are their exponents, would be like this:

places	1	2	3	....	200	201	250
elements	PN	PK	St	....	UN	K	E
	|	|	|		|	|	|
items	"PT"	"2"	"|"	....	"T"	"2"	"|"

As a final example of an embedded clause, consider Example (6) below. The only major difference from (5) is that in this case the embedded clause is placed at the end of the text-sentence. This makes a considerable difference to the information structure and so the intonation:

(6) || he poured himself some water PT2 | because he was feeling thirsty MT1 ||

Fewer intonational elements are generated in (6) than in (5). This is because the embedded clause occurs at the end of the matrix clause, not in the middle of it. Specifically, there is only one set of the final elements: a New element, a Key and an Ender, these being expounded by "MT1 ||".

Let us be specific as to what the elements are in (6), working from left to right. First, the initial "||" is the obligatory Starter that every text-sentence is given. Then the "PT2" (consisting of "PT" + "2") and "|" are the items that expound a Preceding New, a Preceding Key and a Starter. And all three of PN, PK and St are elements of the embedded clause, exactly as they are in (5) above.

So which clause do the elements realized as "MT1" and "||" belong to? The key to the answer lies in the type of New, and so the type of Tonic. The Tonic, as the analysis shows, is a **Mood-bearing Tonic** ("MT"), so the New that it expounds is a Mood-bearing New, and this shows that it is an element of the topmost clause. The semantic feature that has been chosen in generating this sentence introduces a **Cause Adjunct (A/Cau)** that is 'potentially new'. The meaning of 'potentially new' is precisely that it has a strong likelihood of being the final element of the clause (other than the intonational elements).[20] So, in the case of an embedded clause that occurs at the end of a text-sentence (as in this case), the grammar is written in such a way that intonational elements and items are generated for the beginning of the information unit, but not for the end. They are not needed, because the intonational elements of the matrix clause take precedence over those of the embedded clause.

To summarize: the three intonational items that occur at the end of a sentence such as (6) are the Mood-bearing Tonic "MT", its falling Tone "1" and the final "||". All three expound elements of the topmost clause, and the grammar provides that the equivalent elements are not generated for the embedded clause.

Finally, I should point out that broadly the same situation occurs in the case when an Adjunct that is filled by a clause is **thematized**, i.e. placed at the beginning of a clause. An example from §11.3.8.1 is reproduced here:

(7) || because he was feeling rather thirsty/T2 | he poured himself a glass of water/MT1 ||

The difference from Example 6 is that the elements that occur in it at the beginning of the embedded clause would be redundant and so are not generated (i.e. a Preceding Tonic, a Preceding New and a Starter and their exponents).

11.3.10 Summary so far

So far we have distinguished no fewer than thirteen steps that may be involved in generating a single intonation unit. Throughout the description, it has been necessary to 'unpack' the process of realization in a fairly detailed manner, in order to explain it fully. Interestingly, however, the realization rules that implement the many concepts that I have been explaining are elegantly compact. Thus the realization rule to generate the elements and items shown in (2), (3), (4) and (5) above is:

'medial element situation subrule':
St @ 3, E @ 250,
if written then 'written separate information unit subrule',
if spoken
then (St<"|", E<"|",
          K @ 201,
          if neutral separate unit then K<"2",
          PN @ 1, PN<"T",
          PK @ 2, PK<"2",
          if no contrastive newness within situation
          then (UN @ 200, UN<T)   ).

'written separate information unit subrule' :
if unmarked sep inf wr   then (St<",", E<",")
if downgraded sep inf wr   then (St<"(", E<")")
if afterthought sep inf wr   then (St<"-", E<"-")

This is a satisfyingly economical description, especially in that exactly the same rule applies to the embedded clauses in both Examples (2) and (4) and Examples (3) and (5). That is, it is irrelevant that one clause is embedded in a nominal group and the other in a clause.

Moreover, two equivalent but simpler rules generate (i) the sentence-initial embedded clause in (1), in which the first three elements and items are not required, and (ii) the sentence-final embedded clause in (6), in which there is no need to generate the final three elements and their exponents. In both cases the three elements and items are provided by the mother clause.

After the syntax has been stripped away at the end of Step 14, all we shall be left with is a string of items. And at that point no explicit evidence will remain, to tell us whether a particular Tonic occurs as part of a clause or part of a nominal group, just as is the case with the words of the text-sentence.

Yet nominal and other groups are also sources of additional information units. So, while this chapter focuses mainly on the realization of intonation in the clause, we shall now look briefly at the nominal group in its own right.

11.4 Intonation and punctuation in nominal and other groups

Other than the clause, the nominal group is the major source of additional information units. The most frequent case occurs when the unit that fills a qualifier is given a separate information unit, as illustrated in (2) and (4) in §§11.3.8.2 and 11.3.9.

Thus (2a) below, which is reproduced from §11.3.8.2, is a nominal group in which a clause fills the qualifier, with the Starter and Ender both being expounded by commas. Note, then, that the comma after *uncle* is a Starter and not an Ender, because it is introduced as the result of the introduction of the embedded clause *who lives in New Zealand.*

(2a)   her uncle, who lives in New Zealand,

And (4), which is reproduced from §11.3.9, shows the more complex realization of the same choices, as they are realized in a spoken text.

(4) || her uncle PT2 | who lives in New Zealand T2 | is a doctor MT1 ||.

Let us now consider another example of a nominal group in which a new intonation unit is introduced. We find this when co-ordination occurs, as in the written text in (7):

(7)   My brother, his wife and a friend (are coming to the party).

Its equivalent in a spoken text is:

(8) || my brother T2 | his wife T2 | and a friend are coming to the party MT1 ||.

Essentially, the principles described above for an Unmarked New with a simple Tonic in the clause apply here too. So the end of a non-final co-ordinated nominal group might look like this (before the application of the Tonic+Tone conflation rule, as given in the final adjustment rules):

Type B

places	73	74	75
elements	UN	K	E
	|	|	|
items	"T"	"2"	"|"

In other words, this example is different from that of the non-initial embedded clauses that were introduced in §§11.3.8.2 and 11.3.9, in that there is no need in this case to invoke the use of a Preceding New, a Preceding Key and a Starter.

There is another source of an additional unit that we haven't considered so far that is also connected with the nominal group. This occurs when a semantically 'heavy' nominal group is generated, often as the initial element of the clause. Such cases are likely to contain quite a lot of 'new' information, and the Text Planner may decide, on these grounds, to assign it a separate information unit. This, then, is a situation that is quite like what occurs when we thematize an Adjunct that is filled by a clause, e.g. the one we examined in §11.3.8.1. When it occurs it is modelled by a system network and a realization rule that are very similar to those for the semantically 'heavy' thematized Adjunct (which is in turn quite similar to the rule given in §11.3.10).

11.5 The final adjustment rules

11.5.1 An overview

This set of rules constitutes the fourteenth and final step in generating intonation and punctuation. The guiding principle is that any rule that expresses a choice in meaning must be handled in the main realization rules. The present set of rules are relatively minor adjustments to the **form** of the output that must be made in order to ensure that it meets with the conventions of 'good' output text, either spoken or written.

Altogether, these rules have eight sections, so that applying them is not, strictly speaking, a single step. But many of them only apply occasionally, and most involve only minor adjustments. Yet each is vital, if the generator is to produce natural-sounding or natural-looking representations for something approaching the full range of different types of text-sentence. (See Fawcett, 2004b for a detailed account of the final adjustment rules.)

The first six adjustment rules are applied in the order given here, and they are:

1. In spoken and written text: trimming redundant information markers (e.g. reducing two adjacent commas to one).
2. In spoken text: temporary syntax boundary insertion (see below).

3. In spoken text: applying the Tonic+Tone conflation rule (see below).
4. In spoken and written text: minor phonological and graphological adjustment rules (including providing a sentence-initial capital letter when needed, changing "make+ing" to "making", etc).
5. In spoken text: adding the intonation contours for (i) the pretonic and (ii) the tail (the post-Tonic segment) that are indicated by the type of Tonic and Tone.
6. In spoken and written text: stripping the syntax and removing the temporary syntax boundary (see below).[21]

Here we shall focus on the rules that are necessary to adjoin the Tonic and the Tone (both of which are often at this stage still 'parked' at the end of the text-sentence) with the relevant word (i.e. Rules 2, 3 and 6).

11.5.2 In spoken text: inserting a temporary syntax boundary

Rule 2 is only required occasionally, and its purpose is purely pragmatic, i.e. to simplify the operation of the rules. It is only used when a **Contrastive New** is conflated with an element of the clause that is filled by a **unit** (rather than being directly expounded by an item), i.e. when the Tonic is a Type C2.1 Tonic.

The rule first inserts a new element into the structure of the first (and usually only) unit that fills the element with which the CN is conflated. This new element is a **Temporary Starter (TSt)**. Then the rule inserts, as the item that expounds the TSt, a **temporary syntax boundary ("syn|")**. The effect of inserting these temporary additions to the structure is to enable the **Tonic+Tone conflation rule** (to which we come next) to operate on **items** only, i.e. without having to consult the structure of units and elements above the items (words and intonational items). And this makes the rule itself much simpler.

As an example of these temporary additions to the structure, consider the effect on the two nominal groups (ngp) that fill the Agent (Ag) in Figure 11.7.

When these additions have been made to any unit containing a Type C2.1 Tonic, we are ready to apply the Tonic+Tone conflation rule.

This important rule must be applied to every intonation unit, and it has two stages: (i) it joins the **Tone** to its **Tonic** and then (ii) it joins the **Tonic+Tone** to the **word** with which it is to be conflated. These two stages will be described briefly in §§11.5.3 and 11.5.4.

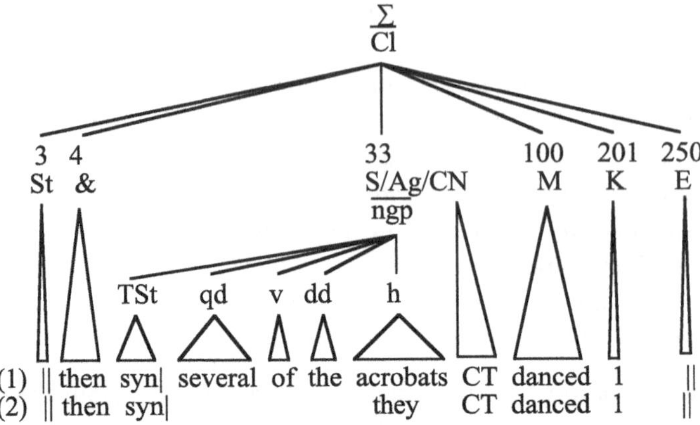

Figure 11.7 A completed clause with a 'contrastively new' element (after inserting a temporary syntax boundary).

11.5.3 In Spoken Text: Stage 1 of the Tonic+Tone conflation rule: Tone to Tonic

In the first stage, the rule simply moves the **Tone** leftwards through the items (assuming a two-dimensional representation of the type used throughout this chapter) until it locates the **Tonic**. The rule then adjoins the Tone to it, e.g. to form "MT1". In most cases the Tonic is immediately to the left of the Tone in the representation on the page, so this is a simple operation. But if the Tonic is a Contrastive Tonic the item is usually much further to the left, and the Tone has to continue inspecting the items to its left until it locates a Tonic, to which it can then be adjoined. The result of this **adjunction** is that the two **intonational items** become one intonational item (just as happens when a suffix such as *ing* is adjoined to *walk,* etc.). So there is no marker of adjunction (as there is for conflation); the two items have been fused into one. Examples of the different types are given below.

We shall refer informally to the new item that is the product of the first stage as the 'Tonic+Tone', since that is the order in which the two items are shown in a representation after being adjoined.

We shall now consider each of the three main types of Tonic.

In a clause that contains a **Mood-bearing Tonic**, the "MT" is immediately to the left of the Tone, and after the Tone has been adjoined to it to create a single intonational item the end of the clause will look like this:

.... MT1 ||

In a clause (or any other unit) that contains an **Unmarked Tonic ("T")** or a **Preceding Tonic ("PT")**, the Tone is similarly adjoined to the "T" or "PT" immediately to its left to form a single item, like this:

.... T2 || or   .... PT2 ||

In a clause (or other unit) that contains a **Contrastive Tonic ("CT")** matters are a little more complicated. A Type C1 Contrastive Tonic is straightforward, because the "CT" is already conflated with the item.

A Type C2.1 "CT" is similarly attached to an element via the CN that it expounds, and the Tonic+Tone conflation rule will attach it to an appropriate item.

A Type C2.2 "CT" will ultimately express its 'contrastive newness' lower in the tree structure as either a Type C1 or a Type C2.1. This will happen when it has been 'copied' down the tree via the realization rules till it reaches the same unit as the word (or morpheme) to which it is to be adjoined (as indicated in the systemic functional logical form input).

We can therefore summarize the structures that contain a Contrastive Tonic and its Tone in two rather (than three) examples (bearing in mind that the unit would not be the topmost unit in the case of a Type C2.2 example):

	Type C1	Type C2.1
place	100	33
element	M/CN	S/Ag/CN
	|	|
item	"kiss/CT1"	"Ivy/CT1"

11.5.4 In Spoken Text: Stage 2 of the Tonic+Tone conflation rule: Tonic+Tone to word

We come now to the second part of the Tonic+Tone conflation rule.

In a clause with a **Mood-bearing Tonic**, the Tonic and its Tone (e.g. "MT1") now move leftwards until they find a word in the intonation unit that can accept a Tonic. However, since most words in English meet this criterion, it is more economical to work from the list of 'inherently weak items', i.e. those that do not accept a Tonic (unless it is a Contrastive

Tonic).[22] These words are commonly thought of as 'grammatical' rather than 'lexical' items, but their key characteristic is that they do not contain an inherently strong syllable, i.e. they do not contain 'word stress'.

Thus, in a clause such as *He still hasn't been noticed by her*, the item "MT1" would move leftwards from its temporary location at the end of the clause to be conflated with the item *noticed* (since both *her* and *by* are inherently weak items), so generating:

|| He still hasn't been noticed/MT1 by her ||.

There are three points to be made. The first is that, in the majority of cases, the movement is, as in the first stage, merely to the item immediately to the left of its current position. But the rule must be expressed in terms that also allow for a longer move, as in cases such as *He STILL hasn't been noticed by her* or when the Tone needs to move further leftwards to join the "CT".

The second point is that, when the intonational item encounters the word with which it will be joined, the 'adjunction' is treated as a type of 'conflation' rather than as a complete 'fusion'. The reason is a pragmatic one: this makes it easier for a program that models the process in a computer to identify the word for search purposes (as is needed for some types of final adjustment. Thus the word is separated from the intonational item "MT1" by a forward slash signifying 'conflation'). So, in a sentence such as *She's arrived*, the relationship between the item "MT1" and the item 'arrived' would be shown like this:

.... arrived/MT1 ||

The situation is similar with a simple **Tonic** ("T") or a **Preceding Tonic** ("PT"). These too move leftwards in the text-sentence, seeking a lexical item with which to be conflated. However, while there can only be one "MT" per sentence (because there can be only one Tone that carries a MOOD meaning), there can be many more than one "T" and "PT", e.g. when there are two or more co-ordinated clauses and/or two or more co-ordinated nominal groups. So this rule must be applied to each intonation unit. However, as with the movement left of a "MT", a "T" or a "PT" can only go as far as the first **intonation unit boundary** that it encounters.[23]

The position is different in the case of a **Contrastive Tonic**. The first difference is that, unlike the cases considered so far, the "CT" is in place already, i.e. it is already conflated with the item that it marks as being 'contrastively new', as in:

|| Ivy did/CT1 kiss Bill ||

The realization in written form would be

Ivy DID kiss Bill.

However, in the case of a Type C2.1 example, the "CT" and its accompanying Tone (so "CT1", "CT2" etc.) usually does have to move leftwards, as it looks for a word with inherent word stress that therefore permits conflation. But it must only go as far as the left syntax boundary of the element with which the CN is conflated, as in the following example.

|| she didn't like syn| the fat/CT1 one ||

Here, the "CT1" began at the end of the clause, because that coincides with the end of the unit that fills the element to which the CN is attached (here, C/Ph/CN, since *the fat one* is the Phenomenon in a Process of 'liking'). Thus the "CT1" has moved leftwards till it found the item *fat* (which has an inherent strong syllable).

But what happens if it doesn't find a word that it is permitted to conflate with, e.g. the spoken version of *Then THEY danced,* as is the case in Example (2) in Figure 11.7? The answer is that the original movement leftwards begins again, but this time without the restriction that the item must not be on the 'inherently weak word list'. The result is that it gets conflated with the immediately preceding item. In the case of Example (2) above, the representation would now be:

|| then syn| they/CT1 danced ||

and finally, after the removal of 'syn|' (see §11.5.5):

|| then they/CT1 danced ||

This concludes the summary of how the Tonic+Tone conflation rule works.

11.5.4.1 A point to note

Perhaps the most intriguing single fact about this rule is that, while both the Tonic and the Tone are likely to have been inserted as elements of the topmost clause (as in the next example), the item with which they are ultimately conflated is very often not one that expounds an element of the topmost clause, but one that expounds an element of a lower unit in the overall tree structure. There is nothing unusual about this, as this very mundane example shows:

|| I told him that I had already eaten my lunch/MT1+ ||

Here the "MT1" is conflated with the item that expounds the head of a nominal group, and this nominal group forms the third layer of structure in this sentence. More specifically, it fills the Complement/Affected of the embedded clause *that I had already eaten my lunch*, and this is in turn the Complement/Phenomenon in the topmost clause, of which *told* is the Main Verb.

11.5.5 In spoken and written text: Stripping away the syntax (and the temporary syntax boundary)

The last major step in generating the intonation or punctuation is to strip away the syntax – in an expanded sense of the term 'syntax' that includes all the elements of structure that are expounded by items of intonation or punctuation. This is also the time when the temporary syntax boundary is removed, having done its work.

After this has been done, all that is left of the generated text-sentence in Figure 11.7 is the string of words and the markers of intonation or punctuation. Thus the output of the sentence whose structure is shown in Figure 11.7 is as in the example below (after applying the final adjustment rules):

|| then several of the acrobats/CT1 danced ||

The last of the 'final adjustment rules' are (i) the addition of appropriate intonational contours on the **pretonic segment** and on the **tail** (anything that comes after the Tonic) and (ii) those adjustments that relate to the sentence's place in the overall structure of the discourse (as outlined in Footnote 21).

After these have done their work, the string of items is ready for the final stage of processing. This takes place in the **speech synthesizer**, and its task is to turn the written representation of the string of items into actual sounds. This complex process will involve detailed phonetic modifications, such as spreading the movement of the Tone throughout the relevant syllable (or syllables).[24]

11.6 Conclusions

11.6.1 Summary: the main concepts introduced in this chapter

Perhaps the best way to summarize this chapter is as in the chart of categories and relationships that are set out in Figure 11.8. It focuses on the concepts that are required to enable this model of how meanings are realized as intonation to work.

There are four sections, each corresponding to one of the four types of **New**, and within each type there are four columns. The first column simply names the categories to which the three concepts to the right belong, and each of the other three columns models a trio of pairs of elements and items, such that the trios are in the relationship to each other that they have before the Tonic+Tone conflation rule applies.

By allowing the repetition of some of the concepts, this summary shows which concepts are used only with one type of 'New' element, and which ones occur with more than one – and sometimes with all four types of 'New'.

MOOD-BEARING NEW (realizes 'new' + MOOD)

Category	Type of **New** and its **Tonic**	Type of **Key** and its **Tones**	**Enders** and **Starters** and their **boundary markers**
element (clause)	MN (Mood-bearing New)	K (Key)	E (Ender)
	expounded by	expounded by	expounded by
item (clause)	"MT" (Mood-bearing Tonic)	"1", "2", "12-", etc (Tones)	"‖" (boundary marker)

UNMARKED NEW (realizes 'new' + INFORMATION STATUS)

Category	Type of **New** and its **Tonic**	Type of **Key** and its **Tones**	**Enders** and **Starters** and their **boundary markers**
element (any unit)	UN (Unmarked New)	K (Key)	E (Ender)
	expounded by	expounded by	expounded by
item (any unit)	"T" (Simple Tonic)	"1", "2", "12-", etc (Tones)	"|" (boundary marker)

PRECEDING NEW (realizes 'new' + INFORMATION STATUS)

Category	Type of **New** and its **Tonic**	Type of **Key** and its **Tones**	**Enders** and **Starters** and their **boundary markers**
element (any unit)	PN (Preceding New)	PK (Preceding Key)	St (Starter)
	expounded by	expounded by	expounded by
item (any unit)	"PT" (Preceding Tonic)	"1", "2", "12-", etc (Tones)	"‖" or "|" (boundary markers)

CONTRASTIVE NEW ('contrastive new' + MOOD or INFORMATION STATUS)

Category	Type of **New** and its **Tonic**	Type of **Key** and its **Tones**	**Enders** and **Starters** and their **boundary markers**
element (any unit)	CN (Contrastive New)	K (Key)	E (Ender)
	expounded by	expounded by	expounded by
item (any unit)	"CT" (Contrastive Tonic)	"1", "2", "12-", etc. (Tones)	"‖"or"|" (boundary markers)

Figure 11.8 A summary of the realizations of the four types of 'Newness' and their associated elements and items.

11.6.2 Some specific innovations in the model described in this chapter

Clearly, the purpose of this chapter has not been to provide a description of intonation in English for use in analysing texts, even though a by-product of this research is a notation for specifying the outputs from the grammar that could be adapted for that application.

The main purpose has been to share with other scholars the insights that we have gained through working on the generation of intonation (and punctuation) in the COMMUNAL Project. We first implemented an 'intermediate' computer model of English intonation (as introduced in Fawcett 1990), and then, in the late 1990s and early 2000s we developed the far more comprehensive model that is described here. The components described here are an integral part of a much more comprehensive version of the GENESYS model for generating syntax, items, intonation and punctuation.

In §11.1.2, I listed five innovations in modelling intonation and punctuation that this work has led to, and in §11.1.4 I showed why the Cardiff Model treats intonation and punctuation as part of the level of **form**, with the role of **segmental phonology** and **orthography** being to **specify** words, not to 'realize' them.

The description of the working model of intonation and punctuation given here illustrates the value of those innovations, and here we shall highlight some of the particularly noteworthy aspects of the model.

First, we have seen the value of having a model in which intonation and punctuation are generated in essentially the same way as syntax, words and morphemes. So we have introduced here, for the first time, a model in which intonation and punctuation are handled in terms of **elements** and the **items** that expound them, just as are the longer-established parts of the lexicogrammar. The result is that the output from the process of generating a text-sentence is a string of items that is made up of both words and either intonational items or items of punctuation.

Second, we have seen how to handle embedded clauses and non-final co-ordinated clauses. A notable feature of this is the neat way in which the new elements of a **Starter**, a **Preceding New** and a **Preceding Key** (together with the intonational items that expound them, e.g. "T", "2" and "|") become parts of the **information unit** that precedes the unit that is currently being generated. The final step in this process is only completed after the application of the **Tonic+Tone conflation rule**, and the representation of the example that we considered in §11.3.8.2, for example, is:

|| her uncle/PT2 | who lives in New Zealand/T2 | is a doctor/MT1 ||

Third, we have seen that the model would be inadequate if we did not recognize the need to have the two elements of (i) a MN or an UN and (ii) a K in the clause, each with its own exponent. In the early version of GENESYS described in Fawcett 1990 the two functions were not distinguished, and that model only worked with the more limited coverage of intonation in that version. The reason why we need both is, as we have seen, that the exponent of K (e.g. a Tone 1) is not necessarily tied to the exponent of the MN (i.e. "MT"). Once a full model of 'contrastive newness' is built into the grammar, so that a "CT" can be conflated with any word in the text-sentence, there will not necessarily be a "MT" in the clause, and the Tone that would in the typical case have been adjoined to the "MT" will instead be adjoined to a "CT". The same principle applies to the UN and its following K; if there is a CN, and so a "CT" instead of a "T", the Tone will in due course be adjoined to the "CT".[25]

A fourth set of new concepts is related to this: it is the three ways in which 'contrastive newness' manifests itself. As we saw in §§11.3.2.3 and 11.3.3.4:

1. the Contrastive New (CN) may be attached to an element of the clause which is directly expounded by an item, as when 'contrastive newness on polarity' is realized in the Operator (e.g. 'She DOES love him'); or
2. the CN may be attached to a Participant Role (such as Agent) or a Circumstantial Role (such as Place) taken as a whole, which may consist of many words (none of which will have been generated at the time when the "CT" itself must be generated); or
3. it may be known from the start that the 'contrastive newness' is to be attached to an element of a unit within the clause, as in *Give the ball to the RED team, not the BLUE one.*

I could describe other advances in modelling intonation and punctuation that we have made during the development of this model, but those mentioned so far are sufficient to demonstrate the following important fact: that the demands of building an explicit model for the generation of text-sentences, which in some parts necessarily becomes quite intricate, may well force one to think again (and often again and yet again!) about some basic principle of the organization of the model. And this sometimes leads the investigator to question assumptions that had earlier been taken as axiomatic. For example, this chapter has asked: Is a language tri-stratal, with 'form' realizing 'meaning' and 'phonology' 'realizing' form? Or does intonation realize meaning directly, so suggesting that segmental phonology **specifies** words rather than realizing them? A responsible scientist of language should always be ready to explore alternative ways of modelling the data, as we have here. This is precisely the process that we should expect in the scientific study of any phenomenon.

There has been a second and very different type of challenge in developing an overall model for generating the intonation and punctuation of English: that of how to hold the whole complicated architecture of this area of the grammar in mind for a considerable period of time, while working out how to relate the various parts to each other in the most functionally logical manner – and while remembering all the time the still wider framework of the overall model into which these particular components have to fit. This is where thinking in terms of building a computer model of the phenomenon helps; computers have wonderful memories and abilities to model relationships!

11.6.3 The need for more work on explicit SFL models of intonation and punctuation

Our work on these major aspects of the GENESYS generator suggests that it is time that models of intonation, like models of the lexicogrammar as a whole, should move forward in two dimensions: (i) beyond 'toy' grammars (with their highly selective coverage), and (ii) beyond 'partial' grammars, (i.e. grammars which deal with only one component at a time, such as a 'grammar of intonation' might claim to be).

Although the above two 'restricted' types of grammar may have their part to play in exploring, developing and testing ideas about how best to model the full complexity of language, our experience in the COMMUNAL Project has been that it is only (i) when one tackles something approaching the full range of the phenomena of an area of language, such as the full intonation system of English, and (ii) when one does so in relation to all the other components of a model of language and its use (e.g. as outlined in Fawcett, forthcoming 2015) that we shall find genuinely adequate solutions to the many challenges presented by natural languages to the scientists whose task it is to investigate the phenomenon that is for many researchers the most fascinating of all: human language.

This chapter, then, reports the findings of a research project that seeks to bring together two of the most promising approaches to discovering the nature of language available to us in the twenty-first century: (i) the use of Systemic Functional Grammar, in which the system networks are seen as choices between the meanings of the language, and (ii) the formalization of our models to the point where they can be tested through implementing them in the computer.

This chapter has illustrated (i) the type of system networks that are needed, (ii) the type of realization rules that are needed (some completely explicitly, though most through relatively informal verbal descriptions), and (iii) the type of representation of the outputs for which we need to aim, as an input to a speech synthesizer. The part of the chapter that is presented in the fullest detail is the part that identifies the concepts that are required to enable the realization rules to function for any grammar of intonation and punctuation that can cover the range of phenomena for which the present model provides. But this model is still far from the state when it cannot be improved, and I look forward to finding a scholar or scholars who will carry this work forward to the next stage.

Acknowledgements

The COMMUNAL Project was supported by grants from the Speech Research Unit at DRA Malvern for over ten years, as part of assignment no. ASO4BP44 on Spoken Language Understanding and Dialogue (SLUD); by ICL and Longman in Phase 1; and throughout by Cardiff University. I thank all these institutions for their invaluable support for this 'blue sky' research.

I would also like to express my thanks to the three friends and colleagues to whom I am most indebted in developing the ideas expressed in this chapter. The first is Michael Halliday, the 'father' of systemic functional linguistics and the linguist to whom I, like many others, owe the basic concepts of my current model of language. The second major debt is to Gordon Tucker, who has worked closely with me for many years in (i) developing the version of systemic functional grammar (SFG) that has come to be known as the Cardiff Grammar, and (ii) in implementing it in the COMMUNAL computer model of language. And, with respect to the body of research described here, there is a third and equally great debt: to Paul Tench, for his insightful modifications of and extensions to Halliday's description of English intonation (Tench 1996a, 1996b).

Finally, I thank the editors of this volume, Wendy Bowcher and Brad Smith, for their tremendous work on suggesting ways to cut down what was originally a monograph-length work to its present length. It is still a very long chapter. Our excuse is that this topic is inherently a large one, and the point of the paper – which is to demonstrate that it is possible to construct a generative systemic functional grammar of intonation and punctuation for English – would be lost if we were not to include a reasonably full description of how that has been done.

Notes

1. There is, however, a need for certain low-level adjustments at the final stage of generation, such as the absorption of any weak syllables at the start of an intonation unit into the 'tail' of the previous one. But the need for such 'final adjustment rules' does not affect the viability of the principles of the model described here.
2. Here I am using the traditional term for this component of language, because it is probably the most widely recognized. But its use should not be taken as implying a position in the debate about the relative strengths of the traditional approach to 'word phonology' and Firthian 'prosodic analysis' – or any other model. My purpose is solely to identify an area of study in linguistics.
3. Throughout this chapter, I shall take for granted a minimal familiarity with the standard units and elements of English syntax in a SFL approach, but I shall try to add an explanatory note on any additional terms derived from the Cardiff Grammar.
4. The final adjustment rules (see §11.5) contain a rule whose function is to 'tidy up' any left-over cases in which two identical items of intonation or punctuation occur together. This solution to the problem has the advantage of using an existing rule rather than creating a new rule for this particular case, and from this viewpoint the present solution is the more economical one. It avoids the need to have a new type of realization rule that must only be invoked for the first sentence of a text (or, more specifically, a turn in the discourse structure).
5. The only way in which a system of 'TONALITY' could be made relevant to the generation of texts would be if we were operating with a model in which we assumed (i) that the Performer (P) first generated a full text-sentence in her/his mind (which could be a page or more in length when transcribed); (ii) that P looked at it from the viewpoint of the Addressee (A) and then decided that it was too long a chunk of information for A to process comfortably as one unit; and (iii) that P then set to work on the task of cutting it up into smaller information units. This is clearly unrealistic!
6. The 'string of words' does in fact have a role in a full model of language. It is as an input to the **parser**, which is the component which carries out the first major step in the long and complex process of understanding. And

that is a very different matter. See Fawcett (1994) for a discussion of the differences between the two processes of generation and understanding.

7. A subsidiary point that is worth noting is that, in these relatively delicate systems, little use is made of the names of systems. In part this is because there is not one system that offers the choice between assigning a separate information unit and not doing so. As we have seen, some separate information units are assigned as the result of a choice in the PROMINENCE system above, and others are dictated by the choice in similar systems elsewhere in the network.

8. Here, however, I can simply say that in (i) a simplex 'topmost' clause or (ii) the final one of a string of two or more co-ordinated 'topmost' clauses, the realization of [no contrastive newness within situation] is the insertion of the element Mood-bearing New (MN), this being expounded by a Mood-bearing Tonic ("MT"). This realization statement is in Rule 1.1 of GENESYS. For other clauses the realization is typically – but not necessarily – the insertion of an Unmarked New (UN), this being expounded by a simple Tonic. For a non-final co-ordinated clause (whether independent or dependent) it is Rule 19.8 that inserts it (and the other elements and items that are the representations of intonation), and for a 'simplex' or 'final co-ordinated dependent' clause it is Rule 99.

9. We shall refer to unembedded clauses that fill the element 'sentence' (Σ) as 'topmost' clauses; this is in contrast with the term 'matrix clause', which is a clause that contains an embedded clause but which is not necessarily a 'topmost' clause. In the model assumed here, a topmost simplex clause may have ellipted elements, and so appear to consist merely of, say, a nominal group. Such short forms may become established conventions, as in the labels on doors. But in its logical form such a form is necessarily a 'proposition' (or, in systemic functional logical form, an event); for example, *EXIT* is an ellipted form of *This is an exit*.

10. This choice in 'information focus' shouldn't be confused with the various systems that occur at various points elsewhere in the grammar, which merely present a choice between making it LIKELY that an element will be marked as 'new' in this way and not doing so. Such features typically have the form [X potentially new], an example being [time position potentially new]. Notice that the element is only POTENTIALLY new; it may be that some other factor will prevent it from receiving the Mood-bearing New (MN), and so the unmarked Tonic (e.g. the addition of a final Adjunct after the element).

11. In the early model of intonation described in Fawcett 1990 and in other descriptions of the process of generation such as Fawcett *et al.* 1993, the only aspects of the meaning that the Performer may present as 'contrastively new' are (i) the 'Polarity' and (ii) the 'Process' (as in *She DID kiss him* and *She didn't KISS him*). With these severe restrictions, it was relatively simple to model contrastive newness. But expanding the grammar to provide for the fact that a CN can occur in any unit has been one of the major challenges

in extending the model towards the goal of comprehensiveness, and it has necessarily introduced considerable additional complexity.

12. Until we have developed the model of intonation to the point where it will be easily interpretable, we shall only use examples that are expressed in terms of the conventions of the written mode, as in the above case.

13. This partial similarity at the level of form has led some scholars, including Halliday and Tench, to treat both as cases of 'unmarked' or 'neutral tonicity' (e.g. in the summary diagram in Tench, 1996a: 152). But that gives too much weight to the level of form. In functional terms, (1) is more like (2) and (3) than it is like (4).

14. We should note that this is the conflation of two items – not of two elements, as occurs frequently in the realizations in syntax. The reason for treating the Tonics as items is to enable them to be treated like other items for 'search' purposes, at a later stage in the process of generation.

15. One alternative to what is proposed here would be to include in the grammar a specific Place, with its own number, for every element that can be made 'contrastive' (which is most of them). But to do this would virtually double the number of elements in each unit for what is a relatively unusual occurrence (perhaps 1–2% of clauses). A slightly preferable alternative would be for the program to be given the power to add a 'supplementary element' (such as '33.1' after '33') after any Place (just as we can add a new realization rule by adding a new digit). This would enable the CN to occur at a Place in the unit immediately after the Main Verb or the Agent (or whatever element it is). This would in turn allow the CN to be expounded by an unattached item, as if it was a separate element. But this would have the serious drawback that we would lose the representation of the fact that the Performer intends the element as a whole to be regarded as contrastively new (and not just the preceding word). The representation shown here seems to provide the clearest picture of the relationship.

16. It would add enormously to the complexity of the procedure if it had to check, for every item that it encountered, to see if it was the initial element of the relevant unit. Indeed, we would have to equip it with a search procedure that would look further up the tree structure to discover what element had originally been marked as 'contrastively new'. There are several possible solutions to the challenge of writing a computer program to model the fact that the grammar must be able to recognize the leftmost item with which the "CT" can be conflated, and we have settled on one that will enable the grammar to perform this procedure correctly, even if the syntax had been stripped away already. Thus there is a small program that consults the tree structure and then inserts into the string of items a new item, i.e. 'syn|' (meaning 'syntactic boundary') at the appropriate place (see Figure 11.7). Finally, I should point out that there is provision in the Tonic+Tone conflation rule for the Tonic+Tone to settle on an inherently weak item when there is no alternative, as in the present case.

17. The context of situation for this sentence is that K is telling her mother about a visit to a theatre to see a performance that mixed circus and dance. Here is the discourse context (with K speaking): || the clowns did all sorts of clever tricks/T2 | and then they did a funny sort of dance/MT1 || then a whole team of acrobats/T2 came on | and did some really cool balancing/ MT1 acts || then several of the acrobats/CT1 danced ||.

18. Our investigations in the COMMUNAL Project of alternative approaches to this matter have shown that, if we did not introduce the Tonic as a separate element, there would be very complex realization rules with very complex conditions. It is a matter of balancing complexity within a rule (which brings with it the danger of making mistakes) against complexity in another part of the model, and only experience can give one a sense of how to make the best decision in these matters.

19. In one sense, then, the intonational aspects of Steps 6 and 7 follow automatically from Step 1. But we treat them here as separate steps, because it is helpful to maintain the parallels between the generation of intonation and punctuation as far as it is logical to do so, and the exponents of the Ender in a written text do not follow automatically from Step 1.

20. This is in contrast with a final Adjunct that gives 'supplementary' information and so has a separate intonation unit, as in || he poured himself some water MT1 | feeling thirsty T1 ||.

21. In addition, however, we need to provide for the following two types of adjustment to a spoken text (which we have not yet implemented in the computer program, however). We adjust the speed of delivery where necessary, to make the gaps between the stressed syllables (which are derived from the inherent word stress of the items) roughly equal, so that the regular beat of the strong syllables approximates to the norm for English (English being a 'stress-timed' language). We also adjust the pitch relative to the place of the text-sentence in the discourse, and mark the last information unit in a turn by a greater fall, so signalling willingness to cede the floor. (Tench 1996a: 23–6, 129).

22. In the GENESYS sentence generator the list of 'inherently weak items' is located in the document for the phonological rules.

23. In the case of certain simple Tonics, such as those found in a postal address, the realization rule places them directly after the items with which they are to be conflated. But such cases do not need to be treated as exceptions, because when they try to move leftwards they cannot, since the item after which they occur is not on the list of inherently weak items (e.g. a word such as 'Road' in a postal address).

24. I should point out that the form of representation used here to indicate intonation was approved as a suitable input to a speech synthesizer by the researchers at the Speech Research Unit at what was then known as DRA Malvern (now privatized as QinetiQ), who were the major sponsors of the project.

25. There is a further major reason why we cannot simply treat all types of New and all types of Tonic in the same way, though it has not been the focus of attention in this chapter. It is that we need to be able to generate different **pretonic segments** and different **tails** (i.e. 'post-tonic segments') for each type. These two tasks are carried out in the final adjustment rules. If the Tonics are not labelled differently, i.e. as "CT" rather than "MT", the computer program will not know when to generate each of the various types.

References

Fawcett, R. P. (1980) *Cognitive Linguistics and Social Interaction: Towards an Integrated Model of a Systemic Functional Grammar and the Other Components of a Communicating Mind.* Heidelberg: Julius Groos.

Fawcett, R. P. (1983) Language as a semiological system: a re-interpretation of Saussure. Invited lecture to the linguistics association of Canada and the United States 1982. In J. Morreall (ed.) *The Ninth LACUS Forum 1982* 59–125. Columbia, SC: Hornbeam Press.

Fawcett, R. P. (1987) The form of a minimal procedural grammar, i.e. a grammar for natural language interaction with a computer. In I. Fleming (ed.) *The Thirteenth LACUS Forum 1986* 381–93. Columbia, SC: Hornbeam Press.

Fawcett, R. P. (1990) The computer generation of speech with semantically and discoursally motivated intonation. In *Proceedings of 5th International Workshop on Natural Language Generation* 164–73. Pittsburgh, PA: University of Pittsburgh.

Fawcett, R. P. (1994) A generationist approach to grammar reversibility in natural language processing. In T. Strzalkowski (ed.) *Reversible Grammar in Natural Language Generation* 365–413. Dordrecht: Kluwer.

Fawcett, R. P. (2004a) *Realizing Meaning in Intonation and Punctuation in English: The GENESYS Model* (COMMUNAL Working Papers no. 19). Cardiff: Computational Linguistics Unit, Cardiff University.

Fawcett, R. P. (2004b) *The Final Adjustment Rules for the Full GENESYS Grammar* (COMMUNAL Working Papers no. 20). Cardiff: Computational Linguistics Unit, Cardiff University.

Fawcett, R. P. (2008) *Invitation to Systemic Functional Linguistics through the Cardiff Grammar: an extension and simplification of Halliday's Systemic Functional Grammar* (3rd edition). London: Equinox.

Fawcett, R. P. (2011a) Problems and Solutions in Identifying Processes and Participant Roles in Discourse Analysis, Part 1: Introduction to a Systematic Procedure for Identifying Processes and Participant Roles. *Annual Review of Functional Linguistics* 3: 34–87.

Fawcett, R. P. (2011b) A semantic system network for MOOD in English (and some complementary system networks). Available from fawcett@cardiff.ac.uk.

Fawcett, R. P. (forthcoming 2015) *An Integrative Architecture of Language and its Use for Systemic Functional Linguistics and Other Theories of Language.* London: Equinox.

Fawcett, R. P., Tucker, G. H. and Lin, Y. Q. (1993) How a systemic functional grammar works: the role of realization in realization. In H. Horacek and M. Zock (eds) *New Concepts in Natural Language Generation* 114–86. London: Pinter.

Halliday, M. A. K. (1967) *Intonation and Grammar in British English.* The Hague: Mouton.

Halliday, M. A. K. (1970) *A Course in Spoken English: Intonation.* Oxford: Oxford University Press.

Halliday, M. A. K. (1985) *An Introduction to Functional Grammar.* London: Arnold.

Halliday, M. A. K. (1994) *An Introduction to Functional Grammar* (2nd edition). London: Arnold.

Halliday, M. A. K. and Matthiessen, C. M. I. M. (2004) *An Introduction to Functional Grammar* (3rd edition). London: Arnold.

Tench, P. (1976) Double ranks in a phonological hierarchy. *Journal of Linguistics* 12: 1–20.

Tench, P. (1996a) *The Intonation Systems of English.* London: Cassell.

Tench, P. (1996b) The fall and rise of the level tone in English. *Functions of Language* 4 (1): 1–22.

Tench, P. and Fawcett, R. P. (1988) *Specification of Intonation for Prototype Generator 2* (COMMUNAL Report no. 6). Cardiff: Computational Linguistics Unit, Cardiff University.

Part E

Interacting with Systemic Phonology

12 Locating the limerick 'Wall Street Irene' and the sonnet 'On his blindness' in the semiotic space between the body as signal generator/receiver and the body as social interactant

William S. Greaves[a]

12.1 Introduction

This chapter defines the semogenic (meaning-making) space between the body as ears and tongue, which handle sound, and as hands and feet, which carry out social activities such as recreational dancing or, more technically, performing a medical procedure on a patient. It introduces Praat software for dealing with sound, discusses the particular Praat TextGrids used in this literary/linguistic analysis, and then explains rhythm of discourse, as these are used to examine the sound and wording of very different literary performances: readings of the limerick 'Wall Street Irene', and of John Milton's sonnet 'On his blindness'. These performances can be heard on the sound files in the electronic supplementary material accompanying this chapter, available for download at [www.equinoxpub.com/systemic-phonology-files].

a **William Southworth Greaves** is Emeritus Professor in the Graduate Programme in English in the Department of English at Glendon College, York University, Toronto, Canada. His research interests include language education, language and primates, and English intonation. He has authored and edited 15 books and manuscripts, including the co-edited volume (with James Benson) *Functional Dimensions of Ape-Human Discourse* (Equinox) and the co-authored volume (with M. A. K. Halliday) *Intonation in the Grammar of English* (Equinox). He has played an active role in the International Systemic Functional Linguistics Association, and in 1982 co-convened in Canada the 9th International Systemic Congress, the first held outside of the UK. He regularly delivers seminars and workshops on English intonation within the systemic functional framework to international audiences.

12.2 Technical matters

This chapter is not written to be read. It is intended to be read and heard. The availability of electronic supplementary material for this chapter makes it possible to demonstrate how we are using Praat to show how language spans the space between the physical sound of a poem being spoken and the cultural context providing the poem's genre. (For a discussion of whether genre constitutes a distinct stratum, see Martin, 1992: 546ff.)

If you have not already done so, please download the files from [www.equinoxpub.com/systemic-phonology-files] and have the files ready to use in order to enjoy the spoken mode of our language while you read about its systems. First, to be sure your sound system is working:

Play 'Sound file 1'

This should only require you to double-click on the file of that name. You should hear a reading of John Milton's 'On his blindness'. If nothing happens, you will need to be sure that your computer has a sound card, that your earphones or speakers are properly connected to your computer, and that the necessary software is functioning. (To stop the sound from playing, press the 'Esc' button.)

This chapter assumes that you are reading and listening from the accompanying sound files, and also invites you to augment your reading by using Praat yourself. Technical details for using Praat are found in the Appendix.

12.3 Situating language

Semogenic space is discussed first in terms of its two physical boundaries: the substances our own bodies interact with in projecting a message (sound, marks and other media) and the 'outside' bodies we encounter in social interaction. The dimensions of the space – context (field, tenor and mode), semantics, lexicogrammar, phonology and phonetics – are familiar from works by Halliday and others working within the systemic functional tradition (e.g. Halliday, 1978; Martin, 1992; Tench, 1996; Halliday and Matthiessen, 2004; Thompson, 2004; Halliday and Greaves, 2008). Just as the visual space of art is understood through the interplay of reading theory and visiting galleries, so our understanding of semantic space grows through encounters with instances of text. There are, of course, a seemingly infinite number of instances. Even given the constraints here – monologic performances of short English poems – the range is extraordinary, encompassing every past such utterance and expanding with every new speaking of a sonnet or other short form. So like any tour of an art gallery, this exploration of semantic space deals with a selection: vocal performances of a particular seventeenth-century object and of a particular twentieth-century object. Understanding the sound of these recitations is handled by direct presentation, using the sound files and Praat TextGrids in the electronic supplementary material, which can be more fully explored with the aid of the Appendix.

Here is a little sketch of a human being:

Humans relate to language in two ways. First, we 'do' language in an eco-social environment (the physical, biological and cultural context of language):

Person as Social Being

A person is a social body, interacting with countless other social bodies: a biological organism enmeshed with countless other biological organisms in various cultures in a material world. Second, at the same time, a person is a 'transmitting/receiving' body (the neuro-physiological environment of speech). We hear, read or (with Braille) feel expressed language:

Person as Signal Receiver

or we express language by speaking, signing or writing it:

Person as Signal Generator

It is never possible to choose between doing language in an eco-social environment *or* transmitting/receiving language in a neuro-physiological environment; we inevitably and inextricably do both:

The languaging person: at the same time social being and signal sender/receiver

So that is where language is located.

In general terms, language potential consists of four different kinds of choice available to us: meaning choices, wording choices, sounding choices and sound choices:

The Choices Language Offers

SEMANTICS

LEXICOGRAMMAR

PHONOLOGY

PHONETICS

But this chapter is concerned with English literary instances, so the tiny figures above represent specific English-speaking cultures (seventeenth-century England and twentieth-century North America). A seventeenth-century English discussion about man's relationship to other animals would be framed in terms of theology; a twentieth-century discussion of the same topic would be highly likely to involve Darwinian evolutionary theory – even if only to argue against it.

12.4 Discourse: the social aspect

Social behaviour involving language is discourse. Through the symbolic power of language we shape our social world by the meanings we exchange with each other. We construe our 'fields of discourse', our goal-directed social actions, through our choices among the categories and relations of ideational semantics; we enact our 'tenors of discourse', our relations with our addressees and our own emotional states, through our choices in interpersonal semantic systems; and we enable our 'text' to emerge by weaving together these ideational and interpersonal meanings into a coherent and relevant message. We can behave socially precisely because we have, through our discourse, created a social context which we share (to a greater or lesser degree) in three dimensions: field, tenor and mode.

CONTEXT

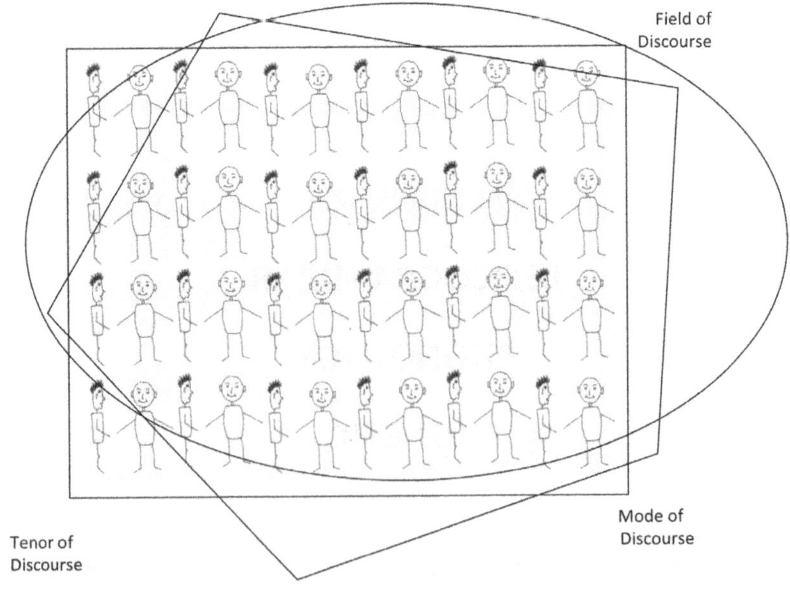

Without such a symbolically created context we would have much less power over the material world we live in. 'Locating' these two poems in semantic space means discussing choices made in all strata. One could begin with any stratum, say phonetics, but context seems a more natural entry point.

Our **fields of discourse** (making meaning to 'do', to reach purposeful goals, e.g. 'doing' engineering) are realized in experiential and logical meanings (e.g. 'the stress level in the beam is ...'), and these meanings allow us to live, for example, in apartment buildings with pre-stressed concrete beams, rather than in caves. These are countless fields because human beings cooperate to achieve innumerable ends: shopping, philosophizing, cooking, babysitting, dating, worshipping, farming, engineering, doing linguistics, yachting, teaching and so on. And these can be thought about in different degrees of generality: broadly, for example, doing science as opposed to arts, or doing physics as opposed to chemistry; or very delicately indeed with very narrow specifications such as, for example, 'the field of radiometric and photometric calibrations'. Such fields are not static: 'Improved detector technology in the past decade, for example, has opened a new era in this field', announces *NIST Technical Note 1438*. Another example of narrow specification can be seen in the following nominal group: 'optical radiation measurement with selected detectors and matched electronic circuits between 200 nm and 20 pm'. A physical act of using an instrument would congruently come into language as a verb, say 'measuring', but here it has come into language as a thing 'measurement' which has been extensively modified and qualified to enable the highly precise meaning necessary to proceed in this field. The 'new era in this field' could not have opened without the ability to create such new meanings. And at such delicacy the English nominal group is stretched to quite wonderful lengths in order to construe the meanings needed. Note, for example, the modification of 'detectors' in 'large area thermal, pyroelectric, photoconductive (PC), and photovoltaic (PV) detectors'. (For a discussion of nominal group structure, see Halliday and Matthiessen, 2004: 312; and for nominalization see Eggins, 1994: 57)

Our **tenors of discourse** (making meaning to 'enact' social relations and to relate to others in giving or receiving either goods and services or information) are realized in interpersonal meanings, for example, a command such as: 'get ready for the inspection tomorrow'. These meanings allow us to interact in ways vastly more complex than even such highly social animals as wolves or elephants. Sometimes we state these relationships quite openly: 'I am the expert'. 'You bore me'. 'Remember, I am your teacher'. 'I am really excited about this topic'. 'I don't believe we've been introduced'.

And our **modes of discourse** (making meaning to 'textualize', to weave field and tenor in the production of a message) are realized in textual meanings, and through lexicogrammatical systems such as Theme, which is defined as the departure point of the message, underlined in this example: <u>Tomorrow</u>, we are having an inspection', which is about 'tomorrow', as opposed to 'We are having an inspection tomorrow', which is about 'we'. In both cases, of course, the speaker and audience are the ones 'having an inspection', and it will take place the day following the speech act. There is no difference in the 'facts', but as statements the change in Theme makes them quite different. (For a discussion of Theme see Thompson, 2004: 141). Creating text allows us to transcend the barrier of time, in the sense of making messages today which can be understood by others in the future. It can also transcend the barriers of space by sending messages which can be understood far from our personal 'here'. Text is created in countless familiar modes which help us to get going when we talk or write, or 'tune in' as we listen or read: lab reports, for example, or exams, recipes and telephone surveys. These familiar text types which make the reader and audience feel 'at home' also include literary genres such as epic, lyric, farce, fable, ode, sonnet and limerick.

A genre is an established way of representing the world to an audience. It weaves Field of Discourse and Tenor of Discourse into a familiar (and therefore processable) form of message. Say 'Once upon a time ...' to a sleepy child at bedtime, and you are off and running in the creation of a bedtime story. But as well as enabling, genres restrict the range of your meaning. Your bedtime story is highly unlikely to contain a nominal group such as 'RTM processable, high temperature (Tg > 600°F), low toxicity matrix resin system'. If it did, it might well put your child to sleep, but not with the good will you intended.

12.5 Using Praat to explore the meaning choices

You can hear the poems we are exploring by simply clicking on the sound files as described in this chapter [go to: www.equinoxpub.com/systemic-phonology-files]. But you will be able to explore the poems much more satisfactorily by using Praat, and the TextGrids contain much more detail than can be included in the body of this chapter (see the Appendix).

Because Praat always presents the physics (soundwaves and spectrograms) at the top of a TextGrid, the ordering of our tiers of analysis (phonetics, phonology, lexicogrammar, semantics, context) will seem upside down to those familiar with, for example Halliday and Matthiessen (2004: 24–5). Phonetic analysis is at the top because it is closest to the physical sound, while contextual analysis is at the bottom because it is closest to the social behaviour of humans. Here is an image of a Praat TextGrid with four tiers: phonology-tone units, lexicogrammar-word, lexicogrammar-clause and context-field.

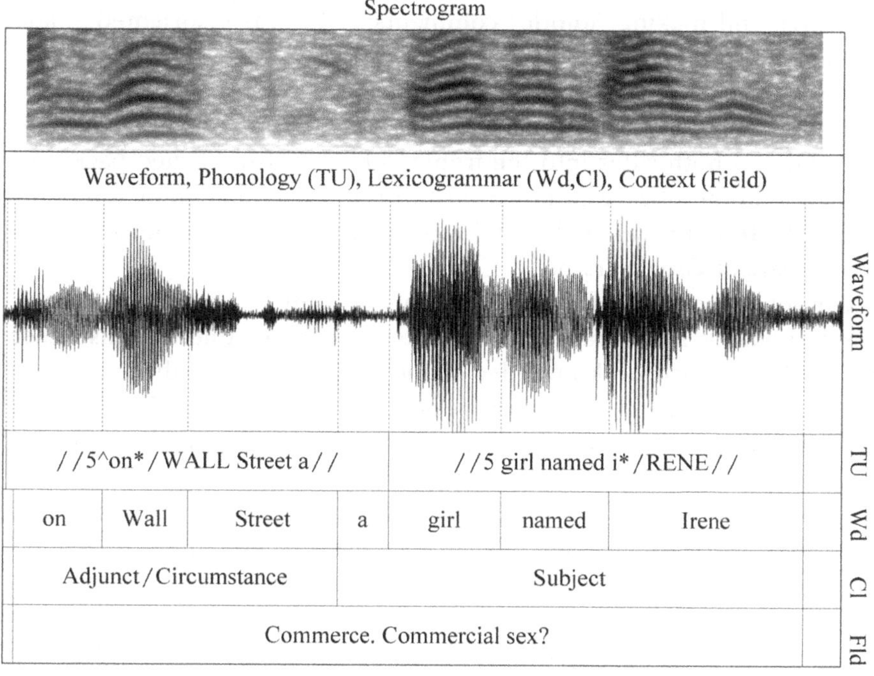

Click on the sound file to hear the line.

Play 'Sound file 2'

12.6 Rhythm

The limerick is a very recognizable component of our eco-social environment. But how do we recognize it? The answer, as with all genres, is spread right through the language strata, but a good way of handling the discussion is to skip directly to the other aspect of the body which frames language: the neuro-physiological environment of speech.

Oliver Sacks, in *An Anthropologist on Mars* (1996), gives an interesting example in the case of 'Greg', a young man who had left his family to join a religious group: 'Although Greg's parents did not have any direct communication from him, they did get occasional reports from the temple – reports filled, increasingly, with accounts of his "spiritual progress," his "enlightenment"' (Sacks, 1996: 44–5). But when Greg's parents visited him after four years 'their lean, hairy son had become fat and hairless; he wore a continual "stupid" smile ... he kept bursting into bits of song and verse and making "idiotic" comments ... he was disoriented – and he was totally blind' (*ibid.*). The cause of Greg's change was not spiritual, but purely physical. Greg had developed 'an enormous midline tumor, destroying the pituitary gland and the adjacent optic chiasm and tracts and extending on both sides into the frontal lobes. It also reached backward to the temporal lobes, and downward to the diencephalon, or forebrain' (*ibid.*) The tumour was benign and was removed, but it had incapacitated a huge part of Greg's brain.

One of the effects of the removal of the tumour was a spectacular loss of memory. For instance, five minutes after being told that his father had died, Greg had no knowledge of the event. However, there was one exception to this loss of memory, related directly to genre. Greg had an excellent memory for one part of his former eco-social environment; he could remember songs from the 1960s. He could not remember songs later than that, but he was still attuned to that particular genre. He 'was able to learn new songs easily, despite his difficulty in retaining any "facts." It seemed as if wholly different kinds – and mechanisms – of memory might be involved' (*ibid.*: 65–6). Rhythm seems to have been an important factor, because 'Greg was also able to pick up limericks and jingles with ease (and had indeed picked up hundreds of these from the radio and television that were always on in the ward)' (*ibid.*: 66).

Sacks illustrates this with a story about how he told Greg the rhyme:

> Hush-a-bye baby,
> Hush quite a lot,
> Bad babies get rabies
> And have to be shot.

Sacks reports how Greg immediately and flawlessly repeated the rhyme, and laughed at it. Greg then compared it with 'something gruesome, like Edgar Allen Poe' (*ibid.*: 66) and asked Sacks whether he had made it up. Sacks then goes on to say that 'two minutes later he could not recall it, until I reminded him of the underlying rhythm. With a few more repetitions, he learned it without cuing and thereafter recited it whenever he met me' (*ibid.*: 66).

Rhythm was such a strong component of Greg's being that it survived the damage caused by his tumour. Moving the body in response to rhythm, as in dancing, is an important element in our physical makeup. What follows is a little exercise in using your body to feel more explicitly the rhythmic pattern inherent in the limerick genre.

12.7 Rhythm in the limerick 'Wall Street Irene'

Literature plays a big role in creating and maintaining cultures, and the limerick as a genre exploits sexual themes and points of view for humorous purposes. Cultures (regional and temporal) differ greatly in the way they handle discourse involving sex. John Donne, for example, was almost a contemporary of Milton's, and his poem 'Batter my heart' weaves together the explicit sexual themes that we find in the limerick 'Wall Street Irene' with the intense personal religious themes that are expressed in Milton's 'On his blindness', in a way many twenty-first-century readers would find rather strange and difficult to understand.

We'll start discussion with the limerick, exploring its powerful rhythm, the 'wedge', which in Greg's case eased meanings into his consciousness which he would otherwise be unable to retain. Here is the actor Sam Neill performing the limerick.[1]

Play 'Sound file 3'

In the following transcriptions foot boundaries are shown by a single slash and tone unit boundaries by a double slash; tonic syllables are upper case and are preceded by an asterisk, and silent Ictus is shown as usual by a caret.

> // ∧ on */ WALL street a // girl named i*/RENE //
> // ∧ made an / offering / somewhat ob*/SCENE //
> // ∧ she / stripped herself */ BARE /
> // ∧ and / offered a */ SHARE /
> // ∧ to / merrill lynch */ PIERCE // fenner and */ BEAN //

In English the foot is a unit of rhythm: it takes place in time and has a two part structure. The first element is Ictus, realized by a 'salient' syllable, which stands out because of one or more of the features, loudness, length and pitch change. This is followed by Remiss, realized by any number of syllables, including zero, which are not salient. If you swing your arm like a pendulum, and snap your fingers at the start of the swing, you will be imitating the structure of a foot. The snap represents the Ictus and the rest of the swing the Remiss. Try it.

SNAP! and the swing continues

To feel the rhythm your pendulum-arm is establishing, do this six times:

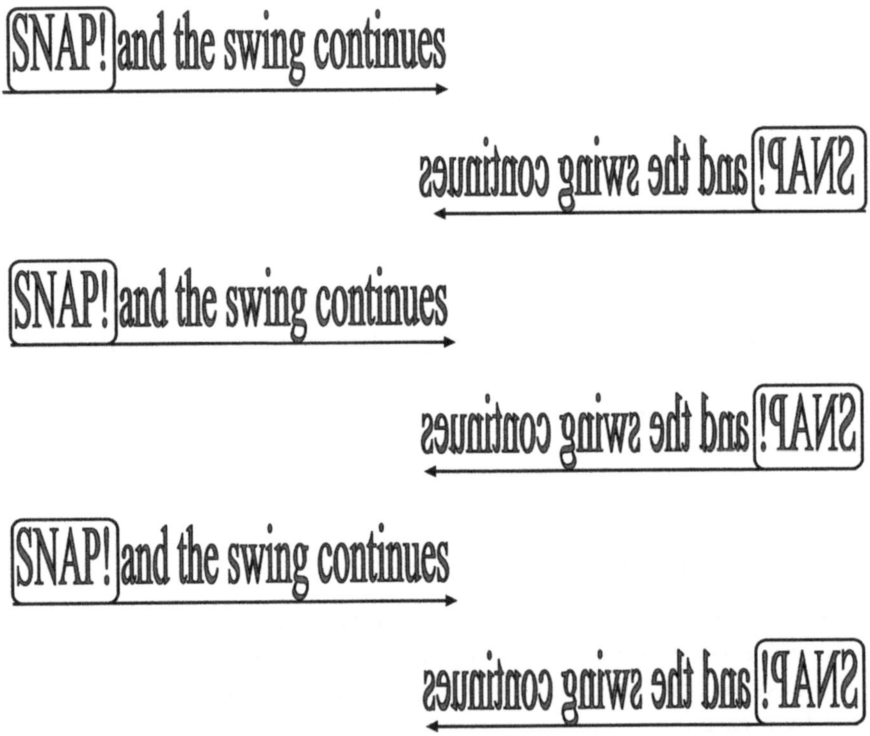

SNAP! and the swing continues

SNAP! and the swing continues

SNAP! and the swing continues

SNAP! and the swing continues

SNAP! and the swing continues

SNAP! and the swing continues

Now begin adding speech sounds, feet from the limerick, starting with the second foot. Say

/WALL street a

out loud. Snap while you say 'WALL' and let the two syllables 'street a' tag along after while you finish the swing.

Play 'Sound file 4'

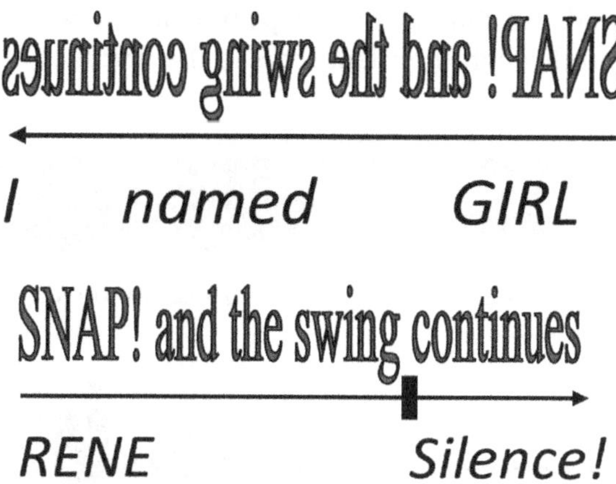

Do this several times. You need to get the feel of co-ordinating the snap with saying the salient syllable /**WALL**.

Now add the next foot. Start with /**WALL street a** and without breaking the rhythm of your arm, flow into /**girl named i**

Play 'Sound file 5'

With the next foot, concentrate on the silence which follows /RENE. The silence may be quite short, as the syllable /RENE will stretch out to accommodate the rhythm.

Play 'Sound file 6'

Finally, we turn to the **first** foot, / ʌ **on** /. It has been held until now because this foot presents a special difficulty. The Ictus is silent, represented in print by a foot boundary / followed by the silent Ictus mark ʌ.

Play 'Sound file 7'

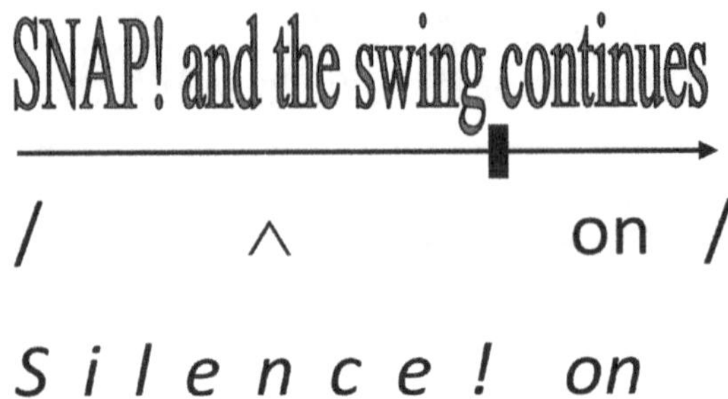

You have to make the snap right at the *beginning* of your swing and hold a long silence until you allow a very short weak non-salient 'on' to emerge at the *end* of the foot.

Here is an exercise in which clicks are added to establish the rhythm. Counting out loud and timing your snaps to coincide with the clicks will flow you into and through the silent Ictus in the first foot of the limerick.

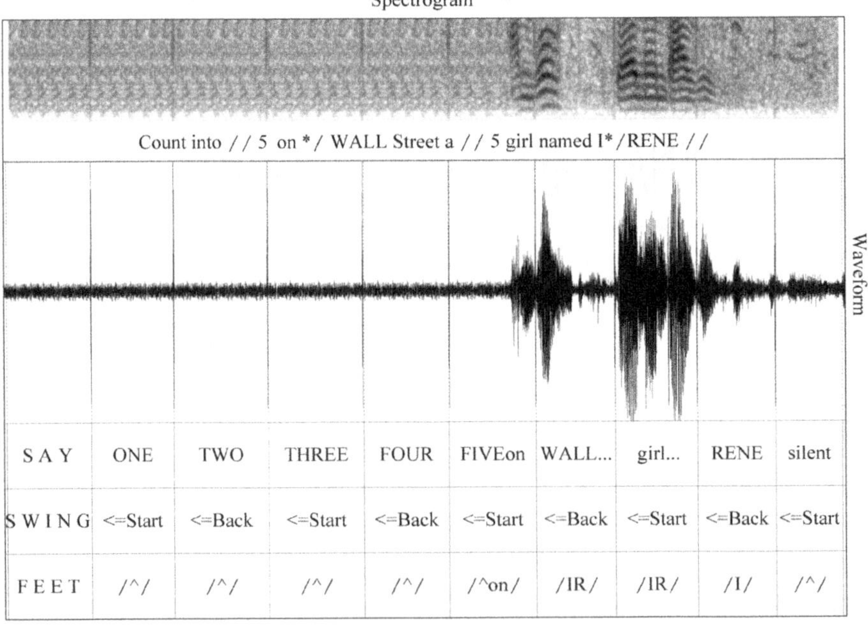

S A Y	ONE	TWO	THREE	FOUR	FIVEon	WALL....	girl...	RENE	silent
S W I N G	<=Start	<=Back	<=Start	<=Back	<=Start	<=Back	<=Start	<=Back	<=Start
F E E T	/∧/	/∧/	/∧/	/∧/	/∧on/	/IR/	/IR/	/I/	/∧/

Play 'Sound file 8'

Now try the first line without clicks: // ∧ [complete silence while you snap and swing your arm] // ∧ [complete silence for most of the swing] on */ WALL street a // girl named i*/RENE //. And now continue on to the second line:

> // ∧ made an / offering / somewhat ob*/SCENE //
> **Play 'Sound file 9'**

12.8 Rhythm and genre

The limerick is a very iconic genre. That is, there is a kind of direct path from the contextual limerick genre to the physical sound of the rhythmic pattern. You can experiment with this. But first we need to add a brief description of the numerals used to represent the tone system choices. In the following transcription the numeral at the beginning of each tone group represents a choice in the system of TONE: 1 = a falling tone; 2 = a rising tone; 3 = a level-rise tone; 4 = a fall-rise tone; 5 = a rise-fall tone. Now try saying the following to a friend:

> // 5 ∧ da / da dada / da dada */ da//
> // 1 ∧ da da / da dada / da da da */ da //
> // 3 ∧ da / da dada */ da /
> // 3 ∧ da / da dada */ da /
> // 1 ∧ da da / da dada / da da da */ da //

If the limerick is part of your shared cultural context, the odds are that your friend will recognize it even without lexicogrammar and semantics. And we could, perhaps, include the limerick a-a-b-b-a rhyme scheme.

> // 5 ∧ da / da dada / da dada */ eh//
> // 1 ∧ da da / da dada / da da da */ eh //
> // 3 ∧ da / da dada */ bee/
> // 3 ∧ da / da dada */ bee /
> // 1 ∧ da da / da dada / da da da */ eh //

This is not unlike the sky-predator alarm call a vervet monkey utters in response to an eagle. The meaning of the sign is a direct association of the content 'sky predator' and the expression (that particular call, among the 27 calls vervets produce). The sound, even with no 'grammar', means 'sky predator', as we know because the other vervets rush to lower levels where they are safe from attack from the air. Just as directly, the // 5 ∧ da / da dada / da dada */da// sound means 'I am a limerick'. But the limerick genre involves far more than simple direct semiotic and material/physical coupling. Every limerick is an instance of discourse; it is the product of choices in all the strata. These choices, because they follow a familiar pattern, confirm our recognition of the genre but at the same time some of them must be startlingly singular in order to cause us to laugh.

The genre involves many expectations: interaction of lexicogrammar and semantics resulting in several fields of discourse; a suspicion that one of those fields will deal with sex or some such usually taboo field; a phonological pattern of five tone units (one for each line), a corresponding lexicogrammatical pattern of five information units; the probability of an existential clause with a circumstance of location in the first line; and a feeling that we will experience pleasure as we encounter the words which are construing meanings in several fields at once. Limericks often (as in this instance) present rather outrageous material which would not be sanctioned if it were not packaged in this particular form. Whether or not it should be so sanctioned is a legitimate social question, but the linguistic fact is that in cultures where the limerick is recognized, pushing the boundaries of acceptable behaviour is a valued part of the game being played. Whether or not the game should be played, and the role that playing it takes in shaping our culture, are, again, legitimate social questions.

12.9 Fields of discourse

The first lexical item, 'Wall Street', is indexical. Although it names an actual street, it is used to refer to American financial markets and financial institutions as a whole. So with that one item we are plunged into the field of finance.

'Offering' doesn't take you into the field in quite the same automatic way. By itself, 'offering' might indicate the field of religion. But when linked with, for example *equity*, a Google search leads to financial activity. With a 'hit' such as 'Issues surrounding venture capital, initial public offering (IPO) and post-IPO equity financing for Canadian small and medium-sized businesses (SMEs)', the field of finance is strongly established by collocation. 'Offering' keeps company with the lexical items 'venture capital', 'initial public offering', 'IPO' (treated differently from initial public offering because of its different graphology and hence, probably, collocational distribution), 'equity financing', 'small and medium-sized businesses', and 'SMEs' (distinct for the same reason as above).

'Offering' is established as a field restricted item by technical nominal group structures. 'Offering' itself is modified by 'initial' and 'public', resulting in a highly technical phrase, as is shown by the acronym 'IPO'. And 'financing' is the head of the splendidly long and technical nominal group 'post-IPO equity financing for Canadian small and medium-sized businesses'. We get 'equity financing' through modification of 'financing' by 'equity', and we get modification of 'equity financing' first by further pre-modification 'initial public offering (IPO) equity financing' and then the whole thing is qualified by 'for Canadian small and medium-sized businesses (SMEs)'. Further Google searching reveals that 'offering' has plenty of financial semantic baggage which it successfully carries into the limerick.

A search on 'share' turns up just as rich an example:

> The shares are to be sold on an instalment basis. The first payment of $6.125 per share (U.S.$4.554 per share for purchasers in the United States) will be payable on the closing of the offering, scheduled for September 22, 1995, the second payment of $4.25 per share will be due on September 23, 1996 and the final payment of $4.25 per share will be due on March 24, 1997.

Merrill, Lynch, Pierce, Fenner & Bean, although consisting of six words, is a single lexical item. When searched, it turned up a little narrative which is quite different from the expository writing above, but just as clear in establishing the field of finance:

> It was all an accident. The hand of fate. I was in law school looking for a law clerk job and answered a want ad. The firm in question, **Merrill, Lynch, Pierce, Fenner & Bean,** was looking for a 'runner' to work between the hours of 9:00 and 1:00, which was perfect for my class schedule. With that many names, how could this firm be anything but an established law firm looking for a clerk to run to court?
>
> Let's face it, I was very innocent. So I ended up on **the floor** of **the Chicago Mercantile Exchange** and my life changed. There was a life force on **that floor** that was magical and exciting, and though I didn't understand what was going on, I wanted to be a part of it. (Leo Melamed, in Kolman, 1996)

The joke in this little account is, of course, precisely that the narrator failed to recognize **Merrill, Lynch, Pierce, Fenner & Bean** as a financial firm, not a law firm. His conversion from law to finance is shown by his comfortable use of **floor** in 'a life force on **that floor** that was magical and exciting'.

The second major field of discourse in 'Wall Street Irene' is commercial sex. In a limerick it doesn't take much to activate this field. Two lexical items, **strip** and **bare** do the job nicely. A search combining these will turn up many examples posted by commercial sex establishments.

The field of commercial sex is construed by language as highly technical as that in the financial examples. Neither 'strip' nor 'bare' alone predicts the field, but when 'strip' modifies 'club', the phrase becomes the lexical **'strip club'**, which in turn can become a modifier as in **'strip club** information site'; or a qualifier as in 'list of **strip clubs'**. This process can lead to long and involved modification as in 'the nation's best **strip clubs** web sites'; and so forth. Although this is not about machinery, or chemicals, or the effect of climate change on population growth, the language is just as technical.

12.10 Exploiting the fields

Many limericks start with 'there was a young X from Y …'. 'Wall Street Irene' begins with a closely related pattern: a location as Circumstance is marked Theme and then followed by the main character, Irene.

// 5 ∧ on */ WALL street a // 5 girl named i*/RENE //

In the next line we find that Irene is Actor, not Existent, and that she was engaged in the creative Process 'make' with 'offering' a Goal. 'Offering' as Goal is perfectly normal in the field of discourse finance.

// 1 ∧ made an / offering / somewhat ob*/SCENE //

But 'offering' is qualified by 'somewhat obscene', which is not normal in the field of finance, and we have to 'tune in' to the field of commercial sex, which with 'strip' and 'bare' takes over completely as field in the next line:

// 1 ∧ she / stripped herself */ BARE /

But then 'offer' and 'share' bring finance back in the next line.

// 1 ∧ and / offered a */ SHARE /

This pivots the limerick. Where 'an offering somewhat obscene' in the second line had presented the two fields in separate parts of the nominal group – first finance and then commercial sex – in this line the single word **'offer'** in collocation with 'share' is fully meaningful as language not unlike **'to be sold on an instalment basis'** within 'the shares are to be sold on an instalment basis'. At the same time, however, in collocation with **'strip'** and **'bare'** in the previous line, we also process 'offer' in the language of service provided to **'strip** club patrons'. The final line continues this fusion by presenting the professionals in the financial field as clients in the commercial sex field:

// 1 ∧ to / merrill lynch */ PIERCE // 1+ fenner and */ BEAN //

12.11 The role of sound

The object we are investigating is a spoken instance of the limerick, in which the sound gives a fair bit of paralinguistic information. There is a lot of background noise: clinking and chatter. This is indexical of the material situational setting, which could well be a bar or other such locale where a raconteur is regaling a close intimate audience at his table. And the quality of his speech contributes to this effect: careful diction, at points whispered, articulate and very deliberate intonation – we could make a fair guess at the tenor of the discourse even when hearing it at a distance and not quite making out the words.

This is indexical information which helps provide a setting. The soundwaves we receive help us to 'feel' the location of the narrator. It is doing the same job as a silent scene presented before the talk begins in a movie. Most of the 'punch' of the limerick, however, comes from its language. Choices in all strata are involved in the humour, but we will conclude the discussion of 'Wall Street Irene' by considering the TONE UNIT in phonology and its counterpart the INFORMATION UNIT in the lexicogrammar. Here is a Praat analysis of the first line:

Spectrogram

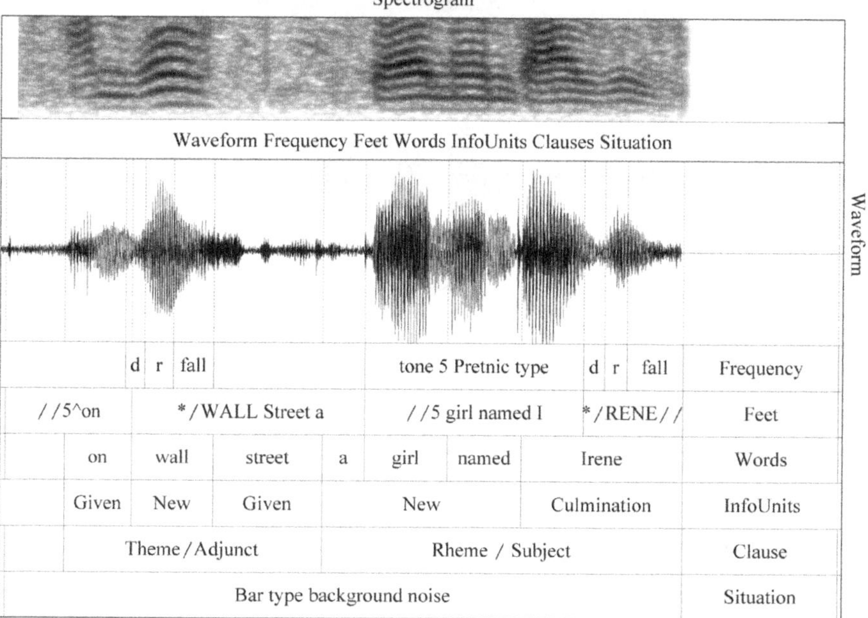

	d	r	fall		tone 5 Pretnic type	d	r	fall	Frequency
//5^on		*/WALL Street a		//5 girl named I		*/RENE//		Feet
	on	wall	street	a	girl	named	Irene	Words
	Given	New	Given		New		Culmination	InfoUnits
	Theme / Adjunct			Rheme / Subject				Clause
	Bar type background noise							Situation

Play 'Sound file 10'

The first clause has been spoken as four tone units – the first two in this line and the third and fourth in the second line. The boundaries of the tone unit // 5 ∧ on */ WALL street a// do not quite coincide with the corresponding information unit 'on Wall Street' because the former is a phonological unit, the latter a lexicogrammatical one. Location of the tonic on */ WALL marks the word 'street' as Given information, and we would include 'on' as part of Given, although the system is specific only in terms of what follows the tonic syllable. (For a discussion of the phonetic characteristics of a tonic syllable see Tench, 1996: 53–5.) But a location somewhere, e.g. **on** a street, or **near** a street, is assumed at the start of a limerick. As new information, 'Wall' highlights this particular street as location, but it is doing more. 'Wall Street' contrasts with, for example, George Street, and introduces finance as a main field of discourse. The next tone unit is not marked. The tonic in // 5 girl named i*/RENE // is in the neutral position. 'Irene' is the last lexical item in the information unit. So we know that 'Irene' is the culmination of new information, but not, precisely, where newness begins. In this case there is no reason to assume that the whole nominal group is not New. Let's listen again.

Spectrogram

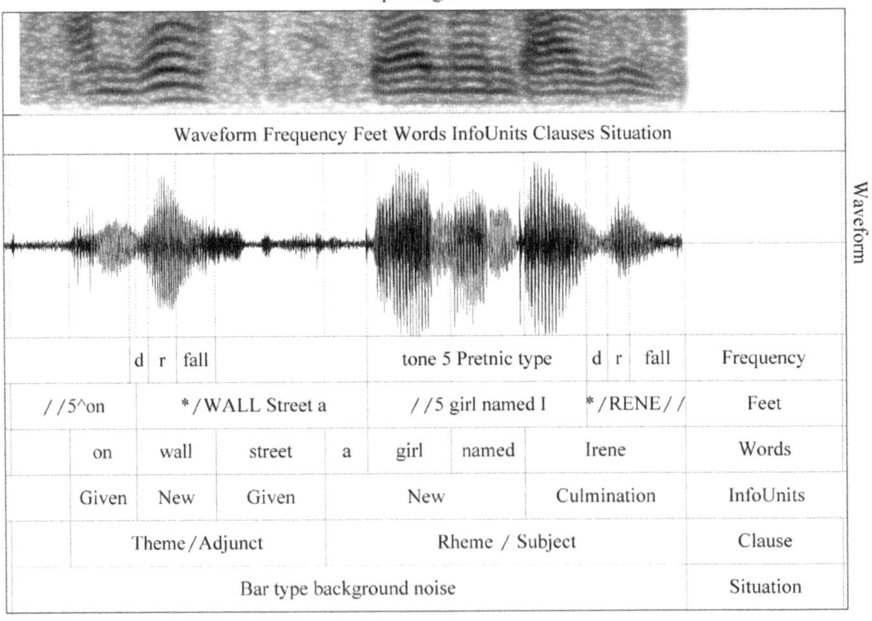

Waveform Frequency Feet Words InfoUnits Clauses Situation								
	d	r	fall	tone 5 Pretnic type	d	r	fall	Frequency
//5^on	*/WALL Street a			//5 girl named I	*/RENE//			Feet
on	wall	street	a	girl	named	Irene		Words
Given	New	Given	New		Culmination			InfoUnits
Theme/Adjunct			Rheme / Subject					Clause
Bar type background noise								Situation

Play 'Sound file 8'

The clause is declarative and positive, but chunking the information with four separate tone units gives the narrator four opportunities to express his polar certainty, rather than just one. First, for the **Circumstance** 'on Wall Street' the narrator selects tone 5: the speaker is not just polar certain, he is enthusiastic, committed. Second, about the **Actor**, 'a girl named Irene', the narrator selects tone 1. He is not particularly committed, but he is polar certain, or definite. Third, for the **Goal** 'an offering' of the **Process** 'made' he selects another tone 1, and fourth, with the secondary tone 1+ of the expansion 'somewhat obscene', he highlights the field joke, that is, he is not only polar certain but is also performing 'obscene' with extra 'oomph'. Placing the Tonic on 'obscene' as the focus draws full attention to this particular lexical item.

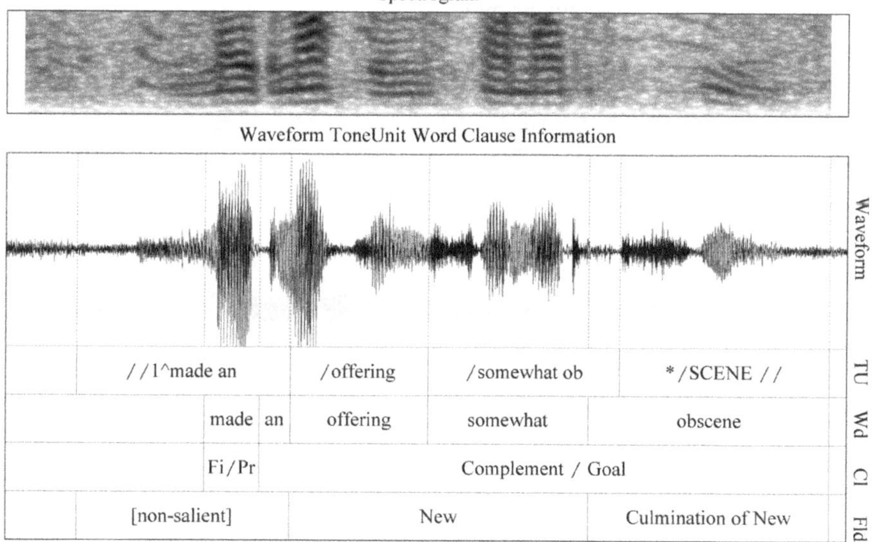

//1^made an	/offering	/somewhat ob	*/SCENE //	TU
made	an	offering	somewhat	obscene	Wd
Fi/Pr		Complement / Goal			Cl
[non-salient]		New		Culmination of New	Fld

Play 'Sound file 11'

The performer could have produced the whole clause as a single tone unit with the tonic on */SCENE, giving us // 1 ʌ on / Wall Street a /girl named I/rene made an / offering / somewhat ob*/SCENE // but the genre makes this improbable. The a-a-b-b-a rhyme scheme and the rhythmic pattern of a single salient syllable concluding each line make a separation of tone units at line ends almost inevitable. And the complexity of the message with its simultaneous fields of discourse, plus the deliberate style of the narrator, lend themselves to multiple information units, guiding the hearer into 'digesting' the message one chunk at a time and also providing a dramatized performance feel: the exaggeration of comedic performance.

The next line is neutral, consisting of one clause conflated with a single tone unit, and the tonic syllable realizes the last lexical item. The tone 1 choice here is doing the unmarked interpersonal work of showing polar certainty for the statement.

The third line is neutral: one tone unit realizing one clause, and the tone 3 choice anticipating the 'and' which ties it to the next. 'She' as an anaphoric pronoun follows a silent Ictus as a given Remiss syllable, and 'bare' culminates the new information: // 3 ∧ she / stripped herself */ BARE //.

Play 'Sound file 12'

The fourth line is much like the third, but the clause extends to the Beneficiary in the final line with an information break which is forced by the genre, as in the cases above.

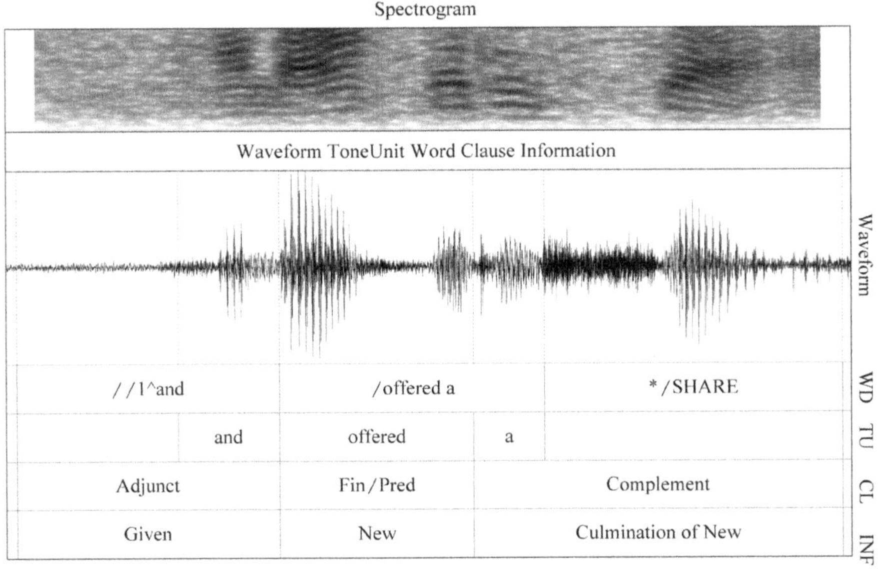

Play 'Sound file 13'

The final line not only presents the Beneficiary as informationally distinct from the rest of the clause, but it breaks the group of stockbrokers into two units. The tone 1 choice for the first simply places it in the concord sequence of polar certain neutral affirmations.

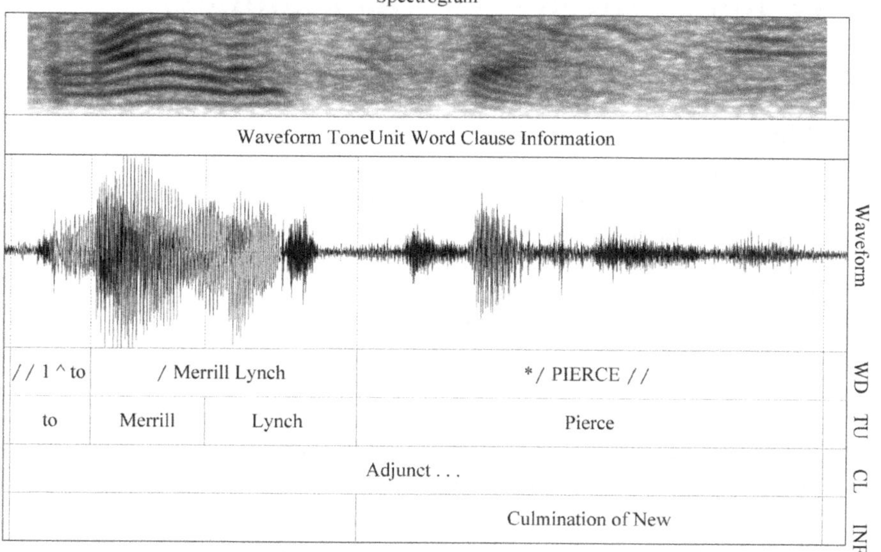

Play 'Sound file 14'

The final unit, // 1+ fenner and */ BEAN // cements the positive declarative mood choice. It does this with two features which heighten the effect. First, in terms of rhythm, there are two extra feet in the line: one a normal foot, and one consisting of a silent Ictus. It is perhaps tempting to propose a line break at the silent Ictus, however ending a line at */ *PIERCE* would violate the a-a-b-b-a rhyme scheme. What the silence does do, however, is add an element of suspense before delivery of the final information unit. The second heightening is achieved through secondary delicacy. A neutral tone 1. is simply a fall that flows from the Pretonic. The tone 1+ which concludes the limerick jumps up from the Pretonic and then falls, with the meaning 'not only am I certain about the polarity, I am somewhat excited, surprised or enthusiastic'.

Play 'Sound file 15'

Here is the whole line.

Play 'Sound file 16'

12.12 John Milton's 'On his blindness'

Play 'Sound file 17'

When I consider how my light is spent
Ere half my days in this dark world and wide,
And that one talent which is death to hide,
Lodg'd with me useless, though my soul more bent
To serve therewith my Maker, and present
My true account, lest he returning chide,
'Doth God exact day-labour, light denied?'
I fondly ask. But Patience, to prevent
That murmur, soon replies: 'God doth not need
Either man's work or his own gifts: who best
Bear his mild yoke, they serve him best. His state
Is kingly; thousands at his bidding speed
And post o'er land and ocean without rest:
They also serve who only stand and wait.'   (John Milton, 1655)

In listening to Robert Speaight's performance of this sonnet[2] we are experiencing a text woven in the 1650s in Protestant England, well removed from our cultural here-and-now. We do not, and can never, directly experience the material situational setting. But because language construes, enacts and enables context, we can, to some degree, recover and share in Milton's culture.

Milton had had his sight taken from him when, at the height of his intellectual powers, he was engaged fiercely in defending God's chosen land (England under Puritan Protestant government) against all and sundry. In this poem he blames God (a grave sin) by asking the question at the heart of the poem: 'Doth God exact day-labour, light denied?' But then he responds to his own question, in the shift from a self-centred perspective to the God-centred perspective that frames the sonnet.

The configurations of field, tenor and mode of a culture organize the bustle and hurly burly of human rushing around. And in the sixteenth and seventeenth centuries in England one of the modes of creating text, of enabling a message to be made, was a special message form consisting of an octave and a sestet: the Petrarchan sonnet. This form lends itself to contrasts in meaning.

12.13 Interpersonal semantics

Interpersonal semantics revolves around the choices of statement (giving information), question (demanding information), command (demanding goods and services) or offer (giving goods and services). 'On his blindness' deals with just two of these. Milton's octave is built around the meaning question: 'Doth God exact day-labour, light denied?' The sestet, on the other hand, is entirely devoted to giving information. One statement follows another.

12.14 Experiential semantics

The experiential semantics of Milton's octave is built around verbal and mental processes. Through these processes he is thinking and stating propositions which are dangerous in the field of discourse of seventeenth-century theology. The sestet on the other hand has participants engaged in material and relational processes which are entirely in accord with the religion of his time.

12.15 Phonetics and genre

If we move from context and culture, language's eco-social environment, to phonetics, language's neuro-physiological environment, we find another shaping factor. The genre of Petrarchan sonnet is recognized directly through the rhyme of the final syllables in its two-part structure: abbaabba in the octave, and cdecde in the sestet. This is very concrete. It is not even as abstract as phonology. It is a matter of the nature of the sound itself.

Someone familiar with the sonnet form in English poetry could listen to a particular stretch of Hungarian and perhaps feel from the sound that it is divided into 'two greater units: (abba) and (ccdd)' (Szigeti, 1995: 294). The hearer might speculate about the poetic nature of whatever it was even though the sound system, the lexicogrammar, the semantics and indeed the culture were largely matters of mystery. But the sound stratum alone could hardly take such an investigator very far into meaningful interpretation.

12.16 Phonology

Phonology sits between sound and wording. Choices in the sounding system are realized in phonetics and they construe lexicogrammatical words, and choices among intonation systems are realized in phonetic shapes and construe information units. The sonnet needs segmental phonemes, of course, to construe its words in the lexicogrammar. But it is the intonational phonology which relates most directly to the sonnet genre. Because the rhyme and rhythm schemes favour single syllable stressed words at the end of each line, there is a tendency to chunk information with a 'culmination of New' occurring at the end of each of the fourteen lines.

12.17 Lexicogrammar

There is a vast amount to say about the lexicogrammar of 'On his blindness'. We are going to focus mainly on one feature: projection.

Projections are clause complexes in which the projecting clause brings the projected one into being. The two clauses are tightly related, of course, but construe 'different worlds'. For example, in the complex 'John thinks Mary will be home by midnight', John's world is in the present time of the speaker and hearer, whereas Mary's world is in a time to come after the speech act.

There are three projections in 'On his blindness':

> I consider ... ,
> I ask ... ,
> Patience replies ... .

The sonnet begins with 'When I consider', a mental Projection tucked away within a Circumstance for the main projection. 'Considering' is a mental process projecting thought (what he considers), and that projected thought is long and complex:

> how my light is spent
> Ere half my days in this dark world and wide,
> And that one talent which is death to hide,
> Lodg'd with me useless, though my soul more bent
> To serve therewith my Maker, and present
> My true account, lest he returning chide ...

Play 'Sound file 18'

Milton here reveals a preoccupation with himself as he dwells on the frustration of being struck blind in full career. The problem at the heart of the octave, which has to be solved in the sestet, is that this self-focus is an act of pride, a sin, the seventh and most deadly.

It becomes theologically worse. Milton follows the mental projection which opens the octave with a verbal one which concludes it; the question he 'asks' is directed inwardly, to himself, but the 'world' he projects is not Milton doing and acting, but God doing and acting; it is God's world. And the locution he projects doesn't praise God (as the seventeenth-century field of discourse would predict); it questions divine justice:

'Doth God exact day-labour, light denied?'

Play 'Sound file 19'

The very long Circumstance for asking his question 'When I consider … lest he returning chide', is in marked position occurring well before the Subject 'I',

Play 'Sound file 20'

and the question itself, 'Doth God exact day-labour, light denied?',

Play 'Sound file 21'

is placed before the projecting clause rather than after it where it would more 'naturally' occur. This leaves the projecting clause 'I fondly ask' to comment on the question rather than simply to launch it. This is hugely important for the octave–sestet structure. While making his way towards the projecting clause through the extensive Theme marked matter, that is, during the process of framing the Circumstance for asking the question and uttering the question itself, Milton as narrator has undergone a reorientation of perspective from self-centred to God-centred. This will be articulated in the sestet, but the Circumstance of manner (fondly, i.e. foolishly) in the projecting clause 'I fondly ask' reveals that his reorientation began at the start of the octave. By the time he gets to the clause which projects his question, Milton already knows that asking that question is wrong.

The sestet is 'launched' with the second, and last, major projection, as 'patience' (an aspect of Milton himself which he has awakened during the octave) 'replies'. Replying is a mental process projecting speech, in this case his own response to his own question, in an internal conversation with himself. Realizing that his question had been 'fond' (i.e. foolish), he does not answer it; rather, he responds to it in the persona of 'patience', an aspect of his character that emerged at the end of his long self-centred Theme in the octave.

Because he can now 'see' clearly beyond the circumference of his own situation, the reply which Patience projects looks outward. The focus is no longer on Milton's brooding mental processes, but rather on 'needing', 'bearing', 'serving', 'being', 'speeding', 'standing' and, crucially, patiently 'waiting':

- God **doth not need** man's work or his own gifts
- Who **bear** mild yoke they **serve**
- God's state **is** kingly
- Thousands **speed** and **post**
- They [[who only **stand** and **wait**]][3] also **serve**

The final process, 'waiting' is carefully presented.

The neutral proposition would be 'they who only stand and wait also serve'. But Milton takes apart the nominal group and delays the qualifier: 'They also serve who only stand and wait'. 'Wait' is now placed in the neutral position to receive the Tonic, which the speaker in this performance indeed gives it.

Play 'Sound file 22'

In doing so the performer must select a tone, and his falling tone 1 adds the certainty of [neutral] KEY to the positive polarity of the declarative clause. Distribution of Given and New comes into play here too, with the single syllable lexical word 'wait' in final position having a very strong unmarked potential to realize the culmination of New information. Intonationally, the speaker in our version makes the most of this potential by breaking the final clause into three information units. The first, *// 13 ^ they */ ALso */ SERVE,*

Play 'Sound file 23'

places the tone 1 of a compound tone 13 on 'also', thus both making it New and associating it through tone with the polar positive mode of the clause. The tone 3 in this compound tone unit is serving its textual role in making 'serve' secondary New rather than Given.

The next tone unit *// 1 ^ who only */STAND //*

Play 'Sound file 24'

places Tonic on the lexical item 'stand' thus giving focus to its contrast with 'speeding' and 'posting' and once again, through selection of tone 1, adding the certainty of the key system to that of the mood selection.

The final tone unit // 1 ∧ and */WAIT //

Play 'Sound file 25'

is spoken quietly and deliberately. There is no need of loudness for intensity. The separate tonality and the certainty of tone 1 do it all.

12.18 Conclusion

The chapter has explored semantic space by situating language between body as social being and the body as signal generator and receiver; by looking at context (field, tenor and mode) as closest to the social body; looking at phonetics (with technical help from Praat) as closest to signal transmission and reception; by making the discussion concrete through focus on two instances broadly similar because they are each monologic performances of short English poems, but very different in terms of temporal provenance and field of discourse; and by providing a detailed discussion of 'Wall Street Irene' in terms of rhythm, rhyme and genre, of the interplay between simultaneous fields of discourse and the role of intonation in exploiting this. The discussion of 'On his blindness' proceeded in terms of interpersonal semantics, experiential semantics, interacting fields of discourse, phonetics and genre, intonational phonology and genre, and lexicogrammar and genre, with a focus mainly on projection and the process types in projecting clauses and in the projected matter. Throughout, sound has been part of the discussion, presented to the eye in the printed soundwaves, spectrograms and pitch lines; to the ear in the sound icons which present the spoken lines when played in the sound files, and to the intellect when the sound and TextGrid in the electronic supplementary material are explored through Praat, as described in the Appendix.

The sound, sounding, lexicogrammar and semantics of Milton's sonnet have taken us, to the degree we have been able to process them with our twenty-first-century version of these potentials, some way out of the contexts in which we currently understand our world. We do not, and can not, perhaps, construe our material situational world as populated with physical angels speeding and posting in the same way that Milton's colleagues could have, but a literary work like 'On his blindness' has probably taken us closer to experiencing it than any number of scholarly accounts of intellectual history could do. And thinking about 'Wall Street Irene', which we can experience quite fully in shared patterns of sound, sounding, lexicogrammar and semantic potential can perhaps make us aware of the darker side of this amusing genre. Much has been said recently about the 'glass ceiling' and other manifestations of sexual oppression in the workplace, and much has, indeed, been done. Nevertheless, viewing women as a useful commodity has hardly vanished from the world's cultures, and experiencing and enjoying literature such as this limerick no doubt plays its part in shaping and maintaining that aspect of the dynamic between our sexes.

Acknowledgements

I would like to acknowledge the help of Dr Bradley Smith and Dr Meena Debashish who worked with me in preparing the presentation on which this chapter is based. I am grateful to Margaret Fink, producer of the movie *For Love Alone*, for permission to use the sound file of Sam Neill (playing James Quick) reciting the limerick 'Wall Street Irene', and to the Arthur and Luce Klein Spoken Arts Collection at the Yale Collection of Historical Sound Recordings, Yale Music Library, Yale University Library for permission to use Robert Speaight's recording of 'On his Blindness'.

Notes

1. 'Wall Street Irene' was performed by Sam Neill playing James Quick in the film *For Love Alone*.
2. John Milton's 'On his Blindness' read by Robert Speaight is available on *Treasury of John Milton*, Spoken Arts, Inc. SA-867 (LP) or SAC-867 (audio-cassette).
3. The pair of square brackets indicates an embedded element such as 'who mistook his wife for a hat' in the nominal group 'the man [[who mistook his wife for a hat]]'.

References

Eggins, S. (1994) *An Introduction to Systemic Functional Linguistics*. London: Pinter.
Eggins, S. and Slade, D. (1997) *Analysing Casual Conversation*. London: Cassell.
Halliday, M. A. K. (1978) *Language as Social Semiotic*. London: Arnold.

Halliday, M. A. K. and Greaves, W. S. (2008) *Intonation in the Grammar of English.* London: Equinox.

Halliday, M. A. K. and Matthiessen, C. M. I. M. (2004) *An Introduction to Functional Grammar* (3rd edition). London: Arnold.

Kolman, J. (1996) The world according to Leo Melamed. *Derivatives Strategy,* April. Available at www.derivativesstrategy.com/magazine/archive/1995-1996/0496qaf753.asp?print (accessed 7 March 2012).

Martin, J. R. (1992) *English Text: System and Structure.* Amsterdam: Benjamins.

Martin, J. R., Matthiessen, C. M. I. M. and Painter, C. (1997) *Working with Functional Grammar.* London: Arnold.

Sacks, O. (1996) The last hippie. In his *An Anthropologist on Mars: Seven Paradoxical Tales* 42–76. New York: Vintage Books.

Szigeti, C. (1995) The metrical heritage of Balassi in seventeenth century Hungarian poetry. *Hungarian Studies* 10(2): 291–306. Available at http://epa.oszk.hu/01400/01462/00017/pdf/291-306.pdf (accessed 17 May 2012).

Tench, P. (1996) *The Intonation Systems of English.* London: Cassell

Thompson. G. (2004) *Introducing Functional Grammar* (2nd edition). London: Arnold.

Appendix

Download and install the latest version of the computer program Praat, freely available from www.fon.hum.uva.nl/praat. If you have it running as you read this chapter, you can explore the TextGrids as you read about them.

If you have not already done so, download the electronic supplementary material accompanying this chapter from [www.equinoxpub.com/systemic-phonology-files]. It contains the sound files and TextGrid files you will need as you use Praat in following this chapter. You can hear the sound files without using Praat, but Praat gives you far more control over what you hear, and, as you become more familiar with Praat, it will give you much more insight into the sound of the poetry.

Run Praat. Then go to Praat Objects and open a sound file from the electronic supplementary material. (Some versions of Praat use the terms 'open' and 'read' in an almost interchangeable way.)

For the limerick, 'read' or 'open' Wall Street Irene.wav. It will then appear as one of the 'objects' in your Praat Objects window. Then 'read' all of the TextGrid files relating to the limerick: Wall Street Irene.TextGrid (for a full analysis), Wall Street Irene_RHYTHM.TextGrid and Wall Street Irene_INTONATION.TextGrid

In Praat Objects, highlight Wall Street Irene.wav. Then hold down the control key and click on Wall Street Irene_RHYTHM.TextGrid. Be sure that only these two files are highlighted.

Click on 'edit'. A screen will appear with a soundwave, a spectrogram, and a number of analysis tiers. At the bottom left corner click on the little square which says 'all'. The full soundwave will now appear, and the full TextGrid, although you will see only a part of what is in each TextGrid segment.

Now you should make a few adjustments. Click on **View**, then **Show Analysis**. Be sure that only the two squares for **Show Pitch** and **Show Spectrogram** have check marks. **Longest Analysis** should be set for about 60.0.

Click on **Spectrogram** and then on **Spectrogram Settings**. Make the **View Range** 25 to 300, and the **Window Length** 0.05.

Click on **Pitch**. Be sure that **Show pitch** is checked. If not, click on it. Then click on **Pitch Settings**, and set the **Pitch range** from 25 to 300. You may have to adjust this a bit to fit the range of the individual speaker. Generally it is helpful to show two or three harmonics (the dark bands) with the blue pitch line centred on the bottom one.

If there is an annoying series of red dots, click on **Formant**, and then on **Show formants**. The check mark on **Show formants** will disappear and the dots will go away.

If there is an annoying series of blue lines, click on **Pulses**, and then on **Show pulses**. The check mark on **Show formants** will disappear and the blue lines will go away.

Now you are ready to hear and see the sound together with its analysis. If you click on any segment in one of the tiers, for example a foot or a clause, the segment will turn yellow, and you will see the full content of the segment at the top of the screen. If you then click on the 'sel' box at the bottom left, the window will fill with just that segment. Click at the top of the screen and you will hear the segment.

All of this will no doubt seem awkward at first, but Praat lets you explore the world of sound in poetry in a way that is quite impossible without it. It's not just seeing the sound, but also the ability to select any segment – foot, syllable, word, poetic line – and hear that precise chunk as you look at its shape.

- *Physical sound* is always represented by the two top bands: a waveform and a spectrogram. A blue line on the spectrogram shows the rise and fall of the speaker's pitch. Praat does the analysis in these two tiers, based on the settings you choose. Below these two you can add as many tiers as you wish, in which you do the analysis. For a study such as this the following inventory will be useful.

- *Phonetics*, our top analysis tier, relates quite directly to the sound above. We use the tier for IPA transcription and also for discussion of sound quality and details of prosodic realization.

- *Phonology*, more abstract than phonetics, is not concerned directly with sound, but with the way language organizes sound. In English every tone unit consists of at least one foot; every foot of at least one syllable; every syllable of at least one segmental phoneme. We could, but do not, have a tier for phonemes. We begin with syllables.
    - *Phonology – syllables transcribed.*
    - *Phonology – syllables structure.*
    - *Phonology – feet transcribed.*
    - *Phonology – feet structure.*
    - *Phonology – tone units transcribed.*
    - *Phonology – tone units structure.*

- *Lexicogrammar* deals with the most abstract analysis – insulated by both phonology and phonetics from the 'real world' of our bodies making and hearing sound (the neuro-physiological environment of speech), and by semantics from the 'real world' of our bodies interacting socially with other bodies (the eco-social environment, the physical, biological and cultural context of language). The four units we deal with are:
    - *Lexicogrammar – words.*
    - *Lexicogrammar – group/phrase.*
    - *Lexicogrammar – clauses.*
    - *Lexicogrammar – information units.*
- *Semantics.* By making choices in our meaning systems, we construe, enact and enable our social context. The TextGrids accompanying this chapter deal mainly with the unit MOVE in the interpersonal meaning system which is shown in the *Semantics – moves* tier. (For a discussion of the relationship between MOVES and other strata see Eggins and Slade, 1997: 184; Martin *et al.*, 1997: 57; and Halliday and Greaves, 2008: 48).
- *Context.* Comments about genre, about fields, tenors and modes.
- *Material situational setting.* Physical social interaction is described in the bottom tier.

To see these yourself with Praat open Wall Street Irene_INTONATION. TextGrid and Wall Street Irene_INTONATION.wav. Be sure only these two are highlighted, and click on edit. Make the adjustments outlined above. As a first step in experimenting with Praat you may want to simplify the TextGrid by clicking on a number of the tiers and removing them (with the tier highlighted, click on the 'Tier' menu and then on 'remove entire tier').

Author index

Subject index

CPSIA information can be obtained at www.ICGtesting.com
Printed in the USA
BVOW09s0444031014

369327BV00004B/9/P